LEARN NEW TESTAMENT GREEK

"We didn't want Greek! Now we want more!!"
Kenyan students after doing
lessons 1–19 in 12 hours of class work

This **comprehensive introduction** to New Testament Greek takes beginners from the first stage of learning to read Greek syllables and words to a stage where they can tackle the Gospels and work at University level:

- It is designed in accordance with the principles by which languages can be learned. It therefore leads people quickly into the reading of biblical passages and sets them free from constant need to consult dictionaries. Students start reading passages of New Testament text with understanding after just one hour of instruction.
- All major forms are explained and used extensively. Basic forms like participles and subjunctives are introduced early on in a simple form and this foundation is built on progressively. So, from an early stage, Greek in genuine New Testament style is encountered.
- Grammatical terminology is progressively introduced and parsing is taught.
- Stems are explored, prepositions are extensively illustrated, understanding of translation is built up, the influence of Hebrew is discussed and textual criticism is introduced.
- As the book was first developed for students in Uganda, it is easier than most books for those whose English is not their first language, and in England people say, 'We can understand it!'

For **students** it contains everything that needs to be learned to read the Greek New Testament with confidence:
- Check columns aid learning and allow progress to be made without mistakes. This is one of the features that make the book ideal for those who study on their own or through distance-learning courses.
- What is begun to be learned in any lesson is consolidated in the lessons that follow.
- Basic words and forms are learned by being seen repetitively in meaningful contexts so students do not become dictionary drudges.
- The contents pages are a learning and revision tool.
- The audio files of lessons 1–21 help with memorization, provides repetition of exercises.
- All grammatical terminology is explained and the Reference Grammar is designed as an aid to parsing.
- Constant practice in translating sentences that are similar, except for a key difference, develops people who can translate accurately.

"*This group of more than 30 students is far ahead of any beginners class I have ever taught before – their enthusiasm burns brightly.*"
A Cambridge tutor when LNTG was first introduced

For **teachers** this is suitable as a resource to teach individual students or large classes of students:
- It invites whole-class participation in reading and in translating. This aids attention and reduces anxiety. It also provides repetition, which is good for establishing memory.
- It enables rapid progress, e.g. lessons 1–17 in ten hours and 1–30 in 26 hours. Progress is pleasure. Rapid progress is excitement!
- It does not demand 'homework'! No out-of-class research and writing is demanded as each class meeting is the learning experience. Only some revision is needed between classes.
- Division into short sections a) encourages a feeling of being able to cope; b) gives a sense of steady progress; c) gives opportunity for movement, word games, songs, visual material, and eye-exercises and rest, to be slotted in; d) stimulates the level of attention.
- Anyone who has used the book to learn can use it to teach someone else, for all that is necessary is to lead someone through the material and help them to keep smiling.

LEARN NEW TESTAMENT GREEK

3rd Edition,
with Accents

John H. Dobson

Free MP3 audio files accompany this book.

PiQUANT editions

BakerAcademic
Grand Rapids, Michigan

Copyright © 1988, 1993, 2005 by John H. Dobson

Third revised edition (updated) and audio files
copyright © 2005, 2007 and 2012 by Piquant
PO Box 83, Carlisle, CA3 9GR, United Kingdom
www.piquanteditions.com
ISBN 978-1-909281-21-9

Previously published in the UK in 1988, 1992 by the Bible Society
Stonehill Green, Westlea, Swindon SN5 7DG, England
Co-published in North America in 1989, 1993, 2005, 2007 by
Baker Academic, a division of Baker Publishing Group
P.O. Box 6287, Grand Rapids, MI 49516-6287
www.bakeracademic.com

All rights reserved.
No part of this publication may be reproduced, stored in a retrieval system, or transmitted in any form or by any means—for example, electronic or mechanical, including photocopying or recording—without the prior written permission of the publisher. The only exception is brief quotations in printed reviews.

British Library Cataloguing-in-Publication Data

Dobson, John H.
Learn New Testament Greek. – 3rd rev. ed.
1.Bible. N.T. – Language, style 2.Greek language, Biblical – Grammar
I.Title
487.4
ISBN 9781909281219

Quotations from the Greek New Testament are from the
United Bible Societies' 4th revised edition, published by the United Bible Societies, copyright © The United Bible Societies, 1966, 1968, 1975, 1983, 1993.

The Greek fonts used to publish this work are available from
www.linguistsoftware.com. +1-425-775-1130.

Cover design by Projectluz
Book design by 2aT (www.2aT.com)

CONTENTS

Preface ix
Introduction xi

1. αβγ – Learning the Letters 1
2. ἐν ἀρχῇ – In the beginning 4
3. ἐστίν – is   ἦν – was 8

Introduction to Lessons 4–6 **12**
4. λέγω – I am saying, I say 13
5. λέγομεν – we are saying, we say 17
6. λόγος – a word   ὁ λόγος – the word 22

7. αὐτός – he   οὗτος – this 27
8. λέγων – saying   ὁ λέγων – the person saying 34
9. καρδία – a heart   ἡ καρδία – the heart 41
10. ἡμεῖς – we   ὑμεῖς – you   ὅς – who 49
11. ὃς ἂν λέγῃ – whoever says
    ἐὰν λέγῃ – if he says
    ἵνα λέγῃ – so that he may say
    λέγωμεν – let us say 56
12. ἔργον – a work   τὸ ἔργον – the work
    ὁ, ἡ, τό – the 63
13. ποιέω (ποιῶ) – I do, I make ⁓ 71
14. ἔλεγεν – he was saying, he used to say ⁓ | 78
15. ἐποίει – he was doing, he used to do ⁓ | 85
16. A to Ω – Alpha to Omega 91
17. πρός, εἰς, ἐν, ἐκ, ἀπό
    ἔρχεται – he comes, he goes 97
18. λέγειν – to say, to be saying ⁓ 101
19. λέγων, λέγουσα, λέγον – saying — 104

Introduction to Lessons 20–25 **111**
20. ποιήσας – having done ⦙ 113
21. ἐποίησα – I did, I made   ἔγραψα – I wrote, I did write ⦙| 120

v

22. βαλών – having thrown   ἐλθών – having gone ⊣   125
23. ἔβαλον – I threw   ἦρα – I picked up ⊣| 132
24. ἐσθίω – I am eating ▬   ἔφαγον – I ate ⊣|
    λέγειν — to be saying ▬   εἰπεῖν — to say •   138
25. καταβαίνοντος αὐτοῦ – while he was coming down
    καταβάντος αὐτοῦ – when he had come down ⊣   143

26. ἀκούσω – I will hear   βαλῶ – I will throw   148
27. Questions: τίς; – who?   τί; – what? why?   153
28. ἄνθρωπος ἀγαθός – a good man
    οἱ ἅγιοι – the saints   158
29. γίνομαι – I become, I happen   γιν ▬
    γενόμενος – having become   γεν ⊣   165
30. ποιῆσαι – to do •   ἐκβαλεῖν – to throw out •   171
31. βαπτίζομαι – I am being baptized ▬
    ἐβαπτιζόμην – I was being baptized ▬| 176
32. ἐβαπτίσθην – I was baptized ⊣|
    βαπτισθείς – having been baptized ⊣   186
33. πεπίστευκα – I have trusted, I trust ⟂ |→
    γέγραπται – it has been written, it is written ⟂ |→
    οἶδα – I know ⟂ |→   191
34. τίθημι – I am putting   δίδωμι – I am giving
    τιθείς – putting ▬   διδούς – giving ▬
    θείς – having put ⊣   δούς – having given ⊣   202

Introduction to Lessons 35–52   **208**

35. καλός – good   καλῶς – well
    εἷς, δύο, τρεῖς – one, two, three   209
36. ἵνα – so that, that
    ἵνα ποιήσῃ – so that he may do •
    ἵνα δῶμεν – so that we may give •   217
37. ὁ Κύριος – the Lord
    τὸν λόγον, τὴν καρδίαν: the accusative case   224
38. ὥστε – with the result that   234
39. τοῦ λόγου, τῆς καρδίας: the genitive case   240
40. τοῦτο ποίησον – do this!   249
41. μὴ κλέψῃς — do not steal •
    μὴ κλαῖε – do not weep, stop crying ▬   255
42. τῷ λόγῳ, τῇ καρδίᾳ: the dative case   260

43. εἰ ἐμερίσθη – if it has been divided ἐὰν μερισθῇ – if it should be divided	269

Introduction to Lesson 44 — 274

44. δίκαιος – righteous δικαιοσύνη – righteousness ἀδικία – injustice, wrong	275
45. νίπτω – I wash (someone or something else) νίπτομαι – I wash (part of myself)	284
46. Translating – Romans 1:1–7	288
47. εἶπες ὅτι ἐσθίει – you said that he was eating	293
48. The Influence of Hebrew and Aramaic	297
49. γένοιτο – let it happen, may it happen δεδώκει – he had given ⁻ |→|	307
50. ἵνα ἡ χαρὰ ὑμῶν ᾖ πεπληρωμένη ACKP...	314
51. Culture and Translation	321
52. Ἄγωμεν ἐντεῦθεν – Let us go on from here	326
Key to Progress Tests	333
Reference Grammar & Accents	335
Appendix: Some Thoughts on the Teaching of Biblical Languages	351
Scripture Index	359
Index of Grammar & Constructions	365
Index of Greek Words	369

Free MP3 audio files that accompany this book can be downloaded at:
http://piquanteditions.com/files/LearnNewTestamentGreek.zip

Symbols

—	continuing action	⋯	repeated action
⊣	completed action	•	single action, or action without specific reference to continuance
|	time line		
⋯|	continued or repeated action in past time	⊣|	completed action or single action in past time

⋰ \|→ action in past time, with a result that continues in present time; e.g. I have written.

⋰ \|→\| past action, that had a result in past time; e.g. I had written.

Abbreviations

GNB	Good News Bible
LXX	Septuagint (Greek Translation of Hebrew Scriptures)
NEB	New English Bible
NIV	New International Version
NJB	New Jerusalem Bible
NRSV	New Revised Standard Version
NLT	New Living Translation
REB	Revised English Bible
JBP	J B Phillips

LEARN NEW TESTAMENT GREEK

PREFACE

The enormous world-wide sales of the second edition of *Learn New Testament Greek* have shown that it is a book that students and tutors are delighted to use. Translations into Portuguese, Korean, Czech, French and Indonesian, and planned translations into Chinese and Urdu illustrate its universal appeal. So why is a third edition needed?

Since I worked on the second edition, I have had 12 years more experience of teaching, and my book *Learn Biblical Hebrew* has been published. In this third edition I have included teaching material that I find brings insight and delight to those who learn. My growing knowledge of Hebrew has enabled me to appreciate the literary skill of the NT writers in a new way. I have also discovered that often a word or passage in the New Testament that is perplexing becomes clear when it is translated back into Hebrew. In this third edition I have tried to share some of the new things I am learning.

I have also found that in the UK and the USA people are pleased to have help in comparing and assessing Bible translations. So I have included some Bible translation assessment exercises. These exercises will at the same time assist tutors using the book for distance learning. They will be able to test progress not only by setting NT texts for translation but also by asking for comments on the variety of translations of a particular passage offered in the exercises.

The greatest delight of my own students comes from reading and understanding biblical passages. I have increased the amount of reading material – especially the amount from the Gospel of St John.

The tape which was available with the first and second editions covered only lessons 2–14. Now with MP3 audio files we can include material from lessons 1–21.

Many tutors have asked that the text should be clearer to read and be accented. This edition has an accented text and is easier to read. In the appendix there is a short section with guidelines and suggestions for those who teach. I am always glad to answer questions about teaching methods and to listen to suggestions for improving the book. Please let me know if you find any errors.

To those of you who want to understand better the Hebraic background to the New Testament I commend the companion volume *Learn Biblical Hebrew* – see page 385 for more information.

Enjoy your learning and teaching,

John H Dobson

INTRODUCTION

The New Testament is a remarkable collection of writings. No book has had a more profound influence on the world's history.

If you wish to study the New Testament, it helps greatly if you are able to read it in the original language. With this course it is possible to *Learn New Testament Greek* quickly, even if you have never attempted to learn a language before. In the first hour you will begin to read and reflect on some New Testament text. After seventeen short lessons you will begin to read longer passages. By the end of the course you will have been helped to read about fifty passages from the New Testament. You will also have a grasp of the structure of the Greek language and its grammar, an ability to use commentaries that refer to the Greek text, and a growing skill as a translator. Because a lot of Greek will be fixed in your long-term memory you will be able to read much of the New Testament without constant reference to a dictionary.

The principles and methods used in *Learn New Testament Greek* ensure that you will make rapid progress with your studies. New information is introduced in small bits, which makes it easy to take in. It is frequently repeated, which makes it easy to remember. You learn words and forms before grammatical descriptions, which is the natural sequence – a child learns 'mouse' and 'mice' before it learns that 'mouse' is a noun and that 'mice' is plural. But because you can work through the course quickly, you can also learn the main grammatical forms and terms quickly, and you will learn how to parse Greek words.

In *Learn New Testament Greek* you will not be asked to memorize long lists of words or grammatical forms. You will rather learn the principles and pointers which enable you to recognize the meaning and function of words which are new to you. This will equip you to tackle even unfamiliar passages of the New Testament with confidence.

Learning New Testament Greek

You can use these lessons for study on your own or with a teacher. Most of the Greek sentences and passages are printed with an English translation on the right-hand side of the page. This means that you can start without any fear of making serious mistakes. We now know that looking at short sentences and phrases in a new language with a translation beside them is an excellent way to start learning a language. You are not cheating when you look at the translation, you are helping yourself learn. And, when you read the Greek with the translation covered, you can uncover it stage by stage to check whether you have understood it.

You will find the *Learn New Testament Greek* audio files a useful aid. You can hear Greek sentences and passages from the first 21 lessons read aloud. Follow the text as you listen: your ears and eyes will work together to fix ideas in your mind.

Use the audio files to get a general idea of the lessons you are going to study. Use it to review lessons you have done.

Instructions and suggestions

1. When you begin a new lesson, first read through it quickly, looking at the English and the Greek. Then work through it carefully, reading and translating the passages given.

2. The 'Translate' section has a line down the middle. Cover the right-hand column, using a plain piece of card or paper.

3. When you have read a line or a group of lines in Greek, move your piece of card a little way down the page and check that you have understood what the Greek means. If you made a mistake, mark that line and learn from it.

   If you do not know and cannot guess the meaning of a word, do not spend a long time looking at it. Use the check-column to find out what it means. Underline it or highlight it.

4. If you find that something in a lesson is not quite clear:
   (a) See if the English translation can help you to understand it
   (b) Continue to the end of the lesson
   (c) Do the next two or three lessons, because what you start to learn in any lesson is confirmed in the lessons that follow
   (d) Review earlier lessons in case there is something you have missed
   (e) Do not feel that you need to learn things the first time you see them. When you learned your own language you did not learn the word for 'Mummy' the first time you heard it. In Greek when you first see

ἐγένετο – 'it came into being', be content with that. You will learn related forms later on and they will be easier because you have seen ἐγένετο.

5. Work at your own speed, but go as fast as you can. At the end of each short section, pause for a moment of relaxation: take a few deep breaths, stretch your body, stand up, then start the next section refreshed.
   If you do two lessons a day, six days a week, you will complete the course in one month. If you do only one lesson a week, you will still finish in a year. Before you start each new session of study, read through the list of contents up to that point. It is a way to review rapidly the major forms you have learned.

6. From lesson 17 onwards you will need a copy of the Greek New Testament (see lesson 52.3 for more details).

7. If you are learning Greek because you wish to read the New Testament, you need not worry about how you pronounce it. The Greek language has changed as time has passed, and there is no single way that can be called the 'right' way to pronounce Greek words. Lessons 1 and 2 give guidelines, but they are not rules. Listen carefully to the audio CD. If your teacher has a different way of pronouncing Greek, listen carefully to your teacher.

8. Words are best learned by being seen in meaningful contexts. Words are flexible symbols. Their meanings vary according to the context in which they are used. So read and re-read the text of the lesson, but above all re-read the New Testament verses and passages.

9. Grammatical terms: when you go through the course for the first time, do not spend time and effort trying to learn them. To do so might hinder your efforts to learn Greek. Leave them for more careful study when you have read more of the New Testament. They will make more sense when you review them later on.

10. In these lessons everything that needs to be learned is written on the pages. So as soon as you have understood a lesson, you can use it to help others to learn; since all you have to do is to lead them through the pages and to help them to smile. Smiles stimulate study!

11. Enjoy your studies and take pleasure in your progress.

Lesson 1

αβγ – Learning the Letters

1.1 The Greek alphabet

The first step in learning New Testament Greek is to recognize the letters of the Greek alphabet. Several are similar to English letters, although this can sometimes be misleading (ρ looks like 'p' but sounds like 'r').

In the first column below, you will find the Greek letters with their closest English equivalents. The second column has groups of Greek letters and tells you how they are pronounced. When you have studied these carefully, try to read the groups of letters in the third column. Cover the fourth column while you read, then use it to check that you have recognized the letters correctly.

Greek letters	Read the groups of letters	Greek groups of letters	English equivalents
α – a			
β – b	αβ – ab	βα αββα	ba abba
γ – g	γαβ – gab	βαγ	bag
δ – d	βαδ – bad	δαβ γαδ δαδ	dab gad dad
ε – e	βεδ – bed	βεγ δεδ αβεδ	beg ded abed
ζ – dz or ds, as in 'cords'	βεζ – bedz	βεζ βεδ γαζ δαζ ζεδ βαδ	bedz bed gadz dadz dzed bad
η – ē ('ai', as in 'air', or 'ay', as in 'say')	γη – gē	βη δη ηδ ηζ ηδεδ αδεδ	bē dē ēd ēdz ēded aded
θ – th	δεθ – deth	βαθ γαθ βεθ	bath gath beth
ι – i	βιδ – bid	βιγ βιζ διδ ηδιδ	big bidz did ēdid
κ – k	κιθ – kith	κιδ κιζ κηκ	kid kidz kēk
λ – l	λιδ – lid	λαδ λεγ βελλ βεθελ	lad leg bell bethel
μ – m	μη – mē	μαθ μηκ καμελ	math mēk camel

1

ν – n	μαν – man	μεν νημ θιν κιν	men nēm thin kin
ξ – x	αξ – ax	εξ μιξ νιξ νικ λαξ λαζ βιξ βιζ	ex mix nix nik lax ladz bix bidz
o – o	οξ – ox	νοδ ναγ μοθ ον	nod nag moth on
π – p	ποπ – pop	πιπ ποξ ποζ πηδ	pip pox podz pēd
ρ – r	ραν – ran	ριπ ριγ πη μαρκ	rip rig pē mark
σ , ς – s (ς is used only at the end of words)	σιπ – sip	σαπ σκιλλ γοσπελ ριβς ναγς σαγς	sap skill gospel ribs nags sags
τ – t	σετ – set	σατ σιτς τηκ τοτ	sat sits tēk tot
υ – 'u' as in French 'lune', or 'oo' as in 'book'; 'w' when it starts a word	βυκ – book	λυκ κυκ τυκ ρυκ υιθ υιν	look kook took rook with win
φ – ph, f	φυτ – foot	φιτ φατ φιστ φοξ	fit fat fist fox
χ – kh	χακι – khaki	χριστος χριστοφερ	khristos khristopher
ψ – ps	λιψ – lips	τιψ ταψ ταπ ριψ	tips taps tap rips
ω – ō 'o', as in 'phone'	φων – phōn	φωτω σωπ σοπ	phōtō sōp sop
ʽ – h (Written over an initial vowel)	ἁτ – hat	ἱτ ἁμ ὁτ ὡπ ἱψ	hit ham hot hōp hips
ʼ (Written over initial vowel when there is no 'h' sound)	ἀτ – at	ἀμ ἰτ ὀν ἠτ ἰλλ ἱλλ ὀψ	am it on ēt ill hill hops

LEARN NEW TESTAMENT GREEK

1.2 Greek you already know

As you begin to read Greek, you will find that you can already understand some words, because there are English words like them. Notice, for example:

ἀπόστολος – apostle   προφήτης – prophet
θρόνος – throne   Χριστός – Christ

Other words you will quickly recognize because English words are derived from them:

θεός – God   **the**ology
λόγος – word   **the**o**logy**, **logic**
ἄνθρωπος – man   **anthropo**logy
ἀρχή – beginning   **arch**aeology
γράφω – I write   **graph**, para**graph**
ἐν – in   **en**try
φῶς – light   **phos**phorus.

You may also know:

Κύριε ἐλέησον Lord have mercy

When you learn Κύριος – Lord, master, owner; you will be aware that in speaking to someone, you say Κύριε.

You may know 'Jesu, joy of man's desiring'; so when you learn Ἰησοῦς – Jesus, this will help you to be aware that someone speaking to Ἰησοῦς will say Ἰησοῦ.

If you know the tune of *Kumbaya* ('Come by here') you may like to use ἔρχου 'Come!' and ὧδε 'here' to sing:

Ἔρχου ὧδε Κύριε (3 times)
ὦ Ἰησοῦ Κύριε.

1.3 Writing the letters

The arrows show you the easiest place to begin when writing a Greek letter.

αβγδεζηθικλμνξοπρστυφχψω

Notes:
1. Do not put a dot over ι .
2. Be careful to make n pointed: ν , and u round: υ .

LESSON 1

Lesson 2

ἐν ἀρχῇ – In the beginning

2.1 The Greek alphabet – small letters

Look again at the alphabet:

α – a	η – ē	ν – n	τ – t
β – b	θ – th	ξ – x	υ – oo, w
γ – g	ι – i	ο – o	φ – ph
δ – d	κ – k	π – p	χ – kh
ε – e	λ – l	ρ – r	ψ – ps
ζ – dz	μ – m	σ, ς – s	ω – ō

2.2

When two vowels come together, they give the following sounds:

αι – i, ai   (as in mile, aisle)
ει – ei   (as in veil)
οι – oi   (as in boil)
αυ – au, ou   (as in out)
ευ – eu, yew (as in feud)
ου – oo   (as in root)
υι – ui, wi   (as in we)
ιη – yē   (as in Yale)

So αἱ is pronounced like 'high', εὑ is pronounced like 'you', and Ἰησοῦς is pronounced 'Yē-soos'.
Note that when two vowels make a single sound at the beginning of a word, the breathing mark ʼ or ʽ is written over the second vowel.

2.3

When γ occurs before κ, χ, or another γ, it is pronounced as 'n' rather than 'g'.

γγ – ng   γκ – nk   γχ – nkh

So ἄγγελος is pronounced rather like 'angle-os'.

2.4

Read the following lines carefully. Start by reading the Greek words while you keep an eye on the English equivalent. Then cover the right-hand column and read the Greek words again. Uncover the right-hand column to check that you are correct. See that you know the sound the letters make. You will learn the meaning of the words in 2.5.

	Cover this column
ἐν ἀρχῇ ἦν ὁ λόγος	en arkhē ēn ho logos
καὶ ὁ λόγος ἦν πρὸς τὸν θεόν	kai ho logos ēn pros ton theon
καὶ θεὸς ἦν ὁ λόγος.	kai theos ēn ho logos.
οὗτος ἦν ἐν ἀρχῇ	hootos ēn en arkhē
πρὸς τὸν θεόν.	pros ton theon

Note that ι can be written underneath α, η and ω: ᾳ ῃ ῳ. It is not pronounced, or is pronounced very lightly. You see it in this lesson in the word ἀρχῇ.

2.5 Words

ἀρχή – beginning	ἦν – he was, it was	καί – and
λόγος – word	ἐν – in	ὁ – the
θεός – God	πρός – towards, with	τόν – the
οὗτος – this, he		

2.6 Read and then translate

Cover up the right-hand column and translate the passage, uncovering the right-hand column to check each line. Do not read the notes below until you have translated the whole passage.

ἐν ἀρχῇ	In (the) beginning[1]
ἦν ὁ λόγος,	was the word,
καὶ ὁ λόγος ἦν	and the word was
πρὸς τὸν θεόν	with (the) God[2]
καὶ θεὸς ἦν ὁ λόγος.	and the word was God.[3]
οὗτος ἦν ἐν ἀρχῇ	He was in the beginning
πρὸς τὸν θεόν.	with God.

Notes:
1. ἐν ἀρχῇ – in beginning. 'In beginning' is not good English. We translate as 'In the beginning'.
2. πρὸς τὸν θεόν – with the God. In English we do not usually use 'the' when referring to God, so we translate as 'with God'.
3. καὶ θεὸς ἦν ὁ λόγος – and the word was God. Notice that the order of words is different in English.

2.7 Translation

You have read and translated John 1.1. You have noticed that ideas in Greek and in English may be expressed in different words. To translate is not to put the words of one language into another: it is to express the meaning of the words in another language.

2.8 The beautiful Hebraic poetic patterning of John 1:1–2

Hebrew poets made use of carefully crafted word patterns and repetition of key words. Sometimes they combined two patterns together. In John 1:1–2 we find terrace patterning and chiasmus. In terrace patterns the last word of one line is used as the first main word of the next line. Many commentators have noticed this in John 1:1 Note λόγος... λόγος and θεόν... θεὸς :

Ἐν ἀρχῇ ἦν ὁ λόγος
   καὶ ὁ λόγος ἦν πρὸς τὸν θεόν
      καὶ θεὸς ἦν ὁ λόγος

But the dominant pattern in 1:1–2 is chiasmus. In a chiasmus there is a step by step forward movement to a central focus and then a balancing step by step backwards to the closure. This produces patterns like ABC C'B'A and ABCDC'B'A'.

```
A      Ἐν ἀρχῇ
  B      ἦν
    C      ὁ λόγος
             καὶ ὁ λόγος
      D      ἦν
        E      πρὸς τὸν θεόν
                 καὶ θεὸς
      D'     ἦν
    C'     ὁ λόγος
             οὗτος
  B'     ἦν
A'     ἐν ἀρχῇ πρὸς τὸν θεόν         A' CLOSURE: A, plus part of the
                                          central focus
```

Note that in an extended chiasmus the most emphatic point is at the centre. This is a feature to be found in some of the parables of Jesus. Here in John 1:1–2 the major emphasis is on the word θεός.

The closure echoes the beginning but is extended by including part of the central focus. This kind of extension in a closure is also a feature of Hebrew poetry.

Note also the threefold use of the key words λόγος and θεός. John 1:3–10 is also a chiasmus, and we shall see a key word repeated three times in verse 3, and a key word three times in verse 10. Verse 10 repeats part of verse 3, helping to mark the closure.

Lesson 3

ἐστίν – is   ἦν – was

3.1

ἐστίν means 'he is', 'she is', or 'it is'.
ἦν means 'he was', 'she was', or 'it was'.

When we translate ἐστίν and ἦν we can only tell whether to use 'he', 'she', or 'it', by reading the passage as a whole.
Compare

(a) Ἰησοῦς ἦν πρὸς τὸν θεόν. ἀληθὴς ἦν.
Jesus was with God. He was true.

(b) Μαρία ἦν πρὸς τὸν θεόν. ἀληθὴς ἦν.
Mary was with God. She was true.

(c) ὁ λόγος ἀληθὴς ἦν καὶ ἀληθής ἐστιν
The word was true and it is true.

Note that the word order is often not the same in English as it is in Greek. For ἀληθὴς ἦν in (a) we do not say 'True he was', but 'He was true'. Compare θεὸς ἦν ὁ λόγος in 2.6. In this sentence ὁ (the) indicates that the subject is λόγος, so we translate it, 'The word was God'.

3.2 Translate

1. Ἰησοῦς ἐστίν.	Jesus is.
2. Ἰησοῦς ἦν.	Jesus was.
3. ὁ λόγος ἦν.	The word was.
4. ὁ λόγος ἐστίν.	The word is.
5. θεός ἐστιν ὁ λόγος.	The word is God.
6. ἀληθής ἐστιν ὁ λόγος καὶ ἀληθὴς ἦν.	The word is true and it was true.
7. ἐν ἀρχῇ ἦν ὁ λόγος, καὶ ἐν ἀρχῇ ἀληθὴς ἦν.	In the beginning the word was, and in the beginning it was true.

3.3 Words

ὁ λόγος – the word
οἱ λόγοι – the words
ὁ Μᾶρκος – Mark
ὁ Ἰησοῦς – Jesus
τοῦ – of the
τοῦ Ἰησοῦ – of Jesus
οὗτος – this, he
οὗτοι – these

οὗτος ὁ λόγος – this word
ἐστίν – he is, she is, it is
εἰσίν – they are
ἦν – he was, she was, it was
ἦσαν – they were
γράφει – he writes, she writes
γράφει τὸν λόγον – he writes the word
γράφει τοὺς λόγους – he writes the words

ἀληθής – true, genuine, real, honest
οὗτοι οἱ λόγοι ἀληθεῖς ἦσαν – these words were true

3.4 Translate

1. ὁ λόγος ἀληθής ἐστιν.	The word is true.
2. οἱ λόγοι ἀληθεῖς εἰσιν.	The words are true.
3. οὗτος ὁ λόγος ἀληθής ἐστιν.	This word is true.
4. οὗτοι οἱ λόγοι ἀληθεῖς εἰσιν.	These words are true.
5. ἀληθὴς ἦν ὁ λόγος.	The word was true.
6. ἀληθὴς ἦν ὁ λόγος τοῦ Ἰησοῦ.	The word of Jesus was true.
7. γράφει τὸν λόγον.	He writes the word.
8. γράφει τοὺς λόγους.	He writes the words.
9. ὁ Μᾶρκος γράφει τοὺς λόγους. γράφει τοὺς λόγους τοῦ Ἰησοῦ. οὗτοι οἱ λόγοι τοῦ Ἰησοῦ ἀληθεῖς εἰσιν.	Mark writes the words. He writes the words of Jesus. These words of Jesus are true.
10. ὁ Ἰησοῦς ἦν πρὸς τὸν θεόν. οὗτος ἦν ἐν ἀρχῇ πρὸς τὸν θεόν.	Jesus was with God. He was in the beginning with God.
11. οὗτοι εἰσιν οἱ λόγοι τοῦ Ἰησοῦ καὶ οἱ λόγοι τοῦ Μάρκου.	These are the words of Jesus and the words of Mark.

3.5

You have begun to learn the following Greek words. Notice the English words that are like them. Many English words are derived from Greek words.

LESSON 3

Greek word	Compare
ἡ ἀρχή – the beginning	archetype – original model
	archaeology – study of things from earlier times
ὁ θεός – God, the God	theism – belief in God
	theology – study of God
ὁ λόγος – the word	logic, theology, archaeology
Ἰησοῦς – Jesus	Jesus
Μᾶρκος – Mark	Mark
ἐν – in	enter, in
ἐστίν – he is, she is, it is	is
εἰσίν – they are	is
γράφει – he writes, she writes	graph, paragraph, graffiti
πρός – to, with	prosthetic

3.6

(a) Using the patterns
   οἱ λόγοι τοῦ Ἰησοῦ – the words of Jesus
   ἡ ἀγάπη τοῦ θεοῦ – the love of God
            and the words from 3.5
   say in Greek:
      The words of Jesus – the words of God – the word of God – the word of Mark – the words of Mark – the love of God – the love of Jesus – the beginning of the word.

(b) Using the patterns
   ἀγαθός ἐστιν ὁ θεός – God is good
   ἀληθὴς ἦν ὁ λόγος – the word was true
   say in Greek:
      God is good – the word is good – Mark is good – the word is true – the word was true – Mark was honest – the word was good.

(c) Learn by heart from 1 Jn 1:5 ὁ θεὸς φῶς ἐστιν (God is light) and from 1 Jn 4:16 ὁ θεὸς ἀγάπη ἐστίν (God is love).

3.7 Progress test 1

Test the progress you have made by reading these questions and writing down which answers you think are correct. For example, in question 1 if you think that Ἰησοῦς ἐστιν means 'Jesus is', write down: 1 (c).

Which translation is correct?

1. Ἰησοῦς ἐστιν.
(a) The word is.
(b) Jesus was.
(c) Jesus is.

2. ὁ λόγος ἦν.
(a) The word was.
(b) The word is.
(c) God was.

3. οὗτός ἐστιν ὁ λόγος
(a) God is the word.
(b) This is the word.
(c) These are the words.

4. οὗτοι οἱ λόγοι ἀληθεῖς εἰσιν
(a) These words are true.
(b) This word is true.
(c) He writes true words.

5. γράφει τοὺς λόγους τοῦ Ἰησοῦ ὁ Μᾶρκος.
(a) Jesus is writing these words.
(b) He is writing the words of Jesus and of Mark.
(c) Mark is writing the words of Jesus.

Now check your answers by looking in Key to Progress Tests on page 333.

INTRODUCTION TO LESSONS 4–6

When you have mastered lessons 4, 5, and 6 you will have made a great advance towards your goal of reading the New Testament in Greek. In each lesson you will learn a few important new forms. You will learn them one small step at a time, but for purposes of reference all the forms are listed here.

In lessons 4 and 5 you will learn the forms of
λέγω – I am saying, I speak:

One person – singular
λέγω – I am saying
λέγεις – you are saying
λέγει – he is saying

More than one person – plural
λέγομεν – we are saying
λέγετε – you are saying
λέγουσιν – they are saying

In lesson 6 you will learn the forms of λόγος – a word, and ὁ – the:

Singular
ὁ λόγος – the word   < subject >
τὸν λόγον – the word   < object >
τοῦ λόγου – of the word
τῷ λόγῳ – with the word

Plural
οἱ λόγοι – the words
τοὺς λόγους – the words
τῶν λόγων – of the words
τοῖς λόγοις – with the words

Lessons 4–6 should be studied as a group. When you do lessons 4 and 5 you will probably have some questions in your mind which you will find answered in lesson 6.

Lesson 4

λέγω – I am saying, I say

4.1

λέγω – I am saying, I say, I speak
λέγεις – you are saying, you say, you speak
λέγει – he is saying, he says, he speaks

Note that the endings show who is speaking:

-ω – I   -εις – you, thou   -ει – he, she, it.

Each of these endings refers to only one person.

Note that as Greek uses the same ending for he, she, or it, λέγει could also mean 'she is speaking', or 'she speaks'. If you are reading a whole passage of Greek, you will be able to tell which is meant. To save space in this book, -ει forms are usually translated as 'he...', but bear in mind that sometimes they could equally well mean 'she...', or 'it...'.

4.2

λέγω – I am saying, I say	The ending
I am speaking, I speak	-ω
γράφω – I am writing, I write	indicates 'I'.

So: λέγω τὸν λόγον – I am saying the word
                      I am speaking the word

γράφω τοὺς λόγους – I am writing the words.

Translate:

1. λέγω τοὺς λόγους.	I am saying the words.
2. τὸν λόγον γράφω.	I am writing the word.
3. γράφω τοὺς λόγους.	I am writing the words.
4. γράφω τοὺς λόγους τοῦ Μάρκου.	I am writing the words of Mark.
5. λέγω λόγους ἀληθεῖς.	I am saying true words.
6. λέγω τὸν λόγον.	I am saying the word.
7. λέγω τὸν λόγον τοῦ θεοῦ.	I am saying the word of God.

4.3 Translation

λέγω – I say, I speak, I tell, I am saying...

Note that when we wish to translate λέγω into English we have to choose from several English words. Consider λέγω αὐτῷ. αὐτῷ means 'to him'. So we may translate λέγω αὐτῷ as 'I say to him', 'I speak to him', 'I tell him', or 'I am telling him'.

In 4.2 no. 7, λέγω τὸν λόγον τοῦ θεοῦ, 'I am speaking God's word' might be a better translation than 'I am saying the word of God'. When you check your own translations by uncovering the right-hand columns in this book, do not ask yourself 'Have I used exactly the same words in my translation?' but 'Have I expressed the same meaning?'

4.4

λέγεις – you are saying, you say
γράφεις – you are writing, you write

The ending -εις indicates **you** (when speaking to one person)

So: λέγεις τὸν λόγον αὐτῷ – you are saying the word to him
λέγεις λόγον αὐτῷ – you are saying a word to him
'Ιησοῦ, λέγεις λόγους – Jesus, you are speaking words.

Translate:

1. λέγεις τοὺς λόγους αὐτῷ.	You are saying the words to him.
2. λέγεις λόγους αὐτῷ.	You are saying words to him.
3. γράφεις τὸν λόγον.	You are writing the word.
4. γράφω λόγον.	I am writing a word.
5. 'Ιησοῦ, λέγεις τοὺς λόγους.	Jesus, you are speaking the words.
6. 'Ιησοῦ, λέγεις τοὺς λόγους τοῦ θεοῦ.	Jesus, you are speaking the words of God.
7. 'Ιησοῦ, λέγεις αὐτῷ τοὺς λόγους τοῦ θεοῦ.	Jesus, you are telling him the words of God.

4.5

λέγει – he is saying, he says.
γράφει – he is writing, he writes
ἀναγινώσκει – he is reading, he reads

The ending -ει indicates **he, she,** or **it**.

So: λέγει τοὺς λόγους τοῦ θεοῦ – he speaks the words of God
ὁ προφήτης λέγει τοὺς λόγους – the prophet speaks the words
ἀναγινώσκει λόγους ὁ Μᾶρκος – Mark reads words
ἀναγινώσκει λόγους ἡ Μαρία – Mary reads words.

Translate:

1. λέγει τοὺς λόγους.	He speaks the words.
2. ὁ προφήτης γράφει τοὺς λόγους.	The prophet writes the words.
3. ὁ Μᾶρκος ἀναγινώσκει τοὺς λόγους.	Mark reads the words.
4. ὁ Μᾶρκος ἀναγινώσκει τοὺς λόγους τοῦ προφήτου.	Mark reads the words of the prophet.
5. λέγω λόγους καὶ ὁ Μᾶρκος γράφει τοὺς λόγους.	I speak words and Mark writes the words.
6. γράφεις λόγους καὶ ὁ προφήτης ἀναγινώσκει τοὺς λόγους.	You are writing words and the prophet is reading the words.

4.6

(a) Using the patterns λέγω τὸν λόγον – I say the word
 and γράφεις τοὺς λόγους – you write the words

 say in Greek:
  I say the word – you say the word – he says the word –
  you write the words – she says the words – I write the words –
  he writes the word – he writes the words – you write the word –
  I say the words.

(b) γενηθήτω – let there be, let it come into being
 ἐγένετο – there was, it came into being

 With your eyes closed or the light switched off say:
  γενηθήτω φῶς (Let there be light).
 Then with the light on or open eyes:
  καὶ φῶς ἐγένετο (and there was light).

(c) ἐγώ I, τὸ φῶς – the light, ὁ κόσμος – the world.
 Learn by heart from John 8:12,
  Ἐγώ εἰμι τὸ φῶς τοῦ κόσμου (I am the light of the world).

4.7 Progress test 2

Which translation is correct?

1. λέγεις τοὺς λόγους.
(a) I am speaking the words.
(b) You are speaking the word.
(c) You are speaking the words.

2. λέγει λόγον.
(a) He speaks a word.
(b) You speak a word.
(c) I speak a word.

3. λέγω λόγους ἀληθεῖς.
(a) He speaks true words.
(b) You speak true words.
(c) I speak true words.

4. ὁ προφήτης γράφει τοὺς λόγους,
(a) He writes the word of the prophet,
(b) The prophet writes the words,
(c) The prophet speaks the words,

5. καὶ ἀναγινώσκεις αὐτούς.
(a) and you read them.
(b) and he reads them.
(c) and she reads them.

Check your answers in Key to Progress Tests on page 333

Lesson 5

λέγομεν – we are saying, we say

5.1

In lesson 4 you learned three forms which indicate a single person:

λέγω – I am saying   -ω – I
λέγεις – you are saying   -εις – you
λέγει – he is saying, she is saying   -ει – he, she, it

Now you will learn three forms which indicate more than one person:

λέγομεν – we are saying   -ομεν – we
λέγετε – you are saying   -ετε – you
λέγουσιν – they are saying   -ουσιν, -ουσι – they

Note the difference between

λέγεις – you say (singular).
and λέγετε – you say (plural).

5.2

λέγομεν – we are saying, we say   The ending
γράφομεν – we are writing   **-ομεν**
ἀναγινώσκομεν – we are reading   indicates **we**.

So: λέγομεν τοὺς λόγους καὶ γράφομεν αὐτούς
     We are saying the words and we are writing them

     γράφομεν τὸν λόγον καὶ ἀναγινώσκομεν αὐτόν
     We are writing the word and we are reading it.

Translate:

1. γράφομεν τὸν λόγον καὶ ἀναγινώσκεις αὐτόν.	We write the word and you read it.
2. γράφει τοὺς λόγους καὶ ἀναγινώσκομεν αὐτούς.	He writes the words and we read them.
3. ὁ προφήτης λέγει τοὺς λόγους τοῦ θεοῦ καὶ γράφομεν αὐτούς.	The prophet speaks the words of God and we write them.

4. λέγομεν τοὺς λόγους τοῦ Ἰησοῦ καὶ γράφει αὐτοὺς ὁ Μᾶρκος. | We speak the words of Jesus and Mark writes them.

5. ὁ Μᾶρκος γράφει τὸν λόγον καὶ ἀναγινώσκομεν αὐτόν. | Mark writes the word and we read it.

5.3

λέγετε – you are saying, you say
γράφετε – you are writing
ἀκούετε – you are hearing

The ending **-ετε** indicates **you**, when addressing more than one person (plural or p)

So: λέγομεν τούτους τοὺς λόγους καὶ ἀκούετε αὐτούς
We speak these words and you hear them

γράφετε τοῦτον τὸν λόγον καὶ ἀναγινώσκω αὐτόν
You write this word and I read it.

Translate:

1. λέγετε τοῦτον τὸν λόγον. | You speak this word.
2. ἀκούετε τοῦτον τὸν λόγον. | You hear this word.
3. γράφετε τούτους τοὺς λόγους καὶ ἀναγινώσκω αὐτούς. | You write these words and I read them.
4. ὁ προφήτης λέγει τούτους τοὺς λόγους καὶ ἀκούετε αὐτούς. | The prophet speaks these words and you hear them.
5. ἀναγινώσκετε τοὺς λόγους τοῦ προφήτου καὶ ἀκούομεν αὐτούς. | You are reading the words of the prophet and we hear them.

5.4

λέγουσιν – they are saying, they say.
ἀκούουσιν – they are hearing
ἀναγινώσκουσιν – they are reading

The ending **-ουσιν** or **-ουσι** indicates **they**.

So: γράφουσιν τοὺς λόγους ἐν τῷ βιβλίῳ
They are writing the words in the book

οἱ προφῆται ἀναγινώσκουσιν τοὺς λόγους τοῦ βιβλίου
The prophets are reading the words of the book.

Translate:

1. οἱ προφῆται γράφουσιν τοὺς λόγους ἐν τῷ βιβλίῳ.	The prophets are writing the words in the book.
2. οἱ προφῆται λέγουσιν τοὺς λόγους τοῦ θεοῦ καὶ ἀκούομεν τοὺς λόγους.	The prophets speak the words of God and we hear the words.
3. ἀναγινώσκετε τοὺς λόγους τοῦ βιβλίου και ἀκούουσιν αὐτούς.	You read the words of the book and they hear them.
4. ἀκούουσιν τοὺς λόγους καὶ γράφουσιν αὐτοὺς ἐν τῷ βιβλίῳ.	They hear the words and they write them in the book.

5.5

Here are the forms of λέγω you have learned:

One person (singular)	More than one person (plural)
λέγω – I say	λέγομεν – we say
λέγεις – you say	λέγετε – you say
λέγει – he says	λέγουσιν – they say

The endings indicate the person:

-ω – I   -εις – you   -ει – he, she, it

-ομεν – we   -ετε – you   -ουσιν – they

The main part, or stem, indicates the meaning:

Verb	Stem
λέγω – I say	λεγ – say
γράφω – I write	γραφ – write
ἀκούω – I hear	ακου – hear
ἀναγινώσκω – I read	αναγινωσκ – read.

5.6 Type of action – continuing or repeated

Compare these two sentences:

(a) I am writing the words – γράφω τοὺς λόγους
(b) I write the words – γράφω τοὺς λόγους

In (a), γράφω describes an action that is going on now; a continuous action. We will represent this continuing present action by a line: — .

In (b), if the sentence is completed by the words 'every day', so that it reads

LESSON 5

'I write the words every day', then γράφω describes a repeated action, or a series of repeated actions. We will represent this kind of repeated action by a series of dots: ···· . So in Greek, a form like λέγω or γράφω may represent either:

        continuing action —

    or repeated action ····

When we translate such forms into English we have to choose either an English form that indicates continuing action: I am saying, I am writing —, or one that indicates repeated action: I say, I write ····

In short passages and single sentences like the ones in these early lessons it is not usually possible to choose one form rather than the other. So if you translate λέγομεν as 'we are saying', and the check-column has 'we say', do not be surprised. You are not wrong; either alternative is an acceptable translation.

5.7

(a) Using patterns like:

    ἀκούομεν τοὺς λόγους – we hear the words
    ἀναγινώσκετε τὸ βιβλίον – you read the book
    and γράφουσιν τὸν λόγον – they write the word

say in Greek:

    We hear the words – you hear the words – you read the book –
    we read the book – they write the book – they write the word –
    you write the word – we write the word – I hear the word –
    he hears the words – she reads the book.

(b) Using χαίρετε Rejoice! or, Greetings! for a group, ὑμῖν to you and χαῖρε when speaking to one person with σοί to you and εἰρήνη peace! shalom! ἀγάπη love, and χαρά joy

Practice the following greetings

The leader says:		The group replies:
χαίρετε		χαῖρε
εἰρήνη ὑμῖν	Peace to you	εἰρήνη σοί
ἀγάπη ὑμῖν	Love to you	ἀγάπη σοί
χαρὰ ὑμῖν	Joy to you	χαρὰ σοί

(c) ὑμεῖς – you (plural)   αὐτοῖς – to them.

From Mt 5:14 learn:
ὑμεῖς ἐστε τὸ φῶς τοῦ κόσμου.   You are the light of the world.

From John 20:19:
καὶ λέγει αὐτοῖς, Εἰρήνη ὑμῖν.   and he says (said) to them,
Peace to you!

5.8 Progress test 3

Which translation is correct?

1. ἀκούουσιν τοὺς λόγους.
(a) We speak the words.
(b) They hear the words.
(c) We hear the word.

2. ἀναγινώσκομεν τὸν λόγον.
(a) They read the word.
(b) We are reading the word.
(c) You are reading the word.

3. γράφετε τὰ βιβλία.
(a) You read the books.
(b) He writes the books.
(c) You write the books.

4. ἀναγινώσκει τὸ βιβλίον.
(a) We read the book.
(b) You read the book.
(c) She reads the book.

5. οἱ προφῆται ἀκούουσι τοὺς λόγους τοῦ θεοῦ.
(a) The prophets hear the words of God.
(b) The prophet hears the words of God.
(c) The prophet hears the word of God.

Check your answers in Key to Progress Tests on page 333.

Lesson 6

λόγος – a word   ὁ λόγος – the word

6.1

In a simple sentence like

ὁ ἀπόστολος	λέγει	τὸν λόγον
The apostle	speaks	the word

there are three main parts: the subject, the verb, and the object.

The apostle – ὁ ἀπόστολος – is the subject,
                               the person who does something
speaks – λέγει – is the verb, indicating the action being done
the word – τὸν λόγον – is the object, the thing done,
                               or affected by the doing.

In English we usually show the subject by putting it before the verb, and the object by putting it after the verb.

In Greek it is usually the ending of the word which shows most clearly whether it is the subject or the object, not the order of words. Usually **-ος** indicates a subject and **-ον** indicates an object.

So: ὁ Μᾶρκος γράφει τὸν λόγον
and   γράφει τὸν λόγον ὁ Μᾶρκος
both mean: Mark writes the word.

When we want to understand a Greek sentence we must always read it right through to the end, keeping alert to notice the various subject and object indicators.

6.2

λόγος – a word   λόγοι – words   -ος   } subject endings
ὁ λόγος – the word οἱ λόγοι – the words -οι
                                             ὁ
                                             οἱ } the (indicating subject)

So: λόγος ἀληθής – a true word
         ὁ λόγος ἀληθής ἐστιν – the word is true.

Translate:

1. λόγοι, λόγος.	Words, a word.
2. ὁ λόγος, οἱ λόγοι.	The word, the words.
3. οἱ λόγοι ἀληθεῖς εἰσιν.	The words are true.
4. ὁ λόγος ἀληθής ἐστιν.	The word is true.

6.3

τὸν λόγον – the word (object)   -ον
τοὺς λόγους – the words (object)   -ους } object endings

τὸν
τοὺς } the (usually indicating object)

So: γράφει τοὺς λόγους – he writes the words
γράφει τοὺς λόγους ὁ ἀπόστολος – the apostle writes the words
ἀκούετε αὐτούς – you hear them.

Translate:

1. γράφει τοὺς λόγους.	He writes the words.
2. λέγομεν λόγους.	We speak words.
3. γράφει λόγον.	He writes a word.
4. γράφει τοὺς λόγους ὁ προφήτης.	The prophet writes the words.
5. λέγετε τοὺς λόγους καὶ ἀκούομεν αὐτούς.	You speak the words and we hear them.
6. γράφεις τὸν λόγον καὶ ἀναγινώσκω αὐτόν.	You write the word and I read it.

6.4

τοῦ λόγου – of the word   -ου
τῶν λόγων – of the words   -ων } endings indicating **of**

τοῦ
τῶν } of the

So: ἡ ἀρχὴ τοῦ λόγου
The beginning of the word

ἀναγινώσκει τοὺς λόγους τῶν προφήτων
He is reading the words of the prophets

LESSON 6

ἀκούετε τὸν λόγον τοῦ ἀποστόλου
You hear the word of the apostle.

Translate:
1. ἡ ἀρχὴ τῶν λόγων. | The beginning of the words.
2. ὁ λόγος τοῦ προφήτου. | The word of the prophet.
3. οἱ λόγοι τῶν προφητῶν. | The words of the prophets.
4. ὁ ἀπόστολος γράφει τοὺς λόγους τοῦ Ἰησοῦ. | The apostle writes the words of Jesus.
5. οἱ λόγοι τοῦ ἀποστόλου ἀληθεῖς εἰσιν. | The words of the apostle are true.
6. ἀκούομεν τοὺς λόγους τῶν ἀποστόλων καὶ γράφομεν αὐτοὺς ἐν τῷ βιβλίῳ. | We hear the words of the apostles and we write them in the book.

6.5

τῷ λόγῳ – by the word, with the word

- ῳ ⎱ endings indicating
- οις ⎰ by, with, to, for, etc.

τῷ ἀποστόλῳ – to the apostle, for the apostle
τοῖς λόγοις – by the words, with the words

τῷ ⎱
τοῖς ⎰ by the, with the, etc.

So: λέγουσιν λόγοις – they speak by means of words
λέγουσιν τοῖς ἀποστόλοις – they say to the apostles
γράφετε ἐπιστολὰς αὐτῷ καὶ λέγομεν αὐτοῖς
You write letters to him and we speak to them.

Translate:
1. λέγω αὐτοῖς. | I am speaking to them.
2. γράφομεν τοὺς λόγους αὐτοῖς καὶ ἀναγινώσκουσιν τοὺς λόγους. | We write the words to them (for them) and they read the words.
3. λέγεις λόγοις. | You speak by means of words.
4. λέγετε τοῖς λόγοις. | You speak by means of the words.
5. ὁ προφήτης λέγει τῷ ἀποστόλῳ τοὺς λόγους τοῦ θεοῦ καὶ ὁ ἀπόστολος γράφει αὐτοὺς ἐν τῷ βιβλίῳ. | The prophet speaks the words of God to the apostle and the apostle writes them in the book.

6.6

(a) Using patterns like:

γράφει τὸν λόγον ὁ Μᾶρκος – Mark writes the word
and ἀναγινώσκουσιν τοὺς λόγους τοῦ Μάρκου – they read the words of Mark

say in Greek

Mark writes the word – the prophet writes the word –
the apostle speaks the words – the apostle reads the words –
they read the words of Mark – they read the words of the apostle –
they write the words of the apostles.

(b) Practice using and responding to these requests or commands

Spoken to more than one person		Spoken to only one person
ἀνάστητε	Stand up!	ἀνάστηθι
κάθητε	Sit down!	κάθου
ἀκούετε	Listen!	ἄκουε

(c) **μένω** I stay, I abide   **ὁ μένων** the person abiding
ἐν in   **ἐν αὐτῷ** in him, in that person

Read 1 John 4:16 b

ὁ θεὸς ἀγάπη ἐστίν, καὶ ὁ μένων ἐν τῇ ἀγάπῃ
ἐν τῷ θεῷ μένει καὶ ὁ θεὸς ἐν αὐτῷ μένει.

(d) Word fun.

Three girls who can help us with Greek:

Agatha is good,	ἀγαθός – good
Catherine is pure,	καθαρός – pure
Ethel is willing.	ἐθέλω or θέλω – I am willing.

6.7 Progress test 4

Which is the better English translation?

1. λέγουσιν τοὺς λόγους οἱ ἀπόστολοι.
(a) They speak the words the apostles.
(b) The apostles speak the words.

2. τὸ βιβλίον ἀναγινώσκει ὁ προφήτης.
(a) The book he is reading the prophet.
(b) The prophet is reading the book.

3. γράφει τούτους τοὺς λόγους ὁ Μᾶρκος.
(a) Mark writes these words.
(b) Mark writes these the words.

4. τοὺς λόγους αὐτοῦ ἀναγινώσκομεν αὐτοῖς.
(a) The words of him we are reading to them.
(b) We are reading them his words.

Check your answers in Key to Progress Tests on page 333.

Lesson 7

αὐτός – he   οὗτος – this

7.1

αὐτός (he) has forms similar to λόγος

αὐτός – he, it   αὐτοί – they

So: αὐτὸς πιστεύει ἀλλὰ αὐτοὶ οὐ πιστεύουσιν
He believes but they do not believe.

Note that πιστεύει by itself means 'he believes'. αὐτός is added for emphasis, usually when 'he' is contrasted with another person or group.

Translate:
1. αὐτοὶ λέγουσιν ἀλλὰ (but) | They are speaking but
   αὐτὸς οὐ λέγει. | he is not speaking.
2. αὐτοὶ γράφουσιν τοὺς λόγους | They are writing the words
   ἀλλὰ αὐτὸς οὐ γράφει αὐτούς. | but he is not writing them.
3. αὐτὸς ἀναγινώσκει τοὺς λόγους ἀλλὰ | He reads the words but
   αὐτοὶ οὐκ ἀναγινώσκουσιν αὐτούς. | they do not read them.

7.2

αὐτόν – him, it   αὐτούς – them

Translate:
1. ἀκούω τὸν λόγον καὶ γράφω αὐτόν. | I hear the word and I write it.
2. ἀκούεις τοὺς λόγους | You hear the words
   καὶ γράφεις αὐτούς. | and you write them.

7.3

αὐτοῦ – of him, of it   αὐτῶν – of them

So: ἀναγινώσκετε τὸ βιβλίον αὐτοῦ
Lit. You are reading the book **of him**.

In English we do not say 'the book of him', so we translate, 'you are reading **his** book'.

Translate:
1. ἀναγινώσκομεν τὸ βιβλίον αὐτοῦ. | We are reading his book.
2. ἀναγινώσκομεν τὸ βιβλίον αὐτῶν. | We are reading their book.
3. ἀκούω τοὺς λόγους αὐτοῦ καὶ γράφω αὐτοὺς ἐν τῷ βιβλίῳ. | I hear his words and I write them in the book.

7.4

αὐτῷ – to him, for him   αὐτοῖς – to them, for them

Translate:
1. λέγω αὐτῷ. | I am speaking to him.
2. λέγω αὐτοῖς. | I am speaking to them.
3. λέγετε αὐτοῖς τοὺς λόγους τοῦ θεοῦ καὶ αὐτοὶ γράφουσιν αὐτούς ἐν τοῖς βιβλίοις αὐτῶν. | You speak to them the words of God and they write them in their books.

7.5

There are many other words with the same endings as αὐτός and λόγος, for example: ἄνθρωπος – a man, a person, somebody.

ἄνθρωπος – a man   <subject>   ἄνθρωποι – men, people
ἄνθρωπον – a man   <object>   ἀνθρώπους – men
ἀνθρώπου – of a man   ἀνθρώπων – of men
ἀνθρώπῳ – to a man, for a man   ἀνθρώποις – to men, for men

The forms of ὁ (the) which go with ἄνθρωπος are the same as those which go with λόγος (see pp22–24). So, τῶν ἀνθρώπων – of the men.

7.6 Words

Some words with endings like λόγος:

Compare

ὁ θεός – the god, God | theist – one who believes God exists
ὁ ἄνθρωπος – the man | anthropology – the study of man
ὁ ἀπόστολος – the apostle, the envoy | apostle – a person sent by someone
ὁ θρόνος – the throne, the seat | throne – a king's seat

ὁ οὐρανός – the sky, heaven
αὐτός – he, it

Uranus – one of the planets
autobiography – a person's life story written by him/herself

Note also:
λέγω τὸν αὐτὸν λόγον – I say the same word
αὐτὸς ὁ θεός – God himself
ἀλλά – but   (ἀλλ' before a vowel)
οὐ, οὐκ, οὐχ – not

Note that οὐ becomes οὐκ before a vowel and οὐχ before ' (h).
So: λέγει αὐτῷ – he speaks to him
οὐ λέγει αὐτῷ – he does not speak to him
λέγει αὐτῇ ἀλλ' οὐ λέγει αὐτοῖς – he speaks to her but he does not speak to them
ἀκούουσιν τοὺς λόγους – they hear the words
οὐκ ἀκούουσιν τοὺς λόγους – they do not hear the words
οὗτος – this man
οὐχ οὗτος – not this man.

7.7 Translate

1. οἱ ἀπόστολοι λέγουσιν τὸν λόγον τοῦ θεοῦ καὶ ἀκούομεν αὐτόν.
   | The apostles speak the word of God and we hear it.

2. οἱ ἄνθρωποι λέγουσιν τοὺς λόγους ἀλλὰ οὐκ ἀκούετε αὐτούς.
   | The men speak the words but you do not hear them.

3. γράφουσιν τοὺς λόγους τοῦ Μάρκου οἱ ἀπόστολοι ἀλλ' αὐτὸς οὐκ ἀναγινώσκει αὐτούς.
   | The apostles write the words of Mark but he does not read them.

4. οὐκ ἀναγινώσκομεν τοὺς λόγους τῶν προφητῶν ἀλλὰ τοὺς λόγους τοῦ ἀποστόλου.
   | We are not reading the words of the prophets but the words of the apostle.

5. ὁ θρόνος τοῦ θεοῦ ἐν τῷ οὐρανῷ ἐστιν, οὐκ ἔστιν ἐπὶ (on) τῆς γῆς (the earth).
   | The throne of God is in heaven, it is not on the earth.

6. ἐν ἀρχῇ ἐποίησεν (made) ὁ θεὸς τὸν οὐρανὸν καὶ τὴν γῆν, καὶ ἐποίησεν τόν ἄνθρωπον ἐπὶ τῆς γῆς.
   | In the beginning God made the heaven and the earth, and he made the man on the earth.

7. καὶ ἐποίησεν ἄνθρωπον.
   | And he made a man.

7.8

οὗτος – this, this man, this person, he

The forms of οὗτος have endings like λόγος. Like the forms of ὁ (the) they begin with τ, except for the subject form.

So: (a) οὗτος ὁ ἄνθρωπος ἀναγινώσκει **τούτους** τοὺς λόγους
τοῖς ἀνθρώποις **τούτοις**
This man is reading these words to these men

(b) **οὗτος** ἦν ἐν ἀρχῇ πρὸς τὸν θεόν
He was in the beginning with God.

Notice that 'this man' may be expressed in Greek either as
οὗτος ὁ ἄνθρωπος (this the man)
or as ὁ ἄνθρωπος οὗτος (the man this).

In sentence (a) both types of word order are found:
οὗτος ὁ ἄνθρωπος – this man
τοῖς ἀνθρώποις τούτοις – to these men.

Translate:

1. οὗτοί εἰσιν οἱ λόγοι.	These are the words.
2. οὗτος ἦν ὁ θρόνος.	This was the throne.
3. οὗτοι ἦσαν οἱ θρόνοι.	These were the thrones.
4. οὗτός ἐστιν ὁ ἀπόστολος.	This is the apostle (or He is …)
5. γράφω τούτους τοὺς λόγους.	I am writing these words.
6. λέγω τοῖς ἀποστόλοις τούτοις.	I am speaking to these apostles.
7. λέγω τούτους τοὺς λόγους τοῦ Ἰησοῦ τοῖς ἀποστόλοις αὐτοῦ καὶ αὐτοὶ γράφουσιν αὐτοὺς ἐν τοῖς βιβλίοις αὐτῶν.	I am speaking these words of Jesus to his apostles and they are writing them in their books.
8. γράφεις τὸν λόγον τοῦτον ἀλλὰ οὗτοι οἱ ἄνθρωποι οὐκ ἀναγινώσκουσιν αὐτόν.	You are writing this word but these men are not reading it.

7.9 Translation

Notice again that the word order in Greek sentences is seldom the same as the word order in a good English translation.
Compare the following:

Greek	Literal English	English
ὁ λόγος οὗτος	the word this	this word
οὗτος ὁ λόγος	this the word	this word
αὐτός ὁ θεός	he the God	God himself
ὁ λόγος αὐτοῦ	the word of him	his word
οἱ λόγοι αὐτῶν	the words of them	their words
ἀδελφοί μου οὗτοί εἰσιν	brothers of me these are	these are my brothers
ὁ τὸν λόγον ἀκούων	the word hearing	he who hears the message

Some writers have suggested that literal translations are good translations, but this is not so. A literal translation may be useful as a first step in helping us to understand the structure of a Greek sentence. We must then think how we can best express its meaning in our own language. While you are learning New Testament Greek, it is probably wise not to use an interlinear version. By making us consider the question 'What does this word mean?' it may distract us from asking, 'How can I express the meaning of this sentence in my language?'

7.10

(a) Using the patterns:
   λέγει τοῦτον τὸν λόγον ὁ Πέτρος   Peter is speaking this word
   ἀναγινώσκομεν τούτους τοὺς λόγους   We are reading these words

   say in Greek
      Peter is speaking this word – Mark is speaking these words –
      the apostle is writing these words – the apostles are writing these words
      – we are reading these words – you (p) are writing this word –
      I am listening to these words – you (s) are listening to this word.

(b) πάντα – all things   δι'αὐτοῦ – through him   χωρίς – apart from
   ἐγένετο – came into being   οὐδὲ ἕν – not one thing
   ὃ γέγονεν – that which has come into being

LESSON 7

Read John 1:3
πάντα δι' αὐτοῦ ἐγένετο
καὶ χωρὶς αὐτοῦ ἐγένετο
οὐδὲ ἓν ὃ γέγονεν.

(c) ὁ κόσμος – the world   οὐκ ἔγνω – it did not know

Read John 1:10
ἐν τῷ κόσμῳ ἦν
καὶ ὁ κόσμος δι' αὐτοῦ ἐγένετο
καὶ ὁ κόσμος αὐτὸν οὐκ ἔγνω.

(d) John 1:3 is the start of a chiasmus. Notice how it is held together by three uses of the same basic verb: ἐγένετο (twice) and γέγονεν (remember the three uses of λόγος and of θεός in 1:1–2).

John 1:10 is the end of the chiasmus. Notice how is is held together by three uses of κόσμος (world, created order): κόσμος (twice) and κόσμῳ.

To make clear (i) that it balances 1:3 and (ii) that it closes the chiasmus, δι'αὐτοῦ ἐγένετο is quoted from verse 3.
(Remember ἐν ἀρχῇ was at the beginning and in the closure in 1:1–2.)

(e) Word fun. Recite loudly:

ἀρχή is beginning
Truth is ἀλήθεια
Kingdom βασιλεία
τέλος is the ending.

(Note: ἀλήθεια – reality, reliability, truth   βασιλεία – kingly power, kingdom)

7.11 Progress test 5

Which translation is correct?

1. λέγομεν λόγους.
(a) We speak words.
(b) They speak words.
(c) We speak the words.

2. λέγετε τούτους τοὺς λόγους.
(a) They speak these words.
(b) You speak their words.
(c) You speak these words.

3. λόγον γράφω.
(a) I hear a word.
(b) I write a word.
(c) You write the word.

4. γράφει τὸν λόγον.
(a) You write the word.
(b) He writes the words.
(c) He writes the word.

5. γράφουσιν τοῦτον τὸν λόγον.
(a) We write this word.
(b) They write these words.
(c) They write this word.

6. ἀναγινώσκεις τοὺς λόγους αὐτοῦ.
(a) You read these words.
(b) You read his words.
(c) You hear his word.

7. οὗτος ἦν ὁ λόγος τοῦ προφήτου καὶ οὗτος ἐστιν ὁ γράφων αὐτόν.
(a) These are the words of the prophet and he is writing it.
(b) This is the word of the prophet and this is the person writing it.
(c) This was the word of the prophet and this is the person writing it.

8. αὐτὸς οὐκ ἔστιν ἐπὶ τῆς γῆς ἀλλ᾽ ἐν τῷ οὐρανῷ.
(a) These are not on the earth but in heaven.
(b) He was not on the earth but in heaven.
(c) He is not on the earth but in heaven.

Check your answers in Key to Progress Tests on page 333.

Lesson 8

λέγων – saying   ὁ λέγων – the person saying

8.1

λέγων – saying (one person: singular)
λέγοντες – saying (more than one person: plural)

So: (a) λέγων τοὺς λόγους γράφει αὐτούς
Saying the words he writes them
or While saying the words he writes them

(b) ἀκούοντες τοῦ Ἰησοῦ πιστεύουσιν αὐτῷ
Hearing Jesus they believe in him
or While they are listening to Jesus they trust in him.

These words λέγων, λέγοντες, ἀκούοντες refer to a continuing action: —

In (a) he writes the words while the act of speaking is going on.
In (b) they believe in Jesus while the act of listening is going on.

Translate:

1. ἀκούοντες τοὺς λόγους τοῦ Ἰησοῦ πιστεύομεν αὐτῷ.	Hearing Jesus' words we believe in him.
2. ἀκούοντες αὐτοῦ πιστεύετε αὐτῷ.	Hearing him you believe in him.
3. ἀκούοντες τοὺς λόγους πιστεύουσιν αὐτοῖς.	Hearing the words they believe them.
4. ἀκούων τοῦ Ἰησοῦ πιστεύεις αὐτῷ.	Hearing Jesus you believe in him.
5. ἀκούων τοῦ Ἰησοῦ πιστεύω αὐτῷ.	Hearing Jesus I believe in him.
6. ἀκούων τοὺς λόγους πιστεύει αὐτοῖς.	Hearing the words he believes them.
7. ἀκούει τοὺς λόγους ἀλλὰ οὐ πιστεύει αὐτοῖς.	He hears the words but he does not believe them.
8. ὑμεῖς ἐστε τὸ φῶς τοῦ κόσμου.	You are the light of the world.

8.2

ὁ λέγων – the person saying   οἱ λέγοντες – the people saying

Note that when ὁ (the) is followed by a form like λέγων, ὁ may be translated as 'the person'.

So: αὐτός ἐστιν ὁ λέγων τὸν λόγον
He is **the person saying** the word

οὗτοι εἰσιν οἱ λέγοντες τοὺς λόγους
These are **the people saying** the words.

Translate:

1. αὐτός ἐστιν ὁ ἀκούων τὸν λόγον.	He is the person hearing the word.
2. οὗτός ἐστιν ὁ γράφων τοῦτον τὸν λόγον.	This is the person writing this word.
3. αὐτοί εἰσιν οἱ λέγοντες τούτους τοὺς λόγους.	They are the people saying these words.
4. ἀκούων τοὺς λόγους γράφει αὐτούς.	Hearing the words he writes them.
5. οὗτοί εἰσιν οἱ ἀναγινώσκοντες τὸ βιβλίον.	These are the people reading the book.

8.3 Translating forms like ὁ λέγων into English

In order to aid our understanding of the Greek, it is helpful to begin by seeing that ὁ λέγων is 'the person saying'. But such an expression is not often used in English. We would usually translate ὁ λέγων as 'he who says', or 'the person who says'.

So οἱ ἀναγινώσκοντες τὰ βιβλία (lit. the people reading the books) may be expressed in English as:

The people who are reading the books

or   Those who read the books

or   The readers of the books.

ὁ ἀπόστολος ὁ γράφων τὸ βιβλίον (lit. the apostle the one writing the book) may be expressed in English as:

The apostle who is writing the book

or   The apostle writing the book.

οἱ προφῆται οἱ τὰ βιβλία ἔχοντες (lit. the prophets the ones the books having) may be expressed in English as:
> The prophets who have the books
> or The prophets with the books.

Translate:

ὁ ἀπόστολος ἀκούει τὸν λόγον τοῦ Ἰησοῦ, καὶ ἀκούων τὸν λόγον γράφει αὐτὸν ἐν τῷ βιβλίῳ. ὁ ἀπόστολός ἐστιν ὁ γράφων τὸ βιβλίον καὶ οἱ λόγοι αὐτοῦ ἀληθεῖς εἰσιν. μακάριοί (blessed) εἰσιν οἱ ἀναγινώσκοντες τὸ βιβλίον αὐτοῦ.	The apostle hears the word of Jesus, and hearing the word he writes it in the book. The apostle is the person writing the book and his words are true. Blessed are those who read his book.

8.4 ὅτι – '...'

ὅτι is a linking word. It may mean 'that' or 'because' (8.7). But another common use of ὅτι is to show the beginning of quoted words. In New Testament Greek there are no inverted commas. ὅτι followed by a capital letter indicates words spoken or quoted.

So: οἱ λέγοντες ὅτι, Ἀπόστολός ἐστιν, ἀληθεῖς εἰσιν
      Those who say, 'He is an apostle', are true.

Note: ὅτι does not always occur before quoted words. In many cases a capital letter is the only indication of quoted or spoken words.

Translate:

1. ὁ λέγων ὅτι Ὁ θεός ἐστιν ἐν τῷ οὐρανῷ, ἀληθής ἐστιν, ἀλλὰ ὁ λέγων ὅτι Ὁ θεὸς οὐκ ἔστιν ἐν τῷ οὐρανῷ, ψεύστης (a liar) ἐστὶν καὶ οἱ λόγοι αὐτοῦ οὐκ ἀληθεῖς εἰσιν.	He who says, 'God is in heaven', is true, but he who says, 'God is not in heaven', is a liar and his words are not true.
2. ὁ λέγων ὅτι Ὁ θεὸς οὐκ ἀγαθός (good) ἐστιν, ψεύστης ἐστὶν καὶ ὁ λόγος τοῦ θεοῦ οὐκ ἔστιν ἐν αὐτῷ.	He who says, 'God is not good', is a liar and the word of God is not in him.
3. ἀγαθοί εἰσιν οἱ λόγοι τοῦ ἀποστόλου καὶ μακάριος (blessed) ὁ ἀναγινώσκων αὐτούς.	The words of the apostle are good and blessed is the person who reads them.

4. μακάριος ὁ λέγων τὸν λόγον τοῦ θεοῦ καὶ μακάριοί εἰσιν οἱ ἀκούοντες. | Blessed is he who speaks the word of God and blessed are those who hear.
5. μακάριοι οἱ τὸν λόγον τοῦ θεοῦ ἀκούοντες καὶ ποιοῦντες (doing). | Blessed are those who hear and do the word of God.

8.5 Words

Verbs with endings like λέγω (see 5.5):

Compare

γράφω – I write, I am writing — graph, anagram
ἀκούω – I hear, I listen — acoustic, acoustics
   ἀκούω τὸν λόγον – I hear the word
   ἀκούω αὐτοῦ – I hear him
ἀποστέλλω – I send out, I send — apostle, apostolic
γινώσκω – I know — know, gnostic, agnostic
εὑρίσκω – I find, I meet — heuristic
ἔχω – I have
λαμβάνω – I take, I receive, I accept
ἀναγινώσκω – I read
πιστεύω – I believe, I trust
   πιστεύω τοῖς λόγοις – I believe the words
   πιστεύω τῷ Ἰησοῦ – I believe in Jesus, I trust Jesus

Other words:
μακάριος – blessed, happy   ἡ Μαρία – Mary
ὁ Φίλιππος – Philip   ὁ Λουκᾶς – Luke

8.6 Translate

1. ἡ Μαρία ἔχει τὸ βιβλίον. | Mary has the book.
2. ἀκούουσιν τὸν λόγον καὶ λαμβάνουσιν αὐτόν. | They hear the word and receive it.
3. γινώσκετε τὸν Ἰησοῦν καὶ πιστεύετε αὐτῷ. | You know Jesus and you trust him.
4. ὁ Ἰησοῦς εὑρίσκει τὸν Φίλιππον καὶ λέγει αὐτῷ ὅτι Μακάριος ὁ εὑρίσκων τοὺς λόγους τοῦ θεοῦ καὶ πιστεύων αὐτοῖς. | Jesus finds Philip and says to him, 'Blessed is he who finds the words of God and believes them.'

5. ὦτα (ears) ἔχων, ἀκούει.	Having ears, he hears.
6. ὦτα ἔχων, οὐκ ἀκούει.	Having ears, he does not hear *or* Though he has ears he does not hear.
7. ὦτα ἔχοντες οὐκ ἀκούουσιν.	Though they have ears they do not hear.
8. γινώσκοντες τὸν Ἰησοῦν πιστεύουσιν αὐτῷ, καὶ λαμβάνουσιν τοὺς λόγους αὐτοῦ.	Knowing Jesus they trust him, and they accept his words.
9. ἀποστέλλει τοὺς ἀποστόλους αὐτοῦ πρὸς τὴν Μαρίαν.	He sends his apostles to Mary.

8.7

(a) Using the pattern:
  οἱ λέγοντες ὅτι ʽΟ θεὸς ἀγαθός ἐστιν τὴν ἀλήθειαν λέγουσιν
  Those who say   'God is good'   are speaking the truth
  and the words ἀγαθός – good, ἅγιος – holy, καθαρός – pure,
  μακάριος – blessed

  say in Greek:
  Those who say, 'God is good' are speaking the truth – those who say 'God is pure' are speaking the truth – those who say, 'God is holy' are speaking the truth – those who say, 'God is blessed' are speaking the truth.

(b) Using the pattern:
  ὁ λέγων ὅτι ʽΟ θεὸς οὐ καθαρός ἐστιν ψεύστης ἐστίν
  The person who says, 'God is not pure' is a liar
  and ψεύστης a liar, and οὐκ before ἁ and οὐχ before ἁ

  say in Greek:
  The person who says 'God is not pure' is a liar – the person who says 'God is not blessed' is a liar – the person who says, 'God is not good' is a liar – the person who says, 'God is not holy' is a liar.

(c) ἡ ζωή – the life   οἱ ἄνθρωποι – mankind

Read John 1:4
   ἐν αὐτῷ ζωὴ ἦν
   καὶ ἡ ζωὴ ἦν τὸ φῶς τῶν ἀνθρώπων
In John 1:1–2 ἦν occurs four times. Here it occurs twice. It is a key word in Jn 1:1–10. It occurs nine times. Repetition of key words is a prominent feature in the Hebrew poetry of the Old Testament.

(d) Word fun:
   Recite   καί is 'and', and ἀλλά 'but'
            οἶκος 'house' and σκηνή 'hut',
            ἐστίν 'is' and εἰσιν 'are'
            ἐγγύς 'near' and μακρός 'far'.
(οἶκος – house, family, household, temple... σκηνή – tent, shelter, hut...)

8.8

Read through carefully, then do progress test 6.

God sends his angel to Mary

ὁ θεὸς ἐν οὐρανῷ ἐστιν. καὶ ἀποστέλλει τὸν ἄγγελον αὐτοῦ ἐκ (from) τοῦ οὐρανοῦ πρὸς τὴν Μαρίαν λέγειν (to speak) τοὺς λόγους αὐτοῦ. καὶ ἔρχεται (comes) ὁ ἄγγελος πρὸς τὴν Μαρίαν καὶ λέγει αὐτῇ (to her) τοὺς λόγους τοῦ θεοῦ. καὶ ἀκούει αὐτοὺς ἡ Μαρία καὶ γινώσκει ὅτι (that) ἀληθεῖς εἰσίν.

Τούτους τοὺς λόγους ἔγραψεν (wrote) ὁ Λουκᾶς ἐν τῷ βιβλίῳ αὐτοῦ, καὶ ἀναγινώσκοντες τὸ βιβλίον εὑρίσκομεν τοὺς λόγους τοῦ ἀγγέλου καὶ τοὺς λόγους τῆς Μαρίας. καὶ πιστεύομεν αὐτοῖς ὅτι (because) ἀληθεῖς εἰσίν.

Μακάριος ὁ ἔχων τὸν λόγον τοῦ θεοῦ καὶ πιστεύων τῷ 'Ιησοῦ. καὶ μακάριοί εἰσιν οἱ ἔχοντες τὸ βιβλίον τοῦ ἀποστόλου καὶ ἀναγινώσκοντες αὐτό.

8.9 Progress Test 6

Answer the following questions on 8.8.

1. Where does the passage say God is?
2. Who is sent to Mary?
3. Whose words does the angel speak to her?
4. What does Mary know about the words?
5. Who wrote these words in his book?
6. Who is reading the book?
7. Whose words do we find in the book?
8. Why do we believe the words?
9. What person is described as being blessed?
10. What people are described as being blessed?

Check your answers in Key to Progress Tests on page 333.

Lesson 9

καρδία – a heart   ἡ καρδία – the heart

9.1

As you study ἡ καρδία, the heart, you will see that the structure is similar to that of λόγος, but there is a difference in the endings, and in the forms for 'the'.

ἡ καρδία – the heart   -α } subject endings
αἱ καρδίαι – the hearts   -αι

ἡ
αἱ } the (indicating subject)

So: ἡ καρδία αὐτοῦ ἀγαθή ἐστιν – his heart is good
καθαραί εἰσιν αἱ καρδίαι αὐτῶν – their hearts are pure.

Translate:

1. καρδία, καρδίαι.	A heart, hearts.
2. αἱ καρδίαι, ἡ καρδία.	The hearts, the heart.
3. ἀγαθαί εἰσιν αἱ καρδίαι αὐτῶν.	Their hearts are good.
4. ἡ καρδία αὐτοῦ οὐκ ἔστιν καθαρά.	His heart is not pure.

9.2

τὴν καρδίαν – the heart   -αν } object endings
τὰς καρδίας – the hearts   -ας

τήν
τάς } the (indicating object)

So: γινώσκεις τὴν καρδίαν αὐτοῦ – you know his heart
καρδίαν ἔχει ἀγαθήν – he has a good heart.

Translate:

1. ὁ θεός γινώσκει τὰς καρδίας τῶν ἀνθρώπων, καὶ γινώσκει τὴν καρδίαν τούτου τοῦ ἀποστόλου.	God knows the hearts of the men, and he knows the heart of this apostle.

2. καρδίαν ἔχεις ἀγαθὴν καὶ λαμβάνεις | You have a good heart and you
τούτους τοὺς λόγους τοῦ θεοῦ. | receive these words of God.

3. καρδίαν ἀγαθὴν ἔχων | Having a good heart
λαμβάνεις τὸν λόγον αὐτοῦ. | you receive his word.

9.3

τῆς καρδίας – of the heart -ας } of
τῶν καρδιῶν – of the hearts -ων

τῆς
τῶν } of the

So: οἱ διαλογισμοὶ τῶν καρδιῶν αὐτῶν
The thoughts of their hearts

αἴρω τοὺς λόγους ἀπὸ τῆς καρδίας αὐτοῦ
I take away the words from his heart.

Translate:

1. γινώσκω τοὺς διαλογισμοὺς | I know the thoughts
τῆς καρδίας αὐτοῦ. | of his heart.

2. αἴρεις τὸν λόγον τοῦ θεοῦ | You take away God's word
ἀπὸ τῆς καρδίας αὐτοῦ. | from his heart.

3. ὁ Ἰησοῦς γινώσκει τοὺς | Jesus knows the
διαλογισμοὺς τῶν καρδιῶν αὐτῶν. | thoughts of their hearts.

4. οὗτοι οἱ διαλογισμοὶ τῆς καρδίας | These thoughts of his heart are
αὐτοῦ οὐκ ἀγαθοί εἰσιν. | not good.

9.4

τῇ καρδίᾳ – with the heart, in the heart -ᾳ } with, by, in, to, for,
ταῖς καρδίαις – with the hearts, in the hearts -αις etc.

τῇ
ταῖς } with the, to the, etc.

The meaning indicated by these endings is usually shown by the rest of the sentence in which they occur (see also 42.1).

So: μακάριος ὁ καθαρὸς τῇ καρδίᾳ
Blessed the pure in heart
or Blessed is the pure in heart
or How blessed the pure in heart!

λέγουσιν ἐν ταῖς καρδίαις αὐτῶν...
They say in their hearts...

Translate:

1. μακάριοι οἱ καθαροὶ τῇ καρδίᾳ.	Blessed are the pure in heart.
2. λέγει ἐν τῇ καρδίᾳ αὐτοῦ ὅτι Ὁ θεός οὐκ ἀγαθός ἐστιν.	He says in his heart, 'God is not good.'
3. μακάριος ὁ ἔχων τὸν λόγον τοῦ Ἰησοῦ ἐν τῇ καρδίᾳ αὐτοῦ.	Blessed is he who has the word of Jesus in his heart.
4. μακάριοι οἱ ἔχοντες τούτους τοὺς λόγους τῶν προφήτων ἐν ταῖς καρδίαις αὐτῶν.	Blessed are those who have these words of the prophets in their hearts.

9.5 Translating καρδία into English

In 9.1–9.4 we have translated καρδία as 'heart'. In many New Testament passages 'heart' is a suitable translation. In Matthew 5:8 we might translate μακάριοι οἱ καθαροὶ τῇ καρδίᾳ as, 'Blessed are the pure in heart', or as, 'How blest are those whose hearts are pure'.

But in Revelation 18:7 ἐν τῇ καρδίᾳ αὐτῆς λέγει cannot be well translated as, 'She says in her heart', because we do not normally use the word 'heart' to refer to our processes of thinking. 'She says in her mind' would perhaps be a better translation, but it is not the most natural way for an English person to express the meaning of ἐν τῇ καρδίᾳ αὐτῆς λέγει. We need to consider translations like 'She says to herself', 'She keeps telling herself', or 'She thinks'.

καρδία in New Testament Greek covers an area of meaning in which we find such English words as heart, mind, thoughts, intentions, attitude.
Those who are translating the New Testament into some other language must consider what words and idioms cover this area of meaning. For example, in some languages thoughts and emotions are described not by a word for the heart but by a word for the abdomen.

9.6

Here are the forms of ἡ καρδία you have begun to learn:

Singular		Plural
ἡ καρδία – the heart	< subject >	αἱ καρδίαι – the hearts
τὴν καρδίαν – the heart	< object >	τὰς καρδίας – the hearts
τῆς καρδίας – of the heart		τῶν καρδιῶν – of the hearts
τῇ καρδίᾳ – with the heart		ταῖς καρδίαις – with the hearts

Note carefully the difference between:
  τῆς καρδίας – of the heart
and τὰς καρδίας – the hearts (object form).

9.7 Words

	Compare
καρδία – heart, mind, attitude	cardiac

Words with the same endings as καρδία:

ἡ ἁμαρτία – the sin, sin	hamartiology
ἡ ἐκκλησία – the congregation, the church	ecclesiastical

(note that ἐκκλησία refers to people, never to a building)

ἡ ἀλήθεια – the truth, reality, what is genuine
    (ἀληθής – true, real, honest)

ἡ βασιλεία – the kingdom, the reign	basilica
(βασιλεύς – king)	
ἡ ἡμέρα – the day	ephemeral
ἡ γῆ – the earth, the land, the soil	geology, geography

Words with the same endings as ἡ γῆ:

ἡ ἐπιστολή – the letter, the epistle	epistle, epistolary

αὐτή – she, it:
 ἡ βασιλεία αὐτῆς – her kingdom
αὕτη – this:
  γράφει ταύτην τὴν ἐπιστολήν
 or γράφει τὴν ἐπιστολὴν ταύτην } he writes this letter
ἐν ταύτῃ τῇ ἡμέρᾳ – on this day

9.8 Translate

1. ὁ Παῦλος γράφει τάς ἐπιστολὰς καὶ ἐν αὐταῖς εὑρίσκομεν τὸν λόγον τῆς ἀληθείας.

   Paul writes the letters and in them we find the word of truth.

2. λέγει ἐν τῇ καρδίᾳ αὐτῆς ὅτι Ἁμαρτίαν οὐκ ἔχω.

   She says to herself, 'I have no sin.'

3. οἱ λέγοντες ὅτι Ἁμαρτίαν οὐκ ἔχομεν, οὐ τὴν ἀλήθειαν λέγουσιν.

   Those who say, 'We have no sin', do not speak the truth.

4. Παῦλος γράφει ἐπιστολὰς ταῖς ἐκκλησίαις ταύταις καὶ ἀναγινώσκομεν αὐτάς.

   Paul writes letters to these churches and we read them.

5. ὁ προφήτης λέγει τοὺς λόγους τοῦ θεοῦ τῇ Μαρίᾳ καὶ αὐτὴ γράφει αὐτοὺς ἐν τῷ βιβλίῳ αὐτῆς.

   The prophet speaks the words of God to Mary and she writes them in her book.

6. καὶ αὕτη ἐστὶν ἡ ἐπιστολὴ ἣν (which) ὁ Παῦλος γράφει καὶ ἀναγινώσκεις αὐτὴν ἐν ταύτῃ τῇ ἡμέρᾳ, καὶ εὑρίσκεις τὸν λόγον τῆς βασιλείας τοῦ θεοῦ ἐν αὐτῇ.

   And this is the letter which Paul is writing, and you are reading it on this day, and you find the word of the Kingdom of God in it.

7. ὁ ἀπόστολος λέγει τὸν λόγον τῇ ἐκκλησίᾳ καὶ οἱ ἄνθρωποι ἀκούουσιν τὸν λόγον τῆς βασιλείας.

   The apostle speaks the word to the congregation and the men hear the word of the Kingdom.

8. ἐν ταύταις ταῖς ἡμέραις ἀκούομεν τὸν λόγον τοῦ Ἰωάννου (of John) καὶ λαμβάνομεν αὐτὸν ἐν ταῖς καρδίαις ἡμῶν (of us). καὶ οὗτός ἐστιν ὁ λόγος τοῦ Ἰωάννου,
   Ὁ λέγων ὅτι Κοινωνίαν (fellowship) ἔχω μετὰ (with) τοῦ θεοῦ, καὶ ἐν τῇ σκοτίᾳ (darkness) περιπατῶν (walking) ψεύστης ἐστὶν καὶ ἡ ἀλήθεια οὐκ ἔστιν ἐν αὐτῷ.
   ἀναγινώσκομεν τούτους τοὺς λόγους ἐν τῇ ἐπιστολῇ αὐτοῦ, καὶ ἀναγινώσκοντες αὐτὴν πιστεύομεν τοῖς λόγοις αὐτοῦ.

   In these days we hear the word of John and we receive it in our minds. This is John's message:
   'He who says, "I have fellowship with God" and walks in the darkness is a liar, and the truth is not in him.'
   We read these words in his letter, and reading it we believe his words.

9.9 Translation

In 9.8 no. 7, we translated ὁ ἀπόστολος λέγει τὸν λόγον τῇ ἐκκλησίᾳ as 'The apostle speaks the word to the congregation'. When we see that he speaks about the Kingdom, we might decide that an alternative translation of λέγει τὸν λόγον would be better. We might translate it as 'preaches the message to the congregation', or as 'preaches to the congregation'. See also 4.3.

9.10

(a) Using words from 9.7 and the pattern:
   αὕτη ἐστιν ἡ ἀγγελία – This is the message

   say in Greek:
      This is the message – this is the sin – this is the kingdom – this is the truth – this is the letter – this is the land.

(b) Using the patterns
      ἀκούομεν ταύτην τὴν ἀγγελίαν – we hear this message
   and γράφουσιν ταύτην τὴν ἐπιστολήν – they are writing this letter

   say in Greek:
      We hear this message – they hear this message – he hears this message – I hear this message – they are writing this letter – you (s) are writing this letter – she is writing this letter – you (p) are writing this letter.

(c) ἡ σκοτία – the darkness, φαίνω – I shine, κατέλαβεν – it overcame...

John 1:4–5	
ἐν αὐτῷ ζωὴ ἦν,	In him was life,
καὶ ἡ ζωὴ ἦν	and the life was
τὸ φῶς τῶν ἀνθρώπων	the light of mankind
καὶ τὸ φῶς ἐν τῇ σκοτίᾳ φαίνει	and the light shines on in the darkness
καὶ ἡ σκοτία αὐτὸ οὐ κατέλαβεν.	and the darkness has not overcome it.

(d) ἀληθινός – genuine, real true φωτίζω – I give light, πᾶς – every
ἐρχόμενος – coming : ἦν ... ἐρχόμενον – it was coming

John 1:9

ἦν τὸ φῶς τὸ ἀληθινόν,	the real light,
ὃ φωτίζει πάντα ἄνθρωπον,	which gives light to everyone,
ἐρχόμενον εἰς τὸν κόσμον.	was coming into the world.

Notice the major theme of verses 4–5 and verse 9 is light, and that τῶν ἀνθρώπων (of mankind, of people) in verses 4–5 is balanced by πάντα ἄνθρωπον (every person) in verse 9. They are two corresponding parts of the chiasmus in verses 3–10.

There is another feature here that can be found in Hebrew poetry. The last word of verse 9 is κόσμος. Look again at verse 10, (7.10 c and d). κόσμος is the key word in verse 10, and is repeated three times. In Ps 115:8 the last words, which close a section about idols, are 'those who trust in them.' This becomes the key word in verses 9–11 where 'trust in the Lord' occurs three times.

(e) Word fun – three more girls who can help us with Greek: Amy, Sue and May.

I am Amy	εἰμι – I am
You are Sue	σύ – you
May is not	μή – not
but 'ay' are you?	εἶ – you are εἶ ; – are you?

9.11 Progress test 7

Which translation is correct?

1. ἐν ταύταις ταῖς ἡμέραις ἀκούομεν τὸν λόγον τοῦ θεοῦ.
(a) In these days we hear the words of God.
(b) On this day we hear the word of God.
(c) In these days we hear the word of God.

2. μακάριοι οἱ ἔχοντες τὸ βιβλίον τοῦ Ἰωάννου καὶ ἀναγινώσκοντες αὐτό.
(a) They have John's book and they read it.
(b) Blessed are those who have John's book and read it.
(c) Blessed is he who has John's book and reads it.

3. λέγει ἐν τῇ καρδίᾳ αὐτοῦ ὅτι Οὐ πιστεύω τῷ 'Ιησοῦ.
(a) He says to himself, 'I do not believe in Jesus.'
(b) He says in his heart, 'I believe in Jesus.'
(c) She says to herself, 'I do not believe in Jesus.'

4. αὗται αἱ ἐπιστολαὶ ἀγαθαί εἰσιν.
(a) This letter is good.
(b) These letters are good.
(c) These letters were good.

5. ἐν ταύταις ταῖς ἐπιστολαῖς τοῦ Παύλου εὑρίσκομεν τὸν λόγον τῆς βασιλείας τοῦ θεοῦ.
(a) In this letter of Paul we find words of the Kingdom of God.
(b) In these letters of Paul we find the word of God's Kingdom.
(c) In Paul's letters we find the word of God's Kingdom.

Check your answers in Key to Progress Tests on page 333.

9.12

In lesson 10 you will see the forms of ἡμεῖς – we, and ὑμεῖς – you.

ἡμεῖς we	< subject >	ὑμεῖς you
ἡμᾶς us	< object >	ὑμᾶς you
ἡμῶν of us		ὑμῶν of you
ἡμῖν for us, to us		ὑμῖν for you, to you

Lesson 10

ἡμεῖs – we   ὑμεῖs – you   ὅs – who

10.1

    ἡμεῖs – we   – εις – subject ending
    ὑμεῖs – you (p)

So: λέγομεν ἡμεῖs καὶ ὑμεῖs ἀκούετε
      We speak and **you** hear.

Translate:

1. τοὺς λόγους γράφομεν ἡμεῖs καὶ ὑμεῖs ἀναγινώσκετε αὐτούς.	**We** are writing the words and **you** are reading them.
2. λέγετε ὑμεῖs καὶ ἡμεῖs ἀκούομεν	**You** are speaking and **we** are listening.

Note that γράφομεν by itself means 'we write'. ἡμεῖs can be added to it for emphasis. This is usually done when 'we' is contrasted with another person or group:

    ἡμεῖs λέγομεν καὶ ὁ Παῦλος ἀκούει
    We are speaking and **Paul** is listening

    τὸ βιβλίον ἀναγινώσκομεν ἡμεῖs ἀλλὰ ὑμεῖs οὐκ ἀκούετε
    We are reading the book but **you** are not listening.

10.2

    ἡμᾶς – us   – ας – object ending
    ὑμᾶς – you

So: ἀποστέλλει ἡμᾶς ὁ θεὸς ἀλλὰ ὑμεῖs οὐ λαμβάνετε ἡμᾶς
      God sends us but you do not receive us.

Translate:

1. ὁ θεός ἐστιν ὁ ἀποστέλλων ἡμᾶς.	God is the one who is sending us.
2. τὸν Μᾶρκον γινώσκομεν ἀλλὰ ὑμᾶς οὐ γινώσκομεν.	We know Mark but we do not know you.

3. ὁ Μᾶρκος γράφει τὸ βιβλίον | Mark writes the book
   καὶ ὑμεῖς ἀναγινώσκετε αὐτό (it). | and you read it.
4. εὑρίσκει ἡμᾶς ὁ Παῦλος | Paul finds us
   ἀλλὰ ὑμᾶς οὐκ εὑρίσκει. | but he does not find you.

10.3

ἡμῶν – of us   – ων – of
ὑμῶν – of you (p)

So: ἀκούοντες τοὺς λόγους ὑμῶν πιστεύομεν αὐτοῖς
Hearing your words **we** believe them.

Translate:

1. ἀκούουσι τοὺς λόγους ἡμῶν. | They hear our words.
2. ἀκούει τοὺς λόγους ὑμῶν. | He hears your words.
3. ἡμεῖς ἀκούομεν τοὺς λόγους αὐτῶν. | We hear their words.
4. αὐτὸς γινώσκει τοὺς διαλογισμοὺς τῶν καρδιῶν ὑμῶν. | He knows the thoughts of your hearts (minds).
5. αὕτη ἐστὶν ἡ ἐπιστολὴ ἡμῶν. | This is our letter.
6. ὁ θεός ἐστιν μεθ' ὑμῶν (with you). | God is with you.
7. ὁ προφήτης μεθ' ἡμῶν ἐστίν. | The prophet is with us.

10.4

ἡμῖν – for us, to us   – ιν – to, for
ὑμῖν – for you, to you (p)

So: λέγω ὑμῖν – I speak to you, I say to you
ποιεῖ ἡμῖν βασιλείαν – he makes a kingdom for us

Note also:
ἀκούοντες τοὺς λόγους ἡμῶν, πιστεύετε ἡμῖν
Hearing our words, you believe **in us**
or Hearing our words, you trust **us**.

Translate:
1. γράφει ἡ Μαρία τοὺς λόγους ἡμῖν. | Mary writes the words for us (to us).

50   LEARN NEW TESTAMENT GREEK

2. λέγει ὑμῖν ὁ προφήτης | The prophet speaks to you
καὶ ὑμεῖς λέγετε ἡμῖν. | and you speak to us.
3. ὁ τούτους τοὺς λόγους λέγων | The person who is saying these words
ἡμῖν οὐ λέγει τὴν ἀλήθειαν. | to us is not speaking the truth.
4. ἡ ἀλήθεια ἐν ὑμῖν ἐστιν | The truth is in you
ἀλλὰ οὐκ ἔστιν ἐν ἡμῖν. | but it is not in us.
5. οἱ λαμβάνοντες τοὺς λόγους | Those who receive your words
ὑμῶν ἐν ταῖς καρδίαις αὐτῶν | in their hearts
εὑρίσκουσιν τὴν βασιλείαν | find the Kingdom
τοῦ θεοῦ. | of God.

10.5

ὅς – who, which (he who)
ἥ – who, which (she who)
ὅ – which, that which, what

So: ὃς ἔχει ὦτα ἀκούει ἡμᾶς – **he who** has ears hears us
ἣ ἔχει ὦτα ἀκούει ὑμᾶς – **she who** has ears hears you
ὃ ἦν ἀπ' ἀρχῆς ἀπαγγέλλομεν ὑμῖν – **that which** was from the
beginning we announce to you

and ὁ λόγος ὃν λέγεις – the word **which** you say
ἡ ἐπιστολὴ ἣν ἀναγινώσκουσι – the letter **which** they read
τὸ βιβλίον ὃ γράφει – the book **which** he writes.

Translate:
1. οὗτός ἐστιν ὁ λόγος ὃν λέγει. | This is the word which he speaks.
2. αὕτη ἐστὶν ἡ ἐπιστολὴ ἣν | This is the letter which they are
γράφουσιν. | writing.
3. τοῦτο ἐστιν τὸ βιβλίον ἐν ᾧ | This is the book in which
ὁ προφήτης γράφει ἡμῖν τοὺς | the prophet is writing for us the
λόγους τοῦ θεοῦ καὶ ὑμεῖς | words of God and you
ἀναγινώσκετε αὐτό. | are reading it.
4. ὃ ἦν ἀπ' ἀρχῆς | That which was from the beginning
ἀπαγγέλλετε ἡμῖν. | you announce to us.

10.6 Accents: ´ ` ˆ

The New Testament was originally written entirely in capital letters (see lesson 16). There were no marks to indicate a high tone (´) or a tone that is not raised (`) or a rising and falling tone (ˆ). The system of marks, called accents, is found in manuscripts from the ninth century AD onwards. You will find them used in printed texts of the New Testament. Note these examples of words which are distinguished from each other by their accentuation:

ἡ – the	ἥ – who, which, she who
ὁ – the	ὅ – that which
εἰ – if	εἶ – you are, thou art
τις – someone	τίς – who?
τι – something	τί – what? why?
μένω – I remain, I stay	μενῶ – I will remain

You can complete this course and read the New Testament without knowing anything more about accents. Those who need further information should consult the appendix on Accents (pp349–350).

10.7 Words

ἡμεῖς – we
ὑμεῖς – you
μετά – with
   μεθ' ὑμῶν – with you
ὁ ἄγγελος – the messenger, the angel
   ἡ ἀγγελία – the message
ἀπό – from
   ἀπ' ἀρχῆς – from the beginning
ἀπαγγέλλω – I announce, I bring back a report, I declare

ὁ Κύριος – the Lord, the owner
ὁ Χριστός – the Anointed One, the Messiah, the Christ
ἡ κοινωνία – the fellowship, the partnership, the sharing
ἡ σκοτία – the darkness
ὅς – who, which, he who
ἥ – who, which, she who
ὅ – which, that which, what
καί – and, also, even

καί is used to link words and sentences together. When καί begins a sentence we may sometimes translate it into English as 'so', 'then', or 'also'. But very often we mark the end of one sentence and the beginning of another simply by using a full stop, followed by a capital letter. When καί is the first word in a Greek sentence we usually do not need any other 'translation' except the full stop. So we can translate καί λέγει αὐτοῖς as 'He says to them'.

10.8 Translate

1. καὶ λέγει αὐτοῖς, "Ὃς ἔχει ὦτα ἀκούει τοὺς λόγους οὓς ἀπαγγέλλουσιν ἡμῖν οἱ ἀπόστολοι.

   He says to them, 'He who has ears hears the words which the apostles announce to us.'

2. καὶ αὕτη ἐστὶν ἡ ἀγγελία ἣν ἀπαγγέλλομεν ὑμῖν ἵνα (so that) καὶ ὑμεῖς κοινωνίαν ἔχητε (you may have) μεθ' ἡμῶν καὶ μετὰ τοῦ Κυρίου Ἰησοῦ Χριστοῦ.

   This is the message which we declare to you so that you also may have fellowship with us and with the Lord Jesus Christ.

3. ὃ ἦν ἀπ' ἀρχῆς ἀπαγγέλλει ἡμῖν ὁ Ἰωάννης καὶ ἀκούομεν τὸν λόγον αὐτοῦ.

   John declares to us that which was from the beginning, and we hear his word (or, we hear what he says).

10.9

Read carefully:

The message which we declare

ὃ ἦν ἀπ' ἀρχῆς ὃ ἀκηκόαμεν (we have heard) ἀπαγγέλλομεν ὑμῖν ἵνα (so that) καὶ ὑμεῖς κοινωνίαν ἔχητε μεθ' ἡμῶν. καὶ ἡ κοινωνία ἡμῶν μετὰ τοῦ κυρίου ἡμῶν Ἰησοῦ Χριστοῦ ἐστιν. καὶ ταῦτα (these things) γράφομεν ἡμεῖς ἵνα καὶ ὑμεῖς γινώσκητε τὸν θεὸν καί τὸν κύριον ἡμῶν Ἰησοῦν Χριστόν. καὶ αὕτη ἐστὶν ἡ ἀγγελία ἣν ἀκηκόαμεν ἀπὸ τοῦ κυρίου καὶ ἀπαγγέλλομεν ὑμῖν ὅτι Ὁ θεὸς φῶς ἐστιν καὶ σκοτία οὐκ ἔστιν ἐν αὐτῷ.

10.10 Translating difficult words

When you come to a difficult word, or one you have forgotten, leave it until you have finished reading the rest of the sentence. Then you may see what it means. For example, in 10.9 you read the word φῶς. When you saw that the sentence said, 'God is φῶς and darkness is not in him', you could probably see that φῶς must mean 'light'.

When you are trying to find out the meaning of a Greek word, see whether it reminds you of any English words. φῶς might remind you of phosphorus (which glows) or of photograph (a picture 'written' by light on the film).

In 10.8 if you have forgotten αὕτη in αὕτη ἐστὶν ἡ ἀγγελία ἣν ἀκηκόαμεν ἀπὸ τοῦ κυρίου do not give up and do not waste time staring at the word αὕτη. By the time you have said, 'αὕτη is the message which we have heard from the Lord', you will probably see or remember that αὕτη means 'this'. In a few of the sentences and reading passages in this course there are words you have not seen before. This is to give you practice in working out the meaning of unknown words. Later on you will learn to use a dictionary or lexicon, but the less you need to use it the quicker you will be able to read.

The passage in 10.9 was based mainly on 1 John 1:1–5. You have already made a great deal of progress towards reading parts of the New Testament in Greek. In lesson 11 you will take another very important step forward as you study the forms ἵνα λέγῃ (so that he may say), ἐὰν λέγῃ (if he says), ὃς ἂν λέγῃ (whoever says), and λέγωμεν (let us say).

10.11

(a) Using patterns like:
  ὃ ἦν ἀπ' ἀρχῆς ἀπαγγέλλομεν ὑμῖν –
  that which was from the beginning we declare to you
  and   ὃ ἀκηκόαμεν ἀπαγγέλλομεν αὐτοῖς –
  that which we have heard   we declare   to them

  say in Greek:
  that which was from the beginning we declare to you – that which was from the beginning you declare to us – that which was from the beginning we declare to them – that which we have heard we declare to them – that which we have heard we declare to you.

(b) Read from:
  1 Jn 1:5   ὁ θεὸς φῶς ἐστιν
  1 Jn 4:16 ὁ θεὸς ἀγάπη ἐστίν
  1 Jn 2:10 ὁ ἀγαπῶν   The person who loves
             τὸν ἀδελφὸν αὐτοῦ   'his' brother
             ἐν τῷ φωτὶ μένει   abides in the light

There is a difficulty when we translate 1 John 2:10 into English.
ὁ ἀγαπῶν can mean 'he who loves' or '**the person who loves.**' ἀδελφός can mean '**fellow Christian**' or 'brother.' In English we have no common

gender word to express 'his or her'. So in translating we may need to use a plural form 'their':

'Those who love their fellow Christians abide in the light'.

(c) Word fun.   Recite:

οὗτος this and αὐτός he,
αὕτη this and αὐτή she,
ὤν is being, λέγων saying,
ποιῶν doing, βαίνων going.

10.12

Revise lessons 4, 5, and 6.

Lesson 11

ὃς ἂν λέγῃ – whoever says
ἐὰν λέγῃ – if he says
ἵνα λέγῃ – so that he may say
λέγωμεν – let us say

11.1

Note the difference between (a) and (b) in the following:
1. (a) You are writing a letter.
   (b) He may be writing a letter.
2. (a) You are the person who is receiving a letter.
   (b) Whoever receives a letter will be happy

Both (a) sentences state a definite fact about a specific person.
Both (b) sentences state something that is not so definite:
   In   1 (b) he may be doing something else,
and in   2 (b) the word 'whoever' does not refer to a specific person.

Now compare these:
3. (a)   ὁ ἄνθρωπος ὃς λέγει τὸν λόγον
         The man **who speaks** the word
   (b)   ὃς ἂν λέγῃ τὸν λόγον
         Whoever speaks the word
4. (a)   ταῦτα ἀπαγγέλλομεν καὶ κοινωνίαν ἔχετε μεθ' ἡμῶν
         We declare these things and **you have** fellowship with us
   (b)   ταῦτα ἀπαγγέλλομεν ἵνα κοινωνίαν ἔχητε μεθ' ἡμῶν
         We declare these things **so that you may have** fellowship with us
5. (a)   ἀκούει τούτους τοὺς λόγους
         He hears these words
   (b)   ἐὰν ἀκούῃ τούτους τοὺς λόγους...
         If he hears these words...
6. (a)   ταῦτα λέγομεν
         We are saying these things
   (b)   ἐὰν ταῦτα λέγωμεν...
         If we are saying these things...
         If we say these things...
         If we keep saying these things...

Notice that each (a) is definite, and each (b) is less definite.
Each verb in (b) has a vowel that is lengthened – compare:

4. (a) ἔχετε (b) ἔχητε
5. (a) ἀκούει (b) ἀκούῃ
6. (a) λέγομεν (b) λέγωμεν

11.2 Words
ταῦτα – these things
ἐάν – if
ὃς ἄν – whoever
ἵνα – so that
ὁ ἀδελφός – the brother
ἡ ἀγάπη – the love

ἐάν ἔχῃ – if he has
ὃς ἄν λαμβάνῃ – whoever receives
ἵνα πιστεύωσιν – so that they may believe
ἡ ἀδελφή – the sister
ἀγαπῶ (ἀγαπάω) – I love:

note the endings of ἀγαπα-ω (α+ω becomes ω, α+ε becomes α):

ἀγαπ -ῶ – I love
ἀγαπ -ᾷς – you love
ἀγαπ -ᾷ – he loves

ἀγαπ -ῶμεν – we love
ἀγαπ -ᾶτε – you (p) love
ἀγαπ -ῶσιν – they love

μή – not

Compare:

οὐκ ἔχομεν – we do not have
ὃς ἄν ἔχῃ – whoever has
ὁ ἀγαπῶν – the person loving *or* he who loves
ὁ μὴ ἀγαπῶν – the person not loving *or* he who does not love

ἐὰν μὴ ἔχωμεν – if we do not have
ὃς ἄν μὴ ἔχῃ – whoever does not have

11.3 ὅς – who   ὃς ἄν – whoever
Translate:

1. οὗτός ἐστιν ὁ ἀδελφὸς | This is the brother
   ὃς λαμβάνει τὴν ἀδελφήν. | who receives the sister.

2. ὃς ἄν λαμβάνῃ τὰς ἀδελφὰς | Whoever receives the sisters
   οὗτος λαμβάνει ἡμᾶς. | (he) receives us.

3. ὃς ἄν πιστεύῃ τῷ ἀγγέλῳ τοῦ | Whoever believes the angel of the
   κυρίου, τῷ κυρίῳ πιστεύει· | Lord believes the Lord:
   ἀλλὰ ὁ μὴ πιστεύων | but the person who does not
   τῷ ἀγγέλῳ | believe the angel
   οὐ πιστεύει τῷ κυρίῳ. | does not believe the Lord.

11.4 ἐάν – if

Translate:

1. ἐὰν ἀγαπῶμεν τοὺς ἀδελφοὺς λαμβάνομεν τὴν ἀγάπην τοῦ θεοῦ ἐν ταῖς καρδίαις ἡμῶν.	If we love the brothers we receive the love of God in our hearts.
2. ἐὰν ταύτην τὴν ἀγγελίαν ἀπαγγέλλωσιν, τὴν ἀλήθειαν λέγουσιν· ἀλλὰ ὁ μὴ λέγων τὴν ἀλήθειαν ψεύστης ἐστίν.	If they declare this message, they are speaking the truth; but the person who does not speak the truth is a liar.

11.5 ἵνα – so that

Translate:

1. ταῦτα ἀπαγγέλλετε ἡμῖν ἵνα κοινωνίαν ἔχωμεν μεθ' ὑμῶν καὶ ἵνα ἀγαπῶμεν τὸν θεόν.	You declare these things to us so that we may have fellowship with you and so that we may love God.
2. ὃ ἦν ἀπ' ἀρχῆς ἀπαγγέλλομεν ὑμῖν ἵνα καὶ ὑμεῖς γινώσκητε τὸν θεὸν καὶ τὸν Κύριον ἡμῶν Ἰησοῦν Χριστόν.	That which was from the beginning we declare to you so that you also may know God and our Lord Jesus Christ.
3. ἀγαπῶ τοὺς ἀδελφοὺς ἀλλὰ οὐκ ἀγαπῶ τὰς ἀδελφάς.	I love the brothers but I do not love the sisters.

11.6 Let us...

Compare

λέγωμεν – let us say   λέγομεν – we say

ἀγαπῶμεν – let us love   ἀγαπῶμεν – we love

μὴ λέγωμεν – let us not say   οὐ λέγομεν – we do not say

μὴ ἀγαπῶμεν – let us not love   οὐκ ἀγαπῶμεν – we do not love

Translate:

1. λέγωμεν τοὺς λόγους.	Let us say the words.
2. ἀναγινώσκομεν τὴν ἐπιστολήν.	We are reading the letter.

3. ἀναγινώσκωμεν τὰς ἐπιστολὰς. | Let us read the letters.
4. πιστεύωμεν τῷ θεῷ | Let us trust in God
   καὶ ἀγαπῶμεν αὐτόν. | and let us love him.
5. γινώσκομεν τοὺς ἀδελφοὺς | We know the brothers
   ἀλλά οὐκ ἀγαπῶμεν αὐτούς. | but we do not love them.
6. γινώσκωμεν τὰς ἀδελφὰς | Let us know the sisters
   και ἀγαπῶμεν αὐτάς. | and let us love them.
7. μὴ ἀγαπῶμεν τὸν Μᾶρκον | Let us not love Mark
   ἀλλὰ ἀγαπῶμεν τὸν Κύριον. | but let us love the Lord.
8. ὃς ἂν λέγῃ ὅτι ῾Αμαρτίαν οὐκ | Whoever says, 'I do not have
   ἔχω, μὴ λαμβάνωμεν τοὺς λόγους | sin', let us not receive his words.
   αὐτοῦ. οὐκ ἀληθεῖς εἰσίν. | They are not true.

11.7 Continuing or repeated action

Note that all the forms of the verb you have learned so far usually represent either continuing action — or repeated action ···· (see 5.6).

So: γράφει   he is writing —   or, he writes ····
ἵνα γράφῃ   so that he may be writing —   or, so that he may write ····
ὁ γράφων   the person writing —   or, he who writes ····

From lesson 20 onwards we shall also study forms which indicate completed action or single action.

11.8

Compare the following forms of λέγω:

Used in definite statements and definite questions		Used in indefinite clauses and indefinite questions
λέγω	I	λέγω
λέγεις	you	λέγῃς
λέγει	he, she, it	λέγῃ
λέγομεν	we	λέγωμεν
λέγετε	you (p)	λέγητε
λέγουσι(ν)	they	λέγωσι(ν)

11.9

(a) Using the patterns

ὃς ἂν ἔχῃ – whoever has   ἐὰν ἔχῃ – if he has
ἵνα ἔχῃ – so that he may have   ἔχωμεν – let us have   μή – not

say in Greek:
Whoever has – so that he may have – if he has – let us have – let us say – if he says – whoever says – so that she may say – if he knows – if he does not know – whoever knows – we hear – let us hear – let us not listen – we say – so that we may not say.

(b) Word fun.   Recite – pointing at parts of your body:

κεφαλή – head, καρδία – heart
μέλος – limb and μέρος – part,
γλῶσσα – tongue and ὦτα – ears,
λέγει – speaks, ἀκούει – hears.

(c) Note: ἀπεσταλμένος παρὰ θεοῦ – sent from God.
ὄνομα – name.   ἦλθεν – he came.   εἰς μαρτυρίαν - for witnessing
πάντες – all, all people   ἐκεῖνος – that, that man, he

Read John 1.6-8

6. Ἐγένετο ἄνθρωπος,   There was a man,
   ἀπεσταλμένος παρὰ θεοῦ,   sent from God,
   ὄνομα αὐτῷ Ἰωάννης·   name to him John.

7. οὗτος ἦλθεν εἰς μαρτυρίαν   He came for witnessing
   ἵνα μαρτυρήσῃ περὶ τοῦ   so that he might bear witness about
   φωτός   the light
   ἵνα πάντες πιστεύσωσιν   so that all people might believe
   δι' αὐτοῦ.   through him.

8. οὐκ ἦν ἐκεῖνος τὸ φῶς   He was not the light
   ἀλλ' ἵνα μαρτυρήσῃ   but – so that he might bear witness
   περὶ τοῦ φωτός.   about the light.

Notes:

1. This is the centre section of John 1:3–10. Its major theme is the witness of John the Baptist. It prepares for 1:19–37 which tells of John's witness.

    The purpose of the witness is stated as 'so that all might believe through him.' This prepares for the whole book which is aimed at helping people to believe (Jn 20:31).

The other main theme of 6–8 is light (φῶς) which is the main theme in 4–5 and 9.

2. All the clauses are short. This is typical of Hebrew poetic style, as is the repetition of key words and phrases.

In verse 6 ὄνομα αὐτῷ 'Ιωάννης (= his name was John) is as strange in Greek as 'name to him John' is in English, but it reflects Hebrew style nicely. At the end of verse 8 'but that he might bear witness to the light' seems to lack the words 'he came': 'but he came so that...' However, ἵνα μαρτυρήσῃ περὶ τοῦ φωτός is quoted from verse 7 where it is introduced by ἦλθεν – he came. It is typical of the brevity of Hebrew poetic style that a word can be sometimes omitted, so long as it can easily be supplied from a line above.

The repetition of ἵνα μαρτυρήσῃ περὶ τοῦ φωτός marks the closure of this section, just as the repetition of ἐν ἀρχῇ in verse 2 helped to mark the closure of the first section. (Look at any Bible translations you have. See if they have a paragraph or stanza break at the end of v2 and at the end of v8.)

11.10 Progress test 8

Which translation is correct?

1. ἐὰν ταύτην τὴν ἀγγελίαν ἀπαγγέλλητε ἡμῖν...
(a) So that we may announce this message to you...
(b) If we declare this message to you...
(c) If you declare this message to us...

2. μὴ ἀγαπῶμεν τοὺς ἀποστόλους ἀλλὰ τὸν Κύριον.
(a) Let us love the apostles of the Lord.
(b) Let us not love the apostles but the Lord.
(c) If we love the apostles we also love the Lord.

3. ταύτῃ τῇ ἡμέρᾳ ὁ ἀδελφὸς καὶ ἡ ἀδελφὴ λαμβάνουσιν τὴν βασιλείαν τοῦ θεοῦ ἐν ταῖς καρδίαις αὐτῶν.
(a) On this day the sister and the brother receive the Kingdom of God in their hearts.
(b) On this day the brother and the sister receive God's Kingdom in their hearts.
(c) These are the brother and the sister who receive God's Kingdom in their hearts.

4. ὃς ἂν ἀναγινώσκῃ τὸ βιβλίον τοῦ Ἰωάννου
οὗτός ἐστιν ὁ ἀγαπῶν αὐτόν.
(a) Whoever reads John's book, he is the one who loves him.
(b) Whoever reads John's book is the one whom he loves.
(c) The man who reads John's book, he is the one he loves.

5. ὃ ἦν ἀπ' ἀρχῆς ἀπαγγέλλουσιν ὑμῖν οἱ ἀπόστολοι
ἵνα κοινωνίαν ἔχητε μεθ' ἡμῶν.
(a) The apostles declare to us that which was from the beginning so that we may have fellowship with you.
(b) The apostles declare to you that which was from the beginning so that you may have fellowship with us.
(c) That which was from the beginning you declare to the apostles so that they may have fellowship with you.

Check your answers in Key to Progress Testson page 333.

Lesson 12

ἔργον – a work   τὸ ἔργον – the work
ὁ, ἡ, τό – the

12.1

You have learned that some Greek words have endings like λόγος while others have endings like καρδία. In this lesson you will study τὸ ἔργον as an example of a third type of Greek word. Some endings are the same as the endings of λόγος but not all.

τὸ ἔργον – the work, the deed – ον	
τὰ ἔργα – the works, the deeds – α	subject endings

τό
τά   the

So: τὸ ἔργον ὃ ποιεῖς – the work which you do, the deed you are doing

τὰ ἔργα ἃ ποιεῖς – the deeds which you do, the works you are doing

τὰ ἔργα ἡμῶν – our deeds, our works, the things we do, the things we have done

τοῦτο τὸ ἔργον – this act, this deed, this task.

Note that the endings -ον (singular) and -α (plural) are found in some English words derived from Greek, e.g. criterion, criteria;
                        phenomenon, phenomena.

You will have noticed that there are several possible ways of translating ἔργον and ἔργα into English. In the right-hand check column we usually put only one translation. For example, for ταῦτά ἐστιν τὰ ἔργα τοῦ θεοῦ, we put 'These are the works of God'. If you translate it as 'These are the deeds of God' or 'These are the things God does', your translation is also correct. When we are translating from the New Testament, the context may help us to decide how to translate. In Matthew 11:2, τὰ ἔργα τοῦ Χριστοῦ means 'The deeds Christ had done' or 'The wonderful things Christ was doing'; but in John 6:28 τὰ ἔργα τοῦ θεοῦ means 'The things God wants us to do'.

Translate:

1. τοῦτό ἐστιν τὸ ἔργον τοῦ θεοῦ.	This is the work of God.
2. τοῦτό ἐστιν τὸ ἔργον ὃ ποιεῖ.	This is the work which he does.
3. ταῦτά ἐστιν τὰ ἔργα τοῦ θεοῦ.	These are the works of God.
4. ταῦτά ἐστιν τὰ ἔργα ἃ ποιοῦσιν.	These are the deeds which they do.

Note that in nos. 3 and 4, ταῦτά ἐστιν must be translated as 'these are', and not as 'these is'. When plural words which take τά as 'the' (e.g. ἔργα) are the subject of a sentence, they are usually followed by a singular form of the verb.

12.2

τὸ ἔργον – the work, the deed   – ον   object   (the same as the
τὰ ἔργα – the works, the deeds   – α   endings   subject endings)

So: ὁ τὸ ἔργον ποιῶν – the person doing the work
ὁ μὴ ποιῶν τὰ ἔργα – the person who does not do the deeds.

Translate:

1. ποιεῖ τὸ ἔργον.	He does the work.
2. ὁ ποιῶν τὰ ἔργα.	The person doing the deeds
3. ὃς ἂν ποιῇ ταῦτα τὰ ἔργα...	Whoever does these acts...
4. ἐὰν ποιῇ τὸ ἔργον...	If he does the work...
5. γράφουσι τὰ βιβλία ἵνα ἀναγινώσκωμεν αὐτά.	They write the books so that we may read them.
6. οὗτοί εἰσιν οἱ μὴ ἀναγινώσκοντες τὰ βιβλία.	These are the people who are not reading the books.

12.3

τοῦ ἔργου – of the work   – ου
τῶν ἔργων – of the works – ων   } of

So: ἡ ἀρχὴ τοῦ ἔργου – the beginning of the work

Translate:

1. ἡ ἀρχὴ τῶν ἔργων τοῦ θεοῦ. | The beginning of the works of God.
2. αὕτη ἐστὶν ἡ ἀρχὴ τοῦ ἔργου. | This is the beginning of the work.
3. αὕτη ἦν ἡ ἀρχὴ τοῦ βιβλίου. | This was the beginning of the book.
4. μὴ ἀναγινώσκωμεν τὰ βιβλία τοῦ ἀδελφοῦ ἡμῶν ἀλλὰ τὰ βιβλία τῆς ἀδελφῆς ὑμῶν. | Let us not read the books of our brother but the books of your sister.

12.4

τῷ ἔργῳ – by the work
τοῖς ἔργοις – by the works

– ῳ
– οις } by, by means of, with, in

So: μὴ ἀγαπῶμεν λόγῳ ἀλλὰ ἔργῳ
Let us not love in word but in deed
γινώσκω αὐτὴν τῷ ἔργῳ ὃ ποιεῖ
I know her by the work which she does
πιστεύω τοῖς ἔργοις αὐτοῦ
I believe in his works *or* I believe the miracles he does.

Translate:

1. γινώσκομεν αὐτὸν τοῖς ἔργοις ἃ ποιεῖ. | We know him by the works which he is doing.
2. πιστεύετε τοῖς ἔργοις αὐτοῦ. | You believe in his works.
3. πιστεύουσι τοῖς ἔργοις ἡμῶν. | They believe our works.
4. ἀναγινώσκεις τοὺς λόγους οὓς γράφω ἐν τῷ βιβλίῳ τούτῳ. | You are reading the words which I am writing in this book.

12.5 Words

Compare

τὸ ἔργον – the work, the deed, the action — energy
τὸ τέκνον – the child
  τὸ τεκνίον – the little child
τὸ εὐαγγέλιον – the good news, the good message, the gospel (never used of a book, always of a communicated message) — evangel, evangelist

τὸ βιβλίον – the book, the document   bibliography
τὸ δαιμόνιον – the demon   demon
ὁ πονηρός – the evil one
    πονηρός – evil, wicked
ποιέω (ποιῶ) – I do, I make   poetry
τοῦτο – this, this thing
    ταῦτα – these, these things
γάρ – for, because (γάρ is the second word in a Greek
    clause or sentence, never the first)

So: ὁ γὰρ μὴ ἀγαπῶν τὸν ἀδελφόν...
        For he who does not love the brother...

        ἦν γὰρ αὐτῶν πονηρὰ τὰ ἔργα
        (Lit. was for of them evil the deeds)
        For their deeds were evil.

12.6 Translate

1. οἱ πιστεύοντες τῷ Ἰησοῦ τέκνα θεοῦ εἰσίν, ἀλλὰ οἱ μὴ πιστεύοντες τέκνα τοῦ πονηροῦ εἰσιν καὶ ποιοῦσιν τὰ ἔργα ἃ αὐτὸς ποιεῖ.	Those who believe in Jesus are children of God but those who do not believe are children of the evil one and they do the deeds which he does.
2. τὰ δαιμόνια πονηρά ἐστιν, πονηρὰ γάρ ἐστιν τὰ ἔργα αὐτῶν.	The demons are evil, for their deeds are evil.
3. οὐκ ἀγαπῶ τούτους τοὺς ἀνθρώπους, ἔστιν γὰρ αὐτῶν πονηρὰ τὰ ἔργα.	I do not love these men, for the things they do are evil (or, for their deeds are evil).
4. Τεκνία, μὴ ἀγαπῶμεν λόγῳ ἀλλὰ ἐν ἔργῳ καὶ ἀληθείᾳ, καὶ γὰρ ὁ θεὸς ἀγάπη ἐστίν.	Little children, let us not love in word but in deed and truth, for God is love.
5. τοῦτό ἐστιν τὸ βιβλίον ὃ γράφει ὁ Μᾶρκος.	This is the book which Mark is writing.
6. ταῦτα γράφει ἐν τῷ βιβλίῳ τούτῳ ἵνα τὸ εὐαγγέλιον γινώσκητε καὶ κοινωνίαν ἔχητε μετὰ τοῦ Κυρίου ἡμῶν.	He writes these things in this book so that you may know the good news and have fellowship with our Lord.

7. καὶ λέγουσιν αὐτῷ οἱ Φαρισαῖοι, Δαιμόνιον ἔχεις καὶ ἐν (through) τῷ ἄρχοντι (ruler) τῶν δαιμονίων ἐκβάλλεις (you cast out) τὰ δαιμόνια. καὶ λέγει αὐτοῖς ὁ Ἰησοῦς, Δαιμόνιον οὐκ ἔχω, ἀλλὰ ποιῶ τὰ ἔργα τοῦ θεοῦ καὶ ἐκβάλλω τὰ δαιμόνια ἐν τῇ δυνάμει (power) αὐτοῦ.

The Pharisees say to him, 'You have a demon and through the ruler of the demons you cast out the demons.' Jesus says to them, 'I do not have a demon, but I do the works of God and I cast out the demons through his power.'

12.7

You have now seen and translated all the forms for 'the'.

Singular

ὁ	ἡ	τό	subject (nominative)
τόν	τήν	τό	object (accusative)
τοῦ	τῆς	τοῦ	of (genitive)
τῷ	τῇ	τῷ	by, with, to, for (dative)

Plural

οἱ	αἱ	τά	subject (nominative)
τούς	τάς	τά	object (accusative)
τῶν	τῶν	τῶν	of (genitive)
τοῖς	ταῖς	τοῖς	by, with, to, for (dative)

The forms in column 1 go with all words which have ὁ = the:
ὁ βασιλεύς – the king; οἱ βασιλεῖς – the kings; ὁ πατήρ – the father; τοῦ πατρός – of the father.
All nouns with ὁ are called masculine.

The forms in column 2 go with all words which have ἡ = the:
ἡ καρδία – the heart; ἡ ἔρημος – the desert; ἡ πόλις – the town; τῆς γῆς – of the earth.
All nouns with ἡ are called feminine.

The forms in column 3 go with all words which have τό = the:
τὸ ὄνομα – the name; τὸ γένος – the tribe; τὸ φῶς – the light; ἐν τῷ φωτί – in the light.
All nouns with τό are called neuter.

LESSON 12

Look at column 4. We can describe ὁ as nominative singular masculine, τήν as accusative singular feminine, τά as nominative or accusative plural neuter, but notice that in ὁ λέγων – the person who says, and οἱ λέγοντες, ὁ and οἱ are not of the masculine gender. They are of common gender – they refer to people, whether male or female.

We shall discuss these grammatical terms in lesson 37 and study them in lessons 37, 39, and 42. It is not necessary to learn them at this stage.

12.8

Forms of οὗτος – this, ὅς – who, and τὸ ἔργον – the work.

Masculine	Feminine	Neuter	
Singular			
οὗτος	αὕτη	τοῦτο	nom
τοῦτον	ταύτην	τοῦτο	acc
τούτου	ταύτης	τούτου	gen
τούτῳ	ταύτῃ	τούτῳ	dat
Plural			
οὗτοι	αὗται	ταῦτα	nom
τούτους	ταύτας	ταῦτα	acc
τούτων	τούτων	τούτων	gen
τούτοις	ταύταις	τούτοις	dat
Singular			
ὅς	ἥ	ὅ	nom
ὅν	ἥν	ὅ	acc
οὗ	ἧς	οὗ	gen
ᾧ	ᾗ	ᾧ	dat
Plural			
οἵ	αἵ	ἅ	nom
οὕς	ἅς	ἅ	acc
ὧν	ὧν	ὧν	gen
οἷς	αἷς	οἷς	dat

Singular	Plural		
τὸ ἔργον	< subject >	τὰ ἔργα	nom
τὸ ἔργον	< object >	τὰ ἔργα	acc
τοῦ ἔργου	< of >	τῶν ἔργων	gen
τῷ ἔργῳ	< by, with >	τοῖς ἔργοις	dat

12.9 Special note

(a) Review 7.10 (b), (c), and (d), 8.7(c), 9.10 (c) and (d), 11.9 (c).

You have read all the verses in John 1:3–10. Now notice how they are structured as a chiasmus, turning on a central axis about John's witness.

A 3.   πάντα δι' αὐτοῦ ἐγένετο,
       καὶ χωρὶς αὐτοῦ ἐγένετο
       οὐδὲ ἕν ὃ γέγονεν.

  B 4-5 ἐν αὐτῷ ζωὴ ἦν,
         καὶ ἡ ζωὴ ἦν
         τὸ φῶς τῶν ἀνθρώπων·
         καὶ τὸ φῶς ἐν τῇ σκοτίᾳ φαίνει,
         καὶ ἡ σκοτία αὐτὸ οὐ κατέλαβεν.

    C 6-8 ἐγένετο ἄνθρωπος ἀπεσταλμένος παρὰ θεοῦ,
           ὄνομα αὐτῷ Ἰωάννης·
           οὗτος ἦλθεν εἰς μαρτυρίαν
           ἵνα μαρτυρήσῃ περὶ τοῦ φωτός,
           ἵνα πάντες πιστεύσωσιν δι' αὐτοῦ.
           οὐκ ἦν ἐκεῖνος τὸ φῶς,
           ἀλλ' ἵνα μαρτυρήσῃ περὶ τοῦ φωτός.

  B' 9 ἦν τὸ φῶς τὸ ἀληθινόν,
         ὃ φωτίζει πάντα ἄνθρωπον
         ἐρχόμενον εἰς τὸν κόσμον.

A' 10 ἐν τῷ κόσμῳ ἦν
       καὶ ὁ κόσμος δι' αὐτοῦ ἐγένετο,
       καὶ ὁ κόσμος αὐτὸν οὐκ ἔγνω.

Notes:

v3 Some manuscripts put a punctuation mark after ἕν, so translators who accept that punctuation continue, 'That which has come into being through him was life.' This is a little difficult to understand, but the major problem is that (a) it does not fit with the author's style of using threefold repetition of key words in a unit or stanza, and that (b) it destroys the balance between verse 3 and verse 10 which the author has signalled by repeating part of verse 3 in verse 10.

vv6–8 Many commentators consider that these verses are a piece of prose inserted into a piece of poetry. It is true that in terms of the Greek sentences, or an English translation, they do not look much like poetry. But the chiastic structure of 1–2 and 3–10 shows us we are dealing with what is basically Hebraic literature.

Hebrew poetry has short lines – often no more than four words, sometimes less. If 6–8 are translated into Hebrew, no line is more than four words. Notice the triple repetition of the theme of witness:

μαρτυρίαν – μαρτυρήσῃ – μαρτυρήσῃ.

Detailed study of the New Testament can only be done by reading it in Greek. You have made a start. The literary background of the New Testament is primarily to be found in the Hebrew scriptures and in the teaching of the rabbis – who nearly all used Hebrew as the language of instruction. You have already begun to see how a knowledge of Hebrew can help us in understanding the New Testament.

Lesson 13

ποιέω (ποιῶ) – I do, I make ----

13.1

ποιῶ – I do, I make, I am doing...   Compare: λέγω
ποιοῦμεν – we do, we make...   λέγομεν

So: ταῦτα ποιοῦμεν – we do these things
      τοῦτο γράφομεν – we write this
      τὰ ἔργα ἃ ποιῶ – the deeds which I do
      οἱ λόγοι οὓς λέγω – the words which I say.

A verbal form like λέγομεν has two parts:
   (a) the stem, λεγ , which indicates the basic meaning
   (b) the ending, -ομεν , which indicates the person.
In the form ποιοῦμεν we have:
   (a) the stem, ποιε
   (b) the ending, -ομεν
but the ε and ο of ποιέομεν have been combined so that ποιέομεν has become ποιοῦμεν.

Similar changes take place in other verbs with stems ending in a vowel (see ἀγαπάω in 11.2). Note that these verbs are written in dictionaries in their full form: καλέω, ἀγαπάω, πληρόω. But in actual use, the vowel of the stem combines with the vowel of the ending to make the shorter or contracted ending, e.g. ποιῶ (I do), ἀγαπῶ (I love) πληρῶ (I fill, I fulfil).

Translate:

1. τοῦτο ποιῶ ἵνα πιστεύῃς.	I am doing this so that you may believe.
2. ταῦτα ποιοῦμεν ἡμεῖς ἵνα καὶ ὑμεῖς πιστεύητε.	We are doing these things so that you also may believe.
3. ταῦτα λέγομεν ἵνα αὐτοὶ ποιῶσιν τὰ ἔργα ἃ ποιοῦμεν.	We speak these things so that they may do the deeds which we do.

13.2

ποιεῖs – you do, you make...   Compare: λέγεις
ποιεῖτε – you (p) do, you make...   λέγετε

Translate:
1. τοῦτο ποιεῖτε. | You are doing this.
2. τὰ ἔργα τοῦ πονηροῦ ποιεῖτε. | You do the works of the evil one.
3. ἐὰν τὰ ἔργα αὐτοῦ ποιῆτε... | If you do his works...
4. τὸ ἔργον αὐτοῦ ποιεῖς. | You are doing his work.
5. ἐὰν τὸ ἔργον τοῦ θεοῦ ποιῇς... | If you do the work of God...

13.3

ποιεῖ – he does, he makes...   Compare: λέγει
ποιοῦσιν – they do, they make...   λέγουσιν

Translate:
1. τοῦτο ποιεῖ ὁ Παῦλος. | Paul is doing this.
2. τοῦτο ποιῶ. | I am doing this.
3. τοῦτο ποιοῦσιν. | They are doing this.
4. Ἰησοῦ, ταῦτα ποιεῖς. | Jesus, you are doing these things.
5. ταῦτα ποιοῦσιν οἱ ἀπόστολοι. | The apostles are doing these things.
6. ὃς ἂν ταῦτα ποιῇ... | Whoever does these things...

13.4 Words

	Compare
καλέω – I call, I invite	call, Paraclete
λαλέω – I talk, I speak	glossolalia
περιπατέω – I walk about, I walk, I live	peripatetic
ζητέω – I seek, I look for	
ἡ γλῶσσα – the tongue, the language	glossary, glossolalia
τὸ φῶς – the light	
τοῦ φωτός – of the light	photograph
τὸ σκότος *or* ἡ σκοτία – the darkness	
ἐγώ – I; μέ – me; μοῦ – of me;	egoism, me
μοί – to me, for me	
σύ – you (thou); σέ – you; σοῦ – of you;	
σοί – to you, for you	

LEARN NEW TESTAMENT GREEK

13.5 Translate

1. οὗτός ἐστιν ὁ ἀδελφός μου.	He (this man) is my brother.
2. αὕτη ἐστὶν ἡ ἀδελφή σου.	She is your sister.
3. ἐγὼ ταῦτα γράφω ἀλλὰ σὺ οὐκ ἀναγινώσκεις αὐτά.	I am writing these things but you are not reading them.
4. ἡ γλῶσσά μου λαλεῖ σοι καὶ τὰ ὦτά σου ἀκούει.	My tongue speaks to you and your ears hear.
5. λαλεῖ ταύταις ταῖς γλώσσαις ἀλλὰ ἐγὼ οὐκ ἀκούω.	He speaks in these languages but I do not understand.
6. καλεῖ σε ὁ Ἰησοῦς ἵνα ἐν τῷ φωτὶ περιπατῇς.	Jesus calls you so that you may walk in the light.
7. οὐ ζητοῦμεν τὴν σκοτίαν ἀλλὰ τὸ φῶς.	We do not seek the darkness but the light.
8. μὴ ζητῶμεν τὴν σκοτίαν ἀλλὰ τὸ φῶς καὶ τὴν ἀλήθειαν.	Let us not seek the darkness but the light and the truth.
9. ὁ θεὸς φῶς ἐστιν καὶ ἐν αὐτῷ σκοτία οὐκ ἔστιν. καὶ καλεῖ σε ὁ θεὸς ἵνα ἐν τῳ φωτὶ περιπατῇς, οἱ γὰρ ἐν τῷ φωτὶ περιπατοῦντες τέκνα θεοῦ εἰσιν, καὶ αὐτὸν Κύριον καλοῦσιν. περιπατῶμεν ἐν τῷ φωτὶ καὶ μὴ περιπατῶμεν ἐν τῷ σκότει.	God is light and in him there is no darkness. God calls you so that you may walk in the light, for those who walk in the light are children of God, and they call him Lord. Let us walk in the light and let us not walk in the darkness.
10. ζητεῖτέ με ἵνα τοὺς λόγους μου ἀκούητε. ἀλλά, ἀδελφοί μου, ἐὰν γλώσσαις λαλῶ ὑμῖν οὐκ ἀκούετε. ὁ γὰρ λαλῶν γλώσσαις οὐκ ἀνθρώποις λαλεῖ ἀλλὰ θεῷ. οὐδεὶς (no one) γὰρ ἀκούει τοὺς λόγους οὓς λέγει.	You seek me so that you may hear my words. But, my brothers, if I speak to you in tongues, you do not understand. For he who speaks in tongues does not speak to men but to God, for no one understands the words he says.

13.6 Punctuation

In most editions of the New Testament (ἡ καινὴ διαθήκη) the following punctuation marks are used:

Compare	Greek	English
1. Comma	,	,
2. Colon	·	: or ;
3. Full stop	.	.
4. Question mark	;	?
5. Apostrophe	ʼ	ʼ

to mark the dropping of a letter:
μετὰ ἐμοῦ becomes μετʼ ἐμοῦ – with me
μετὰ ἡμῶν becomes μεθʼ ἡμῶν – with us.

13.7

Read carefully:

1. Love and light

ὁ ἀγαπῶν τὸν ἀδελφὸν αὐτοῦ ἐν τῷ φωτὶ περιπατεῖ ἀλλὰ οἱ μὴ ἀγαπῶντες τοὺς ἀδελφοὺς ἐν τῇ σκοτίᾳ εἰσὶν καὶ ἐν τῇ σκοτίᾳ περιπατοῦσιν. τεκνία μου, ἀγαπῶμεν ἀλλήλους, ὁ γὰρ θεὸς ἀγάπη ἐστίν· καὶ μὴ ἀγαπῶμεν λόγῳ μηδὲ τῇ γλώσσῃ ἀλλὰ ἐν ἔργῳ καὶ ἀληθείᾳ.

Notes

ὁ ἀγαπῶν – lesson 8.2, 8.3, 11.2
μή – 11.2
τεκνία – 12.5

ἀλλήλους – each other
ἀγαπῶμεν λόγῳ – 12.4
μηδέ – nor

2. Seeking God

καὶ ἐγὼ ταῦτα γράφω σοι ἵνα τὸν θεὸν ζητῇς ἐξ (out of) ὅλης (whole) τῆς καρδίας σου· ὁ γὰρ ζητῶν τὸν θεὸν ἐξ ὅλης τῆς καρδίας αὐτοῦ, εὑρήσει (will find) αὐτόν, καθὼς (as) ἀναγινώσκεις ἐν τῷ βιβλίῳ τοῦ εὐαγγελίου, Ὁ ζητῶν εὑρίσκει. ὃς γὰρ ἂν αὐτὸν ζητῇ εὑρήσει· καὶ μακάριοί εἰσιν πάντες (all) οἱ ζητοῦντες καὶ εὑρίσκοντες αὐτόν.

13.8 Translation

Here is the last line of 13.7.1:
> καὶ μὴ ἀγαπῶμεν λογῷ μηδὲ τῇ γλώσσῃ
> ἀλλὰ ἐν ἔργῳ καὶ ἀληθείᾳ.

This could be translated literally as, 'And not let us love by word nor by the tongue but by deed and by truth.' Of course, this is not how we would naturally express these ideas in English. We must look for better ways to translate.

καὶ μὴ ἀγαπῶμεν is better translated as:
> Let us not love...

or as Let us show love not by...

λόγῳ and γλώσσῃ indicate love shown 'by word' and 'by tongue'. Because New Testament writers, influenced by Hebrew idiom, often put side by side two ideas that we might rather combine, we might translate
> μὴ...λόγῳ μηδὲ τῇ γλώσσῃ

as not by the words we speak with our tongues.

ἐν ἔργῳ and ἀληθείᾳ indicate love expressed 'by deed' and 'by reality'. So we might translate
> ἐν ἔργῳ καὶ ἀληθείᾳ

as by the things we actually do.

We could then translate
> καὶ μὴ ἀγαπῶμεν λόγῳ μηδὲ τῇ γλώσσῃ ἀλλὰ ἐν ἔργῳ καὶ ἀληθείᾳ

as Let us show our love not just by the words we speak but by what we actually do.

In 13.7.2 we read: ὁ γὰρ ζητῶν τὸν θεὸν ἐξ ὅλης τῆς καρδίας αὐτοῦ. This could be translated literally as, 'The person for seeking the God out of whole of the heart of him.' But it is clearly better to translate
> ὁ γὰρ ζητῶν τὸν θεόν

as For the person who seeks God...
or as For he who seeks God...

ἐξ ὅλης τῆς καρδίας αὐτοῦ is better translated 'with his whole heart' than 'out of his whole heart'. But even that is not very natural English. 'Wholeheartedly' or 'with all his heart', are better. So we might translate:
> ὁ γὰρ ζητῶν τὸν θεὸν ἐξ ὅλης τῆς καρδίας αὐτοῦ

as For the one who seeks God wholeheartedly...
or as For he who puts his whole heart into seeking God...

When we translate we must not ask ourselves, 'How can I put these words into my language?' We must ask, 'How can I express the meaning of these words in my language?'

13.9 Forms of ποιέω – I do, I make, and πληρόω – I fill, I fulfil

ποιῶ – I do
ποιεῖς – you do
ποιεῖ – he does
ποιοῦμεν – we do
ποιεῖτε – you do
ποιοῦσιν – they do

πληρῶ – I fill
πληροῖς – you fill
πληροῖ – he fills
πληροῦμεν – we fill
πληροῦτε – you fill
πληροῦσιν – they fill

13.10 Bible translations evaluation (1)

The more Greek you learn, the more you will be able to evaluate and comment on translation of the Bible. For a start we will consider three short passages which you have already read.

(a) In John 6:28 a question is put to Jesus: 'What should we be doing so as to do τὰ ἔργα τοῦ θεοῦ;' Consider these translations of τὰ ἔργα τοῦ θεοῦ.

NRSV (to perform) the works of God
NIV (to do) the works God requires
REB (if our work is to be) the work of God
GNB (to do) what God wants us to do

(b) 1 John 3:18
μὴ ἀγαπῶμεν λόγῳ μηδὲ τῇ γλώσσῃ
ἀλλὰ ἐν ἔργῳ καὶ ἀληθείᾳ.

NRSV   Let us love, not in word or speech, but in truth and action.
NIV   Let us not love with words or tongue, but with actions and in truth.
REB   Love must not be a matter of words or talk, it must be true love that shows itself in action.
GNB   Our love should not be just words and talk, it must be true love which shows itself in action.
NLT   Let us stop just saying we love each other; let us really show it by our actions.
Perhaps: We must show our love not just by the words we say but by what we actually do to help people.

76   LEARN NEW TESTAMENT GREEK

In evaluating these translations remember that in Hebraic style ideas are often placed side by side to build up a picture. So here, λόγος (word) and γλῶσσα (tongue) do not refer to two different or alternative things but to 'the words we speak'. We also need to be aware that in Hebrew a negative statement in part of a linked pair may show the greater importance of the other element. John is not saying that people should stop speaking words that express love.

(c) John 1:1–2

Ἐν ἀρχῇ ἦν ὁ λόγος, καὶ ὁ λόγος, ἦν πρὸς τὸν θεόν,
καὶ θεὸς ἦν ὁ λόγος. οὗτος ἦν ἐν ἀρχῇ πρὸς τὸν θεόν.

NRSV   In the beginning was the Word, and the Word was with God, and the Word was God.[2] He was in the beginning with God.

GNB   In the beginning the Word already existed; the Word was with God and the Word was God.[2] From the very beginning the Word was with God.

NIV   In the beginning was the Word, and the Word was with God, and the Word was God.[2] He was with God in the beginning.

REB   In the beginning the Word already was. The Word was in God's presence, and what God was, the Word was.[2] He was with God at the beginning.

13.11 A verse to learn:

Mark 1:8

Ἐγὼ ἐβάπτισα	I baptized
ὑμᾶς ὕδατι,	you with water
αὐτὸς δὲ	but he
βαπτίσει ὑμᾶς	will baptize you
ἐν πνεύματι ἁγίῳ.	with the Holy Spirit.

Lesson 14

ἔλεγεν – he was saying, he used to say ···· |

14.1

Compare:
    (a) λέγει – he is speaking —, he speaks ····
    (b) ἔλεγεν – he was speaking — |, he used to speak ···· |
(a) refers to a continuing or repeated action in the present
(b) refers to a continued or repeated action in the past:
    ε before the stem of a verb is **a mark of past time.**

Translate:

1. γράφει τὰς ἐπιστολάς.	He is writing the letters.
2. ἔγραφεν ἐπιστολάς.	He was writing letters.
3. λαμβάνει τὸ βιβλίον.	He takes the book.
4. ἐλάμβανεν τὰ βιβλία.	He was taking the books.
5. ἐπίστευεν τῷ Ἰησοῦ.	He was believing in Jesus.
6. πιστεύει τῷ Ἰησοῦ.	He believes in Jesus.
7. ἀκούει λόγους.	He hears words.
8. ἤκουεν τοὺς λόγους.	He was hearing the words.

14.2 Translating forms like ἔλεγεν

ἔλεγεν refers to continued or repeated action in the past.
So it may be translated into English as:
    he was saying — | (continuing action in past time)
    or he used to say ···· | (repeated action in past time)
    But because in English an extended act of speech is usually introduced by 'he said', we can often translate ἔλεγεν as 'he said'.

When we are translating a New Testament passage we have to choose a translation which will fit well in the passage. Consider these possible translations of καὶ ἔλεγεν τοῖς μαθηταῖς :
    So he said to the disciples
    He was saying to the disciples
    He began to say to the disciples
    He went on to say to the disciples

(In our right-hand check column we usually put the forms with 'was' and 'were', but always remember that forms with 'used to' and other similar translations are also possible.)

14.3

ἔλεγεν – he was saying, he said
ἔλεγον – they were saying, they said
ἔβλεπεν – he was looking at
ἔβλεπον – they were looking at

Translate:

1. λέγει τοῖς μαθηταῖς…	He is saying to the disciples…
2. ἔλεγεν τοῖς μαθηταῖς αὐτοῦ…	He was saying to his disciples…
3. ἔλεγον αὐτῷ οἱ μαθηταί…	The disciples said to him…
4. ἔβλεπεν τὸν Ἰησοῦν.	He was looking at Jesus.
5. ἔβλεπον τὸν ἀδελφὸν αὐτοῦ.	They were looking at his brother.
6. βλέπουσιν τὰς ἀδελφὰς αὐτοῦ.	They are looking at his sisters.

14.4

ἔλεγες – you were saying   Compare: λέγεις
ἐλέγετε – you (p) were saying   λέγετε

Translate:

1. ἔγραφες τὴν ἐπιστολὴν ἡμῖν.	You were writing the letter to us.
2. σὺ γράφεις ἐπιστολήν μοι.	You are writing a letter to me.
3. ἔγραφες ταύτην τὴν ἐπιστολήν.	You were writing this letter.
4. ἐγράφετε ἐπιστολάς.	You were writing letters.
5. ἀναγινώσκετε τὰς ἐπιστολάς.	You are reading the letters.
6. ἀνεγινώσκετε τὰς ἐπιστολάς.	You were reading the letters.
7. μὴ ἀναγινώσκωμεν τὴν ἐπιστολὴν ἣν σὺ ἔγραφες.	Let us not read the letter which you were writing.

14.5

ἔλεγον – I was saying   Compare: λέγω
ἐλέγομεν – we were saying   λέγομεν

Note that only the context shows the difference between
ἔλεγον – I was saying, and ἔλεγον – they were saying.

Translate:

1. ἐγὼ Ἰωάννης ἔλεγον ὑμῖν ὅτι Ὁ θεὸς φῶς ἐστιν.	I, John, used to say to you, 'God is light.'
2. ταῦτα ἐλέγομεν ὑμῖν.	We were saying these things to you.
3. ἀγαπῶ σε καὶ ταῦτα ἔγραφόν σοι ἵνα κοινωνίαν ἔχῃς μετά μου.	I love you and I was writing these things to you so that you may have fellowship with me.
4. ταῦτα ἔγραφον ἡμῖν οἱ ἀπόστολοι.	The apostles were writing these things to us (for us).
5. ἐὰν ταῦτα γράφωσιν, τὴν ἀλήθειαν γράφουσιν.	If they are writing these things, they are writing the truth.
6. ἔγραφεν τὰ βιβλία ταῦτα ἡ Μαρία.	Mary was writing these books.

14.6 Summary of forms

A SINGULAR
1. ἔλεγον – I was saying
2. ἔλεγες – you were saying
3. ἔλεγεν – he was saying

PLURAL
1. ἐλέγομεν – we were saying
2. ἐλέγετε – you were saying
3. ἔλεγον – they were saying

B
1. λέγω – I am saying
2. λέγεις – you are saying
3. λέγει – he is saying

1. λέγομεν – we are saying
2. λέγετε – you are saying
3. λέγουσιν – they are saying

Note:
1. The type of action in all these forms in columns A and B is **continuing** or **repeated** action ▬▬ .
2. ε before the stem is **a mark of past time**. So all the forms in column A indicate continued or repeated action in past time ▬▬ ⌐.

3. The **endings** after the stem show the **person**:

	1st person	2nd person	3rd person
Singular	– ον – I	– ες – you	– εν – he, she, it
Plural	– ομεν – we	– ετε – you	– ον – they.

4. The basic stem of the verb is not always its first part. For example, in English 'standing' and 'understanding' have the same basic stem: stand. In Greek verbal forms notice how the ε indicating past time comes immediately before the stem:

	Stem	
λέγω – I am saying	λεγ	ἔλεγον – I was saying
καλῶ – I am calling	καλε	ἐκάλουν – I was calling
ἀναγινώσκει – he is reading	γιν	ἀνεγίνωσκεν – he was reading
περιπατεῖ – he is walking	πατε	περιεπάτει – he was walking
ἀποστέλλουσιν – they are sending	στελλ	ἀπέστελλον – they were sending.

5. In grammar books the forms in column B (p80) of λέγω (I am saying), are called present.
The forms in column A of ἔλεγον (I was saying), are called imperfect.

As we have seen, both the present and the imperfect tenses indicate continued or repeated action, and the type of action is often of more significance than the time. Note that, even in English, to describe 'I go' as in the present tense can be misleading. Study this conversation:

>'Do you go to school?'
>'Yes, I go to school.'

'I go to school' implies:
  (i) I have been to school in the past
  (ii) I go to school now, in the present
  (iii) I expect to continue going to school.

'I go' may be described as being in the present tense, but it refers to past, present, and future time. So in John 15:18:

>Εἰ ὁ κόσμος ὑμᾶς μισεῖ...
>If the world hates you...

μισεῖ (it hates) refers to any hatred 'you' have encountered, do encounter, or will encounter from the world.

LESSON 14

14.7 Words

ἀκολουθέω – I follow
    ἠκολούθει αὐτῇ – he was following her
βλέπω – I look at, I look, I see
διδάσκω – I teach
    ὁ διδάσκαλος – the teacher, the rabbi
    ἡ διδαχή – the teaching, the doctrine
ὁ μαθητής – the learner, the student, the disciple
ἀμήν – truly, verily, amen

14.8 Translate

1. ἀκολουθῶ σοι.	I am following you.
2. ἠκολούθει τῷ Ἰησοῦ ὁ Φίλιππος.	Philip was following Jesus.
3. οἱ μαθηταὶ ἀκολουθοῦσιν τῷ Ἰησοῦ καὶ διδάσκει αὐτούς.	The disciples follow Jesus and he teaches them.
4. ἔβλεπεν ὁ διδάσκαλος τοὺς μαθητάς.	The teacher was looking at the students.
5. οἱ μαθηταὶ ἀκούουσιν τὴν διδαχὴν τοῦ διδασκάλου ἵνα ποιῶσιν τὰ ἔργα ἃ διδάσκει αὐτούς.	The disciples are listening to the teaching of the rabbi so that they may do the deeds which he teaches them.

14.9

Read carefully:
           Disciples were following Jesus

1. Οἱ μαθηταὶ τοῦ Ἰησοῦ ἠκολούθουν αὐτῷ καὶ ἐδίδασκεν αὐτούς. καὶ οἱ μαθηταὶ τοῦ Ἰωάννου ἔλεγον αὐτῷ ὅτι Ἀκούομεν τὴν διδαχὴν τοῦ Ἰησοῦ καὶ ἡ διδαχὴ ἣν διδάσκει ἀληθής ἐστιν.
2. Καὶ ἀφέντες (leaving) τὸν Ἰωάννην ἠκολούθουν τῷ Ἰησοῦ. καὶ ὁ Ἰησοῦς βλέπων αὐτοὺς ἀκολουθοῦντας αὐτῷ ἔλεγεν αὐτοῖς, Τί (what) ζητεῖτε· ἔλεγον αὐτῷ, Ἀκολουθοῦμέν σοι ἵνα τὴν διδαχὴν ἣν σὺ διδάσκεις ἀκούωμεν.
3. Καὶ ἔλεγεν αὐτοῖς ἐν τῇ διδαχῇ αὐτοῦ, Καλεῖτέ με διδάσκαλον καὶ κύριον καὶ καλῶς (well) λέγετε εἰμὶ (I am) γάρ. καὶ ἔλεγεν αὐτοῖς Ἀμὴν ἀμὴν λέγω ὑμῖν, οὐκ ἔστιν μαθητὴς μείζων (greater) τοῦ διδασκάλου αὐτοῦ.

14.10 Translation

In 14.9.2 we read: ἵνα τὴν διδαχὴν ἣν σὺ διδάσκεις ἀκούωμεν. We might translate this literally as 'so that the teaching which you teach we may hear'. But in English:

1. the word order must be changed – 'so that we may hear the teaching which you teach' and
2. 'the teaching which you teach' is not natural English. So the translator must find a better way. Consider:
   (a) so that we may hear the doctrine which you teach
   (b) so that we may listen to your teaching
   (c) so that we may hear what you teach.

A translator must not only ask, 'How can I best express the meaning of these words in my language?' (13.8). He must also ask, 'How can I best express the meaning of these words in my language so that they can be understood by those who will read them or hear them?'

Look again at translations (a), (b), and (c) in the previous paragraph. If we expect our readers to have a good understanding of English, we might choose (a) or (b). If we expected their English to be limited, we would choose (c).

14.11

(a) Note: ἐκεῖνος – that man, he.
εἶπεν – he said
ἀπεκρίθη – he replied
γέγραφα – I have written.

Now read:

Μὴ γράφε,	Don't write,
‛Ο βασιλεὺς τῶν ’Ιουδαίων	'The King of the Judeans
ἀλλ’ ὅτι ἐκεῖνος εἶπεν	but that that man said,
βασιλεύς εἰμι τῶν ’Ιουδαίων.	I am the king of the Judeans.'
ἀπεκρίθη ὁ Πιλᾶτος,	Pilate replied,
"Ο γέγραφα, γέγραφα.	'What I have written, I have written.'

(b) Re-read 10.9 and keep it open as you read

1 John 1:1–3 (᾽Ιωάννου Α 1:1–3)

Notes

ὀφθαλμός – eye
ἐθεασάμεθα – we saw
χεῖρες – hands
ἐψηλάφησαν – they touched
περί – about, concerning

ἐφανερώθη – it was revealed
ἡμέτερος – our
(after ἡμετέρα, in English we need to use the word 'is')

In verse 3 note καὶ ἡ κοινωνία δὲ ἡ ἡμετέρα 'and our fellowship.' Here the added linking word δὲ indicates that in this sentence we have further information about the 'fellowship' that has just been mentioned. So in English we might translate the phrase as: 'Now our fellowship is'.

(c) Word fun:

Recite
    ἡμεῖς we and ὑμεῖς you,
    εἷς is one and δύο two,
    ἐμέ me, and σέ is thee,
    ἕξ is six and τρεῖς is three.

14.12

Revise lessons 7 and 8.

Lesson 15

ἐποίει – he was doing, he used to do ....|

15.1

ἐποίει –   he was doing, he used to do,   ποιεῖ – he does
           he was making,
           he used to make
ἐποίουν – they were doing,   ποιοῦσιν – they do
           they were making

So: τοῦτο ἐποίουν – they were doing this
      ταῦτα ἐποίει ὁ Παῦλος – Paul was doing these things.

Translate:

1. ποίει τὰ ἔργα.	He does the works.
2. ἐποίει τὰ ἔργα ταῦτα.	He was doing these works.
3. βλέπει τὸ ἔργον ὃ ποιοῦσιν.	He sees the work which they do.
4. ἔβλεπεν τὸ ἔργον ὃ ἐποίουν.	He saw the work they were doing.
5. ἐζήτει τοὺς περιπατοῦντας ἐν τῇ σκοτίᾳ.	He was looking for the people walking in the darkness.

15.2

ἐποίεις – you were doing,   ποιεῖς – you do
         you were making
ἐποιεῖτε – you (p) were doing,   ποιεῖτε – you do
          you (p) were making

So: ἐποιεῖτε τὰ ἔργα – you were doing the works

Translate:

1. Ἰησοῦ, ταῦτα ἐποίεις.	Jesus, you were doing these things.
2. ποιεῖς τὰ ἔργα.	You are doing the deeds.
3. τοῦτο ἐποίει ὁ πονηρός.	The evil one was doing this.
4. ταῦτα ἐποιεῖτε.	You were doing these things.
5. ἐζητεῖτε τὸν Ἰησοῦν.	You were seeking Jesus.

6. ἐκάλει τοὺς ἀδελφούς.	He was calling the brothers.
7. ἐκαλεῖτε τοὺς ἀδελφοὺς ὑμῶν.	You were calling your brothers.
8. ἐκάλεις τὰς ἀδελφάς σου.	You were calling your sisters.
9. τοῦτο ποιεῖτε.	You are doing this.

15.3

ἐποίουν – I was doing, I was making   ποιῶ – I do
ἐποιοῦμεν – we were doing, we were making   ποιοῦμεν – we do

So: ψεύστας αὐτοὺς ἐποιοῦμεν – we made them liars
  or, made them out to be liars.

Translate:

1. ψεύστην αὐτὸν ποιοῦμεν.	We make him a liar.
2. ψεύστην ἐποιοῦμεν αὐτόν.	We were making him a liar.
3. ταῦτα ἐλάλουν ἐγὼ ἀλλὰ σὺ οὐκ ἤκουες.	I was saying these things but you were not listening.
4. οἱ μαθηταὶ περιεπάτουν ἐν τῷ φωτί.	The disciples were walking in the light.
5. γλώσσαις ἐλαλοῦμεν ἡμεῖς ἀλλὰ ὑμεῖς οὐκ ἠκούετε.	We were speaking in tongues but you were not understanding.

15.4 Questions

; (a semi colon) is used, in printed Greek texts, as a question mark. It is often sufficient to change a statement into a question:

τοῦτο λέγομεν – We say this   τοῦτο λέγομεν; – Do we say this?
τοῦτο λέγωμεν – Let us say this   τοῦτο λέγωμεν; – Should we say this?
  or Are we to say this?

Translate:

1. προφήτης ἐστίν.	He is a prophet.
2. προφήτης ἐστίν;	Is he a prophet?
3. προφήτης ἦν;	Was he a prophet?

4. προφήτης ἦν.	He was a prophet.
5. ταῦτα ἐζητεῖτε.	You were seeking these things.
6. τοῦτο ἐζητεῖτε;	Were you seeking this?
7. ταῦτα γράφομεν.	We are writing these things.
8. ταῦτα γράφομεν;	Are we writing these things?
9. ταῦτα γράφωμεν.	Let us write these things.
10. ταῦτα γράφωμεν;	Should we write these things?

15.5

ἠγάπα – he was loving, he loved   ἀγαπᾷ – he loves
ἠγαπῶμεν – we used to love, we loved   ἀγαπῶμεν – we love

So: ὁ μαθητὴς ὃν ἠγάπα ὁ Ἰησοῦς – the disciple whom Jesus loved.

Note that when the ε which shows past time is put before a stem that begins with a vowel, the vowel is usually lengthened by being combined with the ε.

So: ἀκούει – he hears   ἤκουεν – he was hearing
       εὑρίσκουσιν – they find   ηὕρισκον – they were finding
       ἔχει – he has   εἶχεν – he had, he used to have

Translate:

1. ἀγαπᾷ ἡμᾶς ὁ θεός.	God loves us.
2. ἠγάπα ὁ Ἰησοῦς τὴν Μάρθαν.	Jesus loved Martha.
3. οὗτος ἦν ὁ διδάσκαλος ὃν ἠγαπᾶτε.	This was the teacher whom you loved.
4. αὐτοὶ ηὕρισκον τὰ βιβλία ἃ εἶχεν ὁ Μᾶρκος.	They were finding the books which Mark had.

15.6 Words

βαπτίζω – I baptize
    ὁ βαπτιστής – the baptist, the baptizer
μαρτυρέω – I bear witness, I give evidence
    ὁ μάρτυς – the witness, the person who gives evidence
    ἡ μαρτυρία – the testimony, the witness, the evidence that is given

τηρέω – I keep watch over, I keep, I guard, I pay attention to
ἡ ἐντολή – the commandment, the command
τίς; – who? which?

Singular	Plural
τίς; – who?	τίνες;
τίνα; – whom?	τίνας;
τίνος; – of whom?	τίνων;
τίνι; – to whom? for whom?	τίσιν;

τί; – what? why?

15.7 Translate

1. Τίς ἐστιν καὶ τί ποιεῖ;
   Μάρτυς ἐστὶν καὶ μαρτυρεῖ
   τῷ Ἰησοῦ.
   'Who is he and what does he do?'
   'He is a witness and he bears witness
   to Jesus.'

2. Τίς ἦν καὶ τί ἐποίει;
   Ὁ βαπτιστὴς ἦν καὶ
   ἐβάπτιζεν τοὺς μαθητὰς αὐτοῦ.
   'Who was he and what was he doing?'
   'He was the baptizer and
   he was baptizing his disciples.'

3. Τίνα ζητεῖτε;
   Τὸν Χριστὸν ζητοῦμεν.
   'Whom do you seek?'
   'We seek the Messiah.'

4. Τίνες εἰσὶν καὶ τί ποιοῦσιν;
   Μαθηταί εἰσιν καὶ τηροῦσιν
   τὰς ἐντολὰς τοῦ Χριστοῦ.
   'Who are they and what do they do?'
   'They are disciples and they keep
   the commandments of Christ.'

5. Τίνι λέγεις; καὶ τίνα αὐτὸν
   καλεῖς; Λέγω τῷ Ἰωάννῳ καὶ
   αὐτὸν τὸν βαπτιστὴν καλῶ.
   'To whom are you speaking? And
   what do you call him?' 'I am speaking
   to John and I call him the Baptist.'

6. Τί ἐδίδασκεν αὐτούς; Ἐν τῇ
   διδαχῇ ἔλεγεν αὐτοῖς, Ἐγὼ
   οὐκ εἰμὶ (I am) ὁ Χριστός, ἀλλὰ
   μαρτυρῶ περὶ (about) αὐτοῦ,
   καὶ ἀληθής ἐστιν ἡ μαρτυρία
   μου ἣν μαρτυρῶ περὶ αὐτοῦ
   ἵνα πιστεύητε αὐτῷ.
   'What was he teaching them?' 'In his
   teaching he said to them, "I am not
   the Messiah, but
   I bear witness about him,
   and my witness is true,
   which I bear about him,
   so that you may believe in him."'

15.8

Read carefully:

Keeping the commandments

Αἱ ἐντολαὶ τοῦ θεοῦ οὐ πονηραὶ εἰσιν, καὶ ἐτήρουν αὐτὰς οἱ ἀπόστολοι καὶ ἐδίδασκον τοὺς ἀνθρώπους ἵνα τὰς ἐντολὰς αὐτοῦ τηρῶσιν. καὶ ἔλεγεν ὁ Ἰωάννης ὅτι Ὁ ἔχων τὰς ἐντολὰς τοῦ θεοῦ καὶ τηρῶν αὐτὰς οὗτός ἐστιν ὁ ἀγαπῶν τὸν θεόν· καθὼς εἶπεν ὁ Ἰησοῦς, Ὁ ἔχων τὰς ἐντολάς μου καὶ τηρῶν αὐτάς, ἐκεῖνός ἐστιν ὁ ἀγαπῶν με. ὃς γὰρ ἂν ἔχῃ τὰς ἐντολὰς αὐτοῦ καὶ μὴ τηρῇ αὐτάς, ἡ ἀγάπη τοῦ θεοῦ οὐκ ἔστιν ἐν αὐτῷ. ἀλλὰ ἐὰν τὰς ἐντολὰς αὐτοῦ τηρῶμεν, ἀληθῶς ἡ ἀγάπη τοῦ θεοῦ ἐστιν ἐν ἡμῖν.

Καὶ τίς ἐστιν ἡ ἐντολὴ αὐτοῦ; αὕτη ἐστὶν ἡ ἐντολὴ αὐτοῦ ἵνα ἀγαπῶμεν ἀλλήλους· καθὼς εἶπεν ὁ Ἰησοῦς, Ἐντολὴν καίνην δίδωμι ὑμῖν ἵνα ἀγαπᾶτε ἀλλήλους, καθὼς ἠγάπησα ὑμᾶς ἵνα καὶ ὑμεῖς ἀγαπᾶτε ἀλλήλους.

Notes

καθώς – as
εἶπεν – ...[he] said
ἐκεῖνος – that, that man, he
ἀληθῶς – truly
ἵνα – that

ἀλλήλους – each other
καινή – new
δίδωμι – I give
ἠγάπησα – I loved

15.9

(a) Using the pattern

ὁ ἔχων τὴν ἐντολὴν καὶ τηρῶν αὐτήν
the one who has the commandment and keeps it

and ποιῶν – 'doing', and καλῶν – 'calling', τηρῶν – 'keeping, protecting'.

say in Greek:
The one who has the commandment and keeps it – the one who has the commandments and does them – the one who calls the apostles and protects them – the one who sees the apostles and loves them – the one who sees the apostle and loves him – the one who hears the commandment and keeps it.

LESSON 15

(b) Using δίδωμι – 'I give', and δίδωσιν – 'he gives', and καινός – 'new', and διαθήκη – 'covenant', and the pattern

ἐντολὴν καινὴν δίδωμι ὑμῖν – I give a new commandment to you

Say in Greek:
I give a new commandment to you – I give a new word to you – I give a new covenant to you – he gives a new commandment to us – he gives a new covenant to us – he gives a new word to you.

(c) Read 15.8 again, then read:

John 13:34 noting καθὼς ἠγάπησα – 'as I loved' or 'as I have loved'

1 John 3:23 noting ἵνα πιστεύσωμεν – 'so that we should believe.'
ὄνομα – 'name, person'. καθὼς ἔδωκεν – 'as he gave'

John 15:9–10 κἀγώ = καὶ ἐγώ – 'and I'. μείνατε – 'Stay!' 'Abide!'
ἐμός – my. ἐὰν τηρήσητε – 'if you keep'. μενεῖτε – 'you will abide'.
τετήρηκα – 'I have kept'.

15.10

Notice these forms for continued action in past time:

	καλέω (I call)	**ἀγαπάω** (I love)	**πληρόω** (I fill)
I	ἐκάλουν	ἠγάπων	ἐπλήρουν
you	ἐκάλεις	ἠγάπας	ἐπλήρους
he	ἐκάλει	ἠγάπα	ἐπλήρου
we	ἐκαλοῦμεν	ἠγαπῶμεν	ἐπληροῦμεν
you	ἐκαλεῖτε	ἠγαπᾶτε	ἐπληροῦτε
they	ἐκάλουν	ἠγάπων	ἐπλήρουν

Lesson 16

A to Ω – Alpha to Omega

16.1 Capital letters

Here is John 1:1–2 in small letters and in capitals:

ἐν ἀρχῇ ἦν ὁ λόγος καὶ ὁ λόγος ἦν πρὸς τὸν θεόν, καὶ θεὸς ἦν ὁ λόγος. οὗτος ἦν ἐν ἀρχῇ πρὸς τὸν θεόν.

ΕΝ ΑΡΧΗΙ ΗΝ Ο ΛΟΓΟΣ ΚΑΙ Ο ΛΟΓΟΣ ΗΝ ΠΡΟΣ ΤΟΝ ΘΕΟΝ ΚΑΙ ΘΕΟΣ ΗΝ Ο ΛΟΓΟΣ ΟΥΤΟΣ ΗΝ ΕΝ ΑΡΧΗΙ ΠΡΟΣ ΤΟΝ ΘΕΟΝ

Here is the title of Mark's Gospel in *minuscule* (small) letters and in *uncials* (capitals):

ἀρχὴ τοῦ εὐαγγελίου Ἰησοῦ Χριστοῦ υἱοῦ θεοῦ.

ΑΡΧΗ ΤΟΥ ΕΥΑΓΓΕΛΙΟΥ ΙΗΣΟΥ ΧΡΙΣΤΟΥ ΥΙΟΥ ΘΕΟΥ

Here are some common words in minuscule and in uncial letters:

ἡμέρα	day	δόξα	glory
ἩΜΕΡΑ		ΔΟΞΑ	
ζωή	life	ἐρωτάω	I ask
ΖΩΗ		ἘΡΩΤΑΩ	
ἔξοδος	exodus	ἐγγύς	near
ἘΞΟΔΟΣ		ἘΓΓΥΣ	

16.2 The alphabet and the names of the letters

α	Α	Alpha	ι	Ι	Iota	ρ	Ρ	Rho
β	Β	Beta	κ	Κ	Kappa	σ, ς	Σ	Sigma
γ	Γ	Gamma	λ	Λ	Lambda	τ	Τ	Tau
δ	Δ	Delta	μ	Μ	Mu	υ	Υ	Upsilon
ε	Ε	Epsilon	ν	Ν	Nu	φ	Φ	Phi
ζ	Ζ	Zeta	ξ	Ξ	Xi (ksi)	χ	Χ	Chi
η	Η	Eta	ο	Ο	Omicron	ψ	Ψ	Psi
θ	Θ	Theta	π	Π	Pi	ω	Ω	Omega

If you learn the order and names of the letters it will help you when you want to look up words in a dictionary or lexicon.

16.3 Uses of capital letters

When the first manuscripts of the New Testament books were written and copied, only capital letters (uncials) were used. Such manuscripts are therefore called uncial manuscripts.

In printed editions of the Greek New Testament, Η ΚΑΙΝΗ ΔΙΑΘΗΚΗ, capital letters are used in three ways.

1. A capital letter is used for the first letter of spoken or quoted words and passages:
    John 1:21 καὶ λέγει, Οὐκ εἰμί. Ὁ προφήτης εἶ σύ;
    He said, 'I am not.' 'Are you the prophet?'
2. A capital letter is used for the beginning of a new paragraph, but not for every new sentence:
    Mark 4:35 Καὶ λέγει αὐτοῖς ἐν ἐκείνῃ τῇ ἡμέρᾳ...
    He said to them on that day...
3. A capital letter is used for names and titles:
    John 1:44 ἦν δὲ ὁ Φίλιππος ἀπὸ Βηθσαϊδά
    Philip was from Bethsaida
    John 1:41 Εὑρήκαμεν τὸν Μεσσίαν, ὅ ἐστιν μεθερμηνευόμενον Χριστός
    We have found the Messiah (which is translated 'Christ').

16.4 Words

εἰμί – I am

Singular	Plural
εἰμί – I am	ἐσμέν – we are
εἶ – you are	ἐστέ – you are
ἐστίν – he is	εἰσίν – they are

δέ – but, and: ἐγὼ δὲ οὐκ εἰμί – but I am not
  (like γάρ and οὖν, δέ is the second word in a sentence or clause)
  ὁ δέ – he   οἱ δέ – they: ὁ δὲ λέγει – he says
οὐδέ – and not, nor: οὐκ εἶ ὁ Χριστὸς οὐδὲ ὁ προφήτης
            – you are not the Messiah nor the prophet
  οὐδὲ...οὐδὲ... – neither...nor...

ἐρωτάω – I ask
   ἠρώτησεν – he asked
   ἠρώτησαν – they asked
εἶπεν – he said
   εἶπαν or εἶπον – they said
οὖν – so, therefore, then
   εἶπεν οὖν αὐτοῖς – so he said to them
   οἱ δὲ εἶπον αὐτῷ, Τίς οὖν σύ; – they said to him, 'Then who are you?'

16.5 Translate

1. οἱ δὲ ἠρώτησαν αὐτόν, Τίς εἶ; | They asked him, 'Who are you?'
ὁ δὲ εἶπεν, Μάρτυς εἰμὶ | He said, 'I am a witness and I
καὶ μαρτυρῶ τῷ Ἰησοῦ. | bear witness to Jesus.'

2. οἱ δὲ εἶπαν, Μάρτυρές ἐσμεν, | They said, 'We are witnesses
ὑμεῖς δὲ τὴν μαρτυρίαν ἡμῶν οὐ | but you do not receive our
λαμβάνετε οὐδὲ ἀκολουθεῖτε τῷ | witness nor do you follow
Ἰησοῦ. | Jesus.'

3. σὺ μαθητὴς εἶ τοῦ Ἰησοῦ καὶ | You are a disciple of Jesus and
αὐτὸν Διδάσκαλον καλεῖς· ἡμεῖς δὲ | you call him 'Teacher'; but we
τοῦ Μωϋσέως ἐσμὲν μαθηταί. | are disciples of Moses.

4. ὑμεῖς ἐστε τὸ φῶς τῶν ἀνθρώπων, | You are the light of men
ἡμεῖς δὲ ἐν τῇ σκοτίᾳ | but we walk in the darkness.
περιπατοῦμεν.

5. οὐδὲ ἐκάλει αὐτοὺς | He was not calling them
οὐδὲ ἐλάλει αὐτοῖς. | nor was he speaking to them.

6. ὁ δὲ εἶπεν αὐτοῖς, Οὐκ εἰμὶ | He said to them, 'I am not
ὁ Ἠλείας. οἱ δὲ ἠρώτησαν αὐτόν, | Elijah.' They asked him,
Τίς οὖν σύ; | 'Who are you then?'

7. οὐκ ἐστὲ ὑμεῖς οἱ καλοῦντές με | You are not the ones calling me
ἀλλὰ ἐγώ εἰμι ὁ καλῶν ὑμᾶς. | but I am the one who is calling you.

8. εἶπεν οὖν αὐτοῖς, Ἐὰν τηρῆτε | So he said to them, 'If you keep
τὰς ἐντολάς μου γινώσκετε | my commandments you know
τὸν θεόν, ὁ γὰρ μὴ τηρῶν | God, for he who does not keep
αὐτὰς οὐδὲ γινώσκει τὸν θεὸν | them neither knows God
οὐδὲ ἀγαπᾷ αὐτόν. | nor loves him.'

16.6

Read carefully:

John's testimony and answers

Καὶ αὕτη ἐστὶν ἡ μαρτυρία τοῦ Ἰωάννου τοῦ Βαπτιστοῦ, ὅτε ἠρώτησαν αὐτόν, Σὺ τίς εἶ; καὶ εἶπεν αὐτοῖς, Ἐγὼ οὐκ εἰμὶ ὁ Χριστός. οἱ δὲ ἠρώτησαν αὐτόν, Τίς οὖν σύ; Ἠλείας εἶ; εἶπεν αὐτοῖς ὁ Ἰωάννης, Οὐκ εἰμί. Ὁ προφήτης εἶ σύ; ὁ δὲ εἶπεν αὐτοῖς, Οὔ. εἶπαν οὖν αὐτῷ, Τίς εἶ; τί λέγεις περὶ σεαυτοῦ; καὶ εἶπεν αὐτοῖς ὁ Ἰωάννης, Ἐγὼ φωνὴ βοῶντος ἐν τῇ ἐρήμῳ, καθὼς εἶπεν Ἠσαΐας ὁ προφήτης. καὶ ἠρώτησαν αὐτὸν λέγοντες, Τί οὖν βαπτίζεις εἰ οὐκ εἶ ὁ Χριστὸς οὐδὲ Ἠλείας οὐδὲ ὁ προφήτης;

Notes
ὅτε – when
σεαυτόν – yourself
βοάω – I shout
βοῶντος – of a person shouting

περί – about
ἡ ἔρημος – the wilderness, the desert
τί οὖν – why then?
εἰ – if   εἶ – you are

16.7 Translating 16.6

(a) οἱ δὲ ἠρώτησαν αὐτόν, Τίς οὖν σύ;
They asked him, 'Who are you then?'

Τίς οὖν σύ is literally 'Who then you?' In English we need:
1. to put in the word 'are', and
2. to put 'then' at the beginning or end of the question:
'Then who are you?' or 'Who are you then?'

(b) Ἐγὼ φωνὴ βοῶντος
Lit. I voice of one shouting
In English: 'I am the voice of a person shouting' or 'I am the voice of someone who is shouting'.

(c) ἠρώτησαν αὐτὸν λέγοντες, Τί...;
Lit. They asked him, saying, 'Why...?'
λέγοντες (saying) indicates that the words they said will follow. In written English we usually indicate this by inverted commas. So we can translate: 'They asked him, "Why...?"' or 'They asked him this question, "Why...?"'

16.8 Read John 1:19–25

As well as the words in 16.6-7 notice:

v19 ἀπέστειλαν – they sent, they had sent (ἀποστέλλω – I send).
  οἱ Ἰουδαῖοι – the Judean (religious) authorities. In John Ἰουδαῖοι means according to its context Judeans, Judean leaders, or Jews.
  οἱ ἱερεῖς – the priests.

v20 ὡμολόγησεν he admitted, he declared. ἠρνήσατο – he denied

v21 Τί οὖν; What then? ὁ προφήτης – the prophet (see Deut 18:15,18).

v22 εἶπαν οὖν – so they said: in John οὖν is a connecting link which usually marks the next step in a narrative. It can be translated as 'so' or 'then'.
  ἵνα ἀπόκρισιν δῶμεν – so that we may give an answer: before ἵνα (so that) we need to supply 'Tell us' (for they continue, 'What do you say about yourself?'). τοῖς πέμψασιν – to the ones who have sent (πέμπω – I send).

v23 ἔφη – he said. (ἡ) ἐρῆμος – wilderness. Εὐθύνατε – make smooth, make straight. (ἡ) ὁδός – road: where roads are rough they must be made smooth if a king is coming.

v24 ἀπεσταλμένοι – sent (people who were sent).

v25 ἠρώτησαν αὐτὸν καὶ εἶπαν αὐτῷ – they asked him and they said to him: this is good Hebraic style, putting side by side the two facts that they asked and that, in asking, they spoke. In English we would say, 'They asked him this question,' or simply, 'They asked him'.

16.9 Progress test 9

Which is the best English translation?

1. ἠρώτησεν αὐτὸν λέγων Τίς οὖν σύ;
   (a) He asked him saying, 'Who then are you?'
   (b) He asked him who he was.
   (c) He asked him, 'Who are you then?'

2. καὶ ἠρώτησαν αὐτὸν καὶ εἶπαν αὐτῷ, Τί οὖν βαπτίζεις εἰ σὺ οὐκ εἶ ὁ Χριστός;
   (a) And they asked him and they said to him, 'Why therefore do you baptize if you are not the Messiah?'
   (b) So they asked him this question, 'Then why do you baptize people if you are not the Messiah?'
   (c) So they questioned him and they said to him, 'If you are not the Messiah why do you baptize?'

3. ἀδελφοί μου, οὐκ ἐντολὴν καινὴν γράφω ὑμῖν.
   (a) Brothers of me, not a commandment new I write to you.
   (b) My brothers, to you I am writing a commandment that is not new.
   (c) My brothers, it is not a new commandment that I am writing to you.

Check your answers in Key to Progress Tests on page 333.

16.10

Note these forms:

Present	Past
εἰμί – I am	ἤμην – I was
εἶ – you are	ἦς or ἦσθα – you were
ἐστίν – he is	ἦν – he was
ἐσμέν – we are	ἦμεν or ἠμέθα – we were
ἐστέ – you are	ἦτε – you were
εἰσίν – they are	ἦσαν – they were

16.11

Revise lessons 9 and 10.

Lesson 17

πρός, εἰς, ἐν, ἐκ, ἀπό,
ἔρχεται – he comes, he goes

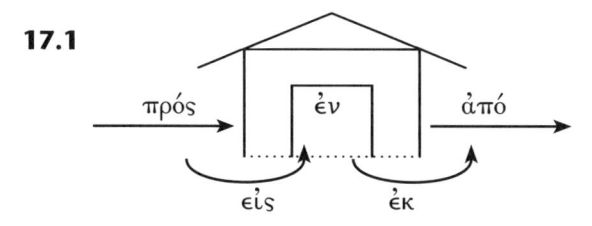

17.1

ἔρχεται – he goes, he comes   ἔρχονται – they go, they come

πρός – to, towards,   ἔρχεται πρὸς τὸν οἶκον
He goes to the house or
He comes towards the house

εἰς – into,   ἔρχεται εἰς τὸν οἶκον
He goes into the house or
He comes into the house

ἐν – in, inside,   ἐν τῷ οἴκῳ εἰσίν
They are in the house

ἐκ – out of,   ἔρχονται ἐκ τοῦ οἴκου
They come out of the house or
They go out of the house

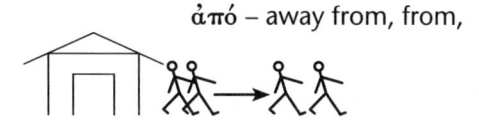

ἀπό – away from, from,   ἔρχονται ἀπὸ τοῦ οἴκου
They go away from the house or
They come away from the house.

17.2 ἔρχεται

ἔρχεται – he goes; she goes; it goes; he comes...

The stem ερχ expresses a continuing movement. In the following diagram a woman is moving from A to B.

A. ————————→ .B
   ἔρχεται

In English, if I am standing at A, I say: 'She is going'. If I am standing at B, I say: 'She is coming.' In English we have a choice of words for this one movement. In Greek the movement is expressed by one word: ἔρχεται. Note also that in English, for the past simple of 'I go' we use a different word: 'I went'. In Greek there are two different stems: ερχ and ελθ.

The stem ερχ indicates continuing or repeated action:

So: ἔρχομαι – I am going, I go.

The stem ελθ indicates completed or single action:

So: ἀπέλθε – go away!   ἐλθών – having come, coming
      ἦλθον – they went.

17.3 Words

ἔρχεται – he goes, he comes
    ἔρχονται – they go, they come
    (Note the endings: – εται – he, she, it; – ονται – they)
πρός – to, towards, up to, with
εἰς – into, in
    εἰς τὸν οἶκον – into the house
ἐν – in, inside, by means of
    ἐν τῷ οἴκῳ – in the house
ἐκ or ἐξ – out of, from
    ἐκ τοῦ οἴκου – out of the house, from the house
ἀπό – away from, from
    ἀπὸ τοῦ οἴκου – (away) from the house
εἰσέρχεται – he goes into
    ἐξέρχεται – he goes out
    ἐξέρχεται ἐκ τοῦ οἴκου – he goes out of the house
    ἀπέρχεται – he goes away
ὁ οἶκος and ἡ οἰκία – the house, the home, the family
ἡ συναγωγή – the synagogue
τὸ ἱερόν – the Temple
ὁ ἱερεύς – the priest
    οἱ ἀρχιερεῖς – the High Priests

ἦλθεν – he went, she went
ἦλθον – they went

17.4 Translate

1. σὺ εἶ ὁ βαπτιστὴς ἀλλὰ ἐγώ εἰμι ὁ ἱερεύς.	You are the baptist but I am the priest.
2. ἐν τῇ συναγωγῇ οἱ μαθηταὶ ἠρώτησαν αὐτόν, Σὺ τίς εἶ; ὁ δὲ εἶπεν, Ὁ ἱερεύς εἰμί.	In the synagogue the disciples asked him, 'Who are you?' He said, 'I am the priest.'
3. ὁ ἱερεὺς ἔρχεται πρὸς τὸ ἱερὸν καὶ εἰσέρχεται εἰς τὸ ἱερόν.	The priest goes to the Temple and he goes into the Temple.
4. Ἔρχονται οἱ ἀπόστολοι εἰς τὸν οἶκον ζητοῦντες τὸν Ἰησοῦν, ἀλλὰ οὐκ εὑρίσκουσιν αὐτὸν ἐν τῷ οἴκῳ. ἐξέρχονται οὖν ἐκ τοῦ οἴκου καὶ ἀπέρχονται ἀπὸ τοῦ οἴκου πρὸς τὴν συναγωγήν, καὶ εὑρίσκουσιν αὐτὸν ἐν τῇ συναγωγῇ. ὁ δὲ Ἰησοῦς ἀποστέλλει αὐτοὺς πρὸς τοὺς Φαρισαίους.	The apostles go into the house looking for Jesus, but they do not find him in the house. So they come out of the house and go away from the house to the synagogue, and they find him in the synagogue. But Jesus sends them away to the Pharisees.
5. λαλεῖ τὸν λόγον τοῦ θεοῦ.	He speaks the word of God.
6. οὐκ ἐλάλει τὸν λόγον, οὐδὲ ἐν τῇ συναγωγῇ οὐδὲ ἐν τῷ ἱερῷ.	He was not speaking the word, neither in the synagogue nor in the Temple.
7. ἔρχεται ὁ ἀπόστολος εἰς τὰς συναγωγὰς ἵνα τὸν λόγον λαλῇ τοῖς ἀνθρώποις ἐν ταῖς συναγωγαῖς.	The apostle goes into the synagogues so that he may speak the word to the men in the synagogues.
8. ἔρχονται οἱ ἀπόστολοι εἰς τὰς οἰκίας ὑμῶν ἵνα τοὺς λόγους τοῦ Ἰησοῦ ἀπαγγέλλωσιν ὑμῖν.	The apostles come into your houses so that they may declare the words of Jesus to you.
9. ὁ ἔχων τὰς ἐντολὰς τοῦ θεοῦ καὶ τηρῶν αὐτάς οὗτός ἐστιν ὁ ἀγαπῶν τὸν θεόν. ὃς δὲ ἂν μὴ τηρῇ αὐτὰς οὐκ ἀγαπᾷ αὐτόν.	He who has the commands of God and keeps them, he is the person who loves God. But whoever does not keep them does not love him.

10. Ὁ δὲ Ἰησοῦς ἦν ἐν τῷ ἱερῷ καὶ ἐδίδασκεν τοὺς μαθητὰς αὐτοῦ. ἦλθον οὖν πρὸς αὐτὸν οἱ Φαρισαῖοι καὶ ἠρώτησαν αὐτόν, Τίς εἶ; ὁ Χριστὸς εἶ σύ; ὁ δὲ εἶπεν αὐτοῖς, Ἐμαρτύρει περὶ ἐμοῦ ὁ Ἰωάννης ἀλλὰ ὑμεῖς οὐκ ἐλαμβάνετε τὴν μαρτυρίαν αὐτοῦ. | Jesus was in the Temple and he was teaching his disciples. So the Pharisees came to him and asked him, 'Who are you? Are you the Messiah?' He said to them, 'John used to bear witness about me but you did not receive his testimony.'

17.5

Read carefully in your Greek New Testament 1 John 1:5–7
(Ἰωάννου Α 1:5–7).

Notes

ἀκηκόαμεν – we have heard
ἀπ᾽ = ἀπό – from
ὅτι – that
οὐδεμία – none, not one, not any
  (οὐδέ – and not, μία – one)
ἐὰν εἴπωμεν – if we should say
ψευδόμεθα – we are lying
ὡς – as
μετ᾽ ἀλλήλων – with each other
τὸ αἷμα – the blood

ἀναγγέλλομεν – we are declaring, we announce
ὁ υἱός – the son
καθαρίζω – I cleanse
  (καθαρός – pure)
ἀπὸ πάσης ἁμαρτίας – from every sin, from all sin
  (πᾶς – every, all).
Compare: ἀπὸ πασῶν τῶν ἁμαρτιῶν – from all the sins.

Lesson 18

λέγειν – to say, to be saying ····

18.1

λέγει – he is saying, he says
ὃς ἂν λέγῃ – whoever says
λέγωμεν – let us say
λέγων – saying
ἔλεγεν – he was saying, he used to say

All these forms of λέγω indicate continuing — or repeated ···· action. Now note another verbal form that indicates continuing or repeated action:

    λέγειν – to be saying, to say ▬
    ἀγαπᾶν – to love ▬

So:

Lk 7:24	ἤρξατο λέγειν πρὸς τοὺς ὄχλους περὶ Ἰωάννου
	He began to speak to the crowds about John
1 Jn 4:20	οὐ δύναται ἀγαπᾶν
	He is not able to love
1 Cor 14:5	θέλω δὲ πάντας ὑμᾶς λαλεῖν γλώσσαις
	But I wish all of you to speak in tongues.

18.2

    ἤρξατο – he began   – ατο – he, she, it
    ἤρξαντο – they began   – αντο – they

So:

Mk 6:2	ἤρξατο διδάσκειν ἐν τῇ συναγωγῇ
	He began to teach in the synagogue
Acts 2:4	ἤρξαντο λαλεῖν ἑτέραις γλώσσαις
	They began to speak in other languages.

Translate:

1. ἤρξατο περιπατεῖν ἐν τῇ συναγωγῇ.	He began to walk about in the synagogue.

2. ἤρξαντο βαπτίζειν τοὺς μαθητὰς αὐτῶν.	They began to baptize their disciples.
3. ἔρχονται πρὸς τὸν οἶκον.	They go to the house.
4. ἤρξατο ἀποστέλλειν τοὺς ἀποστόλους.	He began to send out the apostles.
5. ἔρχεται ἀπὸ τοῦ ἱεροῦ.	He comes from the Temple.

18.3 Words

θέλω – I wish, I want, I am willing (earlier form: ἐθέλω)
    ἤθελεν – he was willing
    τὸ θέλημα – the will (what someone wants)
ἡ ἐξουσία – the authority (the power)
βάλλω – I throw, I put
    ἐκβάλλω – I throw out, I drive out, I send away
κηρύσσω – I preach, I proclaim
ἤρξατο – he began
    ἤρξαντο – they began

18.4 Translate

Ὁ δὲ Ἰησοῦς ἔδωκεν (gave) ἐξουσίαν τοῖς ἀποστόλοις αὐτοῦ κηρύσσειν τὸ εὐαγγέλιον καὶ ἐκβάλλειν τὰ δαιμόνια. καὶ ἤρξατο ἀποστέλλειν αὐτοὺς κηρύσσειν καὶ ἔχειν ἐξουσίαν ἐκβάλλειν τὰ δαιμόνια. Ἤρξαντο οὖν οἱ ἀπόστολοι κηρύσσειν τὸ εὐαγγέλιον τῆς βασιλείας τοῦ θεοῦ λέγοντες, Ἤγγικεν (it has come near) ἡ βασιλεία τοῦ θεοῦ. ὃς ἂν θέλῃ τὸ θέλημα αὐτὸν ποιεῖν, πιστευέτω (let him trust) τῷ Ἰησοῦ. καὶ οἱ ἀπόστολοι ἐμαρτύρουν τῷ Ἰησοῦ ἐν ταῖς συναγωγαῖς καὶ ἐν τῷ ἱερῷ ἀλλὰ οἱ Φαρισαῖοι οὐκ ἤθελον τὴν μαρτυρίαν αὐτῶν λαμβάνειν· αὐτοὶ γὰρ οὐκ ἤθελον τὸ θέλημα τοῦ θεοῦ ποιεῖν.	Jesus gave authority to his apostles to preach the good news and to cast out the demons. Then he began to send them out to preach and to have authority to cast out the demons. So the apostles began to preach the good news of the Kingdom of God saying, 'The Kingdom of God has come near. Whoever wants to do his will, let him trust in Jesus.' The apostles were bearing witness to Jesus in the synagogues and in the Temple but the Pharisees were not willing to receive their testimony; for they themselves were not willing to do the will of God.

18.5

Read carefully Mark 11:27–30 (κατὰ Μᾶρκον 11:27–30).

πάλιν – again
Ἱεροσόλυμα – Jerusalem
περιπατοῦντος αὐτοῦ – as he was walking (lit. his walking)
ποῖος; – what?
ἤ – or, and

ἔδωκεν – he gave
ἐπερωτήσω – I will ask
ἕνα – one
ἀποκρίθητε – Answer!
ἐρῶ – I will say, I will tell

18.6 Progress test 10

Which is the correct translation?

1. τίς ἤρξατο διδάσκειν ἐν τῷ ἱερῷ;
   (a) What did he come to teach in the Temple?
   (b) Who comes to teach in the Temple?
   (c) Who began to teach in the Temple?
2. ἔρχονται οἱ ἀπόστολοι κηρύσσοντες τὸ εὐαγγέλιον.
   (a) The apostles began to preach the gospel.
   (b) The apostles come preaching the gospel.
   (c) The apostles come to preach the gospel.
3. βάλλωμεν τὰ βιβλία εἰς τὴν θάλασσαν.
   (a) We throw the Bible into the sea.
   (b) Let us throw the books into the sea.
   (c) Let us throw the book into the sea.
4. τίς εἶ σὺ καὶ τίνες εἰσὶν οὗτοι;
   (a) Who are you and who is he?
   (b) Who am I and who are these men?
   (c) Who are you and who are these men?
5. οἱ ἱερεῖς οὐκ ἐκάλουν ἡμᾶς εἰς τὴν οἰκίαν ἀλλὰ εἰς τὸ ἱερόν.
   (a) The priests are not calling us into the house but into the Temple.
   (b) We were not calling the priests into the house but into the Temple.
   (c) The priests were not calling us into the house but into the Temple.

Check your answers in Key to Progress Tests.

18.7

Revise lessons 11 and 12.

Lesson 19

λέγων, λέγουσα, λέγον – saying

19.1

Lesson 12.7 gives the three kinds of forms of 'the' in Greek, which indicate masculine, feminine, and neuter nouns. For example:

Masculine	Feminine	Neuter
ὁ ἀνήρ – the man	ἡ γυνή – the woman	τὸ τέκνον – the child
ὁ λόγος – the word	ἡ καρδία – the heart	τὸ ἔργον – the work.

In the same way, λέγων (saying) has three different kinds of endings, according to the gender (masculine, feminine, or neuter) of the word it goes with. Study the following examples:

ἦλθεν ὁ ἀνὴρ ταῦτα λέγων
The man came saying these things

ἦλθεν ἡ γυνὴ ταῦτα λέγουσα
The woman came saying these things

ἦλθεν τὸ τέκνον ταῦτα λέγον
The child came saying these things.

In 8.2 we learned ὁ λέγων – the person saying, he who says.
Now compare these examples of masculine and feminine:

ὁ ποιῶν – the person doing, he who does

ἡ ποιοῦσα – the woman doing, she who does

and note the use of ποιῶν and ὁ ποιῶν and ποιοῦσα and ἡ ποιοῦσα in these examples:

1. (a) βλέπει τὸν ἀπόστολον τοῦτο ποιοῦντα
   (b) βλέπει τὴν γυναῖκα τοῦτο ποιοῦσαν
2. (a) βλέπει τὸν ἀπόστολον τὸν τοῦτο ποιοῦντα
   (b) βλέπει τὴν γυναῖκα τὴν τοῦτο ποιοῦσαν

In 1 attention is directed to what the person is **doing**:
   (a) He sees the apostle **doing** this
   (b) He sees the woman **doing** this

In 2 attention is directed to **the person** who is doing it:
   (a) He sees **the apostle** who is doing this
   (b) He sees **the woman** who is doing this.

Now note:

3. (a) ἔβλεπεν τὰς γυναῖκας τοῦτο ποιούσας
   He used to see the women doing this
   (b) ἔβλεπεν τὰς γυναῖκας τὰς τοῦτο ποιούσας
   He used to see the women **who were** doing this.

In this last sentence the Greek says: 'He used to see the women the (ones) this doing.' We have to express the meaning in an English way: 'He used to see the women who were doing this.'

Translate:

1. βλέπει τοὺς ἀποστόλους ταῦτα ποιοῦντας.	He sees the apostles doing these things.
2. οἱ τοῦτο ποιοῦντες ποιοῦσι τὸ θέλημα τοῦ θεοῦ.	The people who are doing this are doing the will of God.
3. βλέπομεν τὸν ἄνθρωπον τὸν τοῦτο ποιοῦντα.	We see the man who is doing this.
4. ἔρχεται ἡ γυνὴ ταῦτα ποιοῦσα.	The woman comes doing these things.
5. ὁ Μᾶρκος λέγει τῇ γυναικὶ τῇ ταῦτα ποιούσῃ, Τίς εἶ;	Mark says to the woman who is doing these things, 'Who are you?'

19.2 Translating into English

1. Compare sentences (a) and (b):
   (a) ὁ ἀνὴρ ἔρχεται κηρύσσων τὸ εὐαγγέλιον
   (b) ἔρχεται ὁ ἀνὴρ ὁ τὸ εὐαγγέλιον κηρύσσων.

Sentence (a) is literally, 'The man comes preaching the good news.' This is quite clear and understandable English.
Sentence (b) is literally, 'Comes the man the the gospel preaching.' This is not a natural way to express the meaning in English. We must find a better way – perhaps, 'The man who preaches the gospel is coming.'

2. Note ἔχων – having.
In English the idea expressed by ἔχων can often be well expressed by using the word 'with'.

So: βλέπω ἄγγελον ἔχοντα ἐξουσίαν
     I see an angel **with** authority
  or I see an angel **who has** authority

LESSON 19   105

Mk 6:34 ἦσαν ὡς πρόβατα μὴ ἔχοντα ποιμένα
They were like sheep **without** a shepherd
or They were like sheep **that do not have** a shepherd.

19.3 Words

ὁ ἀνήρ – the man, the husband
   ἀγαπᾷς τὸν ἀνδρά σου – you love your husband
ἡ γυνή – the woman, the wife
   ἀγαπᾷς τὴν γυναικά σου – you love your wife
ὁ υἱός – the son, the descendant
ὁ πατήρ – the father, the ancestor, the forefather
   ὁ υἱός τοῦ πατρός – the son of the father
ἡ μήτηρ – the mother
   λέγει τῇ μητρὶ αὐτοῦ – he says to his mother
ἡ φωνή – the voice, the sound
   ἀκούω τὴν φωνήν or ἀκούω τῆς φωνῆς – I hear the voice
δίδωμι – I give
προσκυνέω – I worship, I kneel before, I prostrate myself
   προσκυνῶ αὐτῷ or προσκυνῶ αὐτόν – I worship him,
                          I pay homage to him

19.4 Translate

1. οὗτός ἐστιν ὁ ἀνήρ.	This is the man.
2. εἰσέρχεται ὁ ἀνὴρ εἰς τὴν συναγωγήν.	The man goes into the synagogue.
3. ἔρχεται ὁ ἀνὴρ κηρύσσων τὸ εὐαγγέλιον.	The man comes preaching the gospel.
4. ἀκούομεν αὐτοῦ λέγοντος τοὺς λόγους.	We hear him speaking the words.
5. ἡ μήτηρ καὶ ὁ πατὴρ ἀγαπῶσιν τὸν υἱὸν αὐτῶν καὶ ἀκούουσι τῆς φωνῆς αὐτοῦ.	The mother and the father love their son and they listen to his voice.
6. ἔρχεται ἡ γυνὴ εἰς τὴν οἰκίαν.	The woman comes into the house.
7. ἔρχονται αἱ γυναῖκες πρὸς τὴν οἰκίαν καὶ βλέπουσιν τοὺς ἄνδρας αὐτῶν.	The women come to the house and they see their husbands.

8. δίδωμι τὰ βιβλία τῷ πατρί μου καὶ τῇ μητρί μου. ἐγώ εἰμι ὁ υἱὸς αὐτῶν.	I give the books to my father and to my mother. I am their son.
9. ἔρχεται ὁ πατὴρ ἔχων τὸ βιβλίον.	The father comes with the book.
10. ἔρχεται ὁ πατὴρ ὁ ἔχων τὸ βιβλίον.	The father who has the book comes.
11. δίδωμι ταῦτα τῷ πατρὶ τῷ ἔχοντι τὸ βιβλίον.	I give these things to the father who has the book.
12. ἐκάλει τὸν ἄνδρα τὸν τὸ βιβλίον ἔχοντα.	He was calling the man who had the book.
13. ἔρχεται ἡ γυνὴ ταῦτα λέγουσα.	The woman comes saying these things.
14. ἤρξατο ἡ γυνὴ ταῦτα διδάσκειν.	The woman began to teach these things.
15. εἶπεν οὖν τῷ ἀνδρὶ τῷ ἔχοντι τὸ δαιμόνιον, Τίς εἶ;	So he said to the man who had the demon, 'Who are you?'

19.5 Forms of ὤν – being (εἰμί – I am)

	Masculine		Feminine		Neuter	
Singular						
	(ὁ)	ὤν	(ἡ)	οὖσα	(τό)	ὄν
	(τόν)	ὄντα	(τήν)	οὖσαν	(τό)	ὄν
	(τοῦ)	ὄντος	(τῆς)	οὔσης	(τοῦ)	ὄντος
	(τῷ)	ὄντι	(τῇ)	οὔσῃ	(τῷ)	ὄντι
Plural						
	(οἱ)	ὄντες	(αἱ)	οὖσαι	(τά)	ὄντα
	(τούς)	ὄντας	(τάς)	οὔσας	(τά)	ὄντα
	(τῶν)	ὄντων	(τῶν)	οὐσῶν	(τῶν)	ὄντων
	(τοῖς)	οὖσι(ν)	(ταῖς)	οὔσαις	(τοῖς)	οὖσι(ν)

So: οἱ ὄντες μετ' αὐτοῦ – the people (being) with him
  αἱ λεγοῦσαι – the women saying, the women who say.
Note also ὁ ὤν – he who is, ἡ οὖσα – she who is, τὸ ὄν – that which is.
In translating forms like ὁ ὤν, notice the difference in English between:
(a) βλέπει τὸν υἱὸν τὸν ὄντα ἐν τῇ οἰκίᾳ
  (Lit. He sees the son the one being in the house)
  English: He sees the son who is in the house

LESSON 19

(b) ἔβλεπεν τὸν υἱὸν τὸν ὄντα ἐν τῇ οἰκίᾳ
(Lit. He used to see the son the one being in the house)
English: He used to see the son who was in the house

Look again at the forms of ὤν, οὖσα, and ὄν:
If you place the stem λεγ in front of each, you will find all the forms of λέγων, λέγουσα, and λέγον.
The forms of καλῶν – calling (καλέω) are similar to the forms of λέγων, but the final ε of the stem causes some small changes. Note, for example:

| (ὁ) | καλῶν | (ἡ) | καλοῦσα | (τὸ) | καλοῦν |
| (τοῦ) | καλοῦντος | (τῆς) | καλούσης | (τοῦ) | καλοῦντος |

19.6 Translate

1. οὗτός ἐστιν ὁ ἀνὴρ ὁ ὢν ἐν τῇ οἰκίᾳ. — This (he) is the man who is in the house.
2. ἐβλέπομεν τὸν ἄνδρα ὄντα ἐν τῇ οἰκίᾳ. — We used to look at the man while he was in the house.
3. ἐβλέπομεν τὸν ἄνδρα τὸν ὄντα ἐν τῇ συναγωγῇ. — We used to look at the man who was in the synagogue.
4. ἀκούει τοῦ ἀνδρὸς τοῦ ὄντος ἐν τῷ ἱερῷ. — He hears the man who is in the Temple.
5. λέγει τῇ γυναικὶ τῇ οὔσῃ ἐν τῇ σκοτίᾳ. — He speaks to the woman who is in the darkness.
6. ἐκάλει τοὺς ἄνδρας τοὺς τὸ ἔργον τοῦ θεοῦ ποιοῦντας. — He was calling the men who were doing the work of God.

19.7

Read carefully John 4:17–24 (Κατὰ Ἰωάννην 4:17–24).

ὕπαγε – Go!
φώνησον – Call!
ἐνθάδε – here (to here)
ἀπεκρίθη – she answered
καλῶς – well
ἔσχες – you have had
νῦν – now
εἴρηκας – you have said
Κύριε – Sir (Lord)
θεωρῶ – I see

προσκυνητής – worshipper
ὄρος – mountain
προσεκύνησαν – they worshipped
τόπος – place
ὅπου – where
δεῖ – it is necessary
ὥρα – hour
οἶδα – I know
σωτηρία – salvation
πνεῦμα – spirit

19.8 Progress test 11

Which is the best English translation?
1. ἀπεκρίθη ἡ γυνὴ καὶ εἶπεν, Οὐκ ἔχω ἄνδρα.
    (a) The woman answered and she said, 'I do not have a man.'
    (b) The woman answered and said, 'I do not have a husband.'
    (c) The woman replied, 'I do not have a husband.'
2. καὶ νῦν ὃν ἔχεις οὐκ ἔστιν σου ἀνήρ.
    (a) and now whom you have is not of you a husband.
    (b) and now the man you have is not your husband.
    (c) and now you have a man who is not your husband.
3. ἐν Ἱεροσολύμοις ἐστὶν ὁ τόπος ὅπου προσκυνεῖν δεῖ.
    (a) in Jerusalem is the place where to worship it is binding.
    (b) the place where God should be worshipped is in Jerusalem.
    (c) in Jerusalem is the place where it is necessary to worship.
4. καὶ γὰρ ὁ πατὴρ τοιούτους ζητεῖ τοὺς προσκυνοῦντας αὐτόν.
    (a) and for the Father seeks such people the people worshipping him.
    (b) for it is worshippers like these whom the Father seeks.
    (c) for the Father wants such people to worship him.

Check your answers in Key to Progress Tests on page 333.

19.9 Bible translations evaluation (2)

(a) John 4:16–17

> Λέγει αὐτῇ, Ὕπαγε φώνησον τὸν ἄνδρα σου καὶ ἐλθὲ ἐνθάδε. ἀπεκρίθη ἡ γυνὴ καὶ εἶπεν αὐτῷ, Οὐκ ἔχω ἄνδρα.

NIV He told her, 'Go call your husband and come back.'
'I have no husband,' she replied.

REB 'Go and call your husband,' said Jesus, 'and come back here.'
She answered, 'I have no husband.'

NJB 'Go and call your husband,' said Jesus to her, 'and come back here.'
The woman answered, 'I have no husband.'

NRSV Jesus said to her, 'Go and call your husband and come back.'
The woman answered him, 'I have no husband.'

NLT 'Go and get your husband,' Jesus told her.
'I don't have a husband,' the woman replied.

GNB 'Go and call your husband,' Jesus told her, 'and come back.'
'I haven't got a husband' she answered.

(b) John 5:39 (Note ἐραυνάω – I search, I investigate, I study…)

ἐραυνᾶτε τὰς γραφάς, ὅτι ὑμεῖς δοκεῖτε ἐν αὐταῖς ζωὴν αἰώνιον ἔχειν· καὶ ἐκεῖναί εἰσιν αἱ μαρτυροῦσαι περὶ ἐμοῦ·

NRSV	You search the scriptures because you think that in them you have eternal life, and it is they who testify on my behalf.
NLT	You search the Scriptures because you believe they give you eternal life. But the Scriptures point to me!
NJB	You pore over the scriptures, believing that in them you can find eternal life; it is these scriptures that testify to me.
GNB	You study the scriptures because you think that in them you will find eternal life. And these very scriptures speak about me!
REB	You study the scriptures diligently, supposing that in having them you have eternal life; their testimony points to me.
NIV	You diligently study the scriptures because you think that by them you possess eternal life. These are the Scriptures that testify about me.

Notes

1. ἐν αὐταῖς could mean either 'in them' or 'through them'. Consider whether we should translate: '…that through them you have eternal life.'
2. In 5:39 there are parallels with John 1:7–8 and John 20:31. Consider whether the translations have obscured the parallels in translating μαρτυροῦσαι περὶ and ἔχειν:

	NRSV	NLT	NJB	GNB	REB	NIV
1:7–8	have life	have life	have life	have life	have life	have life
20:31	testify to	witness to	witness to	tell about	testify to	testify concerning

INTRODUCTION TO LESSONS 20–25

Since lesson 2 you have been reading verses and short passages from the New Testament. You have already made good progress towards your aim of being able to read and understand the New Testament in Greek.

In lessons 20–25 you will take another important step forward. So far we have studied chiefly forms which indicate:

continuing or repeated action ⁓ (5.6, 14.6, 18.1).

But you have also successfully translated forms which indicate completed action ⊣ or single action •. For example:

εἶπεν he said ⊣   ἠρώτησαν they asked ⊣
προσεκύνησαν they worshipped ⊣   ἤρξατο he began ⊣
ἀπεκρίθη she answered ⊣   ἀποκρίθητε Answer! •

In lessons 20–25 you will begin to understand forms which indicate completed or single action. These lessons form a group. Study them as a unit. Some parts introduce ideas briefly – they are developed in later lessons. When you reach the end of lesson 25 the basic idea of this group of lessons will be fixed in your mind.

The fundamental idea concerns forms indicating completed action. Our sign for them ends in an upright line to indicate completion ⊣ . You will study forms like:

ποιήσας having done   βαλών having thrown   φαγών having eaten.

You will compare them (col.1) with forms for continuing action (col.2)

      1   2
(a) ποιήσας – having done ⊣   ποιῶν – doing ⁓
(b) βαλών – having thrown ⊣   βάλλων – throwing ⁓
(c) φαγών – having eaten ⊣   ἐσθίων – eating ⁓

Such forms may also mark single or non-continuing action, which we indicate with a single dot •

      1   2
(a) ποιῆσαι – to do •   ποιεῖν – to be doing ⁓
(b) βαλεῖν – to throw •   βάλλειν – to throw ⁓
(c) φαγεῖν – to eat •   ἐσθίειν – to eat ⁓

As you compare columns 1 and 2 you will notice the most common marks of **single** or **completed** action ⊣:

(a) σ or θ between the stem and the ending – see lessons 20 , 21
or (b) a shortened stem (βαλ, not βαλλ) – see lessons 22 , 23
or (c) a different stem (φαγ, not εσθι) – see lessons 22 , 24.

Markers of completed ⊣ or single • action	(a) - σ - - θ -	(b) Short stem	(c) Different stem

In lessons 20–25 you will begin to develop a habit of looking at Greek verbal forms and noticing at once whether they indicate a single or completed action, or whether they indicate a continuing or repeated action. It is important at this stage not to give Greek words grammatical labels which may mislead us. However, from lesson 24 onwards we will progressively introduce and explain more of the technical words used by grammarians. Take note of them, but on your first journey through the course you need not try to learn them.

When you have completed lesson 25 you will have laid the foundations on which your growing knowledge of New Testament Greek will rest.

Lesson 20

ποιήσας – having done ⊣

20.1 ποιήσας – **having done** ⊣   ποιῶν – **doing** —

Compare

> ποιῶν τὸ θέλημα τοῦ θεοῦ – doing the will of God
>
> ποιήσας τὸ θέλημα τοῦ θεοῦ – having done the will of God
>
> τοῦτο ποιήσας ἀπέρχεται – having done this he goes away
>
> τοῦτο ποιήσαντες ἀπέρχονται – having done this they go away

Translate:

1. ταῦτα ποιήσαντες ἀπέρχονται.	Having done these things they go away.
2. τοῦτο ποιήσας εἰσέρχεται.	Having done this he comes in.
3. ἔρχεται ποιῶν τὸ θέλημα τοῦ θεοῦ.	He comes doing the will of God.
4. τὸ θέλημα αὐτοῦ ποιήσας ἀπέρχεται.	Having done his will he goes away.
5. ἔρχονται ποιοῦντες τὸ θέλημα τοῦ θεοῦ.	They come doing the will of God.
6. ἦλθον ἵνα τὸ θέλημα τοῦ θεοῦ ποιῶσιν καὶ τὸ θέλημα αὐτοῦ ποιήσαντες ἀπῆλθον.	They came so that they might do God's will, and having done his will they went away.

20.2

> ὁ ποιήσας – the person having done, he who has done...
>
> οἱ ποιήσαντες – those who have done, those who did...

Compare

ὁ ποιῶν – the person who is doing, he who makes...
οἱ ποιοῦντες – those who are doing, the people who make...

Heb 1:7 ὁ ποιῶν τοὺς ἀγγέλους αὐτοῦ πνεύματα
        The one who makes his angels spirits.

Acts 4:24   σὺ ὁ ποιήσας τὸν οὐρανὸν καὶ τὴν γῆν.
        You (are) the one who made the heaven and the earth.

Translate:

1. ἐγώ εἰμι ὁ τοῦτο ποιήσας.	I am the person who did this.
2. σὺ εἶ ὁ τοῦτο ποιήσας.	You are the one who did this.
3. σὺ εἶ ὁ ποιήσας τὴν γῆν ἀλλὰ αὐτός ἐστιν ὁ μὴ ποιήσας τὴν γῆν.	You are the one who made the earth, but he is the one who did not make the earth.
4. ὑμεῖς εἰσιν οἱ ποιήσαντες τὸ θέλημα τοῦ θεοῦ.	You are the people who have done the will of God.
5. ἐγώ εἰμι ὁ ποιήσας τὸ θέλημα τοῦ θεοῦ ἀλλὰ αὐτοί εἰσιν οἱ μὴ ποιήσαντες αὐτό.	I am the person who has done the will of God, but they are the people who have not done it.

Note that σ between the stem and the ending is the commonest mark of completed or single action. When the stem of the verb ends in a consonant, the added σ changes the consonant. For example:

    κηρύσσω – I preach   κηρύξας – having preached
    σώζω – I save   σώσας – having saved
    πέμπω – I send   πέμψας – having sent.

    The forms of   ποίησας   ποιήσασα   ποιῆσαν   are similar
    to those of   λέγων   λέγουσα   λέγον   (19.5(b)) except that
there is an σ after the stem, and the σ is followed by the vowel α. You will find all its forms in 21.8.

20.3 Translating participles into English: ποιῶν and ποιήσας

English words ending in -ing (for example, doing) are participles. Greek words like ποιῶν (doing) and ποιήσας (having done) are participles. In these sentences the participles are translated literally:

1. (a) ἔρχονται ταῦτα ποιοῦντες.
    They come doing these things.
   (b) τοῦτο ποιήσαντες ἀπέρχονται.
    Having done this they go away.
2. (a) ἦλθεν μαρτυρῶν τῷ Ἰησοῦ.
    He came bearing witness to Jesus.
   (b) μαρτυρήσας ἀπῆλθεν
    Having borne witness, he went away.
3. (a) ἦλθον κηρύσσοντες ἐν ταῖς συναγωγαῖς.
    They went preaching in the synagogues.
   (b) κηρύξαντες ἐξῆλθον ἐκ τῆς συναγωγῆς.
    Having preached they went out of the synagogue.
4. (a) εὑρίσκουσιν αὐτὸν ἐν τῷ ἱερῷ ἀκούοντα τῶν διδασκάλων.
    They find him in the temple listening to the teachers.
   (b) ἀκούσας τῶν διδασκάλων ἀπελεύσεται.
    Having listened to the teachers he will go away.
5. (a) ἤρξατο διδάσκειν αὐτούς.
    He began to teach them.
   (b) διδάξας αὐτοὺς ἀπῆλθεν.
    Having taught them he went away.

You have probably noticed that some of the translations do not express the meaning in a natural English way. Words like ποιῶν (doing), γράφων (writing), and κηρύσσων (preaching) can often be well translated using an English participle (-ing):

> ἦλθεν Ἰωάννης κηρύσσων ἐν τῇ ἐρήμῳ.
> John came **preaching** in the wilderness.

But sometimes we need to use different ways to express the meaning of such participles in English. Consider:

(a) βλέπω ἄγγελον ἔχοντα (having) εὐαγγέλιον.
    I see an angel who has a message of good news.
(b) ὢν (being) ἐν τῇ οἰκίᾳ διδάσκει τοὺς μαθητάς.
    While he is in the house he teaches the disciples.
(c) ὦτα ἔχων (having) οὐκ ἀκούει.
    Though he has ears he does not hear.

Words like ποιήσας (having done), γράψας (having written), and κηρύξας (having preached) usually express completed action. In English we seldom use sentences like, 'Having written the letter, he posted it.' We are more likely to express the same basic idea by:

(a) When he had written the letter he posted it.
Or (b) He wrote the letter and posted it.
So we might translate ἀκούσας τοὺς λόγους ἐξῆλθεν as:
(a) When he had heard the words he went out
Or (b) He heard what was said and went out.

20.4

Notice that participles like ποιήσας, γράψας, and κηρύξας may refer to events or actions which still lie in the future.

So: αὔριον τοῦτο ποιήσας ἀπελεύσεται
      Tomorrow, **having done this**, he will go away
or   Tomorrow, **when he has done this**, he will go away.

ποιήσας is a completed action form. In this sentence it refers to an action that is still in the future, but at the time when the man goes away, the action will have been completed.

It is important to remember that completed or single action forms do not necessarily refer to past time, unless they also have an ε before the stem (lesson 21).

20.5 Translating participles into English: ποιῶν and ποιήσας

    ὁ ποιῶν – the doer   ὁ ποιήσας – the doer •
    he who does —   he who did ⊣
    he who keeps doing ····   he who has done ⊣
    he who was doing ⁓⁓   he who had done ⊣

In lesson 8 we saw that ὁ can mean 'the person'. So ὁ ποιῶν means 'the person doing' or 'the person making'. In English we have several ways in which we might express this meaning—some of them are given above.

Similarly, ὁ ποιήσας means 'the person having done' or 'the person having made'. ποιήσας is a participle that expresses a single or completed action. It also can be translated in a variety of ways. So we can translate ὁ τοῦτο ποιήσας as 'the person who did this', 'the person who has done this', 'the person who had done this', or 'he who will have done this', according to the context in which it comes.

Compare

μακάριοί εἰσιν οἱ τοῦτο ποιοῦντες
– Blessed are those who do this

μακάριοι ἦσαν οἱ τοῦτο ποιοῦντες
– Blessed were those who were doing this

μακάριοί εἰσιν οἱ τοῦτο ποιήσαντες
– Blessed are those who have done this

μακάριοι ἦσαν οἱ τοῦτο ποιήσαντες
– Blessed were those who had done this.

20.6 Translate

1. Τίς ἐστιν ὁ ποιῶν τὸ θέλημα τοῦ θεοῦ; Ὁ τὰς ἐντολὰς αὐτοῦ τηρῶν ἐξ ὅλης τῆς καρδίας αὐτοῦ.	'Who is the person who does the will of God?' 'He who keeps his commandments wholeheartedly.'
2. Τίνες εἰσὶν οἱ ταῦτα ποιήσαντες; Ἀπόστολοί εἰσιν.	'Who are the people who have done these things?' 'They are apostles.'
3. ὁ θεὸς ἐποιεῖ τὸν οὐρανὸν καὶ τὴν γῆν.	God was making the heaven and the earth.
4. ὁ θεὸς ἦν ὁ ποιῶν τὸν οὐρανόν.	God was the one who was making the heaven.
5. Σὺ εἶ ὁ ποιήσας τὴν γῆν.	'You are the one who made the earth.'
6. ἐν τῇ συναγωγῇ προσκυνοῦσιν τῷ ποιήσαντι τοὺς οὐρανούς.	In the synagogue they worship the one who made the heavens.
7. ἐν τοῖς ἱεροῖς προσκυνοῦσιν τοῖς μὴ ποιήσασιν τὴν γῆν.	In the temples they worship those who did not make the earth.

20.7 Words

πέμπω – I send
    πέμπων – sending
    πέμψας – having sent
    ἔπεμψα – I sent
ἐκεῖνος – that, that man, he   (compare οὗτος – this)
    ἐκείνη ἡ ἡμέρα or ἡ ἡμέρα ἐκείνη – that day
ἡ ὥρα – the hour, the time
ἡ ζωή – the life
καθώς – as, according as, in the same way as
μείζων – greater, more important:
    μείζων τούτου – greater than this
    μείζων ἐκείνου – greater than that

20.8 Translate

1. ἐν ταύτῃ τῇ ὥρᾳ ὁ Πατὴρ ἀκούει τὴν φωνὴν τῶν προσκυνούντων αὐτῷ. | In this hour the Father hears the voice of those who are worshipping him.

2. ἐν ἐκείνῃ τῇ ἡμέρᾳ προσκυνήσαντες τῷ Πατρὶ ἐξῆλθον ἐκ τοῦ ἱεροῦ ἐκείνου. | On that day having worshipped the Father they went out from that temple.

3. ὁ προσκυνῶν τὸν θεὸν οὐκ ἐστὶν μείζων τοῦ θεοῦ οὐδὲ ἀπόστολος μείζων τοῦ πέμψαντος αὐτόν. | He who worships God is not greater than God nor is an apostle greater than he who has sent him.

4. ἐν ἐκείνῃ τῇ ὥρᾳ ἦλθεν ὁ Ἰησοῦς ἀπὸ τῆς συναγωγῆς καὶ εἶπεν αὐτοῖς, Καθὼς ἔπεμψέν με ὁ Πατὴρ καὶ ἐγὼ πέμπω ὑμᾶς. | In that hour (At that time) Jesus came from the synagogue and said to them, 'As the Father sent me I also am sending you.'

5. ἦλθες, Ἰησοῦ, ἵνα ζωὴν ἔχωμεν καὶ ἐν σοὶ ζωήν εὑρίσκομεν· σὺ γὰρ εἶ ἡ ἀλήθεια καὶ ἡ ζωή. καὶ μείζων τῶν προφητῶν εἶ, καθὼς εἶπεν ὁ Ἰωάννης. | You came, Jesus, so that we might have life, and in you we find life; for you are the truth and the life. You are greater than the prophets, as John said.

6. ἔπεμπεν αὐτοὺς βαπτίζειν ἄνδρας καὶ γυναῖκας | He used to send them to baptize men and women.

7. μείζονα ἔργα δίδωμι αὐτοῖς ποιεῖν. | I give them greater works to do.

20.9

Read carefully:

Life for the dead

ὁ μὴ τιμῶν τὸν υἱὸν οὐ τιμᾷ τὸν πατέρα τὸν πέμψαντα αὐτόν. Ἀμὴν ἀμὴν λέγω ὑμῖν ὅτι Ὁ τὸν λόγον μου ἀκούων καὶ πιστεύων τῷ πέμψαντί με ἔχει ζωὴν αἰώνιον καὶ εἰς κρίσιν οὐκ ἔρχεται ἀλλὰ μεταβέβηκεν ἐκ τοῦ θανάτου εἰς τὴν ζωήν. ἀμὴν λέγω ὑμῖν ὅτι Ἔρχεται ὥρα καὶ νῦν ἐστιν ὅτε οἱ νεκροὶ ἀκούσουσιν τῆς φωνῆς τοῦ υἱοῦ τοῦ ἀνθρώπου καὶ οἱ ἀκούσαντες ζήσουσιν.

Notes

τιμάω – I honour
αἰώνιος – eternal
κρίσις – judgement
μεταβέβηκεν – he has passed
    (μεταβαίνω – I cross over, I pass)

θάνατος – death
νεκρός – dead
ἀκούσουσιν – they will hear
ζήσουσιν – they will live

Ἀμὴν ἀμὴν λέγω ὑμῖν (truly truly I say to you): in the Gospels this expression draws attention to the importance of what is said. It has the sense of: 'Listen carefully – this is important'.

20.10 Read John 4:1–6 Jesus leaves Judea to go to Galilee, and travels through Samaria

v1 ἔγνω – he knew. πλείων – more. v2 καίτοιγε – and yet, but in fact. v3 ἀφῆκεν – he left (ἀφίημι – I leave). v4 ἔδει – it was necessary. διέρχεσθαι – to travel through. v5 πόλις – town. τὸ χωρίον – the place. v6 ἐκεῖ – there. πηγή – spring, well.
κεκοπιακώς – exhausted, tired out (κοπιάω – I work hard).
ἡ ὁδοιπορία – the journey, the travelling. ἕκτος – sixth.

Note (a) In v4 the linking word δέ does not in this context mean 'but'. It serves to introduce information.

    (b) In v6 ἐκαθέζετο οὕτως (he was sitting like this) is a vivid phrase – one can imagine the storyteller imitating the action as he speaks about it (καθέζομαι – I sit, I am sitting).

20.11

Revise lessons 13 and 14.

Lesson 21

ἐποίησα – I did, I made
ἔγραψα – I wrote, I did write ⸱|

21.1

Compare:

(a) τοῦτο **ποιήσας** – **having done** this: completed or single action ⸱

(b) τοῦτο **ἐποίησα** – **I did** this: completed or single action in past time ⸱|

(a) ἐγράφομεν ἐπιστολάς – we were writing letters ▬ |

(b) ἐγράψαμεν ἐπιστολάς – we wrote letters ⸱|

In (b), (c) and (d) notice the ε before the stem of the verb which is a mark of past time.

21.2

ἐποίησα – I did, I made
ἐποιήσαμεν – we did, we made

ἔγραψα – I wrote, I did write
ἐγράψαμεν – we wrote

Translate:

1. ἐποιήσαμεν τὰ ἔργα ἐκεῖνα.	We did those deeds.
2. μείζονα ἔργα ἐποίησα.	I did greater deeds.
3. ἐπέμψαμεν ἀγγέλους πρὸς αὐτόν.	We sent messengers to him.
4. ἐπέμπομεν αὐτοὺς πρὸς αὐτήν.	We were sending them to her.
5. ἔγραψά σοι τὴν ἐπιστολὴν ταύτην.	I wrote you this letter.
6. ἐγράψαμεν ἐπιστολὰς ὑμῖν;	Did we write letters to you?
7. ταῦτα ποιήσαντες προσεκυνήσαμεν τὸν θεόν.	When we had done these things we worshipped God.
8. ἐγὼ ἐλάλουν γλώσσαις ἀλλὰ σὺ οὐκ ἐλάλησας.	I used to speak in tongues, but you did not speak.

21.3

ἐποίησας – you did
ἐποιήσατε – you (p) did

ἐκήρυξας – you preached
ἐκηρύξατε – you (p) preached

Translate:
1. ἐκηρύξατε τὸ εὐαγγέλιον | You preached the good news
τούτοις τοῖς ἀνδράσιν. | to these men.
2. σὺ δὲ οὐκ ἐκήρυξας αὐτὸ | But you did not preach it
ἐκείναις ταῖς γυναιξίν. | to those women.
3. ταῦτα ἐποιοῦμεν ἡμεῖς | We were doing these things
ἀλλὰ ὑμεῖς οὐκ ἐποιήσατε αὐτά. | but you did not do them.
4. ποιεῖτε ταῦτα τὰ ἔργα ἃ | You are doing these works which
ἐγὼ δίδωμι (I give) ὑμῖν ποιεῖν. | I give you to do.
5. ἀκούσας τὴν φωνὴν τοῦ υἱοῦ μου | Having heard the voice of my son
ἦλθον πρὸς αὐτὸν καὶ ἐδίδαξα | I went to him and I taught
αὐτόν. | him.
6. Ἐδίδαξας τοὺς μαθητάς σου; | 'Did you teach your disciples?'
Ναί, ἐδίδαξα αὐτούς. | 'Yes, I taught them.'

21.4

ἐποίησεν – he did, he made
ἐποίησαν – they did, they made

ἤκουσεν – he heard
ἤκουσαν – they heard

Translate:
1. ἐποίησεν ὁ θεὸς τὴν γῆν. | God made the earth.
2. ἤκουσαν τὸν λόγον τοῦ ἀποστόλου. | They heard the apostle's word.
3. ἠκούσατε αὐτοῦ λέγοντος. | You heard him speaking.
4. ἠκούσατε αὐτῶν λεγόντων; | Did you hear them speaking?
5. ἤρξατο λαλεῖν αὐτοῖς | He began to speak to them
καὶ ἐδίδαξεν αὐτοὺς | and he taught them
τὴν ἐντολὴν τοῦ Πατρός. | the commandment of the Father.
6. ἠκολούθησαν αὐτῷ οἱ ἀδελφοί; | Did the brothers follow him?
7. ἠκολούθουν αὐτῷ οἱ μαθηταί; | Were the disciples following him?

21.5

Note carefully:

1. ἐποίει – he was doing ἤκουεν – he used to hear
   ε before the stem of a verb is a mark of action in past time.

2. ποίησας – having done   γράψας – having written
   ἀκούσας – having heard
   σ between the stem and the ending is a mark
      of single or completed action.

3. ἐποίησα – I did, I had done ἤκουσα – I heard
   ἔγραψα – I wrote   ἐκήρυξα – I preached
   σ between the stem and ending and ε before the stem, are marks of single or completed action in past time ⸴I

   In English, completed action in past time is usually expressed by forms like 'I preached', 'I did', 'I went' (past simple), but sometimes by forms like 'I had preached' (pluperfect / past perfect).
   Notice the translations of ἔγραψα in sentences (a) and (b):

   (a) ἀναγινώσκετε τὴν ἐπιστολὴν ἣν ἔγραψα
   You are reading the letter which **I wrote**

   (b) ἀνεγινώσκετε τὴν ἐπιστολὴν ἣν ἔγραψα
   You were reading the letter which **I had written**.

4. Note that in some verbal forms θ between the stem and the ending marks single or completed action.

   For example: ἀπεκρίθη 'he answered', ἠγέρθη 'he rose',
   ἐβαπτίσθη – 'he was baptized'.

21.6

Read carefully:

   The father preached to his sons and sent a message to his wife

Ἦλθεν οὖν ὁ πατὴρ πρὸς τοὺς υἱοὺς αὐτοῦ καὶ ἐκήρυξεν αὐτοῖς. οἱ δὲ ἤκουσαν τῆς φωνῆς αὐτοῦ ἀλλὰ οὐκ ἠθέλησαν τὸ θέλημα τοῦ θεοῦ ποιεῖν. ἀπῆλθον οὖν εἰς οἶκον αὐτῶν.

Ἐν ἐκείνῃ τῇ ἡμέρᾳ ἔπεμψεν ὁ ἀνὴρ πρὸς τὴν γυναῖκα αὐτοῦ λέγων, Ἐκήρυξα τὸν λόγον τοῖς τέκνοις ἡμῶν ἀλλὰ οὐκ ἠθέλησαν ἀκούειν οὐδὲ ἐπίστευσαν τῷ Κυρίῳ. καὶ ἠρώτησεν αὐτῇ λέγων, Ἐκβάλωμεν αὐτοὺς ἐκ τῆς οἰκίας; ἡ δὲ ἀπεκρίθη λέγουσα, Ὁ θεὸς ἀγάπη ἐστίν, καὶ ἔδωκεν ἡμῖν ἐντολὴν ἵνα ἀγάπωμεν ἀλλήλους. αὕτη ἡ ἐντολὴ μείζων ἐστὶν πάντων τῶν ἐντολῶν. νῦν οὖν τηρῶμεν τὴν ἐντολὴν καὶ μὴ ἐκβάλωμεν αὐτούς.

21.7

Here are the forms of ἐποίησα which you have learned:
  ἐποίησα – I did, I made, I had done, I had made

	Singular (one person)	Plural (more than one)
1st person	ἐποίησα – I did	ἐποιήσαμεν – we did
2nd person	ἐποίησας – you did	ἐποιήσατε – you did
3rd person	ἐποίησεν – he did	ἐποίησαν – they did

21.8

ποιήσας – having done   ὁ ποιήσας – he who has done

	Masculine	Feminine	Neuter
Singular	(ὁ) ποιήσας	(ἡ) ποιήσασα	(τὸ) ποιῆσαν
	(τὸν) ποιήσαντα	(τὴν) ποιήσασαν	(τὸ) ποιῆσαν
	(τοῦ) ποιήσαντος	(τῆς) ποιησάσης	(τοῦ) ποιήσαντος
	(τῷ) ποιήσαντι	(τῇ) ποιησάσῃ	(τῷ) ποιήσαντι
Plural	(οἱ) ποιήσαντες	(αἱ) ποιήσασαι	(τὰ) ποιήσαντα
	(τοὺς) ποιήσαντας	(τὰς) ποιήσασας	(τὰ) ποιήσαντα
	(τῶν) ποιησάντων	(τῶν) ποιησασῶν	(τῶν) ποιησάντων
	(τοῖς) ποιήσασιν	(ταῖς) ποιησάσαις	(τοῖς) ποιήσασιν

With the same endings as ποιήσας: πᾶς – every, all.
Note: πᾶς ἄνθρωπος – every man
 πάντες οἱ ἄνθρωποι – all the men
 πάντες – all, all men, all people
 τὰ πάντα – all things, everything
 πᾶν ὃ ἐποίησας – everything which you have done.

21.9 Read John 4:7–15

v7 ἀντλέω – I draw water.   Δός μοι πεῖν – Please give me a drink
(πίνω – I drink: πιεῖν or πεῖν – to drink).

v8 ἀπεληλύθεισαν – they had gone away.   τροφή – food.
ἀγοράζω – I buy.

v9 αἰτέω – I ask.   συγχράομαι – I use in common with, I associate with.

v10 Εἰ ᾔδεις – if you knew, if you had known. ἔδωκεν ἄν – he would have given.

v11 ἄντλημα – bucket.   τὸ φρέαρ – the well.   βαθύς – deep.
πόθεν ; where from? how?

v12 τὰ θρέμματα – the flocks, herds

v13 διψάω – I am thirsty.

v14 οὐ μὴ διψήσει – (he) will not thirst
εἰς τὸν αἰῶνα – ever (into the age: αἰών – age, eternity).
πηγή – spring (of water).   ἅλλομαι – I leap up.

v15 διέρχομαι – I pass through, I keep coming.   ἐνθάδε – here, to here.

Lesson 22

βαλών – having thrown
ἐλθών – having gone ⌐|

22.1

Study the following pairs:

1. (a) βάλλων – throwing
   (b) βαλών – having thrown
2. (a) λαμβάνων – taking
   (b) λαβών – having taken
3. (a) εὑρίσκων – finding
   (b) εὑρών – having found
4. (a) αἴρων – picking up
   (b) ἄρας – having picked up.

5. (a) γινώσκων – knowing
   (b) γνούς – having known
6. (a) ἀναβαίνων – going up
   (b) ἀναβάς – having gone up
7. (a) διδούς – giving
   (b) δούς – having given

In 1–7 each (a) word refers to a continuing or repeated action ⋯
Each (b) word refers to a completed or single action ⌐
In each pair the stem indicating completed or single action is shorter than the stem indicating continuing or repeated action

So: λαβὼν τὸ βιβλίον   having taken the book
    λαμβάνων τοὺς ἄρτους   taking the loaves
    οἱ ἀναβάντες   the people who have gone up
      εἰς τὸ ἱερόν   into the temple
    οἱ ἀναβαίνοντες   the people who are going up
      εἰς τὸ ἱερόν   into the temple.

Note also:
8. (a) λέγων – saying
   (b) εἰπών – having said
9. (a) ἐρχόμενος – going, coming
   (b) ἐλθών – having gone, having come
10. (a) ἐσθίων – eating
    (b) φαγών – having eaten

11. (a) τρέχων – running
    (b) δραμών – having run
12. (a) φέρων – bringing
    (b) ἐνέγκας – having brought

In 8–12, completed or single action ⤌ is indicated by a different stem.

So: τοῦτο εἰποῦσα ἀπῆλθεν   having said this she went away
    εἰσέρχονται ταῦτα λέγοντες   they come in saying these things
    εἰσὶν ἐν τῇ οἰκίᾳ   they are in the house
    ἐσθίοντες τοὺς ἄρτους   eating the loaves
    φαγόντες τοὺς ἄρτους   having eaten the loaves
    ἀπερχόμεθα   we go away.

22.2 Translate

1. ἐξελθὼν ἀπῆλθεν.	Having gone out he went away.
2. ἐξελθοῦσα ἀπῆλθεν.	Having gone out she went away.
3. ἐξελθόντες ἦλθον πρὸς τὴν οἰκίαν.	Having gone out they went to the house.
4. ἤλθομεν κηρύσσοντες.	We came preaching.
5. κηρύξαντες ἀπήλθομεν.	Having preached we went away.
6. ἔβλεψαν αὐτὸν ἐρχόμενον.	They looked at him as he was coming.
7. ἐξερχόμενοι εἶπον αὐτῷ...	As they were going out they said to him...
8. εὑρὼν αὐτὸν εἶπεν αὐτῷ...	Having found him he said to him...
9. μὴ εὑρόντες αὐτὸν ἀπῆλθον.	Not having found him they went away.
10. μακάριοι οἱ εὑρίσκοντες τὸν Χριστόν.	Blessed are those who find the Messiah.
11. μακάριοι ἦσαν οἱ εὑρόντες αὐτόν.	Blessed were those who had found him.
12. αἴροντες πάσας τὰς ἐπιστολὰς ἐξέρχονται.	Picking up all the letters they go out.
13. ἄρας τὴν ἐπιστολὴν ἐξῆλθεν.	Having picked up the letter he went out.
14. ταῦτα πάντα λαβόντες ἀπήλθομεν.	Having taken all these things we went away.
15. ταῦτα λαμβάνοντες ἀπερχόμεθα.	Taking these things we go away.
16. οἱ ἱερεῖς οἱ ἀναβαίνοντες εἰς Ἱεροσόλυμα...	The priests who are going up to Jerusalem...

17. οἱ ἱερεῖς οἱ ἀναβάντες εἰς Ἰερουσαλήμ...	The priests who had gone up to Jerusalem...
18. ἔρχεται ταῦτα διδούς.	He comes giving these things.
19. ταῦτα δοὺς ἀπέρχεται.	Having given these things he goes away.
20. ταῦτα δόντες ἀπέρχονται.	Having given these things they go away.

22.3 Translating participles

1. Participles such as ποιῶν, βάλλων, or ἐρχόμενος refer to continuing or repeated action ⸺
In a sentence beginning

ἐξερχόμενος εἶπεν τῇ μητρὶ αὐτοῦ...

the action expressed by the participle was *continuing* at the time the action expressed by the verb εἶπεν took place.
In English we do not say
Going out he said to his mother...
but As he was going out, he said to his mother...
or While he was going out, he said to his mother...

2. Participles such as ποιήσας, βαλών, or ἐλθών refer to completed or single action ⊣.
(a) In a sentence beginning

ἐξελθὼν εἶπεν αὐτῇ...

the action expressed by the participle ἐξελθών, was *completed* before the action expressed by the verb εἶπεν took place.
In English we do not usually say
Having gone out he said to her...
but When he had gone out he said to her...
or He went out and said to her...

(b) In another type of completed action, the action expressed by the participle finds its completion in the action expressed by the main verb. See, for example, Mark 5:7:

κράξας φωνῇ μεγάλῃ λέγει...

κράξας is from κράζω (I shout). Its form indicates a completed action. But we would be wrong to translate this either as, 'Having shouted with a loud voice he says...', or as 'He shouted with a loud voice and said...'. Both of these 'translations' wrongly suggest that he shouted first and then spoke

afterwards. But in this case the action indicated by κράξας finds its expression and completion in the action expressed by λέγει so we must translate:
>Shouting with a loud voice he said
>*or* He shouted out.

Compare the use of ἀποκριθείς – answering (once), having answered:
>ἀποκριθεὶς εἶπεν – he replied *or* in reply he said.

We would be wrong if we translated this as 'Having replied, he said' or as, 'He answered and said', because he did not first answer and then speak. The action expressed by the participle ἀποκριθείς finds its completion not before but in the action expressed by the verb εἶπεν.

22.4 Words

εἶδον – I saw
>ἰδών – having seen, seeing
>ἴδε – Look! (used to attract or direct attention)

ὡς – as, like
>ὡς ἦν – as he was
>ὡς ἄγγελοι – like angels, as angels are

καθώς – as, according as (κατά – according to, and ὡς – as)

περί – round, about
>μαρτυρῶ περὶ αὐτοῦ – I bear witness about him
>περιπατέω – I walk about, I walk around, I walk

ἀναβαίνω – I go up, I come up
>ἀναβαίνων – going up
>ἀναβάς – having gone up

καταβαίνω – I go down, I come down
>καταβαίνων – coming down
>καταβάς – having come down

πᾶς – all, every
>πάντες ζητοῦσίν σε – they are all looking for you
>πᾶς ὁ ὄχλος – the whole crowd
>πᾶς λόγος – every word
>πᾶσαι αἱ παραβολαί – all the parables
>τὰ πάντα – everything, all things

22.5 Translate

1. ἰδὼν τὰ πάντα ἐξῆλθεν.	When he had seen everything he went out.
2. ἡ δὲ γυνὴ ἰδοῦσα τὰ πάντα ἐξῆλθεν.	When she had seen everything the woman went out.
3. ὁ θεὸς εἶδεν τὰ πάντα καὶ ἀγαθὰ ἦν.	God saw all things and they were good.
4. περιπατήσαντες ἐν τῷ ἱερῷ ἐξῆλθον ἐκ τοῦ ἱεροῦ πάντες.	When they had walked round in the Temple they all went out of the Temple.
5. οἱ ἀπόστολοι καταβάντες ἀπὸ Ἱεροσολύμων εἰσῆλθον εἰς Καφαρναούμ.	When the apostles had gone down from Jerusalem they went into Capernaum.
6. καταβαίνοντες ἀπὸ Ἱεροσολύμων λέγουσιν αὐτῷ, Τίς εἶ;	As they are coming down from Jerusalem they say to him, 'Who are you?'
7. καταβάντες ἀπὸ Ἱεροσολύμων ἔλεγον αὐτῷ, Τί ποιεῖς; ὁ δὲ ἀποκριθεὶς εἶπεν, Ποιῶ τὸ θέλημα τοῦ Πατρός μου.	When they had come down from Jerusalem they said to him, 'What do you do?' He replied, 'I do the will of my Father.'
8. εἰσὶν ὡς ἄγγελοι καὶ ἀναβαίνουσιν εἰς τὸν οὐρανόν.	They are like angels and they go up into heaven.

22.6

John's witness and teaching

Καὶ ἀναβὰς εἰς Ἰερουσαλὴμ εἶδεν πάντας τοὺς ἱερεῖς ἐρχομένους πρὸς αὐτόν, καὶ ἐμαρτύρησεν αὐτοῖς περὶ τοῦ Χριστοῦ. καὶ ἐδίδασκεν ἐν τῷ ἱερῷ ὡς ἐξουσίαν ἔχων καὶ οὐχ ὡς οἱ Φαρισαῖοι. καὶ εἶπεν πᾶσι τοῖς μαθηταῖς αὐτοῦ, Ἴδε, οὗτοι οὐ λαμβάνουσι τὴν μαρτυρίαν ἣν μαρτυροῦμεν περὶ τοῦ Χριστοῦ, καθὼς εἶπον πάντες οἱ προφῆται.

Καὶ προσκυνήσαντες τῷ θεῷ ἐξῆλθον ἐκ τοῦ ἱεροῦ. καὶ ἐξελθόντες κατέβησαν ἀπὸ Ἰερουσαλήμ. καὶ καταβαίνων ὁ Ἰωάννης εἶδεν τὸν Ἰησοῦν ἀναβαίνοντα. καὶ ἰδὼν αὐτὸν εἶπεν τοῖς μαθηταῖς αὐτοῦ, Ἴδε ὁ 'Αμνὸς (Lamb) τοῦ θεοῦ ὁ καταβὰς ἐκ τοῦ οὐρανοῦ. οὗτος ἔρχεται, καθὼς εἶπον ὑμῖν, ἵνα ποιῇ τὸ θέλημα τοῦ θεοῦ τοῦ πέμψαντος αὐτόν. οἱ δὲ ἀκούσαντες αὐτοῦ λέγοντος καὶ ἰδόντες τὸν Ἰησοῦν ἠκολούθησαν αὐτῷ.

22.7 Progress test 12

Questions on 22.6. The participles are all in the reading passage.
1. Which of the following participles indicate more than one person?
   (a) ἀναβάς, (b) ἐρχομένους, (c) προσκυνήσαντες, (d) καταβαίνων, (e) ἀκούσαντες.
2. Which of the following participles indicate only one person?
   (a) ἔχων, (b) ἐξελθόντες, (c) ἀναβαίνοντα, (d) ἰδών, (e) πέμψαντος, (f) ἰδόντες.
3. Which of these participles indicate completed action?
   (a) ἀναβάς, (b) ἐρχομένους, (c) ἐξελθόντες, (d) καταβαίνων, (e) καταβάς, (f) πέμψαντος, (g) ἀκούσαντες, (h) λέγοντος.
4. Which of these participles indicate continuing action?
   (a) ἐρχομένους, (b) ἔχων, (c) προσκυνήσαντες, (d) ἀναβαίνοντα.

Check your answers in Key to Progress tests on page 333.

22.8

Before you do lesson 23, revise lessons 15–16, and read John 1:43–51 (κατὰ Ἰωάννην 1:43–51).

Words:

τῇ ἐπαύριον – on the next day
πόλις – town
ὁ νόμος – the Torah
Ἰσραηλίτης – a descendant of Israel
ἀληθῶς – truly
δόλος – deceit
πόθεν; – how?
δύναται – it is able
πρό – before

φωνῆσαι – to call
συκῆ – fig tree
ὄψῃ – you shall see
ἐπί – on
ἴδιος – own (one's own, his own, her own)
ἀνεῳγότα – open, opened

Notes

v43 εὑρίσκει – he finds, he meets (here 'he met', *or* 'he found')
Ἀκολούθει μοι – 'Follow me'. or 'Become my follower': a call to become a disciple.   v45 ἐν τῷ νόμῳ – in the Torah: in what we often call the Pentateuch, the most important part of the Jewish scriptures.

v46 εἶναι – to be (εἰμι – I am).

v47 Ἰσραηλίτης – Israelite, descendant of Israel. ἐν ᾧ δόλος οὐκ ἔστιν – in whom there is no deceit: Jacob, who was later named Israel, went to his father μετὰ δόλου (with deceit – LXX Gen 27:35). Nathanael was a genuine 'Israel' person with none of Jacob's deceit.

v48 πόθεν – how? πόθεν express more surprise than πῶς 'how, in what way?' Maybe under the fig tree Nathanael had been meditating on Jacob.

v49 σὺ βασιλεὺς εἶ τοῦ Ἰσραήλ – one of the expectations concerning the Messiah was that he would have insight into people's thoughts and character. Nathanael is so amazed by the insight Jesus has into his nature that he hails him as the King of Israel.

v51 ἀναβαίνοντας καὶ καταβαίνοντας – going up and coming down: we might expect it to be 'coming down (Mk 1:10, Jn 1:32) and going up', but the reference is again to the Jacob story (Gen 28:12) where he saw a ladder καὶ οἱ ἄγγελοι τοῦ θεοῦ ἀνέβαινον καὶ κατέβαινον ἐπ' αὐτῆς.

22.9

διδούς – giving   δούς – having given
ὁ διδούς – the one who gives   ὁ δούς —the one who has given

The following forms are found in the New Testament.
(ὁ) διδούς   (ὁ) δούς
(τὸν) διδόντα   (τὸν) δόντα
(τοῦ) διδόντος   (τοῦ) δόντος
(τῷ) διδόντι
(οἱ) διδόντες

Apart from διδούς and δούς the endings are the same as the forms of ὤν – see 19.5.

Note that the long stem διδο indicates continuing or repeated action. The short stem δο indicates single or completed action.

Lesson 23

ἔβαλον – I threw   ἦρα – I picked up ⊣|

23.1

In 22.1 you saw that in pairs like:
    (a) βάλλων   (a) εὑρίσκων   (a) αἴρων
    (b) βαλών   (b) εὑρών   (b) ἄρας
a shortened stem marks completed or single action.

Now compare:
    (a) ἔβαλλον – I was throwing, I used to throw ⋯|
    (b) ἔβαλον – I threw, I did throw ⊣|

So: (a)   ἔβαλλον τὰ δίκτυα εἰς τὴν θάλασσαν
              I was throwing the nets into the sea
    (b)   ἔβαλον τὸ δίκτυον εἰς τὴν θάλασσαν
              I threw the net into the sea.

Here again the long stem, βαλλ , indicates continuing action.
    The short stem, βαλ , indicates completed action.
    In both ἔβαλλον and ἔβαλον, ε before the stem is a mark of past time.
So in ἔβαλεν (he threw), ἐβάλομεν (we threw), ἔβαλον (they threw),
ἐβαλ – indicates a completed act of throwing, in past time.
    By contrast, βαλών and βάλλων (throwing, casting), have no mark of time.
Note the possible ways of translating μακάριος ὁ βαλὼν τὸ δίκτυον:
    (a) Blessed (is) he who casts the net
    (b) Blessed (was) he who did cast the net
    (c) Blessed (will be) he who will cast the net.

In ὁ βαλών the short stem βαλ indicates a single • or completed ⊣ action, but it does not indicate anything about the time of the action. According to the context in which ὁ βαλών comes, the time may be either (a) present, (b) past, or (c) future.

Now compare:
    ὁ βαλὼν τὸ δίκτυον (single or completed action)
    and ὁ βάλλων τὸ δίκτυον (repeated or continuing action).
When the context shows that it is necessary to emphasize the repetition or continuance of the action expressed by βάλλων, we may need to translate ὁ βάλλων as 'he who keeps casting'.

Compare

μακάριος ἦν ὁ βαλὼν τὸ δίκτυον
Blessed was **he who cast** the net

μακάριος ἦν ὁ βάλλων τὸ δίκτυον
Blessed was **he who kept casting** the net.

23.2 Words

ἁμαρτάνω – I sin (ἁμαρτία – sin)
    ἡμάρτανον – I was sinning
    ἥμαρτον – I sinned: ἥμαρτον εἰς σέ – I sinned against you
αἴρω – I pick up, I take up
    ἦρα – I picked up, I took up: ἦραν λίθους – they took up stones
ὁ λίθος – the stone
ὁ σταυρός – the cross (σταυρόω – I crucify)
ἡ πόλις – the town, the city
    ἐκ τῆς πόλεως – out of the town
    ἔξω – outside: ἔξω τῆς πόλεως – outside the town
ἡ θάλασσα – the sea, the lake
τὸ πνεῦμα – the wind, the spirit, the breath: τὰ πνεύματα – the spirits
ἀκάθαρτος – impure, unclean
ἐρωτάω – I ask
    ἠρώτησα – I asked

23.3

ἔβαλον – I threw
ἐβάλομεν – we threw
Stem: βαλ ⊣

ἔβαλλον – I was throwing
ἐβάλλομεν – we were throwing
Stem: βαλλ ····

Translate:

1. ἐγὼ ἔβαλον λίθον.	I threw a stone.
2. ἄρας τὸν λίθον ἔβαλον αὐτὸν ἔξω.	Having picked up the stone, I threw it outside.
3. ἐβάλλομεν λίθους.	We were throwing stones.
4. ἔξω βάλλομεν αὐτούς.	We are throwing them out (outside).
5. ἐβάλομεν τούτους τοὺς λίθους;	Did we throw these stones?

6. ἐβάλλομεν τοὺς λίθους ἐκείνους. | We were throwing those stones.
7. ἐγὼ ἔβαλλον τὰ δίκτυα εἰς τὴν θάλασσαν ἀλλὰ σὺ οὐκ ἔβαλες αὐτά. | I used to cast the nets into the sea but you did not cast them.

23.4

ἐξέβαλες – you threw out   ἐξέβαλλες —you were throwing out
ἐξεβάλετε – you (p) threw out   ἐξεβάλλετε —you (p) were throwing out

Translate:
1. ἐξεβάλλετε πνεύματα ἀκάθαρτα. | You were casting out unclean spirits.
2. ἐξεβάλετε τὸ πνεῦμα τὸ ἀκάθαρτον; | Did you cast out the unclean spirit?
3. Ἰησοῦ, ἐξέβαλες αὐτὸ ἐκ τοῦ ἀνδρός. | Jesus, you cast it out of the man.
4. ἐξεβάλομεν τὸν ἄνδρα ἐκ τῆς πόλεως. | We expelled the man from the town.
5. ἐξέβαλες αὐτὴν ἔξω τῆς πόλεως. | You drove her outside the town.

23.5

ἔβαλεν – he threw   ἔβαλλεν – he was throwing
ἔβαλον – they threw   ἔβαλλον – they were throwing

Notice the difference between:
　　　　ἄρας τοὺς λίθους ἔβαλον αὐτούς
　　　　Having picked up the stones I threw them.
　And ἄραντες τοὺς λίθους ἔβαλον αὐτούς
　　　　Having picked up the stones they threw them.

ἄρας is singular (one person): it shows that ἔβαλον is 1st person singular – I threw.
ἄραντες is plural: it shows that ἔβαλον is 3rd person plural – they threw.

Translate:
1. ἥμαρτον εἰς τὸν θεὸν πάντες. | They all sinned against God.
2. ἡμάρτανεν εἰς τὸν θεόν. | He was sinning against God.
3. τίς ἥμαρτεν εἰς σέ; | Who sinned against you?
4. εἰσελθόντες εἰς τὴν συναγωγὴν ἐξέβαλον τὰ πνεύματα τὰ ἀκάθαρτα ἐκ τῶν ἀνδρῶν. | They went into the synagogue and cast the unclean spirits out of the men.

23.6

αἴρω – I pick up, I take up, I lift
ἦρα – I picked up, I took up

αἴρων – picking up
ἄρας – having picked up

Translate:
1. αἴρει τὸν σταυρόν. | He takes up the cross.
2. ἦρεν τὸν σταυρὸν αὐτοῦ. | He took up his cross.
3. ἦραν τοὺς σταυροὺς οἱ μαθηταί. | The disciples lifted up the crosses.
4. ἄραντες τοὺς λίθους ἐξῆλθον. | Having picked up the stones they went out.
5. ἄρας τὸν λίθον ἐξῆλθον. | Having picked up the stone I went out.
6. ὃς ἂν μὴ αἴρῃ τὸν σταυρὸν οὐκ ἔστιν μαθητής μου. | Whoever does not keep taking up the cross is not my disciple.

23.7 ε as a mark of past time

We have seen that past time is usually indicated by an ε before the stem, e.g. ἔβαλεν – he threw. Note carefully the following examples:

(a) ἦραν – they picked up   ἠγάπησαν – they loved.
Compare
    ἄρας – picking up (once), having picked up
    ἦραν – they picked up.
The completed action stem of αἴρω is αρ . When ε is put before the stem it is not written εαρ, it becomes ηρ .

LESSON 23

Compare

 αἴρει – he picks up   ἦρεν – he picked up
 ἐρωτᾷ – he asks   ἠρώτησεν – he asked
 ἀγαπᾷ – he loves ἠγάπησεν – he loved
 οἰκοδομέω – I build   ᾠκοδόμησα – I built.

See also 15.5.

(b) ἐξέβαλεν – he threw out ἀπῆλθεν – he went away

You have seen that a word like ἐκβάλλω has three parts:

 1. ἐκ – out, out of (a preposition)
 2. βαλλ – the stem, which indicates throwing ⁝⁝⁝
 3. -ω – the ending.

In ἐξεβάλλομεν (we were throwing out), the ε which indicates past time comes before the stem, not before the preposition. Note the following examples:

Basic meaning	I am ⁝⁝⁝	I was ⁝⁝⁝ |	I did ⫶|
throw out	ἐκβάλλω	ἐξέβαλλον	ἐξέβαλον
announce	ἀπαγγέλλω	ἀπήγγελλον	ἀπήγγειλα
go up	ἀναβαίνω	ἀνέβαινον	ἀνέβην
go down	καταβαίνω	κατέβαινον	κατέβην
answer	ἀποκρίνομαι	ἀπεκρινόμην	ἀπεκρίθην
walk about	περιπατέω	περιεπάτουν	περιεπάτησα
go out	ἐξέρχομαι	ἐξηρχόμην	ἐξῆλθον.

23.8 Translating βάλλω and ἐκβάλλω into English

Words from the Greek stem βαλ cover a fairly wide area of meaning. So in translating βάλλω and ἐκβάλλω, into English we shall often have to choose between several English words, according to the context in the Greek passage.

 βάλλω – I throw, I drop, I put, I bring
 ἐκβάλλω – I cast out, I expel, I drive out, I pull out, I take out,
   I produce.

In John 20:25,

 Ἐὰν μὴ... βάλω τὸν δάκτυλόν μου εἰς τὸν τύπον τῶν ἥλων...
 If I do not **put** my finger into the mark of the nails...

LEARN NEW TESTAMENT GREEK

In Matthew 12:35,
> ὁ πονηρὸς ἄνθρωπος ἐκ τοῦ πονηροῦ θησαυροῦ **ἐκβάλλει** πονηρά
>
> The evil man **produces** evil things from his store of evil
> or The bad man **brings** bad things **out** of his treasure of bad things.

23.9

(a) Read John 9:35–38. Jesus speaks to the healed blind man who was expelled from the Temple.
Words:
Κύριος – master, Lord – Κύριε 'Sir!', or, 'Lord!'
ἵνα πιστεύσω – so that I may believe. ἑώρακας – you have seen.
ἔφη – he said. προσεκύνησεν – he prostrated himself, he worshipped.
Notice that in verse 36 Κύριε is a repectful way of speaking: 'Sir!'

In verse 38 it is nearer to the sense of 'Lord'. In this gospel there is a delight in words that can vary in meaning. It is not usually possible to reproduce such word-play in a translation.

(b) Read John 1:35–39
Words: τῇ ἐπαύριον – on the next day. εἱστήκει – he was standing.
Ἴδε – Look! (ἴδε directs attention: 'There is the Lamb of God!').
στραφεὶς – turning, having turned round.
   θεασάμενος – seeing, having seen.
μεθερμηνεύω – I translate. παρ' αὐτῷ – with him. δέκατος – tenth.

Lesson 24

ἐσθίω – I am eating ···· ἔφαγον – I ate ⊣
λέγειν – to be saying ···· εἴπειν – to say •

24.1

ἐσθίω τὸν ἄρτον – I eat the loaf
ἔφαγον τοὺς ἄρτους – I ate the loaves

Re-read 22.1. Note carefully examples 8–12. In each pair of participles it is a change of stem which shows the change from continuing or repeated action ···· to single or completed action ⊣. In this lesson we study a number of very common verbs in which one stem indicates continuing or repeated action (present stem), but a different stem indicates single or completed action, or action where there is no reference to continuation or repetition (aorist stem). Note carefully the words, stems, and types of action in 24.2.

24.2 Words

Action ····	Present stem	Aorist stem	Action ⊣
ἔρχομαι – I go	ερχ	ελθ	ἦλθον – I went
τρέχω – I run	τρεχ	δραμ	ἔδραμον – I ran
λέγω – I say	λεγ	ειπ	εἶπον – I said
φέρω – I carry	φερ	ενεγκ	ἤνεγκα – I carried
ὁράω – I see	ὁρα	ιδ	εἶδον – I saw
ἐσθίω – I eat	ἐσθι	φαγ	ἔφαγον – I ate

24.3 Translate

1. λαμβάνων τοὺς ἄρτους ἐσθίει αὐτούς.	Taking the loaves he eats them.
2. λαβὼν τὸν ἄρτον ἔφαγεν αὐτόν.	Having taken the loaf he ate it, or He took the loaf and ate it.
3. ἔδραμον οἱ μαθηταὶ πρὸς τὸν Κύριον καὶ προσεκύνησαν αὐτῷ.	The disciples ran to the Lord and worshipped him.
4. ἐξῆλθεν φέρων τοὺς ἄρτους καὶ φαγὼν αὐτοὺς εἰσῆλθεν.	He went out carrying the loaves and when he had eaten them he came in.

24.4

Read carefully:

Mary and some loaves

Τρέχει οὖν Μαρία ἡ Μαγδαληνὴ πρὸς Σίμωνα Πέτρον καὶ λέγει αὐτῷ, Ὁ Λουκᾶς ἦρεν τοὺς ἄρτους ἐκ τοῦ οἴκου μου καὶ ἔδραμεν πρὸς τὴν συναγωγήν. ἀποκριθεὶς δὲ ὁ Πέτρος εἶπεν αὐτῇ, Ἐγὼ οὐκ εἶδον αὐτόν.

Τρέχει οὖν ἡ Μαρία πρὸς τὴν συναγωγὴν καὶ εἰσελθοῦσα ὁρᾷ τοὺς μαθητὰς ἐσθίοντας τοὺς ἄρτους. οἱ δὲ μαθηταὶ φαγόντες τοὺς ἄρτους ἔδραμον ἐκ τῆς συναγωγῆς.

24.5 λέγων – **saying**   εἰπών – **having said**

Forms like:

> ποιῶν – doing   ποιήσας – having done

are called **participles** (see 20.2).

Those which indicate continuing or repeated action ····
> are called **present participles**.

Those which indicate completed or single action ⊣
> are called **aorist participles**.

Continuing or repeated action	Completed or single action
ἐρχόμενος – coming, going	ἐλθών – having come, coming
τρέχων – running	δραμών – having run, running
λέγων – saying	εἰπών – having said, saying
φέρων – carrying, bringing	ἐνέγκας – having brought, bringing
ὁρῶν – seeing	ἰδών – having seen, seeing
ἐσθίων – eating	φαγών – having eaten, eating
ἀποκρινόμενος – answering	ἀποκριθείς – having answered, answering

Translate:

1. εἴδομεν αὐτοὺς ἐρχομένους. | We saw them coming.

2. δραμὼν πρὸς αὐτὴν εἶπεν αὐτῇ, | Running to her he said to her,
Ὁρῶ τοὺς ἄνδρας φέροντας | 'I see the men bringing
γυναῖκα πρός σε. Ἰδοῦσα αὐτοὺς | a woman to you.' Seeing them
εἶπεν αὐτοῖς, Δίδωμι ὑμῖν | she said to them, 'I give to you,
καὶ τῇ γυναικὶ ἐκείνῃ | and to that woman,
τοὺς ἄρτους τούτους. καὶ | these loaves.' So
φαγόντες τοὺς ἄρτους | when they had eaten the loaves
ἀπῆλθον. | they went away.

3. ἤνεγκαν τὸν ἄνθρωπον πρὸς τὸν | They carried the man to Jesus
Ἰησοῦν καὶ ἐνέγκαντες | and when they had brought him
ἀπῆλθον. | they went away.

24.6 λέγειν – to be saying   εἰπεῖν – to say

Forms like the following are called **infinitive**:

λέγειν – to say   ποιεῖν – to be doing, to do ⁞⁞⁞⁞
and εἰπεῖν – to say   ποιῆσαι – to do •

Those which indicate continued or repeated action are called **present infinitive** (whether the time of the action is past, present, or future).
Those which indicate single action, or action without reference to its continuance or repetition, are called **aorist infinitive**.

Continuing action ⁞⁞⁞⁞   **Single action** •

ἔρχεσθαι – to be coming, to come   ἐλθεῖν – to come
τρέχειν – to be running, to run   δραμεῖν – to run
λέγειν – to be saying, to say   εἰπεῖν – to say
φέρειν – to be carrying, to carry   ἐνέγκαι – to carry
ὁρᾶν – to be seeing, to see   ἰδεῖν – to see
ἐσθίειν – to be eating, to eat   φαγεῖν – to eat

Translate:

1. θέλω πάντας τοὺς ἄρτους ἐσθίειν. | I am willing to eat all the loaves.
2. οὐ θέλει τὸν ἄρτον φαγεῖν. | He does not want to eat the loaf.
3. ἦλθεν ταῦτα λέγειν. | He came to say these things.
4. οὐκ ἤθελεν τοῦτο εἰπεῖν | He was not willing to say this.
5. ἤρξαντο προσέρχεσθαι πρὸς τὸν Ἰησοῦν. | They began to come to Jesus.

24.7 Read John 4:27–30, 39–42

v27 ἐπὶ τούτῳ – at this moment, just then.   θαυμάζω – I am amazed.
   μέντοι – however, but.
v28 ἀφῆκεν – she left.   ἡ ὑδρία – water jar (ὕδωρ – water).
v29 Δεῦτε – Come!   πάντα ὅσα – all the things which.
   ἐποίησα – I did, I have done.   μήτι οὗτός ἐστιν – Could he be..?
   (μήτι can introduce a question where the answer is expected to be 'No'; or a question where it is hoped the answer may be 'Yes'. From the context it is clear that the woman hopes he may be the Messiah).
v39 πολλοί – many people.
v40 μεῖναι – to remain, to stay.
v41 πολλῷ πλείους – many more.
v42 οὐκέτι – no longer. σωτήρ – saviour.

24.8 Progress test 13

Which translation is correct?

1. ἤρξαντο διδάσκειν τοὺς ἀκούοντας αὐτῶν.
   (a) They began to teach those who were listening to them.
   (b) They came to teach their disciples.
   (c) He came to teach those who listened to him.

2. ἤνεγκα αὐτὴν πρὸς τοὺς μαθητὰς ἀλλὰ αὐτοὶ οὐκ ἠδύναντο θεραπεύειν αὐτήν.
   (a) They brought her to the disciples and they were able to heal her.
   (b) He brought her to the disciple but he could not heal her.
   (c) I brought her to the disciples but they were not able to heal her.

3. ἀναβάντες εἰς Ἱεροσόλυμα εἰσήλθομεν εἰς τὸ ἱερόν.
   (a) They went up to Jerusalem and went into the Temple.
   (b) Going up to Jerusalem they went into the Temple.
   (c) When we had gone up to Jerusalem we went into the Temple.

4. καταβαινόντων αὐτῶν ἀπὸ Ἱεροσολύμων ἦλθεν γυνὴ πρὸς αὐτόν.
   (a) While they were going down from Jerusalem a woman came to him.
   (b) When they had gone down from Jerusalem a woman came to him.

5. καταβάντων αὐτῶν εἶπεν αὐτοῖς, Ποῦ ἔρχεσθε;
   (a) While they were going down he said to them, 'Where are you going?'
   (b) When they had gone down he said to them, 'Where are you going?'

Which do you think is the better English translation?

6. εὑρὼν αὐτὸν εἶπεν, Σὺ πιστεύεις εἰς τὸν υἱὸν τοῦ ἀνθρώπου;
   (a) Having found him he said, 'Are you believing into the Son of Man?'
   (b) When he found him he said, 'Do you believe in the Son of Man?'

7. ἀπεκρίθη ἐκεῖνος καὶ εἶπεν, Καὶ τίς ἐστιν, Κύριε, ἵνα πιστεύσω εἰς αὐτόν;
   (a) The man replied, 'Sir, who is he, that I may believe in him?'
   (b) That man answered him and said, 'And who is he, Sir, so that I may believe in him?'

8. Which of the following participles indicate continuing or repeated action?
   (a) ἐρχόμενος, (b) ἐλθών, (c) λέγων, (d) ἰδών, (e) ὁρῶν.

9. Which of the following infinitives indicate single action?
   (a) ποιῆσαι, (b) ποιεῖν, (c) δραμεῖν, (d) ἐνέγκαι, (e) φαγεῖν.

Check your answers in Key to Progress Tests on page 333.

24.9

Revise lessons 17 and 18.

Lesson 25

καταβαίνοντος αὐτοῦ – while he was coming down ····
καταβάντος αὐτοῦ – when he had come down ⊣

25.1

Compare:
(a) Mt 17:9 καταβαινόντων αὐτῶν ἐκ τοῦ ὄρους...
   As they were coming down from the mountain...
(b) Mt 8:1 Καταβάντος δὲ αὐτοῦ ἀπὸ τοῦ ὄρους...
   When he had come down from the mountain...

In (a), note:
   the type of action indicated by καταβαίνων (coming down) ····
Literally, καταβαινόντων αὐτῶν means 'them coming down', but that is not good English. According to the context, we shall need a translation like:
   While they were coming down...
   or As they came down...
   or As they are coming down...
So: καταβαίνοντος αὐτοῦ, τοῦτο ποιοῦμεν
   While he **is** coming down, we are doing this

   καταβαίνοντος αὐτου, τοῦτο ἐποιήσαμεν
   While he **was** coming down, we did this.

The order of words in this kind of clause may be either

(1) καταβαίνοντος αὐτοῦ, or (2) αὐτοῦ καταβαίνοντος.
Mark usually uses order (1); John usually uses order (2).

In (b), note:
   the type of action indicated by καταβάς (having come down) ⊣.
Literally, καταβάντος αὐτοῦ means 'Him having come down', but that is not good English. According to the context, we shall need a translation like:
   When he had come down...
   or When he has come down...

So: 1. καταβάντων αὐτῶν ἐποιήσαμεν τοῦτο
When they **had** come down we did this

2. καταβάντων αὐτῶν ποιήσομεν τοῦτο
When they **have** come down we will do this.

In (1) the action expressed by ἐποιήσαμεν is in past time, and the action expressed by καταβάντων was completed before 'we did this'. So we translate: 'When they had come down...'. In (2) the action expressed by ποιήσομεν lies in the future. The action expressed by καταβάντων also lies in the future, but it will be completed before 'we do this'. So we translate: 'When they have come down...'.

25.2 ὤν – being   ὄντος αὐτοῦ – him being

The way we translate a phrase like ὄντος αὐτοῦ will depend on the context.

Compare:
(a) Mk 14:3   ὄντος αὐτοῦ ἐν Βηθανίᾳ...ἦλθεν γυνὴ
While he **was** in Bethany, a woman came
(b) Mk 14:66   ὄντος τοῦ Πέτρου κάτω ἐν τῇ αὐλῇ
While Peter **is** below in the courtyard
ἔρχεται μία τῶν παιδισκῶν τοῦ ἀρχιερέως
there comes one of the servant girls of the High Priest.

(Note ἔρχεται – she comes. In English we would normally use past tenses in telling a story: 'While Peter was down in the courtyard one of the High Priest's serving-maids **came** by.' This use of a present form in a narrative about the past is called the historic present. It occurs frequently in Mark's Gospel.)

Translate:

1. αὐτοῦ καταβαίνοντος οἱ μαθηταὶ εἶπον αὐτῷ...	As he was going down the disciples said to him...
2. καταβάντος αὐτοῦ ἀπὸ Ἰερουσαλὴμ ἀνέβησαν οἱ Φαρισαῖοι πρὸς Ἰερουσαλήμ.	When he had gone down from Jerusalem the Pharisees went up to Jerusalem.
3. εἰσελθόντων αὐτῶν εἰς τὴν πόλιν, ἦλθον πρὸς αὐτὸν αἱ γυναῖκες.	When they had gone into the city the women came to him.

4. ὄντος αὐτοῦ ἐν Βηθανίᾳ ἐν τῇ οἰκίᾳ Σίμωνος ἦλθεν πρὸς αὐτὸν γυνὴ ἔχουσα βιβλίον.	While he was in Bethany in Simon's house, a woman with a book came to him.

25.3

Note that the forms like καταβαίνοντος, καταβάντων, αὐτοῦ and αὐτῶν which you have studied in 25.1–2 are all in the genitive case (see 12.7, 37.1). This construction, in which a noun or pronoun in the genitive case is linked to a participle in the genitive case, e.g., καταβαίνοντος αὐτοῦ, is called the genitive absolute.

25.4 Words

διά – because of, through
    διὰ τί ; – why? (because of what?)
μετά – with, after
    μετά μου or μετ' ἐμοῦ – with me
ἐμβαίνω – I go into, I get in
τὸ πλοῖον – the boat
ἔτι – still
    ἔτι ἐσθιόντων αὐτῶν – while they were (are) still eating;
οὐκέτι, μηκέτι – no longer, not still, never again
δίδωμι – I give
    ἔδωκεν – he gave
μείζων πάντων – greatest of all, most important (lit. greater of all)

25.5 Translate

1. οὐκέτι εἰμὶ ἐν τῇ οἰκίᾳ μετὰ σου.	I am no longer in the house with you.
2. οὐκέτι ταῦτα λέγομεν.	We no longer say these things.
3. μηκέτι ταῦτα λέγωμεν.	Let us no longer say these things.
4. διὰ τί ταῦτα λέγωμεν;	Why should we be saying these things?

25.6

Read carefully:

1. While his brothers ate, Peter went to the boat

ἔδωκεν ὁ Μαθθαῖος ἄρτους αὐτοῖς καὶ ἔτι αὐτῶν ἐσθιόντων ἐξῆλθεν ὁ Πέτρος. καὶ ἐξελθὼν ἀπῆλθεν πρὸς τὸ πλοῖον. καὶ ἐμβάντος αὐτοῦ εἰς τὸ πλοῖον, οἱ ἀδελφοὶ αὐτοῦ φαγόντες πάντας τοὺς ἄρτους ἐξῆλθον πρὸς τὴν θάλασσαν τῆς Γαλιλαίας.

Καὶ ἐμβαινόντων αὐτῶν εἰς τὸ πλοῖον εἶπεν αὐτοῖς ὁ Πέτρος, Διὰ τί ἀκολουθεῖτέ μοι; εἶπον οὖν αὐτῷ, Ἔτι σου ὄντος μεθ᾽ ἡμῶν ἐν τῇ οἰκίᾳ Μαθθαίου εἴπομέν σοι ὅτι Θέλομεν ἐξελθεῖν μετά σου, ἀλλὰ σὺ οὐκ ἤκουσας τοὺς λόγους οὓς ἐλαλήσαμεν.

2. Jesus is thrown out of the Temple

Καὶ ὄντος αὐτοῦ ἐν τῷ ἱερῷ μετὰ πάντων τῶν ἀποστόλων αὐτοῦ, ἦλθον πρὸς αὐτὸν οἱ ἱερεῖς, καὶ προσελθόντες ἠρώτησαν αὐτὸν Διὰ τί διδάσκεις αὐτοὺς ἐν τῷ ἱερῷ; καὶ τίς ἔδωκέν σοι τὴν ἐξουσίαν ταύτην; καὶ ἐξέβαλον αὐτὸν ἔξω. Καὶ ἀπελθόντων αὐτῶν εἶπεν τοῖς μετ᾽ αὐτοῦ οὖσιν, Ἀμὴν λέγω ὑμῖν, πᾶς ὁ πιστεύων εἰς ἐμὲ ἔχει ζωὴν αἰώνιον, ἀλλὰ πάντες οἱ μὴ πιστεύοντες οὐκ ἔχουσιν τὴν ζωὴν οὐδὲ κοινωνίαν ἔχουσι μετὰ τοῦ Πατρός.

Καὶ ἔτι αὐτοῦ λαλοῦντος ἦλθεν πρὸς αὐτὸν γυνὴ καὶ ἠρώτησεν αὐτὸν λέγουσα, Τίς ἐντολὴ μείζων ἐστὶν πάντων τῶν ἐντολῶν; καὶ ἀποκριθεὶς εἶπεν αὐτῇ Ἀγαπήσεις Κύριον τὸν θεόν σου ἐξ ὅλης τῆς καρδίας σου. αὕτη ἡ ἐντολὴ μείζων ἐστὶν πάντων τῶν ἐντολῶν ἃς ἔδωκεν ὁ θεὸς τῷ Ἰσραήλ.

25.7 Bible translations evaluation (3)

(a) John 1:22 Τίς εἶ; ἵνα ἀπόκρισιν δῶμεν τοῖς πέμψασιν ἡμᾶς·
[τί λέγεις περὶ σεαυτοῦ;]

Question: What does the context suggest we need to supply before ἵνα?

NJB   Who are you? We must take back an answer to those who sent us.
NIV   Who are you? Give us an answer to take back to those who sent us.
NRSV Who are you? Let us have an answer for those who sent us.
REB   'Then who are you?' they asked. 'We must give an answer to those who sent us.'

NLT 'Then who are you? Tell us, so that we can give an answer to those who sent us.'
GNB 'Then tell us who you are,' they said. 'We have to take an answer back to those who sent us.'

(b) John 1:29 Ἴδε ὁ ἀμνὸς τοῦ θεοῦ (literally: Look! The Lamb of God)

NRSV	Here is the Lamb of God
NIV	Look, the Lamb of God
REB, GNB	There is the Lamb of God
NJB, NLT	Look! There is the Lamb of God

(c) John 1:48 Πόθεν με γινώσκεις;
Question: Is Nathanael expressing surprise or asking about location?

NRSV	Where did you come to know me?
NJB, NIV, GNB	How do you know me?
REB	How is it you know me?
NLT	How do you know about me?

Lesson 26

ἀκούσω – I will hear   βαλῶ – I will throw

26.1

Compare:

1. (a) ἀκούω – I am hearing
   (b) ἀκούσω – I will hear

2. (a) βάλλω – I am throwing
   (b) βαλῶ – I will throw

3. (a) λέγω – I am saying
   (b) ἐρῶ – I will say

4. (a) ἔρχομαι – I am coming
   (b) ἐλεύσομαι – I will come

Each (b) word refers to action in future time.
   Note the commonest marks of future time:
      1. σ between the stem and the ending
  or 2. a shortened stem
  or 3. a different stem.

These are the same marks as the marks of single action (p112).
   Since action in the future has not yet taken place, it is not normally thought of as continuing action. But some verbs express a state or action which is by its nature continuous, for example:

    ἔσομαι – I will be (εἰμί)
    ἕξω – I will have (ἔχω).

ἔσομαι may be used with a participle which expresses continuing action:
1 Corinthians 14:9, ἔσεσθε ... λαλοῦντες – you will be speaking.

26.2 Words

δοξάζω – I glorify, I praise	Note these forms of ὁ σωτήρ – the saviour
δοξάσω – I will glorify	ὁ σωτήρ
ἡ δόξα – the glory	τὸν σωτῆρα
σῴζω – I save, I rescue, I heal	τοῦ σωτῆρος
σώσω – I will save	τῷ σωτῆρι
σώσας – having saved	(plural forms of σωτήρ do not occur in the New Testament)
ὁ σωτήρ – the saviour	
ἡ σωτηρία – the salvation	

ζάω – I live
  ζήσω – I will live
  ἡ ζωή – the life
  τὸ ζῷον – the living creature
  ζωοποιέω – I make alive

ἐγείρω – I raise, I rise
  ἐγερῶ – I will raise
  ἔρχομαι – I come, I go
  ἐλεύσομαι – I will come, I will go

26.3 Translate

1. πιστεύομεν τῷ θεῷ τῷ ζῶντι καὶ τῷ ζωοποιοῦντι ἡμᾶς.	We trust in the living God who makes us alive.
2. πιστεύσομεν τῷ σωτῆρι.	We will trust in the Saviour.
3. ἀκούσουσιν τὸν λόγον τῆς ζωῆς.	They will hear the word of life.
4. ἀκούσετε καὶ ζήσετε.	You will hear and you will live.
5. ἀκούσαντες ζήσομεν.	When we have heard we will live.
6. ἐγείρει αὐτοὺς ὁ Κύριος.	The Lord raises them.
7. ἐγερεῖ αὐτὸν ὁ σωτήρ.	The Saviour will raise him.
8. σώσει αὐτὴν καὶ αὐτὴ δοξάσει τὸν σώσαντα αὐτήν.	He will save her and she will praise the man who has saved her.
9. σώζει αὐτὴν καὶ αὐτὴ δοξάζει τὸν σώζοντα αὐτήν.	He is saving her and she is praising the man who is saving her.
10. ἐὰν αὐτὴ σώζῃ αὐτόν, αὐτὸς δοξάσει τὴν σώσασαν αὐτόν.	If she saves him, he will praise the woman who has saved him.
11. ἔρχεται ἐν τῇ δόξῃ τοῦ Πατρός.	He comes in the glory of the Father.
12. ἐλεύσεται ἐν τῇ δόξῃ τοῦ θεοῦ καὶ σώσει ἡμᾶς ἀπὸ πασῶν τῶν ἁμαρτιῶν ἡμῶν.	He will come in the glory of God and he will save us from all our sins.
13. οὐ ζητεῖτε τὴν δόξαν τοῦ θεοῦ οὐδὲ ποιεῖτε τὸ θέλημα αὐτοῦ.	You do not seek the glory of God nor do you do his will.
14. οὐ ζητήσομεν τὴν δόξαν τοῦ Κυρίου ἀλλὰ ποιήσομεν τὰ ἔργα τοῦ πονηροῦ.	We will not seek the glory of the Lord but we will do the works of the evil one.
15. μηκέτι ζητῶμεν τὴν δόξαν ἡμῶν ἀλλὰ ἀγαπῶμεν τοὺς ἀδελφοὺς καὶ ποιῶμεν τὸ θέλημα τοῦ θεοῦ ὃς ἐγερεῖ ἡμᾶς καὶ ζωοποιήσει ἡμᾶς.	Let us no longer seek our glory but let us love the brothers and let us do the will of God who will raise us up and will make us alive.

26.4 Some grammatical terms

1. The main forms of the verb which show
    continuing or repeated action ⸺ are called **present**.
    So λέγει (he says), λέγων (saying), λέγειν (to say), are all present.

Forms of the verb that are used in definite statements and definite questions are called **indicative**.

   So ἀκούει (he hears) and ἤκουσεν; (did he hear?) are both indicative.
The forms of λέγω in 5.5 are the present indicative of λέγω.

2. Forms of the verb which show
    continuing or repeated action in past time ⸺ | are called **imperfect**.
    So ἔβλεπεν (he was looking at) and ἔβαλλεν (he was throwing) are both imperfect.

The forms of ἔλεγον in 14.6 are the imperfect indicative of λέγω.
The forms of ἐποίουν in 15.1–3 are the imperfect indicative of ποιέω.

3. Forms of the verb which show
    completed or single action ⸱| are called **aorist**.
    So ἦλθεν (he came), ἐλθών (having come), ἐλθεῖν (to come), ἐποίησεν (he did), ποιήσας (having done), ποιῆσαι (to do), are all aorist.

The forms of ἐποίησα in 21.7 are the aorist indicative of ποιέω.
21.8 gives the forms of the aorist participle of ποιέω.

4. Forms of the verb that show future time are called **future**.
   So: ἀκούσω ἀκούσομεν
       ἀκούσεις ἀκούσετε
       ἀκούσει ἀκούσουσιν

   and βαλῶ βαλοῦμεν
       βαλεῖς βαλεῖτε
       βαλεῖ βαλοῦσιν

are the future indicative forms of ἀκούω and βάλλω.

26.5

Compare these indicative forms:

Meaning	Present	Imperfect	Aorist	Future
I write	γράφω	ἔγραφον	ἔγραψα	γράψω
I teach	διδάσκω	ἐδίδασκον	ἐδίδαξα	διδάξω
I read	ἀναγινώσκω	ἀνεγίνωσκον	ἀνέγνων	ἀναγνώσομαι
I have	ἔχω	εἶχον	ἔσχον	ἕξω
He goes up	ἀναβαίνει	ἀνέβαινεν	ἀνέβη	ἀναβήσεται
They take	λαμβάνουσιν	ἐλάμβανον	ἔλαβον	λήμψονται
They go	ἔρχονται	ἤρχοντο	ἦλθον	ἐλεύσονται
We send	ἀποστέλλομεν	ἀπεστέλλομεν	ἀπεστείλαμεν	ἀποστελοῦμεν

26.6 Translate

1. ἀπέστελλεν τοὺς ἀποστόλους καὶ ἀποστέλλει ἡμᾶς. — He used to send the apostles and he is sending us.
2. ὁ Κύριος ἀπέστειλεν αὐτὴν καὶ ἀποστελεῖ ὑμᾶς. — The Lord sent her and he will send you.
3. ἀναβαίνετε ὑμεῖς καὶ ἡμεῖς καταβησόμεθα. — You are coming up and we will go down.
4. ἐδίδαξά σε καὶ σὺ διδάξεις αὐτοὺς καὶ αὐτοὶ λήμψονται τὴν διδαχήν σοῦ. — I taught you and you will teach them, and they will receive your teaching.
5. γράψετε ἐπιστολὰς καὶ ἡμεῖς ἀναγνωσόμεθα αὐτάς. — You will write letters and we will read them.
6. ἐλεύσονται μετὰ τῶν ἀγγέλων ἐν τῇ δόξῃ τοῦ Πατρός. — They will come with the angels in the glory of the Father.
7. ἔχει ταῦτα τὰ βιβλία ὁ Παῦλος καὶ ἐκεῖνα ἕξει. — Paul has these books and he will have those.

26.7 Read

(a) Read 20.9 again.

(b) Read John 5:19–28
    v19 ἀπεκρίνατο – he replied.   ἀφ' ἑαυτοῦ – from himself (at his own initiative, or, as prompted by his own ideas).   οὐδέν – nothing   ἐὰν μή – unless   ὁμοίως – in a similar way.
    v20 φιλέω – I love.   δείκνυμι – I show.
        θαυμάζω – I am surprised, amazed.
    v21 ὥσπερ – as.   οὕτως – thus, in the same way, so.
    v22 δέδωκεν – he has given.
    v25 νῦν – now.   ὅτε – when.   νεκρός – dead.
    v26 ἐν ἑαυτῷ – in himself
    v28 τὸ μνημεῖον – the tomb.

    In v27 notice: υἱὸς ἀνθρώπου ἐστίν – he is **the** Son of man:-
    (a) When a noun like υἱὸς comes **before** a verb like ἐστίν (he is) it does not need to have the definite article (ὁ, ἡ, *or* τό). Compare Jn 9:5   φῶς εἰμι τοῦ κόσμου. – 'I am **the** light of the world' *with* Jn 8:12 ἐγώ εἰμι **τὸ** φῶς τοῦ κόσμου.
    (b) In contexts where judgement is prominent the background for the use of the term 'the Son of man' is the heavenly figure seen in Daniel's vision (Dan 7:13–14).
    (c) The use of υἱὸς ἀνθρώπου in such a context rather than υἱὸς τοῦ ἀνθρώπου is unusual, but it does occur in Daniel 7:13 in the LXX.

(c) Read John 6:31–33
    v31 πατέρες – forefathers, ancestors.   γεγραμμένος – written.
        ἔδωκεν – he gave.
    v32 δέδωκεν – he has given, he gave.   δίδωσιν – he gives
    v33 διδούς – giving (= who gives)

Lesson 27

Questions: τίς; – who?   τί; – what? why?

27.1 Words

τίς; – who? which? (see 15.6)
τί; – what? why?
   διὰ τί; – for what reason? why?
πότε; – when?
   πότε ἐλεύσεται; – when will he come?
πῶς – how? how is it that?
   πῶς λέγεις; – how is it that you say?
ποῦ; – where?
   ποῦ μένεις; – where are you staying?
πόθεν; – where from? how? (idiomatically: how on earth?)
   πόθεν ἔρχεται; – where does he come from?
   πόθεν με γινώσκεις; – how (on earth) do you know me?
ἀποκρίνομαι – I answer, I reply, I respond.
   ἀπεκρίθη – he answered
   ἀποκριθείς – answering, in reply, in response
        (in response to a question, a person or a situation)
οἶδα – I know (compare οἶδεν – he knows, and εἶδεν – he saw)
δύναμαι – I am able to, I can: δύναται – he can: δύνανται – they can
   δύναται λαλεῖν – he is able to speak
μένω – I abide, I remain, I stay   μενῶ – I will remain
κρίνω – I judge   κρινῶ – I will judge   ὁ κριτής – the judge
οὐδέ or μηδέ – and not, nor
ὅτε – when

27.2 Translate

1. Τί ἐστιν; Οὐκ οἶδα τί ἐστιν.	'What is it?' 'I don't know what it is.'
2. Τί ποιήσεις; Οὐ τί ἐγὼ θέλω ἀλλὰ τί σύ.	'What will you do?' 'Not what I want but what you want.'
3. Τίς ἐστιν καὶ πόθεν ἔρχεται; Οὐκ οἴδαμεν τίς ἐστιν οὐδὲ πόθεν ἔρχεται.	'Who is he and where does he come from?' 'We do not know who he is nor where he comes from.'

4. εἶπον αὐτῷ, Τίνες εἰσὶν καὶ ποῦ μένουσιν; ἀποκριθεὶς εἶπέν μοι, Οὐκ οἶδα τίνες εἰσὶν οὐδὲ ποῦ μένουσιν. | I said to him, 'Who are they and where do they stay?' In reply he said to me, 'I do not know who they are nor where they are staying.'

5. πῶς δύναται Σατανᾶς Σατανᾶν ἐκβάλλειν; | How is Satan able to be casting out Satan?

6. οὐ δύναμαι Σατανᾶν ἐκβαλεῖν. | I cannot cast out Satan.

7. οὐκ οἴδατε πῶς κρίνει τούτους τοὺς ἀνθρώπους ὁ κριτὴς οὐδὲ πότε κρινεῖ ἐκείνους. | You do not know how the judge judges these men nor when he will judge those.

8. ὅτε ἔρχεται ἐρεῖ αὐτοῖς 'Ὑμεῖς ἐστε οἱ ἀδελφοί μου. | When he comes he will say to them, 'You are my brothers'.

9. ἠρώτησεν αὐτὸν, Ποῦ ἐστιν ὁ πατήρ σου; ὁ δὲ ἀπεκρίθη, Σὺ οὐκ οἶδας ποῦ ἐστιν οὐδὲ πόθεν ἔρχεται, ἀλλὰ ἐγὼ οἶδα καὶ δοξάσω αὐτόν. | He asked him, 'Where is your father?' He answered, 'You do not know where he is nor where he comes from, but I know and I will glorify him.'

10. ἠρώτησαν αὐτοὺς λέγοντες, Πόθεν δύνασθε ταῦτα ποιεῖν; ἀπεκρίθησαν οὖν αὐτοῖς οἱ μαθηταί, 'Ὁ Κύριος ὁ πέμψας ἡμᾶς ἐκεῖνος ποιεῖ ταῦτα τὰ ἔργα καὶ μείζονα τούτων ποιήσει ἵνα αὐτὸν δοξάζητε. | They asked them, 'How is it that you are able to do these things?' So the disciples answered them, 'The Lord who sent us does these works and he will do greater ones than these so that you may praise him.'

27.3 Questions beginning with οὐ and μή (not)

Compare:

    (a) 'You can do this, can't you?'
    (b) 'You can't do this, can you?'

The person who asks question (a) expects that the answer will be, 'Yes, I can.' The person who asks question (b) expects that the answer will be, 'No, I can't.' Of course, the answer actually given may be quite different, but that does not matter. It is the expected answer which determines the form of the question.

In questions in Greek:
- (a) οὐ, οὐκ, οὐχ and οὐχί show that the questioner expects the answer, 'Yes'.
- (b) μή and μήτι usually show that the questioner expects the answer, 'No'.

For example:
- (a) οὐ δύνανται ἐκβάλλειν τὰ δαιμόνια;
  They are able to cast out the demons, aren't they?
  or They can cast out the demons, can't they?
- (b) μὴ δύνανται τὸ δαιμόνιον ἐκβαλεῖν;
  They are not able to cast out the demon, are they?
  or They can't cast out the demon, can they?

Study these examples (for some examples, alternative similar translations are given):

Lk 4:22 Οὐχὶ υἱός ἐστιν Ἰωσὴφ οὗτος;
Isn't this man Joseph's son?
Surely he's Joseph's son, isn't he?

Lk 23:39 Οὐχὶ σὺ εἶ ὁ Χριστός;
Are you not the Messiah?
You are the Messiah, aren't you?

Mk 14:19 Μήτι ἐγώ;
It isn't me, is it?
Surely it isn't me?

Jn 4:12 μὴ σὺ μείζων εἶ τοῦ πατρὸς ἡμῶν Ἰακώβ;
You are not greater than our forefather Jacob, are you?

1 Cor 12:29 μὴ πάντες διδάσκαλοι;
They are not all teachers, are they?

Note that in Mark 14:19, John 4:12 and 1 Corinthians 12:29, RSV fails to represent the meaning of μή properly.

Sometimes μή or μήτι is used when the questioner is doubtful (perhaps thinking the answer will be 'No' but hoping it may be 'Yes'):

Mt 12:23 Μήτι οὗτός ἐστιν ὁ υἱὸς Δαυίδ;
Could he be the Son of David?

Jn 4:29 μήτι οὗτός ἐστιν ὁ Χριστός;
Could he be the Messiah?

27.4 Translate

1. οὐ κρινεῖ ὁ θεὸς πάντας τοὺς ἀνθρώπους;	God will judge all men (all the men) won't he?
2. οὐχὶ οὗτός ἐστιν ὁ προφήτης;	This man is the prophet, isn't he?
3. μήτι οὗτός ἐστιν ὁ ἀπόστολος;	Could he be the apostle? *or* He isn't the apostle, is he?
4. οὐκ οἶδας ποῦ μένει;	You know where he is staying, don't you?
5. μὴ πάντες ἀπόστολοι; μὴ πάντες προφῆται; μὴ πάντες γλώσσαις λαλοῦσιν;	They are not all apostles, are they? They are not all prophets, are they? They do not all speak in tongues, do they?

27.5

(a) Read John 3:8–13.

Notes
πνεῖ – it blows
τὸ πνεῦμα – the wind, the spirit
  (it is used in this passage with a double meaning)
ὑπάγω – I go away
οὕτως – thus, so
ὁ γεγεννημένος – the person who has been begotten
  (γεννάω – I beget)
γενέσθαι – to happen (γίνομαι – I become, I happen)
τὰ ἐπίγεια – things on earth   οὐδείς – nobody

(b) Bible translations evaluation (4)

In this section there is a suggestion of the meaning of the Greek, followed by the translations for you to compare with the Greek.

Mark 14:19 Μήτι ἐγώ; – It isn't me, is it?
            or, Surely it isn't me!

NRSV, NIV	Surely, not I?
NLT	I'm not the one, am I?
REB	Surely you don't mean me?
GNB	Surely you don't mean me, do you?

NJB	Not me, surely?

John 4:12 μὴ σὺ μείζων εἶ τοῦ πατρὸς ἡμῶν Ἰακώβ
You are not greater than our ancestor Jacob, are you?

NRSV, NIV, NLT	Are you greater than our father/ancestor Jacob?
NJB	Are you a greater man than our father Jacob?
GNB	You don't claim to be greater than [our ancestor] Jacob, do you?

John 4:29 μήτι οὗτός ἐστιν ὁ Χριστός; Could he be the Messiah?

NRSV	He cannot be the Messiah, can he?
NIV	Could this be the Christ?
REB	Could this be the Messiah?
NLT	Can this be the Messiah?
GNB	Could he be the Messiah?

1 Corinthians 12:29 μὴ πάντες ἀπόστολοι; μὴ πάντες προφῆται;
They are not all apostles, are they? They are not all prophets, are they?

NRSV	Are all apostles? Are all prophets?
NJB	Are all of them apostles? Or all prophets?
REB	Are all apostles? All prophets?
GNB	They are not all apostles or prophets.
NLT	Is everyone an apostle? Of course not. Is everyone a prophet? No.

Lesson 28

ἄνθρωπος ἀγαθός – a good man
οἱ ἅγιοι – the saints

28.1 Nouns and adjectives

Words like

(ὁ)	(ἡ)	(τό)
λόγος	καρδία	ἔργον
ἀνήρ	γυνή	τέκνον
βασιλεύς	πόλις	θέλημα

are called **nouns**.

Gender of nouns:
    Those with ὁ (the) are called **masculine** (m) nouns.
    Those with ἡ (the) are called **feminine** (f) nouns.
    Those with τό (the) are called **neuter** (n) nouns.

Words which can describe nouns, such as:

ἀγαθός – good   μέγας – big   ἀκάθαρτος —impure
κακός – bad   μείζων – bigger   καινός – new
πονηρός – evil   πολύς – much   παλαιός – old
ἀληθής – true   πλείων – more   πᾶς – every

are called **adjectives**.

When an adjective describes a noun it has the same case (37.1), number (singular or plural), and gender as the noun. So:

m	f	n	
ἀγαθὸς λόγος	ἀγαθὴ καρδία	ἀγαθὸν ἔργον	nom s
ἀγαθοῖς λόγοις	ἀγαθαῖς καρδίαις	ἀγαθοῖς ἔργοις	dat p
πάντες βασιλεῖς	πᾶσαι πόλεις	πάντα τέκνα	nom p

28.2 Words
ἅγιος – holy
>τὸ Πνεῦμα τὸ Ἅγιον   or   τὸ Ἅγιον Πνεῦμα – the Holy Spirit
>οἱ ἅγιοι – the holy people, the saints

καινός – new
>ἡ καινὴ διαθήκη – the new covenant
>ἐντολὴν καινὴν δίδωμι ὑμῖν – I give you a new command
>ὅταν αὐτὸ πίνω καινόν – when I drink it new

καλός – good, fine
>ὁ ποιμὴν ὁ καλός – the good shepherd
>καλὸν τὸ ἅλας – salt is good

κακός – bad, evil
>τί κακὸν ἐποίησεν; – what evil did he do?
>ἀποδιδοὺς κακὸν ἀντὶ κακοῦ – returning evil in place of evil

ἄλλος – other
>εἶδεν ἄλλους δύο ἀδελφούς – he saw another pair of brothers
>ὃς ἂν γαμήσῃ ἄλλην – whoever marries another woman
>ἄλλους ἔσωσεν – he saved other people

ὅλος – whole
>ὅλον τὸ σῶμά σου – your whole body
>ἡ οἰκία αὐτοῦ ὅλη – his whole family

πρῶτος – first
>ἦλθεν πρῶτος – he came first

ἔσχατος – last
>ἐν τῇ ἐσχάτῃ ἡμέρᾳ – on the last day

ἴδιος – one's own
>ἦλθεν εἰς τὴν ἰδίαν πόλιν – he went to his own town
>ἤλθομεν εἰς τὴν ἰδίαν πόλιν – we went to our own town
>ἀνέβη εἰς τὸ ὄρος κατ' ἰδίαν – he went up the mountain on his own

28.3
Note carefully the differences between:
(a) ἀγαθὸς ἄνθρωπος
    ἄνθρωπος ἀγαθός   } a good man
(b) ὁ ἄνθρωπος ὁ ἀγαθός
    ὁ ἀγαθὸς ἄνθρωπος   } the good man
(c) ἀγαθὸς ὁ ἄνθρωπος
    ὁ ἄνθρωπος ἀγαθός ἐστιν
    ἀγαθός ἐστιν ὁ ἄνθρωπος } the man is good.

28.4 Translate

1. τό πνεῦμα τὸ ἀκάθαρτον.	The unclean spirit.
2. προφήτης ἅγιος.	A holy prophet.
3. ἅγιος ὁ προφήτης.	The prophet is holy.
4. διδαχὴ καινή.	A new teaching.
5. πᾶσα διδαχὴ καινή.	Every new doctrine.
6. τίς ἡ καινὴ αὕτη διδαχή;	What is this new teaching?
7. εἶπεν τοῖς ἰδίοις μαθηταῖς.	He spoke to his own disciples.
8. πάντες ζητοῦσιν τὴν δόξαν τὴν ἰδίαν.	They all seek their own glory, or All people seek their own glory.
9. καλὸν τὸ ἔργον καὶ οὐ κακόν.	The deed is good and not bad.
10. οὐκ ἦσαν πρῶτοι ἀλλὰ ἔσχατοι.	They were not first but last.
11. οὐχὶ ἦσαν ἔσχατοι;	They were last, weren't they?
12. μήτι εἰσὶν ἔσχατοι;	They aren't last, are they?
13. δύναται ἄλλους διδάσκειν ἀλλὰ τὰ ἴδια τέκνα οὐκ ἐδίδαξεν.	He is able to teach others but he did not teach his own children.
14. ὁ κριτὴς κρίνει τοὺς κακοὺς ἀλλὰ ἀγαθοὺς οὐ κρίνει.	The judge judges the evil people, but he does not judge good people.
15. ἐπίστευσεν αὐτὸς καὶ ἡ οἰκία αὐτοῦ ὅλη.	He himself believed and his whole family.

28.5 καλῶς

καλῶς – well (καλός – good, fine)
ἀληθῶς – truly (ἀληθής – true)
οὕτως – thus, like this, in this way, so (οὗτος – this)

Jn 13:13 καλῶς λέγετε, εἰμὶ γάρ – you say well, for I am

Jn 8:31 ἀληθῶς μαθηταί μού ἐστε – you are truly my disciples

Jn 18:22 οὕτως ἀποκρίνῃ τῷ ἀρχιερεῖ; – do you answer the high priest thus?

Translate:

1. διδασκαλίαν ἀληθῆ διδάσκει.	He is teaching true doctrine.
2. ἀληθῶς ἐδίδασκεν αὐτούς.	He was teaching them truly.
3. αὐτὸς καλῶς ἐδίδαξεν αὐτήν.	He taught her well.

4. ὁ καλὸς καλῶς διδάξει ἡμᾶς.	The good man will teach us well.
5. τί οὗτος οὕτως λαλεῖ; βλασφημεῖ.	Why does he speak in this way? He is blaspheming.

28.6

ὁ, ἡ, τό (the) is called the **definite article**.

Note the way the definite article is used with adjectives:
1. ὁ, ἡ, οἱ, and αἱ usually refer to **people**.

    ὁ and οἱ are masculine or common gender – they refer to men, or to people in general.

    ἡ and αἱ are feminine – they refer to women.

So: οἱ πρῶτοι – the first, those who are first
        οἱ ἅγιοι – the holy ones, the saints (used chiefly of angels and of Christian people).

Compare
    ὁ λέγων – he who says, the person who says
    ἡ λέγουσα – she who says.

2. τό and τά refer to **things**.

    τὸ ἅγιον – that which is holy
    τὰ ἴδια – one's own things, one's own home
    τὰ ἔσχατα – the last things, the final state
    ποιῶ τὰ κακά – I do what is evil, I do evil things.

Compare
    τὰ ὄντα – the things which are (see lesson 19.5)
    ἔδωκεν καὶ τοῖς σὺν αὐτῷ οὖσιν
      – he gave also to those who were with him
      (τοῖς οὖσιν – to the people being).

28.7 Translate

1. μακάριοι οἱ ἔσχατοι οἱ γὰρ ἔσχατοι ἔσονται πρῶτοι.	Blessed are those who are last, for the last shall be first.
2. ἦσαν οἱ πρῶτοι ἔσχατοι καὶ οἱ ἔσχατοι πρῶτοι.	The first were last and the last first.

3. ἀληθῶς λέγεις ὅτι μακάριός ἐστιν ὁ μετὰ τοῦ Ἰησοῦ. | You say truly that he who is with Jesus is blessed.
4. μακάριοι ἦσαν οἱ εἰσελθόντες εἰς τὸ ἱερὸν τὸ ἅγιον· αὐτοὶ γὰρ εἶδον τὴν δόξαν τοῦ θεοῦ. | Blessed were those who had gone into the holy Temple, for they saw the glory of God.
5. οὐχὶ τὰ ἀγαθὰ ποιεῖ ὁ καλός; | The good man does good, doesn't he?
6. ἀγαθοὶ καὶ ἅγιοι οἱ ἔχοντες τὴν ἐντολὴν τὴν καινὴν καὶ τηροῦντες αὐτήν. | Good and holy are those who have the new commandment and keep it.
7. ὁ θεὸς ἐποίησεν τὰ πάντα ἐκ τῶν μὴ ὄντων. | God made all things (everything) out of things that were not in existence.
8. Ἡρῴδης ἔλεγεν ὅτι Ἰωάννης ἐστίν. ἄλλοι δὲ ἔλεγον ὅτι Ἠλείας ἐστίν. ἄλλοι δὲ ἔλεγον Οὐχ οὗτός ἐστιν ὁ Χριστός; | Herod said, 'He is John.' But others said, 'He is Elijah', and others said, 'This man is the Messiah, isn't he?'

28.8

Read Revelation 21:1–3 and John 7:45–52.

(a) Notes on Revelation 21:1–3:

ἡτοιμασμένος – prepared
  (ἑτοιμάζω – I prepare,
   ἕτοιμος – ready)
ἡ νύμφη – the bride
κεκοσμημένος – adorned

ὁ νυμφίος – the bridegroom
ἡ σκηνή – the tent, the tabernacle, the dwelling
ἔσται – he will be
αὐτὸς ὁ θεός – God himself

(b) Notes on John 7:45–52. The Temple police are rebuked by the High priests, who are then challenged by Nicodemus.

v45 οἱ ὑπηρέται – The (Temple) police : ὑπηρέτης – 'assistant, servant' has a wide range of meanings.   ἄγω – I bring, I go.
v46 οὐδέποτε – never v47 πεπλάνησθε – you have been led astray.   ἄρχων – ruler, member of the Sanhedrin.
v49 ἐπάρατος – cursed, under God's curse.
v50 τὸ πρότερον – previously
v51 κρίνει τὸν ἄνθρωπον – judges **a** man: the Greek uses τὸν (the) which marks something as specific, since in any particular case a particular person is involved. Such use of the article is common in Hebrew.

v52 ἐραύνω – I search. Notice in v52 the contempt expressed for Galilee. See also 1:46, 7:41. In 19:19 Ἰησοῦς ὁ Ναζωραῖος ὁ βασιλεὺς τῶν Ἰουδαίων – 'Jesus of Nazareth, the king of the Judeans', the mention of his Galilean origin was perhaps an added reason for the anger of the High Priests.

28.9 Progress test 14

Which translation is correct?
1. εἶπεν φωνῇ μεγάλῃ, Καλὸν τὸ ἅλας.
   (a) They said in a great voice that the salt was good.
   (b) He said in a loud voice, 'This salt is bad.'
   (c) He said in a loud voice, 'Salt is good.'
2. ἔτι αὐτῶν ταῦτα λεγόντων ἀπῆλθεν ἀπὸ τοῦ ἱεροῦ.
   (a) When they had said these things he went out of the Temple.
   (b) While he was still saying these things he went away from the Temple.
   (c) While they were still saying these things he went away from the Temple.
3. καταβάντος αὐτοῦ ἀπὸ τοῦ ὄρους, ἠρώτησαν αὐτὸν λέγοντες, Μὴ σὺ μείζων εἶ τοῦ Ἰακώβ;
   (a) When he had come down from the mountain they asked him this question, 'You are not greater than Jacob, are you?'
   (b) While he was coming down from the mountain she asked him, 'You are greater than Jacob, aren't you?'
   (c) When he had gone up the mountain they spoke to him. 'Are you greater than Jacob?' they asked.
4. αὗταί εἰσιν αἱ λέγουσαι ὅτι Οἱ πρῶτοι ἔσονται ἔσχατοι καὶ οἱ ἔσχατοι πρῶτοι.
   (a) She was the person who said that the first would be last and the last first.
   (b) These are the women who keep saying, 'The first will be last and the last will be first.'
   (c) These are the women who said, 'The last will be first and the first last.'

5. Which of the following words are present indicative?
   (a) λέγοντες, (b) λέγει, (c) γράφομεν, (d) γράψας, (e) γράφεις, (f) καταβαίνων, (g) καταβάς, (h) καταβαίνετε.
6. Which of the words in question 5 are participles?

Check your answers in Key to Progress Tests on page 333.

28.10

Revise lessons 21 and 22. For a summary of important adjectival forms see Reference Grammar R5 (pp339–340).

Lessons 29–34 form a group. Study them as a unit. When you have completed the group the important ideas in it will have begun to be established in your mind.

Lesson 29

γίνομαι – I become, I happen γιν ⁓⁓⁓⁓
γενόμενος – having become γεν ⊣

29.1

γίνομαι – I become, I come into being, I am made, I happen
γιν is the stem which shows continuing or repeated action
γεν is the stem which shows completed or single action

So:
γιν ⁓⁓⁓⁓	γεν ⊣
γινόμενος – becoming	γενόμενος – having become
γίνεται – it happens	ἐγένετο – it happened
γίνεσθαι – to be happening	γενέσθαι – to happen.

Note the endings of the present indicative of
γίνομαι – I happen, I become

Singular	*Plural*
γίνομαι – I become	γινόμεθα – **we** become
γίνῃ – **you** become	γίνεσθε – **you** (p) become
γίνεται – **he** becomes	γίνονται – **they** become.

ἔσομαι (I will be), and λήμψομαι – I will take, I will receive, have the same endings. They are future indicative.

The endings of **δύναμαι** – I can, I am able, are similar:

Singular	*Plural*
δύναμαι – I can	δυνάμεθα – we can
δύνασαι – you can	δύνασθε – you (p) can
δύναται – he can	δύνανται – they can.

29.2 Words

ἔρχομαι – I go
    ἐλεύσομαι – I will go
    ἦλθον – I went
δύναμαι – I am able to
    δυνήσομαι – I will be able
    ἐδυνάμην *or* ἠδυνάμην – I could

ἄρχομαι – I begin
    ἠρξάμην – I began
ἀποκρίνομαι – I answer, I respond (to a statement, question, or situation)
    ἀποκριθήσομαι – I will answer
    ἀπεκρίθην – I answered
πορεύομαι – I travel, I go
    ἐπορευόμην – I was going
    ἐπορεύθην – I went
προσεύχομαι – I pray
    προσηυχόμην – I was praying
    προσηυξάμην – I prayed
ἅπτομαι – I touch
    ἡψάμην – I touched
    ἥψατο τῶν ὀφθαλμῶν αὐτῆς – he touched her eyes
πάλιν – again

29.3 Translate

1. δυνάμεθα τοῦτο ποιεῖν.	We can do this.
2. οὐ δυνάμεθα ταῦτα ποιεῖν;	We can do these things, can't we?
3. ἔρχεσθε πάλιν εἰς τὴν πόλιν.	You go into the town again.
4. ἐὰν θέλῃς, δύνασαι Σατανᾶν ἐκβάλλειν.	If you want to, you can cast out Satan.
5. πῶς δύναμαι Σατανᾶν ἐκβαλεῖν;	How am I able to cast out Satan?
6. πόθεν ἔρχονται καὶ ποῦ πορεύονται;	Where are they coming from and where are they going?
7. οὐκ οἴδαμεν πόθεν ἔρχῃ οὐδὲ ποῦ μένεις.	We do not know where you come from nor where you are staying.
8. ἡμεῖς οὐκ ἁπτόμεθα αὐτοῦ καὶ αὐτὸς οὐκ ἥψατο αὐτῆς.	We are not touching him and he did not touch her.
9. καὶ ἐγένετο ἐν ἐκείναις ταῖς ἡμέραις ἦλθεν Ἰωάννης βαπτίζων ἐν τῇ ἐρήμῳ. καὶ ἐβάπτισεν τὸν Ἰησοῦν καὶ φωνὴ ἐγένετο ἐκ τῶν οὐρανῶν λέγουσα, Σὺ εἶ ὁ υἱός μου.	It happened in those days that John came baptizing in the desert. He baptized Jesus and there was a voice from heaven saying, 'You are my Son.'

29.4 Infinitives

Continued or repeated action ⋯	Single action •
ἔρχεσθαι – to be going, to go	ἐλθεῖν – to go
γίνεσθαι – to happen, to be	γενέσθαι – to happen, to be
προσεύχεσθαι – to be praying, to pray	προσεύξασθαι – to pray
ἀποκρίνεσθαι – to be answering	ἀποκριθῆναι – to answer

(These are present infinitive)   (These are aorist infinitive)

29.5 Translate

1. οὐ δύνανται προσεύξασθαι.	They are not able to pray.
2. ἤρξαντο προσεύχεσθαι.	They began to pray.
3. πῶς δύναται τοῦτο γενέσθαι;	How can this happen?
4. εἰσῆλθον εἰς τὸ ἱερὸν τὸ ἅγιον προσεύξασθαι καὶ ἠρξάμην προσεύχεσθαι.	I went into the holy Temple to pray and I began to pray.
5. οὐκ ἐδύναντο ἀποκριθῆναι.	They were not able to answer.
6. μὴ δύνασθε ἀποκριθῆναι;	You can't answer, can you?
7. ἔρχεται πάλιν πρὸς αὐτὸν ἡ γυνὴ καὶ ζητεῖ αὐτοῦ ἅψασθαι.	The woman comes to him again and seeks to touch him.
8. ἀρχόμεθα πάλιν ταῦτα γράφειν.	We are beginning again to write these things.

29.6 Past tenses

Continued or repeated action in past time ⋯ |	Completed or single action in past time ⌐|
ἠρχόμην – I was coming	ἦλθον – I came
ἐπορεύου – you were travelling	ἐπορεύθης – you traveled
προσηύχετο – he was praying	προσηύξατο – he prayed
ἥπτοντο – they were touching	ἥψαντο – they touched
ἐγίνετο – it was, it came	ἐγένετο – it happened

(These are imperfect indicative)   (These are aorist indicative)

Lesson 29

29.7

Here are the imperfect and aorist indicative endings of προσεύχομαι (I pray), and πορεύομαι (I travel, I go):

	I	You	He	We	You (p)	They
Imperfect						
προσηυχ- } ἐπορευ-	-όμην	-ου	-ετο	-όμεθα	-εσθε	-οντο
Aorist						
προσηυξ-	-άμην	-ω	-ατο	-άμεθα	-ασθε	-αντο
ἐπορευθ-	-ην	-ης	-η	-ημεν	-ητε	-ησαν

Translate:

1. ἐπορεύοντο πρὸς αὐτὸν ἀπὸ πασῶν τῶν πολέων.	They were going to him from all the towns.
2. ἐξελθόντες ἐπορεύθησαν πάλιν εἰς τὰς ἄλλας πόλεις.	When they had gone out they went again to the other towns.
3. εἰσελθὼν εἰς τὸ ἱερὸν προσηύχετο.	He went into the Temple and prayed (began to pray).
4. εἰσελθὼν προσηύξατο.	He went in and prayed.
5. ἤρχοντο πρὸς αὐτὴν καὶ ἥπτοντο αὐτῆς.	They were coming to her and touching her, *or* People kept coming to her and touching her.
6. ἦλθον πρὸς αὐτὸν καὶ ἥψαντο αὐτοῦ.	They came to him and touched him.
7. ταῦτα ἐν Βηθανίᾳ ἐγένετο.	These things took place in Bethany.
8. ἐπορεύθης εἰς τὴν Γαλιλαίαν.	You travelled into Galilee.
9. ἐγὼ προσηυχόμην ἀλλὰ σὺ οὐ προσηύξω.	I was praying but you did not pray.

29.8 Participles

Continuing or repeated action ·····	Completed or single action ┤
ἐρχόμενος – coming, going	ἐλθών – having come, having gone
γινόμενος – happening	γενόμενος – having happened
προσευχόμενος – praying	προσευξάμενος – having prayed
πορευόμενος – journeying	πορευθείς – having journeyed
ἀρχόμενος – beginning	ἀρξάμενος – having begun
(These are present participles)	(These are aorist participles)

Notice that we seldom translate a Greek participle simply by an English participle. For example:

ὁ ἄνθρωπος ὁ ἐρχόμενος
the man **who is coming**

πορευομένων δὲ αὐτῶν, ἀπήγγειλάν τινες τοῖς ἀρχιερεῦσιν ἅπαντα τὰ γενόμενα
While they were on their way, some people announced to the High Priests all the things that had happened.

ἐκείνη πορευθεῖσα ἀπήγγειλεν τοῖς μετ' αὐτοῦ γενομένοις
She went and told the news **to those who had been** with him.

Note that we must translate aorist participles into English in different ways, depending on whether:
    (a) the action is completed before the action of the main verb
or (b) the action is completed in the action of the main verb.

So: (a) προσευξάμενος ἐξῆλθεν
    When he had prayed he went out.
  (b) προσευξάμενος εἶπεν, Σὺ Κύριε ἀγαθὸς εἶ
    In his prayer he said, 'Lord, you are good'
or He prayed, 'You, Lord, are good.'

Translate:

1. προσευξάμενοι ἀπήλθομεν.	When we had prayed we went away.
2. προσευξάμενοι εἴπομεν, Ἡμεῖς ἁμαρτάνομεν ἀλλὰ σὺ ἀγαπᾷς ἡμᾶς καὶ ἐσόμεθα μετά σου ἐν τῇ δόξῃ τῆς βασιλείας σου.	In our prayer we said, 'We are sinning but you love us and we shall be with you in the glory of your kingdom.'
3. πορευθέντες ἀπὸ τῆς πόλεως εἶπον αὐτῷ, Σὺ ἀγαθὸς εἶ τοῖς μετά σου γινομένοις. ὁ δὲ ἀποκριθεὶς εἶπεν, Τί με καλεῖτε ἀγαθόν;	When they had gone away from the town they said to him, 'You are good to those who are with you.' But he replied, 'Why do you call me good?'
4. πῶς δύναται ταῦτα γενέσθαι;	How can these things happen?
5. ἤκουσεν Ἡρώδης τὰ γινόμενα πάντα.	Herod heard all the things that were happening.
6. ἤκουσεν Ἡρώδης τὰ γενόμενα πάντα.	Herod heard all the things that had happened.

29.9

Read carefully:

Ἦλθεν πάλιν εἰς τὸ ἱερὸν καὶ προσηύχετο. καὶ ἐγένετο ἔτι αὐτοῦ προσευχομένου ἦλθον πρὸς αὐτὸν οἱ ἀρχιερεῖς καὶ εἶπαν αὐτῷ, Διὰ τί ἡμεῖς οὐ δυνάμεθα ταῦτα τὰ ἔργα ποιῆσαι ἃ σὺ δύνασαι ποιεῖν; αὐτὸς δὲ οὐκ ἀπεκρίθη αὐτοῖς. πάλιν οὖν ἠρώτησαν αὐτὸν λέγοντες, Πόθεν ἦλθες καὶ ποῦ ἐλεύσῃ; ὁ δὲ ἀποκριθεὶς εἶπεν αὐτοῖς, Ὑμεῖς οὐκ οἴδατε, ἀλλὰ ὁ πιστεύων ἐν ἐμοὶ ἐκεῖνος οἶδεν.

29.10

(a) Forms like ἁγιασθήτω 'may it be treated as holy' are discussed in lesson 40, section 4.

(b) Read: Matthew 6:9–13 'So pray like this.'
  v9 Πάτερ – the form used when speaking to a father (see 37.2)
  v10 ἁγιασθήτω – may it be treated as holy, may it be honoured
    ἐλθέτω – let it come (the commoner form is ἐλθάτω)
    ἡ βασιλεία – the kingly rule (a rule that brings justice, help and
        salvation to people)
  In vv9–10 note the three balanced petitions. The phrase ὡς ἐν οὐρανῷ καὶ ἐπὶ γῆς refers to the group of three, and forms a natural closure to the first section of the prayer.
  v11 ἐπιούσιος – the meaning is uncertain! Suggestions: (a) for the coming day, (b) daily, (c) basic, ordinary. We might translate: 'Give us today the food we need'.
  v12 ἄφες – forgive!   (τὸ) ὀφείλημα – what is owed, debt; wrong, sin.
    ὀφειλέτης – debtor, offender.
  v13 μὴ εἰσενέγκῃς – do not carry [us] along into.
    πειρασμός – testing, temptation   ῥῦσαι – rescue, save
    ἀπὸ τοῦ πονηροῦ – from evil, or, from the evil one.

Lesson 30

ποιῆσαι – to do • ἐκβαλεῖν – to throw out •

30.1
Compare the words in column A with those in column B:

1.   A ⁞⁞⁞⁞   B •

ποιέω – I do	ποιεῖν	ποιῆσαι	to do
σώζω – I save	σώζειν	σῶσαι	to save
πιστεύω – I believe	πιστεύειν	πιστεῦσαι	to believe
ἀγαπάω – I love	ἀγαπᾶν	ἀγαπῆσαι	to love
ζάω – I live	ζῆν		to live
πέμπω – I send	πέμπειν	πέμψαι	to send
διδάσκω – I teach	διδάσκειν	διδάξαι	to teach
προσεύχομαι – I pray	προσεύχεσθαι	προσεύξασθαι	to pray

2.

ἐκβάλλω – I throw out	ἐκβάλλειν	ἐκβαλεῖν	to throw out
πάσχω – I suffer	πάσχειν	παθεῖν	to suffer
λαμβάνω – I take	λαμβάνειν	λαβεῖν	to take
αἴρω – I pick up	αἴρειν	ἆραι	to pick up
καταβαίνω – I go down	καταβαίνειν	καταβῆναι	to go down
δίδωμι – I give	διδόναι	δοῦναι	to give

3.

λέγω – I say	λέγειν	εἰπεῖν	to say
ἐσθίω – I eat	ἐσθίειν	φαγεῖν	to eat
ἔρχομαι – I go	ἔρχεσθαι	ἐλθεῖν	to go
φέρω – I bring	φέρειν	ἐνέγκαι	to bring
ὁράω – I see	ὁρᾶν	ἰδεῖν	to see

4.

εἰμί – I am	εἶναι		to be

Note in column B three marks of single action, or of action without reference to its continuance:

    1. σ after the stem   *or* 2. a shorter stem   *or* 3. a different stem

All the forms in columns A and B are called **infinitive**.

Those in column A are called **present infinitive** because they indicate continued or repeated action.

Those in column B are called **aorist infinitive** because they indicate single action, or an action considered in itself without reference to its continuance.

In English usage we do not usually draw so much attention to the type of action. So we normally translate both ποιεῖν ⁓ and ποιῆσαι • as 'to do'. However, when the context seems to demand emphasis on the continuing nature of the action we may translate ποιειν as 'to be doing' or 'to keep doing'.

30.2 Translate

1. θέλω αὐτοὺς πέμψαι πρός σε.	I want to send them to you.
2. ἤρχοντο σώζειν ἡμᾶς ἀπὸ τῶν ἁμαρτίων ἡμῶν.	They used to come to save us from our sins.
3. οὐκ ἤλθομεν σῶσαι τοὺς ἁγίους ἀλλὰ τοὺς πονηρούς.	We did not come to save the holy people but the evil people.
4. οὐκ ἦλθεν καλέσαι ἀγαθοὺς ἀλλὰ κακούς.	He did not come to call good people but bad people.
5. ἤρξαντο φέρειν τὰ τέκνα πρὸς τὸν Ἰησοῦν.	They began to carry the children to Jesus.
6. ἤρξαντο φέρειν αὐτοὺς ποῦ ἤκουον ὅτι Ἰησοῦς ἐστιν.	They began to carry them where they heard that Jesus was.
7. οὐκ ἐδύναντο αὐτὸν ἐνέγκαι πρὸς τὸν σωτῆρα.	They were not able to carry him to the Saviour.
8. ἤρξατο προσεύχεσθαι.	He began to pray.
9. ἀγαπῶμεν τοὺς ἀδελφούς, τὸ γὰρ ἀγαπᾶν τοὺς ἀδελφοὺς καλόν ἐστιν καὶ οὐ κακόν.	Let us love the brothers, for to love the brothers is good and not bad.

30.3 Words

κατά – according to
    κατὰ τὸν νόμον – according to the Law
    κατ' ἰδίαν – privately, on one's own
    καθ' ἡμέραν – daily
καθώς – according as, as, just as
οὕτως – thus, so
παρά – (1) beside, along by
    παρὰ τὴν θάλασσαν – by the sea, along the shore
παρά – (2) contrary to
    παρὰ τὸν νόμον – against the Law
ὅτι – that, because
πάσχω – I suffer
    πάσχειν – to be suffering
    παθεῖν – to suffer
δέω – I bind
    δεῖ – it is binding, it is necessary
ἔξεστιν – it is lawful, it is permitted (ἐξουσία – authority)
    πάντα ἔξεστιν – everything is lawful,
                  all kinds of things are permitted
πολύς – much (πολύς, πολλή, πολύ)
    πολλοί – many people
    πολύ – much
    πολλά – many things, much
    πολλὰ παθεῖν – to suffer many things, to suffer much
τὸ λέγειν – speaking, speech (lit. 'the to speak')
    καλὸν τὸ λέγειν – speaking is good
    ἐν τῷ λέγειν αὐτόν – while he is (was) speaking
    διὰ τὸ ἔχειν αὐτούς – because they have (had)
    διὰ τὸ μὴ ἔχειν – because of not having
    ἐμοὶ τὸ ζῆν Χριστός – for me to live is Christ
οἱ υἱοὶ Ἰσραήλ – the sons of Israel, the people of Israel

30.4 Translate

1. δεῖ αὐτοὺς πολλὰ παθεῖν. | It is necessary for them to suffer much.

2. δεῖ ὑμᾶς πολλὰ παθεῖν καθὼς ὁ Κύριος ὑμῶν ἔπαθεν. | You are bound to suffer greatly just as your Lord suffered.

3. οὐκ ἔξεστίν σοι τούτους τοὺς ἄρτους φαγεῖν· παρὰ τὸν νόμον ἐστὶν ὅτι ἅγιοί εἰσιν. | It is not lawful for you to eat these loaves. It is against the Law because they are holy.

4. ἔξεστιν αὐτοῖς φαγεῖν τοὺς ἄρτους ὅτι ἱερεῖς εἰσιν. | They are permitted to eat the loaves because they are priests.

5. οὐκ ἔξεστίν μοι τοῦτο ποιῆσαι ὅτι τὸ τοῦτο ποιεῖν παρὰ νόμον ἐστίν. | It is not permissible for me to do this because doing this is against the Law (unlawful).

6. δεῖ ταῦτα γενέσθαι καθὼς εἶπον οἱ προφῆται. | These things are bound to happen as the prophets said.

7. παραπορευομένων αὐτῶν παρὰ τὴν θάλασσαν ἦλθεν πρὸς αὐτὸν λεπρός. | As they were going along beside the sea a leper came to him.

8. καθὼς Μωϋσῆς ἐδίδαξεν πολλοὺς τῶν υἱῶν Ἰσραὴλ οὕτως δεῖ τὸν υἱὸν τοῦ ἀνθρώπου διδάξαι μαθητὰς πολλούς. | As Moses taught many of the people of Israel, so it is necessary for the Son of Man to teach many disciples.

9. καὶ ἐν τῷ διδάσκειν αὐτὸν παρὰ τὴν θάλασσαν πολλοὶ ἐπίστευσαν αὐτῷ. | As he was teaching beside the lake many people believed in him.

10. διὰ τὸ μὴ προσεύξασθαι οὐ λαμβάνουσιν, ἀλλὰ οἱ προσευχόμενοι κατὰ τὸ θέλημα τοῦ θεοῦ οὗτοι λήμψονται. | Because of not praying people do not receive, but those who pray according to the will of God, they will receive.

11. καὶ ἔτι αὐτῶν ὄντων ἐν τῇ πόλει, πάλιν εἶπεν αὐτοῖς κατ' ἰδίαν ὅτι Οἱ θέλοντες πρῶτοι εἶναι ἔσονται ἔσχατοι καὶ πολλοί εἰσιν ἔσχατοι οἳ ἔσονται πρῶτοι. | While they were still in the city, he said to them again privately, 'Those who want to be first shall be last, and many are last who shall be first.'

30.5

(a) Read John 1:11–13

v11 εἰς τὰ ἴδια – to his own place.   οἱ ἴδιοι – his own people.
παραλαμβάνω – I take along, I receive, I accept.

v12 ὅσοι – as many as, all who.   γενέσθαι – to become, to be.
τὸ ὄνομα – the name (which indicates the person,
and the person's nature and honour)

v13 αἷμα – blood.   ἡ σάρξ – the flesh, the person, sexual desire.
γεννάω – I beget, I am the father of (in passive: I am born).

Note that in John 1:3–18 there are two major chiastic structures:

vv3–10 and vv14–18 (see lesson 47). At the centre, between them, are these verses. At the centre of these verses, in verse 12, we find the phrase: τοῖς πιστεύουσιν εἰς τὸ ὄνομα αὐτοῦ. It is typical of Hebrew poetic style to put the most important point at the centre. This point is recalled in 20:31 (the closure of the main part of the Gospel) in the words ἵνα πιστεύοντες ζωὴν ἔχητε ἐν τῷ ὀνόματι αὐτοῦ – 'so that believing you may have life through his name.'

(b) Read John 20:30–31

v30 πολλά – many   (πολύς – much).   ἄλλα – other.
σημεῖα – signs, miracles (σημεῖον, when it refers to the miracles done by Jesus, implies that they were actions that had meaning).
γεγραμμένος – written.

v31 γέγραπται – have been written (a singular verb because the subject ταῦτα 'these things' is neuter plural – see 12.1)

30.6

Revise lessons 23 and 24.

Lesson 31

βαπτίζομαι – I am being baptized ‾‾‾‾
ἐβαπτιζόμην – I was being baptized ‾‾‾‾ |

31.1

βαπτίζομαι – I am being baptized, I am baptized
παραδίδομαι – I am being betrayed, I am handed over

The endings of βαπτίζομαι are the same as those of γίνομαι (29.1):

	Singular	Plural
1st person	–ομαι – I	–ομεθα – we
2nd person	–η – you	–εσθε – you
3rd person	–εται – he, she, it	–ονται – they

So: βαπτιζόμεθα – we are being baptized
παραδίδονται – they are being betrayed, they are being handed over.

31.2

βαπτίζομαι ὑπὸ τοῦ ἀποστόλου – I am being baptized **by the apostle**
κρινόμεθα ὑφ' ὑμῶν – we are being judged **by you**

When the action of the verb is done by a person, ὑπό = by.
Note: ὑπό becomes ὑπ' before a vowel, ὑφ' before ' (h).

Translate:

1. βαπτίζονται ὑπὸ Ἰωάννου.	They are being baptized by John.
2. κρίνεται ὑπὸ τοῦ Κυρίου.	He is being judged by the Lord.
3. Ἰησοῦ, παραδίδῃ ὑπὸ τοῦ Ἰούδα.	Jesus, you are being betrayed by Judas.
4. βαπτίζεται ὑπ' αὐτοῦ ἡ γυνή.	The woman is being baptized by him.
5. ἀγαπώμεθα ὑπὸ τοῦ θεοῦ.	We are loved by God.
6. βαπτίζεσθε πάντες ὑπὸ Ἰωάννου τοῦ βαπτιστοῦ.	You are all being baptized by John the Baptist.
7. οὐ βαπτίζομαι ὑφ' ὑμῶν.	I am not being baptized by you.
8. ἔρχονται πρὸς Ἰωάννην ἵνα βαπτίζωνται ὑπ' αὐτοῦ.	They come to John so that they may be baptized by him.

31.3

βαπτίζομαι ὕδατι or βαπτίζομαι ἐν ὕδατι – I am baptized **with water**

When the action of the verb is carried out by means of a thing, 'by' or 'with' is shown:

(a) by the form, or case, of the word – the dative case

So: βαπτίζεται ὕδατι – he is baptized **with water**

τῇ ἀληθείᾳ σώζεσθε – you are being saved **by the truth**

(b) by ἐν (followed by a word in the dative case)

So: βαπτίζομαι ἐν ὕδατι – I am being baptized **with water**

ἀποκτείνεται ἐν μαχαίρῃ – he is being killed **with a sword**.

There seems to be a similar use of ἐν in 2 Corinthians 5:19:

...ὅτι θεὸς ἦν ἐν Χριστῷ κόσμον καταλλάσσων ἑαυτῷ

...that God was **by means of Christ** (*or* **through Christ**) reconciling the world to himself.

31.4 Words

τις – someone, anyone, a
  τινές – some people, some
τι – something, anything
εἷς – one
  Like ὁ, ἡ, τό (12.7), εἷς has three forms: εἷς, μία, ἕν.
So: εἷς ἀνὴρ ἀγαπᾷ μίαν γυναῖκα – one man loves one woman
  μία γυνὴ ἀγαπᾷ ἕνα ἄνδρα – one woman loves one man
οὐδείς and μηδείς – no one, nobody
οὐδέν and μηδέν – nothing
δύο – two, δέκα – ten, δώδεκα – twelve, τρεῖς – three, τριάκοντα – thirty,
  τριακόσιοι – three hundred
τὸ ὄνομα – the name
  τοῦ ὀνόματος – of the name
τὸ ὕδωρ – the water
  τοῦ ὕδατος – of the water
τὸ ὄρος – the mountain
ἄλαλος – dumb (λαλέω – I speak)
ἡ πίστις – the faith, the trust
  διὰ πίστεως – through faith
ἡ χάρις – the grace: grace, graciousness, favour
  When used with reference to God, χάρις indicates his attitude of loving favour and his consequent loving action.
παραδίδωμι – I hand on, I hand over
  παραδίδωμι τὴν παράδοσιν – I hand on the tradition

31.5 Translate

1. ἔρχεταί τις πρὸς τὸ ὕδωρ.	Someone is coming to the water.
2. βαπτίζει τινὰ ὕδατι.	He baptizes someone with water.
3. βαπτίζεται ἐν ὕδατι ὑπό τινος.	He is baptized with water by someone.
4. ἔρχεται γυνή τις πρὸς τὸ ὄρος.	A woman is coming towards the mountain.
5. ἐκ Ναζαρὲτ δύναταί τι ἀγαθὸν ἐλθεῖν;	Is anything good able to come from Nazareth?
6. ἐκ τῆς Γαλιλαίας δύναταί τι ἀγαθὸν εἶναι;	Can anything good be from Galilee?
7. ἐάν τις φάγῃ ἐκ τούτου τοῦ ἄρτου ζήσει εἰς τὸν αἰῶνα.	If anyone eats from this loaf he will live for ever.
8. ἔρχεται εἷς τῶν μαθητῶν καὶ βαπτίζεται ὕδατι ὑπὸ Ἰωάννου ἐν τῷ ὀνόματι τοῦ θεοῦ.	One of the disciples comes and is baptized with water by John in the name of God.
9. τῇ χάριτι σωζόμεθα διὰ πίστεως, καὶ οὐδεὶς σώζεται τοῖς ἔργοις αὐτοῦ.	We are being saved by grace through faith and no one is being saved by the deeds he does.
10. καταβαινόντων τῶν δώδεκα ἐκ τοῦ ὄρους, αὐτὸς ἀνέβη εἰς τὸ ὄρος κατ' ἰδίαν.	While the twelve were coming down from the mountain, he went up the mountain on his own.
11. ἄλαλός ἐστιν καὶ οὐ δύναται μηδὲν μηδενὶ λέγειν περὶ τῆς πίστεως αὐτοῦ.	He is dumb and is not able to say anything to anyone about his faith.

31.6 ἐβαπτιζόμην – I was being baptized ⁝ I

Here are the endings of ἐβαπτιζόμην. Note the ε in front of the stem which indicates past time:

	Singular	Plural
1st person	-ομην – I	-ομεθα – we
2nd person	-ου – you	-εσθε – you (p)
3rd person	-ετο – he, she, it	-οντο – they.

Translate:

1. ἐξεπορεύοντο πρὸς αὐτὸν οἱ Ἱεροσολυμῖται πάντες καὶ πολλοὶ ἐβαπτίζοντο ὑπ' αὐτοῦ. | All the people of Jerusalem were going out to him and many were baptized by him.
2. ἔρχονται οἱ δώδεκα καὶ λέγουσιν ὅτι Τρεῖς ἔχομεν ἄρτους καὶ τριάκοντα ἰχθύας. | The twelve come and say, 'We have three loaves and thirty fishes.'
3. οἱ δύο ἀπόστολοι ἐπέμποντο ὑπὸ τοῦ Κυρίου καὶ ἐποίουν τὰ ἔργα αὐτοῦ. | The two apostles were being sent by the Lord and they were doing his works.
4. οὐδεὶς σώζεται τοῖς ἰδίοις ἔργοις ἀλλὰ ἐσωζόμεθα τῇ χάριτι τοῦ θεοῦ. | No one is being saved by his own deeds but we were being saved by the grace of God.

31.7

βαπτίζεσθαι – to be baptized
βαπτιζόμενος – being baptized

So: ἐν τῷ βαπτίζεσθαι αὐτόν... – while he was being baptized...

βαπτιζομένων αὐτῶν, ἦλθεν γραμματεύς τις
As they were being baptized a scribe came

Ἰησοῦς ὁ λεγόμενος Χριστός
Jesus, the man called the Messiah.

Translate:

1. οὐκ ἤλθομεν βαπτίζεσθαι ἀλλὰ βαπτίζειν. | We did not come to be baptized but to baptize.
2. εἶδεν αὐτοὺς βαπτιζομένους. | He saw them being baptized.
3. τρεῖς ἀπόστολοι ἀποστέλλονται ὑπὸ τοῦ Κυρίου. | Three apostles are being sent by the Lord.
4. οἱ προφῆται φερόμενοι ὑπὸ Πνεύματος Ἁγίου ἐλάλησαν. | The prophets spoke as they were carried along (*or* being carried along) by the Holy Spirit.
5. οἱ ἅγιοι δύνανται ὑπὸ τοῦ Πνεύματος τοῦ Ἁγίου φέρεσθαι. | The saints are able to be carried along by the Holy Spirit.

6. εἰσῆλθεν εἰς ἄνθρωπος εἰς τὴν οἰκίαν καὶ ἔμεινεν ἐν τῇ οἰκίᾳ ἡμέρας τριάκοντα καὶ μίαν. | One man went into the house and he stayed in the house for thirty-one days.

31.8 Read Mark 11:9-11

v9 προάγω – I go in front.   ἔκραζον – they shouted, they kept calling out. Ὡσαννά – a word expressing hope and exultation, from Hebrew *hoshia'na* – please save (us) ! See Psalm 118:25.

v10 ὕψιστος – most high: ἐν τοῖς ὑψίστοις – in the highest (places) – used with reference to heaven (as God's dwelling place).

v11 περιβλέπομαι – I look round at.   ὀψία, *or* ὀψέ – late.
ἤδη – already

31.9 Grammatical terms for verbal forms

This section and 33.12 are for reference. Do not expect to learn them all at once. You will not need to know grammatical terms in order to read and translate the New Testament. You may need to know them when you are studying commentaries which refer to the Greek text. Several forms are included here for the purpose of reference although you have not learned them yet. Do not spend time studying them now. You will come to them in later lessons.

A. Mood

1. Verbal forms which make a definite statement or question are called **indicative**.

So: λέγει – he says
ἐβλήθησαν – they were thrown
ἦν – he was
ἄγομεν ; – are we going?

are all in the **indicative** mood.

2. Verbal forms which make an indefinite statement or question are called **subjunctive**.

So: (ἐὰν) λέγῃ – (if) he says
(ἐὰν) εἴπῃ – (if) he should say
ἄγωμεν – let us go
ἄγωμεν ; – should we go?

are all in the **subjunctive** mood.
(Other uses of the subjunctive will be studied in later lessons.)

3. Verbal forms which express a direct command are called *imperative*.
   So: ποίησον – do!
   ἔξελθε – go out!
   δός – give!
   βάλλε – keep throwing!
   are all in the **imperative** mood. (See lessons 40 and 41.)

4. Verbal forms which express 'to…' are called **infinitive**.
   So: ποιεῖν – to be doing
   ποιῆσαι – to do
   βαπτίζεσθαι – to be being baptized
   βαπτισθῆναι – to be baptized
   are all in the **infinitive** mood.

5. A verbal form that can describe a noun is called a **participle**.
   So: ποιῶν – doing
   ποιήσας – having done
   ἐρχόμενος – coming
   βαπτισθείς – having been baptized
   are all **participles**.

B. Tense

1. Forms which express continuing or repeated action are called **present** ⁃⁃⁃
   So: ποιεῖ – he does
   ποιῶμεν – let us do
   ποιεῖν – to do
   ποιῶν – doing
   are all **present**.

2. Forms which express continuing or repeated action in past time are called **imperfect** ⁃⁃⁃ |
   So: ἐποίει – he was doing
   ἤρχετο – he was coming
   ἐβαπτίζετο – he was being baptized
   are all **imperfect**.

LESSON 31

3. Forms which express completed or single action are called **aorist** ⊣
    So: ἐποίησεν – he did
      βάλωμεν; – should we throw?
      φαγών – having eaten
      βαπτισθῆναι – to be baptized
    are all **aorist**.

4. Forms which express action in future time are called **future**
    So: ποιήσομεν – we shall do
      ἐλεύσονται – they will come
      ἔσεσθαι – to be
    are all **future**.

5. Forms which express action in the past which has a continuing result are called **perfect** ⊤ |→
    So: πεποίηκα – I have done
      γέγραπται – it has been written
      γέγραφθαι – to have been written
      γεγραμμένος – having been written
      δέδωκεν – he has given
    are all **perfect**. (See lesson 33.)

6. Forms which express action in the past which had a continuing result which is also in the past are called **pluperfect** ⊤ |→|
    So: πεπιστεύκειν – I had trusted
      δεδώκει – he had given
    are **pluperfect**. (See lesson 49.7.)

C. Voice

1. Forms which normally express action done by the subject (usually to someone or something else) are called **active**.
    So: βάλλω – I throw
      ἔβαλον – I threw
      βάλλων – throwing
      βάλλειν – to throw
      βάλλε – throw!
      νίπτω – I wash (someone or something else)
    are all **active**.

2. Forms which normally express action done to the subject by someone or something else are called **passive**.
   So: βάλλομαι – I am being thrown
   ἐβλήθην – I was thrown
   βληθῆναι – to be thrown
   βληθείς – having been thrown
   are all **passive**.

3. Forms which normally express action done by the subject and involving the subject rather than anyone else are called **middle**.
   (See lesson 45.1–4.)
   So: ἔρχομαι – I come
   πορεύεσθαι – to travel
   προσηυξάμην – I prayed
   προσεύξασθαι – to pray
   προσευχόμενος – praying
   προσευξάμενος – having prayed, praying
   νίπτομαι – I wash (myself, or part of myself)
   are all **middle**.

Putting together A, B, and C we can partly describe verbal forms as follows:

λέγει – he says	present indicative active
εἴπωμεν – let us say	aorist subjunctive active
ἔρχεσθαι – to be coming	present infinitive middle
βληθῆναι – to be thrown	aorist infinitive passive
γράψας – having written	aorist participle active
ἐρχόμενος – coming	present participle middle
γεγραμμένος – written, having been written	perfect participle passive

31.10 Progress test 15

1. Which of the following infinitives indicate continuing or repeated action?

(a) διδάξαι   (e) ἀγαπᾶν   (h) βάλλειν
(b) διδάσκειν   (f) ζῆν   (i) καταβαίνειν
(c) ἐλθεῖν   (g) προσεύξασθαι   (j) καταβῆναι
(d) ἔρχεσθαι

2. Which of the following infinitives indicate single • action?

    (a) κηρύξαι   (e) γράψαι   (h) ἔρχεσθαι
    (b) κηρύσσειν   (f) ἆραι   (i) βάλλεσθαι
    (c) ἐσθίειν   (g) ἐλθεῖν   (j) βληθῆναι
    (d) φαγεῖν

3. Which of the following participles indicate continuing or repeated action?

    (a) γινόμενος   (e) κρίνων   (h) πάσχων
    (b) γενόμενος   (f) τρέχων   (i) παθών
    (c) σώζοντες   (g) δραμών   (j) πορεύμενοι
    (d) σώσαντες

4. Which of the following forms are passive?

    (a) βαλεῖν   (e) βαπτίζειν   (h) ἐβάπτισεν
    (b) βληθῆναι   (f) βαπτίζεσθαι   (i) βαπτιζόμενος
    (c) βαπτίζομαι   (g) ἐβαπτίσθη   (j) βαπτίζων
    (d) βαπτίζω

Which is the best English translation?

5. Ἐγένετο ἄνθρωπος ἀπεσταλμένος παρὰ θεοῦ, ὄνομα αὐτῷ Ἰωάννης.
    (a) A man was sent from God whose name was John.
    (b) There was a man. He had been sent by God. His name was John.
    (c) A man came who had been sent by God. His name was John.

6. οὗτος ἦλθεν εἰς μαρτυρίαν ἵνα μαρτυρήσῃ περὶ τοῦ φωτὸς ἵνα πάντες πιστεύσωσιν δι' αὐτοῦ
    (a) This came into witnessing so that he might witness about the light so that all might believe through him.
    (b) He came as a testimony to bear witness to the light to bring all people to faith.
    (c) He came for the purpose of bearing witness, to bear witness to the light so that through him all people might believe.

Check your answers in Key to Progress Tests on page 333.

31.11

(a) Read 10.9

(b) Read 1 John 1.
- v1 ἀκηκόαμεν – we have heard (perfect), ἑωράκαμεν – we have seen. ὀφθαλμός – eye. ἐθεασάμεθα – we saw (aorist). χείρ – hand. ἐψηλάφησαν – they touched (aorist).
- v2 ἐφανερώθη – it was revealed (aorist passive). ἀπαγγέλλομεν – we declare (present). αἰώνιος – age-long, eternal.
- v3 Notice the order of ἑωράκαμεν and ἀκηκόαμεν – as he draws his thoughts to a conclusion John reverses the order we find in verse 1. He is using chiasmus. ἡμέτερος – our (ἡμεῖς – we).
- v4 γράφομεν ἡμεῖς – **we** write: notice the emphatic '**we**' (see lesson 10.1).
  ἡ χαρὰ ὑμῶν – 'your joy', or ἡ χαρὰ ἡμῶν – 'our joy'? (see 50.7).
- v5–7 see 17.5
- v8 ἑαυτοὺς πλανῶμεν – we lead ourselves astray, we deceive ourselves.
- v9 ὁμολογέω – I confess. πιστός – trustworthy, faithful.
  δίκαιος – just, righteous (note that because the function of a judge was to do his best to put things right, righteousness and salvation are often closely linked concepts in the Old Testament).
  ἵνα ἀφῇ – and so he forgives (see C. F. D Moule, *An Idiom-Book of New Testament Greek,* p142).
  ἀδικία – wrongdoing. πᾶς – every, every kind of.

Lesson 32

ἐβαπτίσθην – I was baptized ⊣ |
βαπτισθείς – having been baptized ⊣

32.1

Compare:
1. (a) ἐβάπτισα – I baptized   (aorist indicative active)
   (b) ἐβαπτίσθην – I was baptized   (aorist indicative passive)
2. (a) ἐποίησεν – he did, she did, it did
   (b) ἐποιήθη – it was done |

Note that where the aorist active has σ between the stem and ending, the aorist passive usually has θ between the stem and ending.

The endings are

– ην	I	– ημεν	we
– ης	you	– ητε	you
– η	he, she, it	– ησαν	they

Compare also:
  ἐβαπτιζόμεθα – we were being baptized   (imperfect indicative passive)
  ἐβαπτίσθημεν – we were baptized   (aorist indicative passive).

Translate:

1. ἐβαπτίσθητε ὑπ' αὐτοῦ;	Were you baptized by him?
2. ἐσώθημεν ἀπὸ τοῦ πονηροῦ.	We were saved from the evil one.
3. οὐδεὶς ἐσώθη.	No one was saved.
4. πότε ἐπέμποντο;	When were they being sent?
5. ποῦ ἐπέμφθησαν;	Where were they sent?
6. σὺ ἠγαπήθης.	You were loved.
διὰ τί ἐγὼ οὐκ ἠγαπήθην;	Why was I not loved?

32.2

Compare these infinitives (1) and participles (2):

1. (a) βαπτισθῆναι   to be baptized   •   (aorist passive)
   (b) βάπτισαι   to baptize   •   (aorist active)
   (c) βαπτίζεσθαι   to be baptized ⸺ (present passive)
   (d) βαπτίζειν   to baptize ⸺ (present active)

2. (a) βαπτισθείς   having been baptized ⸱| (aorist passive)
   (b) βάπτισας   having baptized ⸱| (aorist active)
   (c) βαπτιζόμενος   being baptized ⸺ (present passive)
   (d) βαπτίζων   baptizing ⸺ (present active).

Translate:

1. οὐκ ἦλθεν βαπτισθῆναι ἀλλὰ βαπτίζειν.	He did not come to be baptized but to baptize.
2. βαπτισθεὶς ἐξῆλθεν βαπτίζων πάντας τοὺς πιστεύοντας.	When he had been baptized he went out baptizing all the believers.
3. ἐξῆλθον οὖν πρὸς αὐτὸν πάντες βαπτισθῆναι καὶ ἐβαπτίσθησαν ὑπ' αὐτοῦ καὶ βαπτισθέντες ἀπῆλθον πρὸς τὴν πόλιν.	So they all went out to him to be baptized and they were baptized by him. When they had been baptized they went away to the town.
4. οὐκ ἐβαπτίσθημεν ὑπὸ Παύλου; καὶ οὐχὶ μείζονές ἐσμεν τῶν βαπτισθέντων ὑπὸ Σίμωνος;	Were we not baptized by Paul? And are we not more important than those who have been baptized by Simon?
5. καλοῦσιν αὐτὸν καὶ κρίνουσιν αὐτὸν οἱ κριταὶ ὅτι πολλὰ ἐποιεῖ παρὰ τὸν νόμον.	They call him and the judges judge him because he was doing many things against the Law.
6. κληθέντος αὐτοῦ, ἔκρινεν αὐτὸν ὁ Πιλᾶτος κατὰ τὸν νόμον τῶν Ῥωμαίων.	When he had been called, Pilate judged him according to the law of the Romans.

32.3 βαπτισθήσομαι – I shall be baptized

Compare

σώσω – I shall save (future indicative active)
σωθήσομαι – I shall be saved (future indicative passive).

Note that θησ between the stem and the ending is a mark of the future passive.

Translate:

1. ὁ πιστεύσας καὶ βαπτίσθεις σωθήσεται.	The person who has believed and been baptized will be saved.
2. οἱ μὴ πιστεύσαντες κριθήσονται.	Those who have not believed will be judged.
3. τοῦτο ποιηθήσεται.	This will be done.
4. ταῦτα ἐποιήθη.	These things were done.
5. καλοῦμεν τὸ ὄνομα αὐτοῦ Ἰησοῦν ἀλλὰ υἱὸς θεοῦ κληθήσεται.	We call his name Jesus but he shall be called the Son of God.

32.4 Words

Subject form (nominative)	Meaning	'Of' form (genitive)	Subject form (nominative)
Singular		*Singular*	*Plural*
ἡ κεφαλή	the head	τῆς κεφαλῆς	αἱ κεφαλαί
ὁ ὀφθαλμός	the eye	τοῦ ὀφθαλμοῦ	οἱ ὀφθαλμοί
τὸ οὖς	the ear	τοῦ ὠτός	τὰ ὦτα
τὸ στόμα	the mouth	τοῦ στόματος	τὰ στόματα
ἡ χείρ	the hand, the arm	τῆς χειρός	αἱ χεῖρες
ὁ πούς	the foot, the leg	τοῦ ποδός	οἱ πόδες
τὸ σῶμα	the body	τοῦ σώματος	τὰ σώματα
τὸ μέλος	the limb	τοῦ μέλους	τὰ μέλη
τὸ μέρος	the part	τοῦ μέρους	τὰ μέρη
ἡ σάρξ	the flesh	τῆς σαρκός	αἱ σάρκες

τυφλός – blind
κωφός – deaf, deaf and dumb
χωλός – lame

πίπτω – I fall
    ἔπεσεν – he fell
    προσέπεσεν αὐτῷ – he fell before him
    προσέπεσεν πρὸς τοὺς πόδας αὐτοῦ – he fell at his feet
θεραπεύω – I heal
ἐκτείνω – I stretch out
κρατέω – I take hold of, I grasp, I seize, I arrest
    ἐκράτησεν τῆς χειρὸς αὐτῆς – he took hold of her hand
    οἱ στρατιῶται ἐζήτουν αὐτὸν κρατῆσαι – the soldiers were
                                                 seeking to arrest him

32.5 Translate

1. ἡ χεὶρ καὶ ὁ ποὺς μέλη εἰσὶν τοῦ σώματος.	The arm and the leg are limbs of the body.
2. τὸ στόμα καὶ τὰ ὦτα μέρη εἰσὶν τῆς κεφαλῆς.	The mouth and the ears are parts of the head.
3. οὐ δύναται βλέπειν τι τοῖς ὀφθαλμοῖς αὐτοῦ· τυφλὸς γάρ ἐστιν.	He cannot see anything with his eyes, for he is blind.
4. οὐ δύνανται περιπατεῖν· χωλοὶ γάρ εἰσιν.	They cannot walk, for they are lame.
5. οὐκ ἐδύναντο λόγον ἀκοῦσαι τοῖς ὠσὶν αὐτῶν· κωφοὶ γὰρ ἦσαν. ἀλλὰ νῦν ἀκούουσιν, ὁ γὰρ Ἰησοῦς ἐθεράπευσεν αὐτούς.	They were not able to hear a word with their ears, for they were deaf. But now they (can) hear, for Jesus healed them.
6. ἐκτείνας τὴν χεῖρα αὐτοῦ ἐκράτησεν τοῦ ποδὸς αὐτῆς.	Stretching out his hand he took hold of her foot.
7. ὦτα ἔχοντες, οὐκ ἀκούετε; καὶ ὀφθαλμοὺς ἔχοντες οὐ βλέπετε;	You have ears, can't you hear? You have eyes, can't you see? (Having eyes, do you not see?)
8. πόδας ἔχοντες οὐ περιπατοῦσιν καὶ στόματα ἔχοντες οὐκ ἐσθίουσιν, εἴδωλα γάρ εἰσιν.	Though they have legs (feet) they do not walk, and though they have mouths they do not eat, for they are idols.

32.6

Read carefully:

A blind man was healed

ἦν δὲ ἄνθρωπός τις λεγόμενος Βαρτιμαῖος. τυφλὸς ἦν καὶ οὐκ ἐδύνατο οὐδὲν βλέψαι τοῖς ὀφθαλμοῖς αὐτοῦ. οὗτος ἐλθὼν προσέπεσεν πρὸς τοὺς πόδας τοῦ Ἰησοῦ. καὶ αὐτὸς ἐκτείνας τὴν χεῖρα ἥψατο τῶν ὀφθαλμῶν αὐτοῦ. καὶ ἐθεραπεύθη ὁ τυφλὸς καὶ ἀνέβλεψεν. καὶ πολλοὶ χωλοὶ καὶ κωφοὶ ἦλθον πρὸς αὐτὸν καὶ ἐθεράπευσεν αὐτούς. τοὺς κωφοὺς ἐποίησεν ἀκούειν καὶ τοὺς χωλοὺς περιπατεῖν.

32.7

Read 1 Corinthians 12:12–21 (Πρὸς Κορινθίους Α 12:12–21).

Notes

καθάπερ – just as
εἴτε...εἴτε... – whether...or...
δοῦλος – slave
ἐλεύθερος – free
ποτίζω – I cause to drink, I give to drink
παρὰ τοῦτο – for this reason
ἀκοή – hearing
εἰ – if

ὄσφρησις – smelling
ἕκαστος – each
χρεία – need
ἔθετο – he put, he has put
μὲν...δὲ... – on the one hand...
    on the other hand...
    (see also 49.4.7).

32.8

Revise lessons 25 and 26.

For a summary of important noun forms you may consult the Reference Grammar (pp336–337).

Lesson 33

πεπίστευκα – I have trusted ⸱| →
γέγραπται – it has been written, it is written ⸱| →
οἶδα – I know ⸱| →

33.1

Study the following sentences:
(a) πεπίστευκα ὅτι σὺ εἶ ὁ Χριστός
    I have believed that you are the Messiah
    or I believe that you are the Messiah
(b) ἤγγικεν ἡ βασιλεία τοῦ θεοῦ
    The Kingdom of God has come near
(c) ἡ πίστις σου σέσωκέν σε
    Your faith has saved you
(d) χάριτί ἐστε σεσῳσμένοι
    By grace you are saved
    or You have been saved by grace
(e) ὡς γέγραπται ἐν τῷ Ἡσαΐᾳ
    As it has been written in Isaiah
    or As it is written in Isaiah.

In these sentences the verbal forms πεπίστευκα, ἤγγικεν, σέσωκεν, σεσῳσμένοι, and γέγραπται all refer to (1) an action or state in the past which has (2) a present or continuing result ⸱|→.

(a) πεπίστευκα indicates   (1) I believed   (2) I still believe
(b) ἤγγικεν indicates   (1) it came near (2) it is near
(c) σέσωκεν indicates   (1) you were saved   (2) you are safe
                         or (1) you were made well   (2) you are well
(d) σεσῳσμένοι indicates   (1) having been saved   (2) being still safe
(e) γέγραπται indicates (1) it was written   (2) it can still be
                                                              read.

Such verbal forms which indicate a past state or action with a present or continuing result are described as being in the *perfect* tense (31.9 B5). When we translate these perfect tense forms into English, if the emphasis is on the past action we can usually use forms with 'has' or 'have' in English:

ὃ γέγραφα, γέγραφα – what I have written, I have written.

But if the context shows that the emphasis is on the present result, we may use a present tense in English:

ὡς γέγραπται – as it is written, as it stands written,
　　　　　　　as Scripture says.

οἶδα (I know) is perfect in form, but present in meaning.

So:　　οὐκ οἴδαμεν – we do not know　　εἰδώς – knowing
Compare:　　οἶδεν – he knows　　ᾔδειν – I knew.

33.2

The perfect indicative active of πιστεύω – I believe – is πεπίστευκα – I have believed (and I still believe).

Note the endings:

	Singular	Plural
1st person	–α – I	–αμεν – we
2nd person	–ας – you	–ατε – you
3rd person	–εν – he, she, it	–ασιν – they.

γέγραφα (I have written), οἶδα (I know), ἤγγικα (I have come near) and other perfect active forms have the same endings.

Note that the perfect indicative active is usually marked by some of the following:
1. ε before the stem, as in other past tenses
2. κ between the stem and the ending
3. α in the ending (except 3rd person singular)
4. Repetition, or reduplication, of the initial consonant of the stem before the ε that marks past time.

33.3 Words

δίδωμι – I give
　　ἔδωκα – I gave
　　δέδωκα – I have given
καλῶς – well
　　καλῶς ἔχω – I am well
ἀληθῶς – truly
λαμβάνω – I take, I receive
　　εἴληφα – I have received

θνῄσκω – I die
    τέθνηκα – I have died, I am dead
τὸ μνημεῖον – the tomb
τὸ τάλαντον – the talent: silver, worth over £100,000
    (a denarius was a day's wage for Jewish labourers, and a talent was worth 10,000 denarii)
    ἓν τάλαντον – one talent   πέντε τάλαντα – five talents

33.4 Translate

1. πέντε τάλαντα ἔδωκέν σοι ὁ βασιλεύς, ἐγὼ δὲ ἓν τάλαντον εἴληφα.	The king gave you five talents but I have received one talent.
2. ζωὴν αἰώνιον δέδωκεν ἡμῖν ὁ θεός.	God has given eternal life to us.
3. πεπιστεύκαμεν ὅτι σὺ εἶ ἀληθῶς ὁ σωτὴρ τοῦ κόσμου.	We have believed that you are truly the Saviour of the world.
4. ἐγὼ γινώσκω ὑμᾶς καὶ ὑμεῖς ἐγνώκατε καὶ πεπιστεύκατε τὴν ἀγάπην ἣν ἔχει ὁ θεὸς ἐν ἡμῖν.	I know you and you have known and believed the love which God has for us.
5. οἶδεν ἡ γυνὴ τὸν σωτῆρα ἐν ᾧ πεπίστευκεν.	The woman knows the Saviour in whom she has believed.
6. ὃ γέγραφα, καλῶς γέγραφα.	What I have written, I have written well.
7. οἴδασιν ἀληθῶς τίς ἐστιν καὶ ποῦ μένει.	They know truly who he is and where he is staying.
8. σὺ καλῶς πάντα πεποίηκας καὶ ἡμεῖς καλῶς ἔχομεν.	You have done all things well and we are well.

33.5

πεπιστευκώς – having believed
    οἱ πεπιστευκότες – those who have believed
τεθνηκώς – having died
    ἡ τεθνηκυῖα – the woman who has died
εἰληφώς – having taken, having received
εἰδώς – knowing

Each of these verbal forms is a perfect participle active. They indicate past action with a continuing result. So οἱ ἐσχηκότες (ἔχω – I have) means 'the people who have had and still have'. Compare:

Mt 25:20 ὁ τὰ πέντε τάλαντα λαβών
 The man who had received the five talents

Mt 25:24 ὁ τὸ ἓν τάλαντον εἰληφώς
 The man who had received one talent

λαβών is an **aorist** participle. It indicates a completed action:
 'he did receive them.'
εἰληφώς is a **perfect** participle. It indicates a past action with a continuing result: 'he had received it and he still had it.'
Note also: πεπιστευκέναι – to have believed, εἰδέναι – to know.
These are perfect infinitive active.

33.6 Translate

1. ἐξῆλθεν ὁ τεθνηκὼς ἐκ τοῦ μνημείου, καὶ ἐξελθόντος αὐτοῦ οἱ μαθηταὶ ἀπῆλθον πρὸς τὴν πόλιν εἰπεῖν τὸ γεγονὸς τοῖς οὖσιν ἐν τῇ πόλει.	The man who had died came out from the tomb. When he had come out, the disciples went away to the town to tell the people in the town what had happened.
2. οὐ δύνανται ἀποκριθῆναι μὴ εἰδότες τὰς γραφάς.	They are not able to answer, (because of) not knowing the Scriptures.
3. οὐκ εἰσελεύσονται εἰς τὴν βασιλείαν τοῦ θεοῦ διὰ τὸ μὴ αὐτοὺς πεπιστευκέναι εἰς τὸν υἱὸν αὐτοῦ.	They will not enter into the Kingdom of God because they have not believed in his Son.
4. μακάριοι οἱ πεπιστευκότες· αὐτοὶ σωθήσονται διὰ τῆς χάριτος τοῦ θεοῦ.	Blessed are those who have believed: they shall be saved through the grace of God.
5. οἱ καλῶς ἔχοντες εἶδον τὸν ἐσχηκότα τὸν δαιμόνιον καὶ ἐχάρησαν εἰδότες ὅτι ἐθεραπεύθη ὑπὸ τοῦ Ἰησοῦ.	Those who were well saw the man who had had the demon and they rejoiced, knowing that he had been healed by Jesus.

33.7

γέγραπται – it is written
γεγραμμένος – written
γεγράφθαι – to have been written
τετέλεσται – it has been completed
πεπληρωμένος – fulfilled

So: οἶδα ταῦτα γεγράφθαι ὑπὸ τῶν προφητῶν
     I know these things to have been written by the prophets
 or I know that these things were written by the prophets.

Translate:

1. εὑρίσκει ταῦτα γεγράφθαι ὑπὸ τῶν ἀποστόλων καὶ οἶδεν ὅτι ἀληθή ἐστιν.	He finds that these things were written by the apostles and he knows that they are true.
2. καὶ ἐγένετο, καθὼς γεγραμμένον ἐστίν.	And it happened, just as it is written.
3. πεπλήρωται, καθὼς γέγραπται ἐν τῷ Ἠσαΐᾳ τῷ προφήτῃ.	It has been fulfilled, as it is written in (the book of) Isaiah the prophet.
4. χάριτί ἐστε σεσῳσμένοι καὶ οὐκ ἐξ ἔργων ὑμῶν.	You are saved by grace and not as a result of what you have done.
5. ἡ μήτηρ εὗρεν τὸ δαιμόνιον ἐξεληλυθὸς ἐκ τοῦ τέκνου αὐτῆς.	The mother found the demon (already) gone out from her child.

33.8 Range of usage of the perfect tense

Usually in the New Testament perfect verbal forms are used as in classical Greek for past action that involves a continued result, e.g. ἑωράκαμεν καὶ μαρτυροῦμεν (1 Jn 1:3) – we have seen and bear witness. ἑωράκαμεν implies more than 'we saw'. It implies that we still remember what we saw and can act in the light of that knowledge.

But sometimes perfect verbal forms are used in a way that makes them nearer to a simple past (or aorist). For example:

   Jn 6:32   οὐ Μωϋσῆς δέδωκεν ὑμῖν τὸν ἄρτον ἐκ τοῦ οὐρανοῦ –
               It was not Moses who gave you the bread from heaven.
               Here δέδωκεν is reflecting the aorist ἔδωκεν in verse 31
               and seems to have the same meaning.

   1 Jn 4:14   ὁ πατὴρ ἀπέσταλκεν τὸν υἱόν – the father sent the son.
               Here the perfect ἀπέσταλκεν seems to function like the
               aorist ἀπέστειλεν in 1 John 4:10 καὶ ἀπέστειλεν τὸν
               υἱὸν αὐτοῦ – and he sent his son.

We may compare this with the use of the aorist κατέλαβεν in John 1:5.
καὶ τὸ φῶς ἐν τῇ σκοτίᾳ φαίνει – and the light shines on in the darkness
καὶ ἡ σκοτία αὐτὸ οὐ κατέλαβεν – and the darkness has not overcome it.

The present φαίνει suggests that we are concerned not simply with an action in the past but with an ongoing situation.

When we consider this range of usage of perfect and aorist verbs we must remember that languages are usually used more flexibly than any 'rules' we can make to describe them. We may also wonder whether in the New Testament the use of Greek verbs is influenced by the Hebrew which was probably the language of the home for most of its writers.

33.9 Words

ὁ λαός – the people
ὁ ὄχλος – the crowd
ὁ καιρός – the time, the opportunity
ὁ βασιλεύς – the king
ὁ νόμος – the Law (often: the Law of Moses, the Torah)
ὁ γραμματεύς – the scribe, the teacher of the Law
ὁ ἀρχιερεύς – the chief priest
ἡ δύναμις – the power, the ability, the miracle (δύναμαι – I am able)
τὸ ἔθνος – the race, the nation
    τὰ ἔθνη – the nations, the Gentiles
ἐγγίζω – I come near
    ἐγγύς – near
πληρόω – I fulfil
    πλήρης – full

33.10 Translate

1. οἴδαμεν ὅτι οἱ γραμματεῖς ἐδίδασκον τὸν λαὸν τὸν νόμον καθὼς αὐτοὶ ἐδιδάχθησαν. | We know that the scribes used to teach the people the Law just as they themselves had been taught.

2. πεπλήρωται ὁ καιρὸς καὶ ἤγγικεν ἡ βασιλεία τοῦ βασιλέως τῶν βασιλέων. | The time has been fulfilled and the Kingdom of the King of kings has come near.

3. ἦλθον οὖν οἱ ἀρχιερεῖς καὶ οἱ γραμματεῖς πρὸς τὸν Ἰησοῦν καὶ ἠρώτησαν αὐτόν, Τί γέγραπται ἐν τῷ νόμῳ περὶ τοῦ Χριστοῦ;

So the chief priests and the teachers of the Law came to Jesus and asked him, 'What is written in the Law about the Messiah?'

4. τὰ ἔθνη οὐκ οἴδασιν τὸν νόμον τοῦ Μωϋσέως καὶ ἡμεῖς οὐ τηροῦμεν αὐτόν.

The Gentiles do not know the Law of Moses and we do not keep it.

5. περιεπάτει παρὰ τὴν θάλασσαν καὶ εἶδεν Σίμωνα καὶ ἐκάλεσεν αὐτόν. καὶ προβὰς ὀλίγον εἶδεν ὄχλον πολὺν καὶ εἶπεν αὐτοῖς φωνῇ μεγάλῃ, Ἀκούετε ἤγγικεν ἡ βασιλεία τοῦ θεοῦ καὶ ἡ δύναμις αὐτοῦ.

He was walking along by the lake and he saw Simon and called him. Having gone a little further on, he saw a large crowd and said to them in a loud voice, 'Listen, the reign of God has come near and his power.'

33.11 Translation: πεπλήρωται ὁ καιρός (Mark 1:15)

In sentence 2 in 33.9 we translated πεπλήρωται ὁ καιρός rather literally as, 'the time has been fulfilled'. In Mark 1:15 RSV translates similarly, 'the time is fulfilled.' But what does this mean in English? We often think of prophecy being fulfilled, but not naturally of time being fulfilled (except perhaps in the sense of a period of service being brought to an end). 'The time is fulfilled' is 'translation English' rather than real English. So we have to ask ourselves, 'In Mark 1:15 what does πεπλήρωται ὁ καιρός really mean, and how can we best express the meaning in English?'

καιρός means time in the sense of 'opportunity' or 'special time'.

NIV translates: 'The time has come', which is clear and natural English but does not express the very important meaning of πληρόω (I fulfil). Most often in the New Testament πεπλήρωται and similar forms draw attention to the fulfilment of the great promises made by God to the Israelites in Old Testament times (Lk 24:44, Acts 13:32–33). We must include this important idea in our translation. We might translate πεπλήρωται ὁ καιρός as 'the time of fulfilment has come.'

33.12 Grammatical terms

To **parse** a verb is to describe its precise verbal form, by identifying its person, number, tense, mood, and voice.

1. Person

I and **we** are called **first person**.
Thou and **you** are called **second person**.
He, **she**, **it**, and **they** are called **third person**.
So: λέγω , λέγομεν are first person
λέγεις , λέγετε are second person
λέγει , λέγουσιν are third person.

2. Number

I, **you** (**thou**), **he**, **she**, and **it**, all refer to one person or thing; they are called **singular**.
We, **you**, and **they**, all refer to more than one; they are called **plural**.
So: λέγω, λέγεις, λέγει   are all singular
λέγομεν, λέγετε, λέγουσιν are all plural
λέγει is third person singular
λέγετε is second person plural.

3. Tense

Tense	Examples
Present	ποιῶ, βάλλω, λέγω, ἔρχομαι
Imperfect	ἐποίουν, ἔβαλλον, ἔλεγον, ἠρχόμην
Future	ποιήσω, βαλῶ, ἐρῶ, ἐλεύσομαι
Aorist	ἐποίησα, ἔβαλον, εἶπον, ἦλθον
Perfect	πεποίηκα, βέβληκα, εἴρηκα, ἐλήλυθα
Pluperfect	πεποιήκειν, βεβλήκειν, εἰρήκειν, ἐληλύθειν

4. Mood

Mood	Examples
Indicative	λέγει, λέγομεν, εἶπεν, ἐποίησεν, ἐποιήθη
Subjunctive	λέγῃ, λέγωμεν, εἴπῃ, ποιήσῃ, ποιήθῃ
Imperative	ποίησον, ἔξελθε, διανοίχθητι
Infinitive	λέγειν, εἰπεῖν, ποιῆσαι, ἔρχεσθαι, βαπτισθῆναι
Participles	λέγων, εἰπών, ποιήσας, ἐρχόμενος, βαπτισθείς

(For optative, see 49.1–3)

5. Voice

Voice	Examples
Active	ποιῶ, ποιῇ, ποιήσαι, ποιήσας
Middle	ἔρχομαι, ἔρχεσθαι, ἐρχόμενος, ἀπεκρίθη
Passive	ἐβαπτίσθην, βαπτισθῆναι, βαπτισθείς

Parsing verbal forms

Putting together 1–5 above:

λέγομεν (we say) is 1st person plural present indicative active of λέγω

βάλωμεν (let us throw) is 1st person plural aorist subjunctive active of βάλλω

ποίησον (do!) is 2nd person singular aorist imperative active of ποιέω

βαπτισθῆναι (to be baptized) is aorist infinitive passive of βαπτίζω

ἔρχεσθαι (to come) is present infinitive middle of ἔρχομαι

λέγων (saying) is nominative singular masculine present participle active of λέγω.

When parsing a verbal form we need first to translate it literally and then to decide whether it is:

    (a) indicative, subjunctive, imperative, or optative

    (b) infinitive

or (c) a participle.

For (a) indicative, subjunctive, imperative, or optative, we must give:
person, number, tense, mood, and voice.

For (b) infinitive, we must give:
tense, mood, and voice.

For (c) a participle, we must give:
case, number, gender (37.1), tense, mood, and voice.

33.13 Progress test 16

Which is the correct translation?

1. ἀπεστέλλοντο οἱ μαθηταὶ ὑπὸ τοῦ κυρίου βαπτίζειν ὑμᾶς.
   (a) The disciples send us from the Lord to be baptized.
   (b) The disciples were being sent by the Lord to baptize you.
   (c) The disciples are sent by the Lord to baptize you.

2. πάντα τὰ μέλη τοῦ σώματος πολλὰ ὄντα ἕν ἐστιν σῶμα.
   (a) All the limbs of the body, being many, are in the body.
   (b) While the limbs of the body are many, it is one body.
   (c) All the limbs of the body, though they are many, make up one body.
3. Σὺ εἶ Σίμων, σὺ κληθήσῃ Κηφᾶς ὃ ἑρμηνεύεται Πέτρος.
   (a) You are Simon, you will be called Cephas (which is translated 'Peter').
   (b) You were Simon, you will be called Cephas, which means 'Peter'.
   (c) You are Simon, you will become Cephas (which is translated 'Peter').

Which is the best English translation?

4. διὰ τὸ αὐτὸν πολλάκις πέδαις καὶ ἁλύσεσιν δεδέσθαι καὶ διεσπάσθαι ὑπ' αὐτοῦ τὰς ἁλύσεις καὶ τὰς πέδας συντετρῖφθαι.
   (a) Because of him many times with fetters and with chains to have been bound, and to have been torn apart by him the chains and the fetters to have been smashed.
   (b) Because he had been many times bound with fetters and chains and the chains to have been broken by him and the fetters smashed.
   (c) Because many times he had been bound with fetters and chains but had torn the chains apart and smashed the fetters.

Which is the correct description of the following verbal forms from questions 1–4?

5. ἀπεστέλλοντο (1)
   (a) First person plural aorist indicative active of ἀποστέλλω
   (b) Third person plural imperfect indicative passive of ἀποστέλλω
   (c) Third person plural present indicative passive of ἀποστέλλω

6. ὄντα (2)
   (a) Third person plural present indicative of εἰμί
   (b) Nominative singular masculine present participle of εἰμί
   (c) Nominative plural neuter present participle of εἰμί

7. κληθήσῃ (3)
   (a) Third person singular aorist indicative passive of κλαίω.
   (b) Second person singular aorist indicative passive of καλέω.
   (c) Second person singular future indicative passive of καλέω.

8. δεδέσθαι (4)
   (a) Perfect infinitive passive of δέω (I bind).
   (b) Second person plural perfect indicative passive of δέω
   (c) Third person singular perfect indicative active of δέω

Check your answers in Key to Progress Tests on page 333.

33.14

(a) Read 16.8 again – John 1:19–25

(b) Read John 1:26–28
   v26 μέσος – middle, in the middle.   ἕστηκεν – (he) stands
   v27 ὀπίσω – after, behind   ἄξιος – worthy
       λύω – I untie   ἱμάς – strap   ὑπόδημα – sandal
   v28 πέραν – across, on the opposite side
       ὅπου ἦν ὁ Ἰωάννης βαπτίζων : since ἦν is an all-purpose past tense we have to choose between two possible translations:
          (a) In Bethany across the Jordan, where John **was** baptising
       or (b) In Bethany, across the Jordan from where John **had been** baptising.

Lesson 34

τίθημι – I am putting   δίδωμι – I am giving
τιθείς – putting ┅   διδούς – giving ┅
θείς – having put ⊣   δούς – having given ⊣

34.1 Words

τίθημι – I put, I place, I put down, I appoint
   τιθέναι – to put ┅
   θεῖναι – to put •
   ἐπιτίθημι – I place on, I put on (ἐπὶ – on)
δίδωμι – I give, I present
   δίδωσιν – he gives
   δίδου – give! keep giving! ┅
   δός – give! •
   παραδίδωμι – I hand over, I betray, I hand on (παρά – alongside)
   παραδοθῆναι – to be handed over, to be arrested
   παράδοσιν παραδοῦναι – to hand on a tradition or teaching
ἵστημι – I cause to stand, I set up, I stand
   ἕστηκα – I stood
   ἀνίστημι – I stand up, I rise (ἀνά – up)
    ἀναστάς – having got up, rising •
   παρίστημι – I stand beside
   ὁ παρεστηκώς – the bystander
   ἀποκαθίστημι – I restore
    ἀπεκατεστάθη ἡ χεὶρ αὐτοῦ – his arm was restored (Mk 3:5)
ἵημι
   ἀφίημι – I leave, I allow, I forgive, I let, I let go
   συνίημι – I understand
   συνῆκα – I understood
φημί – I say
   ἔφη – he said
ἀπόλλυμι – I destroy, I spoil, I ruin
   ἀπώλεσα – I destroyed
   ἀπολέσαι – to destroy •
   ἀπωλόμην – I perished

34.2 Translate

1. ἐπιτίθημι τὰς χειράς μου ἐπὶ τῆς κεφαλῆς αὐτοῦ.	I am laying my hands on his head.
2. δίδομεν τὰ βιβλία τῷ μαθητῇ καὶ δίδωσιν αὐτὰ τῷ ἀρχιερεῖ.	We give the books to the disciple and he gives them to the High Priest.
3. οἱ ἀδελφοὶ διδόασιν τοὺς ἄρτους ἡμῖν ἵνα δίδωμεν αὐτοὺς τοῖς ἱερεύσιν.	The brothers give the loaves to us so that we may give them to the priests.
4. Ἰούδας Ἰσκαριὼθ ἐστιν ὁ παραδιδοὺς τὸν Ἰησοῦν.	Judas Iscariot is the person who is betraying Jesus.
5. ἀφίετε αὐτοῖς πολλὰ ποιεῖν.	You allow them to do many things.
6. ὁ θεὸς ἀφίησιν ἡμῖν πάντας τὰς ἁμαρτίας ἡμῶν καὶ ζωὴν δίδωσιν ἡμῖν ἐν Χριστῷ.	God forgives us all our sins and gives us life through Christ (in Christ).
7. Ἰησοῦ, ἀπόλλυς πάντα τὰ ἔργα τοῦ πονηροῦ.	Jesus, you are destroying all the works of the evil one.
8. εἶπον τῷ Ἰησοῦ, Οὐχὶ σὺ εἶ ὁ βαπτιστής; ὁ δὲ ἔφη αὐτοῖς, Οὐκ εἰμί	They said to Jesus, 'You are the baptizer, aren't you?' He said to them, 'I am not.'

34.3 διδο ⁓   δο ⊣

In βάλλειν (to throw, to be throwing), βαλεῖν (to throw),
αἴρων (picking up), and ἄρας (having picked up),
  the longer stems βαλλ and αιρ indicate repeated or continuing action;
  the shorter stems βαλ and αρ indicate single or completed action.

Compare

δίδου – give! keep giving!	δός – give!
διδούς, διδοῦσα, διδόν – giving	δούς, δοῦσα, δόν – having given
διδόναι – to give, to keep giving	δοῦναι – to give
	δοθῆναι – to be given.

So: τὸν ἄρτον **δίδου** ἡμῖν καθ᾽ ἡμέραν – give us the bread every day
   τὸν ἄρτον **δὸς** ἡμῖν σήμερον – give us the bread today.

LESSON 34

Note the following words and forms carefully:

Verb	Continued or repeated action stem	Completed or single action stem
τίθημι – I put	τιθε	θε
δίδωμι – I give	διδο	δο
ἵστημι – I set up, I stand	ἱστα	στα
ἀφίημι – I forgive, I leave (ἀπο + ἱημι)	ἱε	ἑ
ἀπόλλυμι – I destroy	ολλ	ολ
δείκνυμι – I show	δεικνυ	δεικ

So: τιθείς – putting, placing
ἐπιτίθησιν – he is placing on
δίδοτε – give!
δίδωσιν – he gives
ἤφιεν– he was allowing
ἕστηκεν – he is standing*
εἱστήκει – he was standing *
ἀπολλύμεθα – we are perishing
δείκνυμι – I show
δεικνύειν – to show

θείς – having put, putting
ἐπέθηκεν – he put on
δότε – give!
ἐδόθη – it was given
ἀφῆκεν – he allowed
ἔστη – he stood*
ἀναστάς – having stood up*
ἀπολέσαι – to destroy
δείξω – I will show
δεῖξαι – to show.

*see top of page 345

34.4 Translate

1. ἐπιθεὶς αὐτῇ τὰς χειρὰς αὐτοῦ ἐθεράπευσεν αὐτήν. | He laid (lit. having laid) his hands on her and healed her.

2. ἐπέθηκεν τὰς χειρὰς αὐτῆς ἐπὶ τοῦ ποδὸς αὐτοῦ καὶ ἀπεκατεστάθη ὁ ποὺς αὐτοῦ. | She laid her hands on his foot (leg) and his foot (leg) was restored.

3. εἶπεν αὐτῇ ὁ Ἰησοῦς,'Ἀφέωνταί σοι αἱ ἁμαρτίαι σου. | Jesus said to her, 'Your sins are forgiven you.'

4. ἀναστὰς ἦλθεν εἰς τὴν πόλιν καὶ ἔδειξεν ἑαυτὸν τῷ ἱερεῖ. | He got up and went into the city and showed himself to the priest.

5. ἀναστᾶσα ἦλθεν εἰς τὴν πόλιν δεῖξαι ἑαυτὴν τῷ ἱερεῖ. | She got up and went into the city to show herself to the priest.

6. ἀναστάντες ἐξήλθομεν ἐκ τῆς πόλεως. | We got up and went out of the city.

7. ἔδωκεν τὸν ἄρτον τῇ γυναικί. | He gave the loaf to the woman.
8. δέδωκεν ἡμῖν
τούτους τοὺς ἄρτους. | He has given us
these loaves.
9. οἱ παρεστηκότες εἶπον ὅτι
Μωϋσῆς δέδωκεν ἡμῖν τὸν νόμον.
ὁ δὲ ἔφη, Οὐ Μωϋσῆς ἔδωκεν
ὑμῖν τὸν νόμον ἀλλὰ ὁ Πατήρ
μου δίδωσιν ὑμῖν τὸν νόμον τὸν
ἀληθινόν. | The bystanders said,
'Moses has given us the Law.'
He said, 'It was not Moses who
gave you the Law, but my Father
is giving you the true Law.'
10. εἷς τῶν μαθητῶν αὐτοῦ εἶπεν
αὐτῷ, Ἡ μήτηρ σου καὶ
οἱ ἀδελφοὶ ἑστήκασιν ἔξω. | One of his disciples said
to him, 'Your mother and
brothers are standing outside.'
11. λαβὼν ἄρτον καὶ δοὺς αὐτοῖς
εἶπεν, Τοῦτο ἐστιν τὸ σῶμά μου. | Taking a loaf and giving it to them
he said, 'This is my body',
12. οἱ Φαρισαῖοι οὐ διδόασιν ἡμῖν
τὴν ζωὴν τὴν αἰώνιον
ἀλλὰ Ἰησοῦς ζωὴν δέδωκεν ἡμῖν. | The Pharisees are not giving us
eternal life,
but Jesus has given us life.
13. ἐκάλεσεν αὐτοὺς ὁ Ἰησοῦς καὶ
ἀφέντες τὸν πατέρα αὐτῶν
ἐν τῷ πλοίῳ ἠκολούθησαν αὐτῷ. | Jesus called them and
leaving (having left) their father
in the boat, they followed him.
14. ἔφη αὐτῷ ὁ βασιλεύς, Οὐ
δύναμαι ἀναστὰς ἄρτους δοῦναι
σοι. | The king said to him, 'I cannot
get up and give you loaves.'
15. ἦλθεν δοῦναι τὴν ψυχὴν (life)
αὐτοῦ καὶ εἶπεν ὅτι Ἐξουσίαν
ἔχω θεῖναι τὴν ψυχήν μου καὶ
ἐξουσίαν ἔχω πάλιν λαβεῖν αὐτήν. | He came to give his life,
and he said, 'I have authority
to lay down my life and
I have authority to take it again.'
16. οὐκ ἀκούετε οὐδὲ συνίετε. | You do not listen, nor do you
understand.
17. οὐκ ἀκούετε οὐδὲ συνίετε; | Do you not listen, nor understand?
18. οὐ συνῆκαν τί τὸ θέλημα
τοῦ θεοῦ ἀλλὰ ἐζήτουν πῶς
ἀπολέσωσιν τὸν Χριστόν. | They did not understand what
God wanted, but they were seeking
how they might destroy the
Anointed One.

34.5

Read Mark 2:22.

Notes

οἶνος – wine ῥήγνυμι – I break
ἀσκός – wineskin ῥήξει – it will burst
εἰ δὲ μή – but if not, otherwise

34.6 Translation – areas of meaning

Hardly any word in English is exactly the same in meaning and usage as any Greek word. So when we are translating a Greek word into English we must always be ready to think carefully.

For example, φόβος covers a fairly wide area of meaning for which we use in English such words as 'fear', 'respect', and 'reverence'. Very often 'fear' will do as a translation, but not always. In 1 John 4:18 we may translate φόβος οὐκ ἔστιν ἐν τῇ ἀγάπῃ as 'There is no fear in love'. But in translating Acts 9:31, πορευομένη τῷ φόβῳ τοῦ Κυρίου, we must ask ourselves, 'Were the members of the Christian community, the ἐκκλησία, walking or living in fear of the Lord or in reverence for him?' It is clear from the context that they revered him rather than feared him. So we might translate as 'Walking in reverence for the Lord', or 'Living in reverence for the Lord'.

Look again at Mark 2:22, especially the words

καὶ ὁ οἶνος ἀπόλλυται καὶ οἱ ἀσκοί

REB and then the wine and the skins are both lost.
GNB and both the wine and the skins will be ruined.

You will see that the REB and GNB translators both had difficulty in translating ἀπόλλυται. ἀπόλλυμι covers a wide area of meaning for which we use several English words including: I destroy, I spoil, I ruin.

In Mark 2:22 ἀπόλλυται combines the ideas of being lost and being ruined. When a wineskin bursts it is ruined but not lost; so the REB translation is not very good. When wine flows out over the floor it is lost rather than being ruined; so the GNB translation is not very good. In an English translation we really need two different verbs to express (a) what happens to the wine, and (b) what happens to the skins. We might translate:

The wine is spilled and the skins are spoiled.

This translation has a similarity of sound in the words 'spilled' and 'spoiled' which fits the proverbial nature of the saying.

34.7

(a) Read John 1:29–34

v29 τῇ ἐπαύριον – on the next day.   βλέπει – he sees, (he saw).
αἴρω – I take up, I take away.   v30 ὑπὲρ οὗ – about whom.
ὀπίσω – after.   ἔμπροσθεν – in front of, before, ahead of.
πρῶτος – first (in importance or in time).
v31 κἀγώ = καὶ ἐγώ – and I.   διὰ τοῦτο – for this reason, for this purpose.   ἵνα φανερωθῇ – that he might be revealed.
v32 τεθέαμαι – I have seen, I saw.   ὡς – as, like
περιστερά – a dove.
v33 οὐκ ᾔδειν – I had not known, I did not know.

Because οἶδα is a perfect form that functions as a present (I know) it has only one past form ᾔδειν. In this context where the sign that brought knowledge has already been mentioned, it is natural to translate it as 'I had not known'.

(b) Read John 1:35–39 again, using notes in 23.9 (b)

34.8

Revise lessons 27 and 28.

INTRODUCTION TO LESSONS 35–52

You have learned to understand most of the basic forms found in the Greek New Testament. Now you will build on the foundation you have laid. Use these lessons as a background to more extensive reading of the New Testament.

Many of the points we study will be illustrated by quotations from the New Testament. Where new words occur, see if you can tell their meaning from the English translation.

When you consider the translations that are given, think whether you would translate in the same way. For example, in 35.3 δεῖ τὸν υἱὸν τοῦ ἀνθρώπου πολλὰ παθεῖν has been translated, 'It is necessary for the Son of Man to suffer much.' This is to help students to recall that δεῖ means 'it is binding' or 'it is necessary,' and παθεῖν means 'to suffer.' You may prefer to translate, 'The Son of Man is bound to suffer greatly', or 'The Son of Man must undergo many sufferings.'

Several of the lessons in this part of the course introduce wide fields of study. They reach areas that other courses for beginners do not reach. Notice what these lessons say, but do not feel that you must understand everything the first time you read through these lessons. Some are included for reference purposes. All of them will become more meaningful as you read more of the New Testament in Greek.

Lesson 35

καλός – good   καλῶς – well
εἷς, δύο, τρεῖς – one, two, three

35.1

In English, the words 'bad' and 'good' are adjectives. The words 'badly' and 'well' are adverbs. Compare carefully:

Adjectives	Adverbs
καλός – good	καλῶς – well
κακός – bad	κακῶς – in an evil way
	(κακῶς ἔχω – I am ill)
ὀρθός – upright, straight	ὀρθῶς – properly, correctly
ὅμοιος – like	ὁμοίως – similarly, in the same way
περισσός – excessive, surplus	περισσῶς – exceedingly, very much
	ἐκπερισσῶς – very excessively
περισσότερος – greater, more excessive	περισσοτέρως or περισσότερον – more excessively, more
δίκαιος – righteous, just	δικαίως – righteously, justly
ἀληθής – true	ἀληθῶς – truly
ταχύς – quick	ταχύ or ταχέως – quickly
τάχιστος – very quick, quickest	τάχιστα – very quickly
	ὡς τάχιστα – as quickly as possible
εὐθύς – straight, level	εὐθύς or εὐθέως – immediately, at once, next, then
Note also: οὗτος – this	οὕτως – thus
	οὕτως...ὥστε... – so much...that...

35.2 Translate

1. οἱ δίκαιοι δικαίως ἐποίησαν καὶ ὁμοίως ὁ πονηρὸς κακῶς ἐλάλησεν. | The just men acted justly and similarly the evil man spoke in an evil way.

2. ἀληθῶς λέγεις ὅτι οἱ κακῶς ἔχοντες χρείαν (need) ἔχουσιν ἰατροῦ. | You say truly that those who are ill have need of a doctor.

3. καὶ εὐθὺς ἐθεράπευσεν τὸν κωφὸν ὁ ἰατρὸς καὶ ὀρθῶς ἐλάλει.

Immediately (then) the doctor healed the dumb man and he began to speak properly.

4. εἶδεν ὁ Ἰησοῦς τὴν Μαρίαν καὶ εὐθὺς ἐκάλεσεν αὐτὴν καὶ αὐτὴ ἠκολούθει αὐτῷ.

Jesus saw Mary and immediately he called her and she followed (began to follow) him.

5. οὕτως ἠγάπησεν ὁ θεὸς τὸν κόσμον ὥστε τὸν υἱὸν αὐτοῦ ἔδωκεν ἵνα πᾶς ὁ πιστεύων εἰς αὐτὸν μὴ ἀπόληται ἀλλ' ἔχῃ ζωὴν αἰώνιον.

For God so loved the world that he gave his Son so that everyone who believes in him should not perish but have eternal life.

35.3

πολύ or πολλά – much, greatly: πλεῖον – more
ὀλίγον – a little (ὀλίγος – little, ὀλίγοι – few)
μόνον – only
μᾶλλον – rather, much more

These are adjectival forms. We often need to use an adverb when translating them into English.

Note:

Lk 7:47 ἠγάπησεν πολύ
She loved much or She loved greatly

Lk 7:42 τίς οὖν αὐτῶν πλεῖον ἀγαπήσει αὐτόν;
So which of them will love him more?

Mk 5:36 Μὴ φοβοῦ, μόνον πίστευε
Do not fear, only believe

Mk 5:38 θεωρεῖ...κλαίοντας καὶ ἀλαλάζοντας πολλά
He sees people crying and wailing loudly

Mk 8:31 δεῖ τὸν υἱὸν τοῦ ἀνθρώπου πολλὰ παθεῖν
It is necessary for the Son of Man to suffer much

Rev 5:4 ἔκλαιον πολύ
I wept much

Mk 5:26 μηδὲν ὠφεληθεῖσα ἀλλὰ μᾶλλον εἰς τὸ χεῖρον ἐλθοῦσα
Not having been helped at all but rather having become worse

Acts 4:19 Εἰ δίκαιόν ἐστιν... ὑμῶν ἀκούειν μᾶλλον ἢ τοῦ θεοῦ
If it is right to listen to you rather than to God

Mk 10:48   ὁ δὲ πολλῷ μᾶλλον ἔκραζεν
           He shouted out much more
           or He shouted out all the more
           or He began to shout even louder
Lk 11:13   πόσῳ μᾶλλον ὁ πατὴρ ὁ ἐξ οὐρανοῦ δώσει
           πνεῦμα ἅγιον τοῖς αἰτοῦσιν αὐτόν
           How much more will the heavenly Father give the
           Holy Spirit to those who ask him
Mk 1:19   προβὰς ὀλίγον
           Having gone on a little way
Mk 6:31   ἀναπαύσασθε ὀλίγον
           Rest for a little while
Lk 7:47   ᾧ δὲ ὀλίγον ἀφίεται, ὀλίγον ἀγαπᾷ
           But to whom little is forgiven, he loves little
           or But he loves little to whom little is forgiven.

Translate:

1. εἶπεν ἡμῖν, Ἐγώ εἰμι τὸ φῶς τοῦ κόσμου. ἀπήλθομεν οὖν ἀπ' αὐτοῦ ἠγαπήσαμεν γὰρ μᾶλλον τὸ σκότος ἢ τὸ φῶς.	He said to us, 'I am the light of the world.' So we left him, for we loved the darkness rather than the light.
2. ἀναστὰς εἰσῆλθεν εἰς τὴν συναγωγὴν καὶ εὐθὺς ἐδίδασκεν αὐτοὺς πολλά, καὶ ἔλεγεν, Μακάριόν ἐστιν διδόναι μᾶλλον ἢ λαμβάνειν.	He got up and went into the synagogue. Then he taught them many things, and he said, 'It is blessed to give (to keep giving) rather than to receive.'

35.4

Note that the following phrases and words can often be best translated into English using adverbs rather than a preposition and a noun:
   μετὰ χαρᾶς – with joy; joyfully, gladly
   μετὰ σπουδῆς – with enthusiasm, with energy; enthusiastically,
               energetically
   ἐπ' ἀληθείας – in truth; honestly, truly, certainly
   καθ' ἡμέραν – each day; daily
   παρρησίᾳ – with boldness; boldly, openly.

When we translate a Greek adverb we may sometimes use an adjective in English:

Jn 1:47 Ἴδε ἀληθῶς Ἰσραηλίτης – Look, truly a descendant of Israel.

We might translate:
   There is a man who is a genuine descendant of Israel.

35.5

Adverbs ending with –θεν usually show the place someone or something comes from:
   ἦλθεν ἐκεῖθεν – he came **from there**
   ἐλεύσεται ἄνωθεν – he will come **from above**
   ἔρχονται πάντοθεν – they are coming **from all directions**
   ἐλήλυθα ἀλλαχόθεν – I have come **from another place**.

Note also:
   ὄπισθεν – behind, after
   ἔμπροσθεν – before, in front of
   ἔσωθεν – inside, within, from within
   ἄνωθεν – from above; from the beginning, over again.

Adverbs ending with –χου usually show where someone is going:
   ἄγωμεν ἀλλαχοῦ – let us go elsewhere
   ἐξελθόντες ἐκήρυξαν πανταχοῦ – they went out and preached everywhere
   καθὼς πανταχοῦ διδάσκω – as I teach in every place.

Adverbs ending with –τε usually show the time at which something happened:
   τότε – then, at that time
   εἶτεν or εἶτα – then, next
   ποτέ – at one time, at any time, once, formerly, ever
   πάντοτε – always, on every occasion
   οὐδέποτε, μηδέποτε – never.

Read carefully:

Ἐξῆλθεν ἀλλαχοῦ μετὰ χαρᾶς καὶ αὐτοῦ ἐξελθόντος ἐκεῖθεν τότε εἶπον οἱ μαθηταὶ παρρησίᾳ λέγοντες, "Ἄγωμεν πανταχοῦ καὶ πάντοτε διδάσκωμεν μετὰ σπουδῆς καὶ μηδέποτε παραδίδωμεν ἀλλήλους τῷ βασιλεῖ. εἶτα πάλιν ἐξῆλθον κηρύσσοντες τὸν λόγον ἐπ' ἀληθείας καὶ διδάσκοντες τοὺς ἀνθρώπους καθ' ἡμέραν ἐν ταῖς συναγωγαῖς τὴν ἄνωθεν διδασκαλίαν.

35.6 Numbers

εἷς – one   πρῶτος – first   ἅπαξ – once

You have seen that εἷς (one) has different forms for masculine, feminine, and neuter:

The one: ὁ εἷς, ἡ μία, τὸ ἕν.

Mk 10:37 Δὸς ἡμῖν ἵνα εἷς σου ἐκ δεξιῶν καὶ εἷς ἐξ ἀριστερῶν καθίσωμεν
Grant that we may sit **one** at your right and **one** at your left

Jn 10:16 γενήσονται μία ποίμνη, εἷς ποιμήν
They shall become **one** flock, **one** shepherd

Mt 5:18 ἰῶτα ἓν ἢ μία κεραία
One iota or **one** stroke of a letter.

Many number words are easy to translate because there are similar English words. For example:

πρῶτος – first: prototype (τύπος – form, example, mark)
δεύτερος – second: Deuteronomy (νόμος – Law, Torah)
τρεῖς – three: triad, tricycle (κύκλος – circle)
ἕξ – six: hexagon (γωνία – corner)
χίλιος – thousand: Chiliasm (belief in a thousand year reign of Christ)
μύριοι – ten thousand: myriads.

Note these common number words:

Units 1; 2...	Tens 10; 20...	Hundreds 100; 200...	Thousands 1,000; 2,000...	Order first...	Times once...
1 εἷς	δέκα	ἑκατόν	χίλιος	πρῶτος	ἅπαξ
2 δύο	εἴκοσι	διακόσιοι	δισχίλιοι	δεύτερος	δίς
3 τρεῖς	τριάκοντα		τρισχίλιοι	τρίτος	τρίς
4 τέσσαρες	τεσσαράκοντα	τετρακόσιοι		τέταρτος	
5 πέντε	πεντήκοντα	πεντακόσιοι			
6 ἕξ	ἑξήκοντα				
7 ἑπτά			ἑπτακισχίλιοι	ἕβδομος	ἑπτάκις
8 ὀκτώ					
9 ἐννέα	ἐνενήκοντα				
10 δέκα			μύριοι	δέκατος	δεκάκις

LESSON 35

Note also:
> ἕνδεκα – 11 δεκατέσσαρες – 14
> δώδεκα – 12 πέντε καὶ δέκα – 15
> ὁ ἑκατοντάρχης – the centurion, the captain

Jn 21:11 τὸ δίκτυον...μεστὸν ἰχθύων ἑκατὸν πεντήκοντα τριῶν
The net full of fish, one hundred and fifty-three.

Translate:

1. ἑξήκοντα καὶ τέσσαρες.	Sixty-four.
2. πεντακόσιοι εἴκοσι καὶ ὀκτώ.	Five hundred and twenty-eight.
3. ἑπτακισχίλιοι ἑκατὸν καὶ δέκα	Seven thousand, one hundred and ten.
4. ὁ πρῶτος καὶ ὁ ἕβδομος καὶ ὁ δέκατος.	The first, and the seventh, and the tenth.
5. ἐποίησεν τοῦτο οὐκ ἅπαξ οὐδὲ δὶς οὐδὲ τρὶς ἀλλὰ ἑπτάκις.	He did this not once, nor twice, nor three times, but seven times.
6. τότε προσελθὼν ὁ Πέτρος εἶπεν αὐτῷ, Κύριε, ποσάκις ἁμαρτήσει εἰς ἐμὲ ὁ ἀδελφός μου καὶ ἀφήσω αὐτῷ; ἕως ἑπτάκις; λέγει πρὸς αὐτὸν ὁ Ἰησοῦς, Οὐ λέγω σοι ἕως ἑπτάκις ἀλλὰ ἕως ἑβδομηκοντάκις ἑπτά.	Then Peter came to him and said to him, 'Lord, how often shall my brother sin against me and I forgive him? Up to seven times?' Jesus said to him, 'I do not say to you "up to seven times" but "up to seventy seven times".'

35.7

Read John 1:35–42.
> στραφείς – having turned round (στρέφω – I turn)
> θεάομαι – I see
> μεθερμηνεύω – I translate
> ἤγαγεν – he brought (ἄγω – I bring)
> Πέτρος – Peter

35.8 Progress test 17

Which is the correct translation?
1. παρακαλοῦσιν αὐτὸν ἵνα ἐπιθῇ αὐτῇ τὴν χεῖρα.
   (a) They beg him to lay his hands on her.
   (b) They beg him to lay his hand on her.
   (c) They ask him to give her his hand.
2. εἶτα πάλιν ἔδωκεν αὐτοῖς τεσσαράκοντα ἄρτους.
   (a) Then again she gave them four loaves.
   (b) Then a second time she took the forty loaves from them.
   (c) Then again she gave them forty loaves.
3. ἀπήγγειλαν ταῦτα πάντα τοῖς ἕνδεκα καὶ ἠπίστουν αὐταῖς.
   (a) They reported the news to the Twelve and they believed them.
   (b) The men reported all these things to the Twelve and they did not believe them.
   (c) The women reported all these things to the Eleven and they did not believe them.

Which is the best English translation?
4. Καλῶς, Διδάσκαλε, ἐπ' ἀληθείας εἶπες ὅτι εἷς ἐστιν καὶ οὐκ ἔστιν ἄλλος πλὴν αὐτοῦ.
   (a) 'Well, Teacher, in truth you said that he is one and there is not another except him.'
   (b) 'Well said, Teacher; you said truly that he is one and there is no one else beside him.'
   (c) 'Well said, Teacher. You were right in saying that God is one and there is no other except him.'
5. Τὸ θυγάτριόν μου ἐσχάτως ἔχει, ἵνα ἐλθὼν ἐπιθῇς τὰς χεῖρας αὐτῇ ἵνα σωθῇ καὶ ζήσῃ.
   (a) 'My daughter is dying. Please come and lay your hands on her so that she may be healed and live.'
   (b) 'My daughter has a terminal illness. I am asking that having come you should put your hands on her so that she might be saved and live.'
   (c) 'My daughter is near the end. I want you to come and put your hands upon her so that she may be saved and she may live.'

Study these translations of 1 Corinthians 10:23, and answer questions 6–10:

πάντα ἔξεστιν, ἀλλ' οὐ πάντα συμφέρει· πάντα ἔξεστιν ἀλλ' οὐ πάντα οἰκοδομεῖ.

(a) All things are allowed, but not everything is fitting; all things are allowed, but not everything builds up.

(b) Everything is permissible, but not everything is beneficial. Everything is permissible, but it is not everything that builds people up.

(c) There are all kinds of things that are not forbidden by God's Law, but they are not all positively good. There are all kinds of things which are not forbidden by God's Law, but they are not all positively helpful.

(d) We can do all kinds of things – but not everything is good. We can do all kinds of things – but not everything is helpful.

6. Which of these translations would you choose for people whose knowledge of English is limited?
7. Which of these translations would you choose for people with a wide knowledge of English?
8. In which translation does the translator make the greatest effort to interpret the meaning?
9. Which translation follows the Greek words most literally?
10. If we wanted to translate 1 Corinthians 10:23 into some other language, which of the English translations should we consider using as we try to decide how to express the meaning in the third language?

Check your answers in Key to Progress Tests on page 334.

Lesson 36

ἵνα – so that, that
ἵνα ποιήσῃ – so that he may do •
ἵνα δῶμεν – so that we may give •

36.1

The present subjunctive active forms of λέγω are given in 11.8, column (b). In lesson 11 you learned the most common uses of the present subjunctive. For example:

> ἵνα γράφῃς – so that you may write
> ἐὰν γράφωσιν – if they write
> ὃς ἂν γράφῃ – whoever writes
> γράφωμεν – let us write

Now compare:

1. (a) ἦλθεν ἵνα ταῦτα **ποιῇ**
    He came so that he might do these things
   (b) ἦλθεν ἵνα τοῦτο **ποιήσῃ**
    He came so that he might do this.

In (a) ποιῇ indicates repeated actions. It is **present** subjunctive.
In (b) ποιήσῃ indicates a single action. It is **aorist** subjunctive.

2. (a) προσέφερον αὐτῷ τὰ παιδία ἵνα αὐτῶν **ἅπτηται**
    They were bringing the children to him so that **he might touch** them

   (b) προσῆλθον αὐτῷ πολλοὶ ἵνα αὐτοῦ **ἅψωνται**
    Many people came to him so that **they might touch** him.

In (a) ἅπτηται indicates repeated action. He kept touching the children as people kept on bringing them. ἅπτηται is 3rd person singular **present** subjunctive middle of ἅπτομαι (I touch).
In (b) ἅψωνται indicates single action. Many people came to him but each needed to touch him only once. ἅψωνται is 3rd person plural **aorist** subjunctive middle of ἅπτομαι.

3. (a) Τίσιν διδῶμεν;
    To which people should we be giving?
   or To whom should we keep giving?
   (b) Δῶμεν ἢ μὴ δῶμεν;
    Should we give or should we not give?

In (a) διδῶμεν indicates continued or repeated action. διδῶμεν is 1st person plural **present** subjunctive active of δίδωμι (I give).

In (b) δῶμεν indicates the act of giving without reference to its repetition or continuity. δῶμεν is 1st person plural **aorist** subjunctive active of δίδωμι.

36.2 Words

ἀποθνῄσκω – I die
    ἀπέθανον – I died
    τέθνηκα – I have died, I am dead
ὁ θάνατος – the death
    θανατόω – I kill, I put to death, I cause to be killed
ὁ αἰών – the age
    αἰώνιος – eternal, age long
    εἰς τὸν αἰῶνα – forever
νεκρός – dead
    ὁ νεκρός – the dead man
    νεκρόω – I put to death, I mortify
ὁ δοῦλος – the slave, the servant
    ἡ δουλεία – the slavery
    δουλεύω – I serve (as a slave)
    δουλόω – I enslave, I cause to be a slave
ὁ διάκονος – the servant
    ἡ διακονία – the service, serving
    διακονέω – I serve, I look after, I care
νῦν – now
ὅτε – when
    ὅταν – whenever, when
    τότε – then
    πότε; – when?
ἕως – until (when the time is definite)
    ἕως ἄν – until (when the time is indefinite)
διά – through, by means of
    δι' αὐτοῦ – through him

36.3 Translate

1. ἦλθεν ἵνα ὁ κόσμος σωθῇ· καὶ ἀπέθανεν ἵνα ἐν τῷ αἰῶνι τῷ ἐρχομένῳ ζωὴν αἰώνιον ἔχωμεν δι' αὐτοῦ.

   He came so that the world might be saved; and he died so that in the coming age we might have eternal life through him.

2. μήτι ὁ διάκονος ἔρχεται ἵνα διακονήθῃ; οὐχὶ ἔρχεται ἵνα διακονῇ;

   Does a servant come so that he may be served? Doesn't he come so that he may serve?

3. ὁ δοῦλος οὐ μείζων ἐστὶν τοῦ κυρίου αὐτοῦ οὐδὲ ὁ διάκονος μείζων τοῦ βασιλέως.

   A slave is not greater than his master nor is a servant greater than the king.

4. μήτι ὁ δοῦλος μείζων ἐστὶν τοῦ πέμψαντος αὐτόν;

   The slave is not greater than the man who sent him, is he?

5. ὅτε ἦλθεν πρὸς τὸν πατέρα εἶπεν αὐτῷ ὁ πατήρ, Ὁ ἀδελφός σου οὗτος νεκρὸς ἦν καὶ ἔζησεν. ἀπολωλὼς ἦν, νῦν δὲ εὑρέθη.

   When he came to his father, his father said to him, 'Your brother here was dead and came alive. He was lost, but now he has been found.'

6. ὅταν ὁ υἱὸς τοῦ ἀνθρώπου ἐκ νεκρῶν ἀναστῇ αἰώνιον δόξαν δώσει πᾶσιν τοῖς πεπιστευκόσιν εἰς τὸ ὄνομα αὐτοῦ.

   When the Son of Man has risen from the dead he will give eternal glory to all who have believed in his name.

36.4

Read carefully:

1. Seven brothers – one wife

ἑπτὰ ἀδελφοὶ ἦσαν· καὶ ὁ πρῶτος ἔλαβεν γυναῖκα. καὶ ἀποθνήσκων οὐκ ἀφῆκεν τέκνον. καὶ ὁ δεύτερος ἔλαβεν αὐτὴν καὶ ἀπέθανεν. καὶ ὁ τρίτος ὡσαύτως καὶ ὁ τέταρτος καὶ ὁ πέμπτος καὶ ὁ ἕκτος καὶ ὁ ἕβδομος. καὶ οἱ ἑπτὰ οὐκ ἀφῆκαν τέκνον. ἔσχατον πάντων καὶ ἡ γυνὴ ἀπέθανεν.

2. A girl asks the king for John's head

εἶπεν ὁ βασιλεὺς αὐτῇ, Αἴτησόν με ὃ ἐὰν θέλῃς καὶ δώσω σοι. καὶ ἐξελθοῦσα εἶπεν τῇ μητρὶ αὐτῆς, Τί αἰτήσωμαι; ἡ δὲ ἔφη, Τὴν κεφαλὴν Ἰωάννου τοῦ βαπτίζοντος. καὶ εἰσελθοῦσα εὐθὺς πρὸς τὸν βασιλέα εἶπεν αὐτῷ, θέλω ἵνα δῷς μοι τὴν κεφαλὴν Ἰωάννου τοῦ βαπτιστοῦ. Καὶ ἀποθανόντος τοῦ Ἰωάννου, ἦλθον οἱ μαθηταὶ αὐτοῦ καὶ ἦραν τὸ πτῶμα (corpse) αὐτοῦ καὶ ἔθηκαν αὐτὸ ἐν μνημείῳ (tomb).

Also read John 3:13–21.

v13 εἰ μή – if not, except.
v14 ὑψόω – I lift up   ὁ ὄφις – the snake
v16 μονογενής – only (only child) – used in NT 8 times with reference to an only son (e.g. Lk 7:12) and once of an only daughter (Lk 8:4)
v18 ἤδη κέκριται – (he) has already been judged.
v20 φαῦλος – bad, worthless.   πράσσω – I do.   ἐλέγχω – I reprove, I convict, I show to be wrong.
v21 φανερόω – I reveal.   ἐργάζομαι – I do, I work, I bring about.
   ἐν θεῷ – through God (by his help). This use of ἐν is perhaps a Hebraism. Compare Psalm 18:29, in LXX where it is Psalm 17:30,
   καὶ ἐν τῷ θεῷ μου   ὑπερβήσομαι τεῖχος
   and with the help of my God   I shall get over a wall.

36.5 So that...; to...

Clauses of purpose or aim are expressed

1. By ἵνα followed by a verb in the subjunctive:

Mk 1:38 Ἄγωμεν ἀλλαχοῦ...**ἵνα καὶ ἐκεῖ κηρύξω**
   Let us go somewhere else so that I may preach there also
   (κηρύξω is 1st person singular aorist subjunctive active of κηρύσσω)
1 Jn 1:4 ταῦτα γράφομεν ἡμεῖς **ἵνα ἡ χαρὰ ὑμῶν ᾖ πεπληρωμένη**
   We write these things so that your joy may be full
   (ᾖ is 3rd person singular present subjunctive of εἰμί – I am).

2. By the infinitive (to...):

Mk 2:17 οὐκ ἦλθον **καλέσαι** δικαίους
   I did not come to call righteous people
   (καλέσαι is aorist infinitive active of καλέω – I call)
Jn 21:3 Ὑπάγω **ἁλιεύειν**
   I am going off to fish
   (ἁλιεύειν is present infinitive active of ἁλιεύω – I fish)

Mk 10:45 οὐκ ἦλθεν διακονηθῆναι ἀλλὰ διακονῆσαι
He did not come in order to be served but in order to serve
(διακονηθῆναι is aorist infinitive passive of διακονέω – I serve; διακονῆσαι is aorist infinitive active).

3. By εἰς or πρός followed by τό (the) and the infinitive:
Mk 13:22 ποιήσουσιν σημεῖα...πρὸς τὸ ἀποπλανᾶν
   They will do signs so as to deceive
or They will work miracles with the aim of deceiving
(ἀποπλανᾶν is present infinitive active of ἀποπλανάω – I deceive, I lead astray, I cause to err)
2 Cor 1:4 ὁ παρακαλῶν ἡμᾶς ἐπὶ πάσῃ τῇ θλίψει ἡμῶν εἰς τὸ δύνασθαι ἡμᾶς παρακαλεῖν τοὺς ἐν πάσῃ θλίψει
The one who comforts us in every kind of trouble we bear so that we may be able to comfort those who are in any kind of trouble
(δύνασθαι is present infinitive middle of δύναμαι – I am able).

4. By ὅπως followed by a verb in the subjunctive:
Mt 2:8 ἀπαγγείλατέ μοι, ὅπως κἀγὼ ἐλθὼν προσκυνήσω αὐτῷ
Bring back a message to me so that I also may go and worship him
(προσκυνήσω is 1st person singular aorist subjunctive active of προσκυνέω, κἀγώ is καὶ ἐγώ)
Acts 9:2 ὅπως ἐάν τινας εὕρῃ...ἀγάγῃ εἰς Ἰερουσαλήμ
So that, if he should find some people...he might bring them to Jerusalem
(ἀγάγῃ is 3rd person singular aorist subjunctive active of ἄγω – I lead, I bring).

36.6 ἵνα and ὅπως – so that

ὅπως basically means 'how'. So while ἵνα focuses attention on the *purpose* of an action, ὅπως focuses attention also on the way it is to be carried out. So ὅπως can sometimes be translated 'so that in this way...'. See, for example, 2 Corinthians 8:14,

ἵνα καὶ τὸ ἐκείνων περίσσευμα γένηται εἰς τὸ ὑμῶν ὑστέρημα, ὅπως γένηται ἰσότης
So that also their surplus may meet your lack,
so that in this way there may be equality.

36.7 ἵνα

ἵνα is a word that links clauses or parts of sentences together. Care must be taken in translating it, as the links it expresses are of several different kinds. Always read the whole sentence carefully before you decide how to translate ἵνα.

1. ἵνα is most commonly used to show purpose:
Mk 3:14 καὶ ἐποίησεν δώδεκα **ἵνα ὦσιν** μετ' αὐτοῦ
He appointed twelve so that they might be with him.

2. ἵνα is used to introduce a request:
Mk 5:18 παρεκάλει αὐτόν...**ἵνα** μετ' αὐτοῦ **ᾖ**
He begged him that he might be with him
Mk 5:23 **ἵνα** ... **ἐπιθῇς** τὰς χεῖρας αὐτῇ
Please lay your hands on her
Jn 17:15 οὐκ ἐρωτῶ **ἵνα ἄρῃς** αὐτοὺς ἐκ τοῦ κόσμου
ἀλλ' **ἵνα τηρήσῃς** αὐτοὺς ἐκ τοῦ πονηροῦ
I do not ask that you should take them out of the world
but that you should keep them from the evil one.

3. ἵνα is used to introduce a command or prohibition:
Jn 15:12 αὕτη ἐστὶν ἡ ἐντολὴ ἡ ἐμή, **ἵνα ἀγαπᾶτε** ἀλλήλους
This is my commandment – that you should love one another
 or My commandment is this: love one another
Mk 3:12 πολλὰ ἐπετίμα αὐτοῖς **ἵνα** μὴ αὐτὸν φανερὸν **ποιήσωσιν**
He sternly ordered them not to make him known
Mk 6:8 παρήγγειλεν αὐτοῖς **ἵνα** μηδὲν **αἴρωσιν**
He ordered them that they should take nothing
 or He told them not to take anything.

4. ἵνα – 'that', describing or explaining what comes before it:
Jn 4:34 Ἐμὸν βρῶμά ἐστιν **ἵνα ποιήσω** τὸ θέλημα τοῦ πέμψαντός με
My food is to do the will of him who sent me
 or My food is that I should do the will of the one who sent me
Jn 17:3 αὕτη δέ ἐστιν ἡ αἰώνιος ζωή, **ἵνα γινώσκωσιν** σὲ τὸν μόνον ἀληθινὸν θεόν
And this is eternal life that they should know you the only true God
 or Eternal life is this: to know thee who alone art truly God.

5. ἵνα may also indicate a result or consequence:
Jn 9:2   τίς ἥμαρτεν...ἵνα τυφλὸς γεννηθῇ;
   Who sinned, that he was born blind?
or Whose sin caused him to be born blind?
Gal 5:17 ταῦτα γὰρ ἀλλήλοις ἀντίκειται, ἵνα μὴ ἃ ἐὰν θέλητε ταῦτα ποιῆτε
   For these are opposed to each other so that you do not do the things which you wish to do.

Because ἵνα may indicate a result rather than a purpose aimed at, it is not always easy to know how to translate it. Consider these two possible translations of Matthew 26:56.

τοῦτο δὲ ὅλον γέγονεν ἵνα πληρωθῶσιν αἱ γραφαὶ τῶν προφητῶν
(a) This all happened so that what the prophets had written might be fulfilled.
(b) This all happened and so what the prophets had written was fulfilled.

36.8 Bible translations evaluation (5)

Consider these translations of John 3:21 (b)
ἵνα φανερωθῇ αὐτοῦ τὰ ἔργα ὅτι ἐν θεῷ ἐστιν εἰργασμένα
Notice how the translators have handled the Hebraism ἐν θεῷ (with God's help). Note also that in the opening of the verse ὁ ποιῶν 'the person doing' is common gender, so several translators use a plural in translation, since 'they' is common gender.

NJB so that what he is doing may plainly appear as done in God.
NRSV so that it may clearly be seen that their deeds have been done in God.
JBP to make it plain that all he has done has been done through God.
NLT so everyone can see that they are doing what God wants.
GNB in order that the light may show that what they did was in obedience to God.
REB so that it may be clearly seen that God is in all they do.

Which of these seem to be paraphrases rather than translations?
Do any of them seem to reflect accurately what is said in the Greek text?

36.9
Revise lessons 29 and 30.

Lesson 37

ὁ Κύριος – the Lord
τὸν λόγον, τὴν καρδίαν: the accusative case

37.1 Cases

In 12.7 you studied the four main cases (nominative, accusative, genitive, and dative) and their commonest functions. Here are the singular forms of ὁ Κύριος – the Lord:

ὁ Κύριος	the Lord (subject form)	nominative case
Κύριε	O Lord (person spoken to)	vocative case
τὸν Κύριον	the Lord (object form)	accusative case
τοῦ Κυρίου	of the Lord	genitive case
τῷ Κυρίῳ	to the Lord, for the Lord	dative case

Abbreviations: nom, voc, acc, gen, dat
Number: κύριος is nom singular (s)
          κύριοι is nom plural (p).
Gender: λόγος is masculine (m or masc)   ὁ is masc
        καρδία is feminine (f or fem)   ἡ is fem
        ἔργον is neuter (n or neut)   τό is neuter

Parsing nouns, adjectives, and participles:
   Give the case, number, gender, and nom s of nouns, pronouns, and adjectives.
   Give the case, number, gender, tense, mood, and voice of participles.

So: καρδιῶν is gen. p. fem. of καρδία (a heart)
   μοί is dat s of ἐγώ (I)
   ἀγαθαί is nom p f of ἀγαθός (good)
   ποιήσας is nom s m aor part act of ποιέω (I do)
   ἐρχόμενα is nom or acc p n pres part middle of ἔρχομαι (I come, I go).

37.2 The vocative case

Κύριε (Lord! *or* O Lord) is the vocative singular of Κύριος. The vocative is the form used when a person is spoken to. Ἰησοῦ is the vocative form of Ἰησοῦς. In English hymns and prayers we sometimes use the form 'Jesu' when we are speaking to him.

Compare these nominative and vocative singular forms:
  Κύριος – Lord   Κύριε – 'Lord!'
  Ἰησοῦς – Jesus   Ἰησοῦ – 'Jesu'
  πατήρ – father   Πατέρ – 'Father'
  γυνή – woman   Γυναί – 'Woman'

Sixteen times in the New Testament the vocative is introduced by ῏Ω :
Mt 15:28   ῏Ω γύναι, μεγάλη σου ἡ πίστις
            O woman, great is your faith
Mk 9:19   ῏Ω γενεὰ ἄπιστος
            O faithless generation!

When ῏Ω is used, it usually indicates that the speaker or writer is moved by emotion, which may be of concern, respect, surprise, or of disappointment.

37.3 The accusative case

λόγον – λόγους,   καρδίαν – καρδίας,   βασιλέα – βασιλεῖς,
γυναῖκα – γυναῖκας,   σέ – ἡμᾶς,   τόν, τήν, τούς, τάς
are all in the accusative case.

Uses of the accusative case

1. The accusative case is most often used for the object of the verb:
Mk 15:29   ὁ καταλύων τὸν ναόν
           The person who destroys the Temple.

2. When a verb is followed by two accusatives we sometimes add a preposition when we translate into English:
Mk 5:7   ὁρκίζω σε τὸν θεόν
           I adjure you by God
Mk 4:10   ἠρώτων αὐτὸν ... τὰς παραβολάς
           They asked him about the parables
Jn 4:46   ὅπου ἐποίησεν τὸ ὕδωρ οἶνον
           Where he made the water into wine
       or Where he made the water wine
Acts 13:5 εἶχον δὲ καὶ Ἰωάννην ὑπηρέτην
           They also had John as their assistant.

3. **When a verb is followed by a noun in the accusative that expresses the same basic meaning, we may need an adverb or adverbial phrase to express the sense of the accusative noun:**

Mt 2:10   ἐχάρησαν χαρὰν μεγάλην (a great joy)
          They rejoiced greatly

Mk 4:41   ἐφοβήθησαν φόβον μέγαν (a great fear)
          They were terribly afraid
    or They were overcome with awe.

4. **The accusative case may be used to describe or qualify other words or ideas:**

Jn 6:10   οἱ ἄνδρες τὸν ἀριθμὸν ὡς πεντακισχίλιοι
          The men, in number about five thousand

Acts 25:10   Ἰουδαίους οὐδὲν ἠδίκησα
          I have done no wrong to the Jews

Heb 2:17   πιστὸς ἀρχιερεὺς τὰ πρὸς τὸν θεόν
          A faithful high priest in his service to God
          (τά is accusative plural neuter of ὁ– the)

5. **When we translate some Greek verbs which are followed by an accusative case, we need a preposition before the noun in English:**

πιστεύομαι – I am entrusted (with):

Gal 2:7 πεπίστευμαι τὸ εὐαγγέλιον
      I have been entrusted with the gospel

εὐλογέω – I bless, I bless God (for), I thank God (for):

Mk 8:7 εὐλογήσας αὐτά
      Having blessed God for them
  or Having given thanks for them

γονυπετέω – I kneel, I fall on my knees (before):

Mt 17:14 γονυπετῶν αὐτόν
      Kneeling before him.

6. **The accusative often shows length of time or space:**

Jn 11:6   τότε μὲν ἔμεινεν ἐν ᾧ ἦν τόπῳ δύο ἡμέρας
          Then he stayed in the place where he was for two days

Mk 1:19   προβὰς ὀλίγον εἶδεν Ἰάκωβον
          Having gone forward a little way he saw James

Lk 24:13 ἦσαν πορευόμενοι εἰς κώμην ἀπέχουσαν
σταδίους ἑξήκοντα ἀπὸ Ἰερουσαλήμ
They were on their way to a village which was sixty stades
away from Jerusalem   (60 stades is about 11 kilometres).

7. **The accusative case is sometimes used with the infinitive in recording what someone says or thinks:**

Mk 8:29 Ὑμεῖς δὲ τίνα με λέγετε εἶναι;
But whom do you say that I am?
(It would be poor English to translate: But whom do you say me to be?)

Mk 1:34 ὅτι ᾔδεισαν αὐτὸν Χριστὸν εἶναι
Because they knew him to be the Christ
or Because they knew that he was the Messiah.

8. **The accusative case is used after many prepositions:**

εἰς ἄφεσιν – for forgiveness
παρὰ τὴν θάλασσαν – beside the sea.

We study these prepositions in 37.4–15. (Other prepositions are followed by a genitive or dative case. See lessons 39.2–13 and 42.2–7 respectively.)

37.4 Prepositions followed by an accusative case

πρός – to, towards, up to, by, close to, with; against
εἰς – into, to, in, as far as; for, with a view to
ἀνά – up, upwards; in, at the rate of
κατά – down; according to, during, about, along
ὑπέρ – above
ὑπό – under
ἐπί – on, on top of, on to; against, at
περί – round, around, about
παρά – beside, along, at the side of
μετά – after
διά – because of

The basic meaning of most of these prepositions concerns **movement towards** something, or a position reached as a result of such movement. The following diagram may help you to learn these basic meanings:

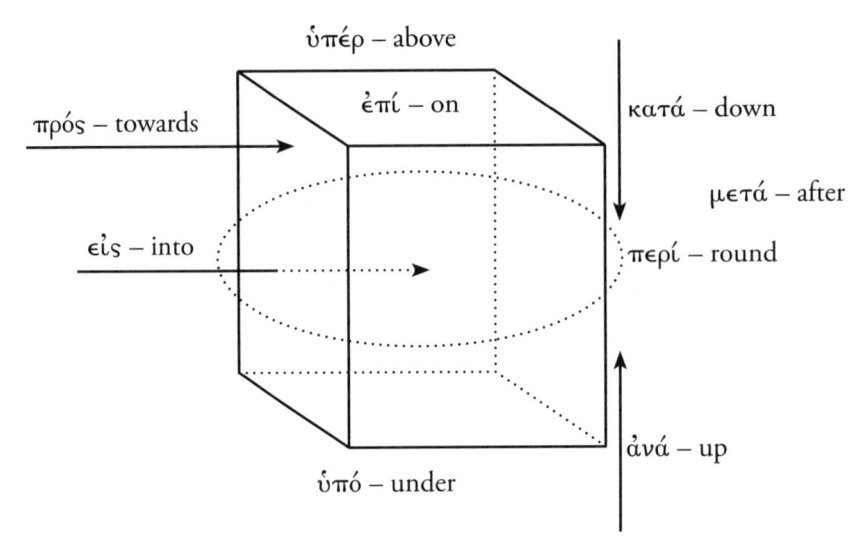

Diagram of prepositions with a cube:
- ὑπέρ – above
- ἐπί – on
- πρός – towards
- εἰς – into
- κατά – down
- μετά – after
- περί – round
- ἀνά – up
- ὑπό – under

Translate:

1. ἔρχεσθε εἰς τὴν πόλιν.	You are going into the town.
2. περιπατοῦμεν παρὰ τὴν θάλασσαν.	We are walking about beside the sea.
3. ἔστιν ἐπὶ τὴν γῆν καί εἰσιν ὑπὸ τὴν γῆν.	He is on the earth and they are under the earth.
4. ἦν ὑπὲρ τοὺς οὐρανοὺς καὶ ἦσαν οἱ ἄγγελοι περὶ αὐτὸν κύκλῳ.	He was above the heavens and the angels were round him in a circle.
5. ἐγὼ ἀναβαίνω εἰς Ἱεροσόλυμα, ἀλλὰ σὺ καταβαίνεις ἀπὸ Ἱεροσολύμων.	I am going up to Jerusalem, but you are going down from Jerusalem.
6. μετὰ δύο ἡμέρας ἦλθεν ἡ γυνὴ λέγουσα, Νῦν πιστεύω διὰ τὸν λόγον σου.	After two days the woman came saying, 'Now I believe because of what you have said.'

37.5 πρός

πρός – to, towards, by, close to, with, against

Mt 14:28 κέλευσόν με ἐλθεῖν πρός σε
Command me to come to you

Mk 4:1 πᾶς ὁ ὄχλος πρὸς τὴν θάλασσαν...ἦσαν
The whole crowd were beside the lake

Mk 6:3 καὶ οὐκ εἰσὶν αἱ ἀδελφαὶ αὐτοῦ ὧδε πρὸς ἡμᾶς;
Are not his sisters here with us?
Mk 12:12 ἔγνωσαν ... ὅτι πρὸς αὐτοὺς τὴν παραβολὴν εἶπεν
They knew that he had spoken the parable against them.

37.6 εἰς

εἰς – into, in, as far as, for, for the purpose of, so as to
Jn 3:13 οὐδεὶς ἀναβέβηκεν εἰς τὸν οὐρανὸν
no one has gone up into heaven
Mk 13:16 ὁ εἰς τὸν ἀγρόν
The person in the field
Mk 7:31 ἦλθεν...εἰς τὴν θάλασσαν τῆς Γαλιλαίας
He went to Lake Galilee
or He went as far as the Sea of Galilee
Mk 6:8 ...ἵνα μηδὲν ἄρωσιν εἰς ὁδόν
...that they should take nothing for the journey
Mk 14:55 ἐζήτουν κατὰ τοῦ Ἰησοῦ μαρτυρίαν εἰς τὸ θανατῶσαι αὐτόν.
They were seeking testimony against Jesus so as to put him to death.

37.7 παρά

παρά – beside, along, at the side of, against, contrary to, compared with, more than
Mk 1:16 παράγων παρὰ τὴν θάλασσαν
Going along beside the lake
Mk 4:4 ἔπεσεν παρὰ τὴν ὁδόν
It fell along the footpath
Mk 10:46 ἐκάθητο παρὰ τὴν ὁδόν
He was sitting at the side of the road
Acts 18:13 Παρὰ τὸν νόμον ἀναπείθει οὗτος τοὺς ἀνθρώπους σέβεσθαι τὸν θεόν
This man is persuading men to worship God in a way that is against the Law
Rom 1:26 αἵ τε γὰρ θήλειαι αὐτῶν μετήλλαξαν τὴν φυσικὴν χρῆσιν εἰς τὴν παρὰ φύσιν
For their women exchanged the natural use (of their bodies) into that which is against what is natural

LESSON 37

Lk 13:2 Δοκεῖτε ὅτι οἱ Γαλιλαῖοι οὗτοι ἁμαρτωλοὶ παρὰ πάντας τοὺς Γαλιλαίους ἐγένοντο;
Do you think that these Galileans were sinners more than all the Galileans?

or Do you consider that these Galileans were worse sinners than anyone else in Galilee?

37.8 ἀνά

ἀνά – up, upwards

ἀνά occurs with the meaning 'up' in many compound verbs.

For example:
ἀναβαίνω – I go up, I travel up to
ἀνίστημι – I raise up, I rise up
ἀναφέρω – I offer up, I bear
 ἀνενέγκαι – to offer up (aorist infinitive)
ἀναβλέπω – I look up, I see, I see again
ἀνοίγω – I open up, I open.

ἀνά is not often used on its own in the New Testament, but note the following phrases:
ἀνὰ δύο – in twos
ἀνὰ πεντήκοντα – in groups of fifty
ἀνὰ δηνάριον – at the rate of one denarius
ἀνὰ μέσον – in the middle
ἀνὰ εἷς ἕκαστος – each one.

37.9 κατά

κατά – down; according to
καταβαίνω – I go down
κάθημαι – I am sitting down
κατεσθίω – I consume, I eat
κατάκειμαι – I lie down
καθίζω – I sit down
κατοικέω – I dwell, I live
τὸ εὐαγγέλιον κατὰ Μᾶρκον – The Good News, according to Mark

Mk 7:5 κατὰ τὴν παράδοσιν τῶν πρεσβυτέρων
According to the tradition of the elders

Mk 15:6 Κατὰ δὲ ἑορτὴν ἀπέλυεν αὐτοῖς ἕνα δέσμιον
At each festival he used to release for them one prisoner

Note also: καθώς – according as, as; καθὼς γέγραπται – as it is written.

37.10 ὑπό

ὑπό – under

Mk 4:21 Μήτι ἔρχεται ὁ λύχνος ἵνα ὑπὸ τὸν μόδιον τεθῇ;
Does a lamp come so that it may be put under the meal-tub?
Jn 1:48 ὄντα ὑπὸ τὴν συκῆν εἶδόν σε
I saw you while you were under the fig tree
Rom 6:14 οὐ γάρ ἐστε ὑπὸ νόμον ἀλλὰ ὑπὸ χάριν
You are not under Law but under grace.

37.11 ὑπέρ

ὑπέρ – above, more than
Phil 2:9 τὸ ὄνομα τὸ ὑπὲρ πᾶν ὄνομα
The name which is above every name
Lk 6:40 οὐκ ἔστιν μαθητὴς ὑπὲρ τὸν διδάσκαλον
A student is not superior to the teacher.

37.12 ἐπί

ἐπί (ἐπ', ἐφ') – on to, on, at, over, against
Mk 4:5 ἄλλο ἔπεσεν ἐπὶ τὸ πετρῶδες
Other (seed) fell onto the rocky ground
Mk 2:14 εἶδεν Λευὶν ... καθήμενον ἐπὶ τὸ τελώνιον
He saw Levi sitting at the customs office
Mt 27:45 σκότος ἐγένετο ἐπὶ πᾶσαν τὴν γῆν
There was darkness over all the land
Mk 3:24 ἐὰν βασιλεία ἐφ' ἑαυτὴν μερισθῇ...
If a kingdom should be divided against itself...

37.13 περί

περί – round, around, about
Mk 3:32 ἐκάθητο περὶ αὐτὸν ὄχλος
A crowd was sitting round him
Mk 4:10 ἠρώτων αὐτὸν οἱ περὶ αὐτόν
His companions questioned him
Mk 6:48 περὶ τετάρτην φυλακὴν τῆς νυκτὸς ἔρχεται.
About the fourth watch of the night he comes.

37.14 μετά

μετά – after

Jn 5:1 Μετὰ ταῦτα ἦν ἑορτὴ τῶν Ἰουδαίων
After these things there was a festival of the Jews

Mk 9:31 μετὰ τρεῖς ἡμέρας ἀναστήσεται
After three days he will rise again.

'A week later' may be expressed either as: μεθ' ἡμέρας ἕξ – after six days (counting only the six days in between – Matthew 17:1),
or as: μεθ' ἡμέρας ὀκτώ – after eight days (counting the first Sunday, six days in between, and the second Sunday – John 20:26).

37.15 διά

διά – because of, on account of, for the sake of
διὰ τί; – why? because of what?

Jn 4:41 πολλῷ πλείους ἐπίστευσαν διὰ τὸν λόγον αὐτοῦ
Far more believed because of his word

Mk 2:27 Τὸ σάββατον διὰ τὸν ἄνθρωπον ἐγένετο
The Sabbath was made for the sake of man

Mk 4:5 διὰ τὸ μὴ ἔχειν βάθος γῆς
Because of not having any depth of earth.

Jn 8:46 διὰ τί ὑμεῖς οὐ πιστεύετέ μοι;
Why do you not believe in me?

37.16

Read carefully:

Your wife and another man

Καλὴ ἡ γυνή σου· ἀλλὰ πονηρά ἐστιν. διὰ τί οὐκ ἔστιν ἐν τῇ οἰκίᾳ; Ἐξῆλθεν παρὰ τὴν θάλασσαν καὶ ἔβλεψεν ἄνδρα ἄλλον καὶ εἰσῆλθεν εἰς τὴν οἰκίαν αὐτοῦ, καὶ νῦν πρὸς αὐτόν ἐστιν. Ἐξελεύσῃ ἐπὶ τὸν ἄνδρα ἐκεῖνον ἀποκτεῖναι αὐτόν; Οὔκ, ἀλλὰ οἴσω αὐτὸν πρὸς τὸν κριτὴν καὶ ὁ κριτὴς αὐτὸν κρινεῖ ὅτι ὑπὸ νόμον ἐσμέν, καὶ κρινεῖ αὐτὸν κατὰ τὸν νόμον. οὐ γὰρ κρινεῖ αὐτὸν παρὰ τὸν νόμον ὁ κριτὴς ὅτι οὐκ ἔστιν ὁ κριτὴς ὑπὲρ τὸν νόμον. μετὰ δὲ ταῦτα ἡ γυνή μου μενεῖ ἐν τῇ οἰκίᾳ μου οὐδὲ ἐλεύσεται περὶ τὴν πόλιν οὐδὲ καθίσει ἐπὶ τὸν θρόνον τὸν ὑπὸ τὴν συκῆν.

37.17

Read John 9:1–12   The Healing of a man born blind.

v1 παράγω – I go along, I pass by.   γενετή – birth.
v2 ὁ γονεύς – the parent.
v3 ἐν αὐτῷ – in him, or, through him.
v4 ἕως – while.
v5 ὅταν – when, while, as long as.   ὦ – I am (present subjunctive of εἰμι).
v6 πτύω – I spit.   χαμαί – on the ground.   πηλός – mud.
  ἐπιχρίω – I smear on.
v7 νίψαι – wash (yourself)!   ἡ κολυμβήθρα – the pool.
v8 ὁ γείτων – the neighbour.   ὁ προσαίτης – the beggar
v9 ὅμοιος – like.
v10 ἠνεῴχθησαν – they were opened (In Greek it is a passive form, but in LXX it sometimes represents a Hebrew Niphal which functions as a middle verb – 'they opened' or 'they came open'.)
v11 ἀναβλέπω – I look up, I become able to see.

Lesson 38

ὥστε – with the result that

38.1

ὥστε – so that, with the result that, so
Note carefully the following sentences:

Mt 12:22 καὶ ἐθεράπευσεν αὐτόν, ὥστε τὸν κωφὸν λαλεῖν.
Translated literally this is:
>And he healed him, so that the dumb to speak.

This is not how we express the meaning of the Greek in English. We do not use the infinitive 'to speak'. We need a translation more like:
>He healed him so that the dumb man spoke.

Or, since λαλεῖν shows continuing action,
>He healed him, so that the dumb man began to speak.

Mk 9:26 ἐγένετο ὡσεὶ νεκρός, ὥστε τοὺς πολλοὺς λέγειν ὅτι ἀπέθανεν
Translated literally:
>He became as if dead, so that the many to be saying that he had died.

In English we need a translation like:
>He became like a corpse, so that most people said, 'He has died.'

Note also:
οὕτως...ὥστε... – so much that...

Jn 3:16 οὕτως...ἠγάπησεν ὁ θεὸς τὸν κόσμον, ὥστε τὸν υἱὸν τὸν μονογενῆ ἔδωκεν.
>God loved the world so much that he gave his only Son.

38.2 Words

ὥστε – so that, with the result that, so as to; so, then, therefore
  οὕτως...ὥστε... – to such an extent that..., so much that...
ὅσος – as much, how great
  ὅσοι – all who
  ὅσα – whatever
τοιοῦτος – such, of such a kind, so great
ἐξίσταμαι – I am amazed

κράζω – I shout
    ἀνακράζω – I shout out
ἀποκτείνω – I kill
    ἀπέκτεινα – I killed
τὸ σάββατον or τὰ σάββατα – the Sabbath day, the week
ἡ ψυχή – the life, the spirit, the person
μέγας, μεγάλη, μέγα – big, large, great
    φωνῇ μεγάλῃ – in a loud voice, loudly

38.3 Translate

1. ἔκραξεν φωνῇ μεγάλῃ ὥστε ἀκούειν αὐτοῦ πάντας ὅσοι ἦσαν ἐν τῇ οἰκίᾳ ἐκείνῃ.

   He shouted loudly so that all who were in that house heard him.

2. ἐθεράπευσεν αὐτοὺς τοῖς σάββασιν ὥστε τοὺς Φαρισαίους ζητεῖν ὅπως αὐτὸν ἀποκτείνωσιν.

   He healed them on the Sabbath day so that the Pharisees began to look for a way to kill him.

3. καὶ λέγει αὐτοῖς, Ἔξεστιν τοῖς σάββασιν ἀγαθὸν ποιῆσαι ἢ κακοποιῆσαι, ψυχὴν σῶσαι ἢ ἀποκτεῖναι;

   He said to them, 'Is it legal on the Sabbath day to do good or to do evil, to save life or to kill?'

4. οὕτως ἠγάπησεν ἡμᾶς ὥστε δοῦναι τὴν ψυχὴν ὑπὲρ ἡμῶν· τοιαύτη ἐστὶν ἡ ἀγάπη αὐτοῦ.

   He loved us so much that he gave his life for us: his love is as great as that.

5. οἱ δὲ ἰδόντες αὐτὸν περιπατοῦντα ἐπὶ τὴν θάλασσαν ἀνέκραξαν. καὶ ἔλεγεν αὐτοῖς, Εἰρήνη ὑμῖν· ἐγώ εἰμι, ὥστε ἐξίστασθαι πάντας.

   Seeing him walking on the lake they shouted out. He said to them, 'Peace be with you: it is I', so that they were all amazed.

38.4 Uses of ὥστε

1. ὥστε and the infinitive – clauses of result:

Mt 12:22 ἐθεράπευσεν αὐτόν, ὥστε τὸν κωφὸν λαλεῖν καὶ βλέπειν
           He healed him, so that the dumb man could speak and see

Mk 2:12   ἐξῆλθεν ἔμπροσθεν πάντων, ὥστε ἐξίστασθαι πάντας καὶ δοξάζειν τὸν θεόν
           He went out before them all, so that they were all amazed and praised God

Mk 3:20   συνέρχεται πάλιν ὄχλος, ὥστε μὴ δύνασθαι αὐτοὺς μηδὲ ἄρτον φαγεῖν
The crowd came together again, so that they were not able even to eat bread
or Such a crowd gathered again that they could not even eat a meal (συνέρχεται is a historic present – cf. 25.2).

2. ὥστε and the indicative – clauses of logical result:

Mk 2:27–28 Τὸ σάββατον διὰ τὸν ἄνθρωπον ἐγένετο...ὥστε κύριός ἐστιν ὁ υἱὸς τοῦ ἀνθρώπου καὶ τοῦ σαββάτου
The Sabbath was made for the good of man, so the Son of Man is Lord even of the Sabbath

Gal 4:6–7 ἐξαπέστειλεν ὁ θεὸς τὸ πνεῦμα τοῦ υἱοῦ αὐτοῦ εἰς τὰς καρδίας ἡμῶν...ὥστε οὐκέτι εἶ δοῦλος ἀλλὰ υἱός
God sent the Spirit of his Son into our hearts...you are therefore no longer a slave but a son.

3. οὕτως...ὥστε..., τοσοῦτος...ὥστε..., πολύς...ὥστε...
such that,   so great that,   so much that:

Mk 2:2   καὶ συνήχθησαν πολλοὶ ὥστε μηκέτι χωρεῖν
Many people were gathered together so that there was no longer room
or So many people came together that there was no space left

Mt 15:33 ἄρτοι τοσοῦτοι ὥστε χορτάσαι ὄχλον τοσοῦτον
Enough loaves to satisfy such a large crowd.

38.5 Because... ὅτι and διά in clauses of cause or reason

Cause and reason are expressed

1. By ὅτι followed by a verb in the indicative:

Mk 1:34   οὐκ ἤφιεν λαλεῖν τὰ δαιμόνια, ὅτι ᾔδεισαν αὐτόν
He was not allowing the demons to speak because they knew him.

2. By διά followed by a verb in the infinitive:

Mk 4:5   εὐθὺς ἐξανέτειλεν διὰ τὸ μὴ ἔχειν βάθος γῆς
It came up quickly because it had no depth of soil

Phil 1:7 καθώς ἐστιν δίκαιον ἐμοὶ τοῦτο φρονεῖν ὑπὲρ πάντων ὑμῶν διὰ τὸ ἔχειν με ἐν τῇ καρδίᾳ ὑμᾶς
As it is right for me to feel this about you all because I have you in my heart.

38.6 Grammatical terms

Clauses of purpose, aim, or intended result are called **final** clauses.

So in Mark 1:38, Ἄγωμεν ἀλλαχοῦ εἰς τὰς ἐχομένας κωμοπόλεις, ἵνα καὶ ἐκεῖ κηρύξω (Let us go elsewhere to the neighbouring country towns so that I may preach there also); ἵνα και ἐκεῖ κηρύξω is a final clause.

Clauses of actual result are called **consecutive** clauses.

So in Mark 15:5, ὁ δὲ Ἰησοῦς οὐκέτι οὐδὲν ἀπεκρίθη, ὥστε θαυμάζειν τὸν Πιλᾶτον (Jesus still made no reply, so Pilate was amazed); ὥστε θαυμάζειν τὸν Πιλᾶτον is a consecutive clause.

38.7 Translating ψυχή

In the New Testament the word ψυχή covers a wide area of meaning. Like the Hebrew word *nephesh* it may refer to person, self, life, or spirit. In choosing how to translate ψυχή into English we must consider carefully the passage in which it occurs.

In Mark 3:4, ψυχὴν σῶσαι means 'to save life': it is the opposite of ἀποκτεῖναι (to kill). Also in Mark 8:35–37, we may consider that 'life' is the nearest equivalent to ψυχή, since taking up one's cross (v34) implies readiness to die.

But in Matthew 26:38, Περίλυπός ἐστιν ἡ ψυχή μου (my ψυχή is very sad) and John 12:27, Νῦν ἡ ψυχή μου τετάρακται (now my ψυχή is disturbed), Jesus is saying that he is saddened and distressed at the very core of his being. Here 'heart' may be the best equivalent English idiom: 'My heart is crushed with sorrow', 'Now my heart is deeply troubled.'

Note also Philippians 1:27, μιᾷ ψυχῇ συναθλοῦντες τῇ πίστει τοῦ εὐαγγελίου (with one ψυχή, struggling side by side for the faith of the gospel). Here one might translate μιᾷ ψυχῇ as 'in unity of spirit' or 'with a single purpose'.

In 1 Corinthians 15:45, ψυχὴ ζῶσα is more or less equivalent to 'a living person'. But note that in 1 Corinthians 15:44–46, the adjective ψυχικός is contrasted with πνευματικός (spiritual). So perhaps here the nearest English equivalent of ψυχικός is 'physical'.

In all our efforts to understand the New Testament in Greek and to translate it into our own languages, we must never limit ourselves to the simple question, 'What is the meaning of this Greek word?' We must always be asking ourselves, 'What is the meaning of the word **in this passage** and how can I express it most accurately and intelligibly in my own language?'

38.8 Read John 9:13-23.

v13 ἄγω – I bring, I lead.

v14 ἀνέῳξεν – he opened (ἀνοίγω – I open).

v16 παρὰ θεοῦ – from God. ἁμαρτωλός – sinful, sinner.

τοιοῦτος – such great.   τὸ σημεῖον – the sign, the miracle.

τὸ σχίσμα – the division.

v18 οἱ Ἰουδαῖοι – the Judeans: here as in other instances in John, it refers particularly to the Judean religious authorities.   ἕως ὅτου – until.

v19 ἄρτι – now.

v21 ἤ – and   (in other contexts ἤ may mean: or).

v21 ἡλικία – age, maturity

v22 συντίθεμαι – I arrange, I agree.   ἀποσυνάγωγος – excluded from the synagogue: the lightest form of exclusion lasted for seven days, or thirty days if pronounced by the Head of the Sanhedrin; the severest was a ban of indefinite duration.

38.9 Progress test 18

Which translation is correct?

1. ἄγωμεν καὶ ἡμεῖς ἵνα ἀποθάνωμεν μετ' αὐτοῦ.
   (a) Let us go away because we shall die with him.
   (b) Let us also go so that we may die with him.
2. προσκόπτει ὅτι τὸ φῶς οὐκ ἔστιν ἐν αὐτῷ
   (a) He stumbles because the light is not in him.
   (b) He stumbles when the light is not in him.
3. πᾶς γὰρ ὁ φαῦλα πράσσων μισεῖ τὸ φῶς ὅτι οὐ ποιεῖ τὴν ἀλήθειαν.
   (a) For everyone who does evil hates the light so that he does not act rightly.
   (b) For everyone who does evil things hates the light because he does not act rightly.

Which is the best English translation?

4. πολλὰ ἐπετίμα αὐτῷ ἵνα μὴ αὐτὸν φανερὸν ποιήσῃ.
   (a) He ordered him many things so that he should not make him manifest.

(b) He rebuked him sternly not to make him known.

(c) He gave him strict orders not to make him known.

5. τὰ κύματα ἐπέβαλλεν εἰς τὸ πλοῖον, ὥστε ἤδη γεμίζεσθαι τὸ πλοῖον.

   (a) The waves began to spill over into the boat, so that it was already filling up with water.

   (b) The waves were beating against the boat and spilling into it, so that it was already getting swamped.

   (c) The waves used to beat into the boat so that already the boat was weighed down.

6. ἐγὼ τίθημι τὴν ψυχήν μου ἵνα πάλιν λάβω αὐτήν.

   (a) I place my soul in order to take it again.

   (b) I lay down my spirit so that I may take it again.

   (c) I lay down my life so that I may take it again.

7. Read carefully through the sentences in 3–6 in this test and write down all the Greek words that are in the accusative case.

Check your answers in Key to Progress Tests on page 334.

38.10

Revise lessons 31 and 32.

Lesson 39

τοῦ λόγου, τῆς καρδίας: the genitive case

39.1

λόγου – λόγων, τῆς καρδίας – τῶν καρδίων, τινος – τινων, ποιοῦντος – ποιούσης and ποιούντων are all in the genitive case.

Uses of the genitive case

1. The genitive case is most often used to show that one thing is closely related to another, usually in some way possessed by it or belonging to it:

Jn 1:12 τέκνα θεοῦ – children of God
Jn 1:19 ἡ μαρτυρία τοῦ Ἰωάννου
John's testimony *or* The witness given by John
Jn 1:27 οὗ οὐκ εἰμὶ ἐγὼ ἄξιος ἵνα λύσω αὐτοῦ
τὸν ἱμάντα τοῦ ὑποδήματος
Of whom I am not worthy to untie the strap of his sandal
Eph 1:13 ἐσφραγίσθητε τῷ πνεύματι τῆς ἐπαγγελίας
(Lit. You were sealed by the Spirit of the promise)
You were sealed by the promised Spirit.

The nature of the relationship shown by the genitive case can often only be discovered by a careful study of the passage in which it comes. For example, ἡ ἀγάπη τοῦ θεοῦ (the love of God) may mean, 'God's love' or 'love for God'. In 1 John 4:9, ἡ ἀγάπη τοῦ θεοῦ means 'God's love for us'. In 1 John 5:3, ἡ ἀγάπη τοῦ θεου means 'Our love for God'. See also lesson 12.1.

In Mark 1:4, we should not translate βάπτισμα μετανοίας as 'a baptism of repentance' (AV, RSV, NJB, NIV) since repentance is not something that can be baptized. We need a translation more like 'a baptism in token of repentance' (NEB) or 'baptism for those who repented'. GNB restructures the whole sentence to express the meaning of μετανοία more clearly: 'Turn away from your sins and be baptized.'

2. The genitive case may be used to show time during which something is done:

Mk 5:5 διὰ παντὸς νυκτὸς καὶ ἡμέρας ... ἦν κράζων
Constantly, by night and by day, he was shouting

Lk 18:12 νηστεύω δὶς τοῦ σαββάτου
I fast twice during each week.

3. The genitive case may be used to show separation from:

Eph 2:12 ἦτε τῷ καιρῷ ἐκείνῳ χωρὶς **Χριστοῦ** ἀπηλλοτριωμένοι **τῆς πολιτείας** τοῦ Ἰσραὴλ καὶ ξένοι **τῶν διαθηκῶν** τῆς ἐπαγγελίας
You were at that time apart from Christ, alienated from the citizenship of Israel, and strangers from the covenants of God's promise.

4. The genitive is often used when things are compared:

Mt 27:64 ἔσται ἡ ἐσχάτη πλάνη χείρων **τῆς πρώτης**
The last deception will be worse than the first

Jn 8:53 μὴ σὺ μείζων εἶ **τοῦ πατρὸς** ἡμῶν Ἀβραάμ;
Surely you are not greater than our forefather Abraham?

1 Cor 13:13 μείζων δὲ **τούτων** ἡ ἀγάπη
But the greatest of these is love

Jn 7:31 μὴ πλείονα σημεῖα ποιήσει **ὧν** οὗτος ἐποίησεν;
Will he do more miracles (signs) than those which this man has done?

5. The genitive is used for price or cost:

Jn 12:5 Διὰ τί ... οὐκ ἐπράθη **τριακοσίων δηναρίων**;
Why was it not sold for three hundred denarii?

6. The genitive is used after many verbs, especially those which have to do with hearing, touching, feeling, remembering, sharing, lacking, and departing:

Mk 9:7 ἀκούετε **αὐτοῦ**
Hear him! (Listen to him!)

Mk 1:31 ἤγειρεν αὐτὴν κρατήσας **τῆς χειρός**
He raised her up having taken hold of her hand

Mt 26:75 ἐμνήσθη ὁ Πέτρος **τοῦ ῥήματος** Ἰησοῦ εἰρηκότος
Peter remembered the word Jesus had said

Rom 3:23 ὑστεροῦνται **τῆς δόξης** τοῦ θεοῦ
They fall short of the glory of God

Lk 22:35 μή **τινος** ὑστερήσατε;
You didn't lack anything, did you?

7. The genitive is used after υἱός:

(a) Mt 4:6   Εἰ υἱὸς εἶ τοῦ θεοῦ, βάλε σεαυτὸν κάτω
If you are the Son of God, throw yourself down
Mt 22:42   τίνος υἱός ἐστιν;
Whose son is he?
Gal 3:7   υἱοί εἰσιν Ἀβραάμ
They are descendants of Abraham.

(b) Eph 5:6   ἔρχεται ἡ ὀργὴ τοῦ θεοῦ ἐπὶ τοὺς υἱοὺς **τῆς ἀπειθείας**
The wrath of God comes upon those who disobey him
or The wrath of God comes upon those who are rebels
2 Thess 2:3   ὁ ἄνθρωπος τῆς ἀνομίας, ὁ υἱὸς **τῆς ἀπωλείας**
(Lit. the man of lawlessness, the son of destruction)
This has been translated in many different ways, e.g.
NEB   Wickedness in human form, the man doomed to perdition
NJB   The wicked One, the lost One
NIV   The man of lawlessness, the man doomed to destruction
GNB   The Wicked One who is destined for hell.

In the (a) examples, υἱός is used in its normal Greek sense of 'son', or 'descendant'.

In the (b) examples, υἱός is used in a different way, following a Hebrew idiom. A son usually has a nature similar to that of his father. So υἱὸς τῆς ἀπειθείας (son of disobedience) means a person whose nature it is to disobey, a person whose true character is revealed in the way he constantly disobeys God.

It is sometimes very difficult to know the best way to translate υἱός into English – compare the different attempts to translate 2 Thessalonians 2:3 given above. We must be particularly careful in using 'children' as a translation of υἱοί. In 1 Thessalonians 5:5 we might translate υἱοὶ φωτός ἐστε as 'You are children of light.' The knowledge that Paul says this to the readers and hearers of the letter makes it clear that he is not talking about children, but about Christian people of all ages. In Ephesians 5:6 it would be misleading to translate 'The wrath of God comes upon the children of disobedience' (see AV). It might make the reader or hearer think that God's wrath comes on children who are disobedient. It does not mean this. It refers to people who persistently disobey God.

In Mark 2:19, οἱ υἱοὶ τοῦ νυμφῶνος (the sons of the bridegroom's house) refers to the custom of the bridegroom's friends meeting at his house before going in procession to fetch the bride from her home. We do not have exactly the same custom in England. We can translate οἱ υἱοὶ τοῦ νυμφῶνος as 'the bridegroom's friends' or 'the friends gathered at the bridegroom's house'. It would be misleading to translate as 'the wedding guests', since Mark 2:19–20 only mentions the bridegroom (at a time when he has not yet brought the bride home), while in English 'wedding guests' suggests the presence of both bride and bridegroom.

8. Genitive with a participle – genitive absolute:
Mt 9:33   ἐκβληθέντος τοῦ δαιμονίου ἐλάλησεν ὁ κωφός
          When the demon had been cast out, the dumb man spoke.
For this common usage of the genitive case, see 25.1–3.

39.2 Prepositions followed by a genitive case

ἀπό – away from, from

ἐκ – out of, as a result of

*διά – through, by means of, after

*μετά – with, among

*περί – about (as in 'speak about', 'pray about')

*παρά – from the side of, from

*κατά – down from, against, throughout

*ἐπί – on, in, in the time of, on account of, up to

*ὑπέρ – for, on behalf of

ἀντί – in the place of, instead of

ὀπίσω – behind, after

πρό – before

ἔμπροσθεν – in front of, before

*ὑπό – by (when something is done by a person)

χωρίς – without, apart from

Those prepositions marked * are also used with the accusative case (see 37.4, 7, 9–15). Their meaning is different when they are followed by a genitive case.

The basic meaning of many of the prepositions followed by the genitive concerns movement away from something, or a position away from something else:

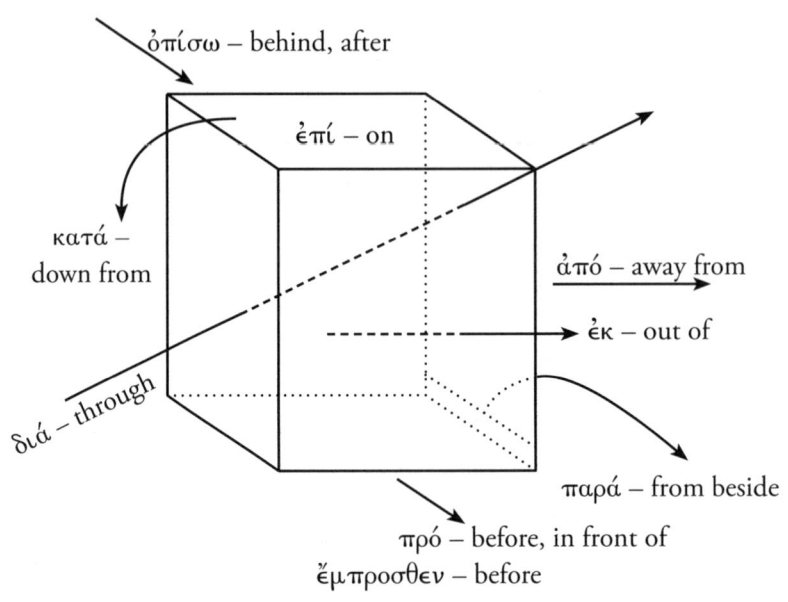

ὀπίσω – behind, after
ἐπί – on
κατά – down from
ἀπό – away from
ἐκ – out of
διά – through
παρά – from beside
πρό – before, in front of
ἔμπροσθεν – before

Translate:

1. ὀπίσω μου.	Behind me, after me.
2. πρὸ τῆς οἰκίας.	In front of the house.
3. κατέβη ἐκ τοῦ οὐρανοῦ.	He came down from heaven.
4. ἐξῆλθεν παρὰ τοῦ θεοῦ.	He went out from God.
5. τὰ ἐπὶ τῆς γῆς.	The things on the earth.
6. ἀπήλθομεν ἀπὸ Ναζαρέθ.	We went away from Nazareth.
7. ἤλθετε διὰ τῆς Γαλιλαίας.	You went through Galilee.
8. ὁ ὀπίσω μου ἐρχόμενος.	The one coming after me.

39.3 ὀπίσω

ὀπίσω – behind, after

Mk 8:33 Ὕπαγε ὀπίσω μου
Go away behind me (*or better,* Go away from me)

Mk 8:34 Εἴ τις θέλει ὀπίσω μου ἐλθεῖν...
If someone wishes to follow after me...

Jn 12:19 ὁ κόσμος ὀπίσω αὐτοῦ ἀπῆλθεν
For the world has gone off after him

Note: εἰς τὰ ὀπίσω – backwards, back.

39.4 πρό

πρό – before
Mt 5:12 οὕτως γὰρ ἐδίωξαν τοὺς προφήτας τοὺς πρὸ ὑμῶν
For thus they persecuted the prophets who were before you
Mk 1:2 Ἰδοὺ ἀποστέλλω τὸν ἄγγελόν μου πρό προσώπου σου
See, I am sending my messenger before your face (ahead of you)
Gal 2:12 πρὸ τοῦ γὰρ ἐλθεῖν τινας ἀπὸ Ἰακώβου...
For before some people came from James...

39.5 κατά

κατά – down, down from; against
Mk 5:13 ὥρμησεν ἡ ἀγέλη κατὰ τοῦ κρημνοῦ εἰς τὴν θάλασσαν
The herd rushed down the cliff into the lake
Mk 11:25 ἀφίετε εἴ τι ἔχετε κατά τινος
Forgive if you have something against someone
or Forgive if you have anything against anyone.

39.6 παρά

παρά – from (from or beside a person)
Mk 8:11 ζητοῦντες παρ' αὐτοῦ σημεῖον ἀπὸ τοῦ οὐρανοῦ
Seeking from him a sign from heaven
Mk 3:21 οἱ παρ' αὐτοῦ ἐξῆλθον
His relatives went out
Mk 5:26 δαπανήσασα τὰ παρ' αὐτῆς πάντα
Having spent all her wealth
(τὰ παρ' αὐτῆς – the things from beside her,
  her possessions, her money)
Jn 9:16 Οὐκ ἔστιν οὗτος παρὰ θεοῦ ὁ ἄνθρωπος
This man is not from God.

39.7 διά

διά – through, by means of, after
Mk 9:30 παρεπορεύοντο διὰ τῆς Γαλιλαίας
They were travelling through Galilee

Mk 14:21 οὐαὶ δὲ τῷ ἀνθρώπῳ ἐκείνῳ δι' οὗ ὁ υἱὸς τοῦ ἀνθρώπου
παραδίδοται
But alas for that man through whom the Son of Man is betrayed
Heb 9:12 διὰ δὲ τοῦ ἰδίου αἵματος εἰσῆλθεν ἐφάπαξ
He entered in once for all by means of his own blood
(ἐφάπαξ means 'once for all', i.e. once without need for
repetition. It does not mean 'once and for all people')
Mk 14:58 διὰ τριῶν ἡμερῶν ἄλλον ἀχειροποίητον οἰκοδομήσω
After three days I will build another not made by hand
 or In three days I will build another not made by human hands
(διά, when it refers to a period of time, often means 'after',
but sometimes means 'through', 'throughout', 'in', 'during a
period of time').

Note: διὰ παντός – all the time, continually.

39.8 ἐπί

ἐπί – on, in, in the time of, over…

Mk 2:10 ἀφιέναι ἁμαρτίας ἐπὶ τῆς γῆς
To forgive sins on earth
Mk 8:4 Πόθεν τούτους δυνήσεταί τις
ὧδε χορτάσαι ἄρτων ἐπ' ἐρημίας;
How will anyone be able to satisfy these people
with bread here in the wilderness?
Mk 12:14 ἐπ' ἀληθείας τὴν ὁδὸν τοῦ θεοῦ διδάσκεις
You teach the way of God truly
Acts 11:28 ἥτις ἐγένετο ἐπὶ Κλαυδίου
Which happened in the time of Claudius
Acts 7:27 Τίς σε κατέστησεν ἄρχοντα … ἐφ' ἡμῶν;
Who appointed you as ruler over us?
Mk 12:26 οὐκ ἀνέγνωτε ἐν τῇ βίβλῳ Μωϋσέως ἐπὶ τοῦ βάτου;
Have you not read in the book of Moses
in the passage about the bush?
Rev 21:16 ἐμέτρησεν τὴν πόλιν τῷ καλάμῳ
ἐπὶ σταδίων δώδεκα χιλιάδων
He measured the city with a reed,
reaching a total of twelve thousand furlongs
(Note: 'furlong' is the nearest English equivalent to the Greek 'stade'. It is
a term not often used today, so GNB converts to a more modern system

of measurement – 2,400 kilometres. But as 12 and 1,000 are symbolic numbers in Revelation, it seems better to retain the original figure).

39.9 μετά

μετά – with, among (nearly always with a person)

Mk 1:13 ἦν μετὰ τῶν θηρίων
He was with the wild animals

Mk 1:36 Σίμων καὶ οἱ μετ' αὐτοῦ
Simon and his companions

Mk 2:16 Ὅτι μετὰ τῶν τελωνῶν καὶ ἁμαρτωλῶν ἐσθίει;
Why does he eat with the tax-collectors and sinners?

Mk 6:25 εἰσελθοῦσα...μετὰ σπουδῆς πρὸς τὸν βασιλέα ᾐτήσατο...
Coming in with haste to the king she asked...
or She hurried in to the king and asked...

39.10 περί

περί – about, concerning

Mk 1:30 καὶ εὐθὺς λέγουσιν αὐτῷ περὶ αὐτῆς
At once they told him about her

Mk 10:41 ἤρξαντο ἀγανακτεῖν περὶ Ἰακώβου καὶ Ἰωάννου
They began to be annoyed about James and John

Phil 2:20 τὰ περὶ ὑμῶν μεριμνήσει
He will be concerned for your affairs
(τὰ περὶ ὑμῶν – the things concerning you, your affairs, your welfare).

39.11 ὑπέρ

ὑπέρ – for, on the side of, on behalf of, about

Mk 9:40 ὃς γὰρ οὐκ ἔστιν καθ' ἡμῶν ὑπὲρ ἡμῶν ἐστιν
For the person who is not against us is on our side

Mk 14:24 Τοῦτό ἐστιν τὸ αἷμά μου τῆς διαθήκης τὸ ἐκχυννόμενον ὑπὲρ πολλῶν
This is my blood of the covenant which is poured out on behalf of many

Jas 5:16 εὔχεσθε ὑπὲρ ἀλλήλων
Keep praying for each other
or Pray for one another

Jn 1:30 οὗτός ἐστιν ὑπὲρ οὗ ἐγὼ εἶπον...
This is the man about whom I said...

39.12 ἀντί

ἀντί – instead of, in place of, as a substitute for, for

Mt 2:22   Ἀρχέλαος βασιλεύει...ἀντὶ τοῦ πατρὸς αὐτοῦ Ἡρῴδου
           Archelaus reigns in place of his father Herod
Mk 10:45 δοῦναι τὴν ψυχὴν αὐτοῦ λύτρον ἀντὶ πολλῶν
           To give his life as a ransom for many
Lk 11:11 καὶ ἀντὶ ἰχθύος ὄφιν αὐτῷ ἐπιδώσει;
           And instead of a fish will he give him a snake?
Note: ἀνθ' ὧν – therefore, wherefore, because
Lk 1:20 ἀνθ' ὧν οὐκ ἐπίστευσας τοῖς λόγοις μου
           Because you did not believe my words.

39.13 ὑπό

ὑπό – by (by a person)
Mk 1:5   ἐβαπτίζοντο ὑπ' αὐτοῦ
         They were being baptized by him
Rom 15:24 ἐλπίζω...θεάσασθαι ὑμᾶς καὶ ὑφ' ὑμῶν προπεμφθῆναι ἐκεῖ
           I hope to see you and by you to be sent on there.

39.14

(a) Read John 9:24–34

  v24 ἐκ δευτέρου – a second time.   ὃς ἦν τυφλὸς – who had been blind.
     Δὸς δόξαν τῷ θεῷ – Give glory to God: an idiom meaning 'Speak
                 the truth before God' (see Josh 7:19)
  v27 μὴ καὶ ὑμεῖς – would you perhaps also...? (see 27.3 Mt 12:23)
  v28 λοιδορέω – I revile, I abuse.
  v30 τὸ θαυμαστόν – something amazing.
  v31 θεοσεβής – pious, devout, religious.
  v34 ὅλος – whole, complete

(b) Read John 9:35–38 again – see 23.9 (a)

(c) Read John 9:39–41

  v39 τὸ κρίμα – the judgement:
     εἰς κρίμα – for judgement, for the purpose of judging.
  v41 εἰ τυφλοὶ ἦτε – if you were blind.
     οὐκ ἂν εἴχετε – you would not have.

Lesson 40

τοῦτο ποίησον – do this!

40.1

Compare:

(a) εἶπεν αὐτῷ, Τοῦτο **ποίει.**
   He said to him, 'Do this!'

   εἶπεν αὐτῇ, **Αἶρε** τοὺς λίθους.
   He said to her, 'Pick up the stones!'

   εἶπεν αὐτοῖς, Τοῦτο **ποιεῖτε.**
   He said to them, 'Do this!'

   εἶπεν αὐταῖς, **Αἴρετε** τοὺς λίθους.
   He said to them, 'Pick up the stones!'

(b) εἶπεν αὐτῷ, Τοῦτο **ποίησον.**
   He said to him, 'Do this!'

   εἶπεν αὐτῇ, **Ἆρον** τὸν λίθον.
   He said to her, 'Pick up the stone!'

   εἶπεν αὐτοῖς, Τοῦτο **ποιήσατε.**
   He said to them, 'Do this!'

   εἶπεν αὐταῖς, **Ἄρατε** τὸν λίθον.
   He said to them, 'Pick up the stone!'

In (a) the commands expressed by ποίει, ποιεῖτε, αἶρε, and αἴρετε are commands to do actions that are repeated (done more than once). ποίει, ποιεῖτε, αἶρε, and αἴρετε are *present imperative*.

In (b) the commands expressed by ποίησον, ποιήσατε, ἆρον, and ἄρατε are commands to do a single action. ποίησον, ποιήσατε, ἆρον, and ἄρατε are *aorist imperative*.

So (a) in Luke 22:19,

   τοῦτο **ποιεῖτε** εἰς τὴν ἐμὴν ἀνάμνησιν
   Do this in remembrance of me

ποιεῖτε is a command to do it often, to keep on doing the action. We might translate it as, 'Keep doing...'.

But (b) in John 2:5,

   ὅ τι ἂν λέγῃ ὑμῖν **ποιήσατε**
   Whatever he says to you, **do** it

ποιήσατε is a command to do the action, without reference to its repetition.

Compare also:

Lk 11:3 τὸν ἄρτον ἡμῶν τὸν ἐπιούσιον **δίδου** ἡμῖν τὸ καθ' ἡμέραν
   Keep giving us our daily bread each day

Mt 6:11 τὸν ἄρτον ἡμῶν τὸν ἐπιούσιον **δὸς** ἡμῖν σήμερον
   Give us our daily bread today.

δίδου – give, keep giving, is present imperative ▰▰▰▰
δός – give, is aorist imperative •

Notice that in Greek the imperative is used both for commands and for requests.

So in John 4:16,
φώνησον τὸν ἄνδρα σου καὶ ἐλθὲ ἐνθάδε
Call your husband and **come** here.
But in John 4:15,
Κύριε, δός μοι τοῦτο τὸ ὕδωρ
Sir, **please give** me this water
and John 4:7,
Δός μοι πεῖν   (lit. give me to drink)
Please give me a drink.

40.2 Words
ὧδε – here
ἐκεῖ – there
	ἐκεῖθεν – from there
ὁράω – I see
	ὁρᾶτε μή... or βλέπετε μή... – see that you do not, beware lest
ἴδε – look! (used to attract or direct attention: 'see!' 'Look, there is...',
'	Look, here is...')
ἑαυτόν – himself
	ἐμαυτόν – myself, σεαυτόν – yourself,
	ἑαυτούς – themselves, ourselves, yourselves
ἀλλήλους – each other, one another
	ἄλλος – other, another
χαίρω – I rejoice, I greet
	λίαν ἐχάρην – I rejoiced greatly
	χαῖρε, χαίρετε – hail, hello, greetings! rejoice!
ἡ χαρά – the joy (distinguish from χάρις – grace, undeserved love)
φέρω – I bear, I carry, I bring
	ἐνέγκαι – to bring (aorist infinitive)
	προσφέρω – I carry to, I offer
	προσήνεγκεν – he offered
ἡ μετάνοια – repentance, turning from sin to God
	μετανοέω – I repent, I change my attitude

μετά indicates change. νοια indicates attitude of mind. So in μετάνοια and μετανοέω the emphasis is on change of attitude and action, on turning from a life centred on self to a life centred on God. In the English word 'repentance' there is more of an emphasis on sorrow for past wrong, and in the Latin *penitentia* there is more emphasis on punishment for wrongdoing. So, while μετάνοια and repentance both suggest the combination of sorrow for sin and turning from it, the emphasis in μετάνοια is more on the change or turning.

40.3 Translate

1. λέγω τούτῳ, Ἔλθε ὧδε καὶ ἔρχεται, καὶ ἄλλῳ Πορεύθητι ἐκεῖ καὶ πορεύεται, καὶ ἄλλῳ, Ἔνεγκε τοῦτο καὶ φέρει καὶ τῷ δούλῳ μου Ποίησον τοῦτο καὶ ποιεῖ. | I say to this man, 'Come here' and he comes, to another, 'Go there' and he goes, to another 'Bring this' and he brings it, and to my slave, 'Do this' and he does it.

2. χαίρετε ἐν Κυρίῳ καὶ ἀγαπᾶτε ἀλλήλους, καθὼς εἶπεν ἡμῖν, Ἀγαπᾶτε ἀλλήλους· καθὼς ἐγὼ ἠγάπησα ὑμᾶς. καὶ ἀγαπῶμεν τοὺς ἐχθροὺς ἡμῶν, γέγραπται γάρ, Ὁρᾶτε μή τις κακὸν ἀντὶ κακοῦ τινι ἀποδῷ. | Rejoice in the Lord and love each other, as he said to us: 'Love each other, as I have loved you.' And let us love our enemies, for it is written: See that no one gives back evil to anyone in return for evil.

3. εἶπεν Σίμωνι, Ὕπαγε ἁλιεύειν καὶ τὸν ἀναβάντα πρῶτον ἰχθὺν ἔνεγκε ὧδε, ἵνα φάγωμεν. | He said to Simon, 'Go to fish, and the first fish that comes up, bring here so that we may eat.'

4. ἐάν τινες ὑμῖν εἴπωσιν, Ἴδε, ὧδε ὁ Χριστός ᾖ, Ἴδε ἐκεῖ, μὴ πιστεύετε, ἀλλὰ εἴπατε αὐτοῖς, Μετανοεῖτε καὶ πιστεύετε ἐν τῷ εὐαγγελίῳ. | If any people say to you, 'Look! Here is the Messiah' or 'Look! He is there', do not believe but say to them, 'Repent and believe the Good News.'

40.4

ἀκολουθείτω – he must followἀράτω – he must pick up
ἀκολουθείτωσαν – they must followἐλθάτω – he must come,
let him come

Compare:
1. (a) εἶπεν αὐτῷ, 'Ἀκολούθει μοι – he said to him, 'Follow me!'

(b) εἶπεν αὐτοῖς, 'Ἀκολουθείτω μοι – he said to them, 'He must
follow me'
2. (a) εἰ θέλεις ὀπίσω μου ἐλθεῖν, ἆρον τὸν σταυρόν σου
If you want to follow me, take up your cross

(b) εἴ τις θέλει ὀπίσω μου ἐλθεῖν, ἀράτω τὸν σταυρὸν αὐτοῦ
If anyone wishes to follow me, he must take up his cross
or If someone wishes to come after me, let him take up his cross.

In 1(a) and 2(a) the speaker addresses a command directly to the person he wishes to obey it.

In 1(b) and 2(b) the same action is required, but the person who is to do it is not spoken to directly.

Note also the different types of action:

In 1(b) ἀκολουθείτω is in the present tense because the action of following is an action that is to be continued.

In 2(b) ἀράτω is in the aorist tense because the action of picking up is a single action.

In English we do not have a verbal form exactly similar to ἀκολουθείτω, so in translating we use '**he must** follow' or '**let him** follow.'

So in Mark 13:15,
ὁ ἐπὶ τοῦ δώματος μὴ καταβάτω μηδὲ εἰσελθάτω
τι ἆραί ἐκ τῆς οἰκίας αὐτοῦ
The man on the roof must not go down nor must he go in
to take anything out of his house.

But in Mark 15:32,
ὁ Χριστὸς ὁ Βασιλεὺς Ἰσραὴλ καταβάτω νῦν ἀπὸ τοῦ σταυροῦ
Let the Messiah, the King of Israel, come down now from the cross.

When we use 'let' in this way it does not mean 'allow'. Because 'let' has several meanings in English a translator must often avoid it, so that the meaning is not ambiguous.

Compare

ἐπίτρεψον αὐτῷ ἀπελθεῖν
Let him go away. **Give him permission** to go away
ἄφες αὐτὸν ἀπελθεῖν
Let him go away. **Allow him** to go away
ἀπελθάτω
Let him go away. **He must** go away.

In each case the second translation makes the meaning clear.

40.5 Translate

1. εἰ τις θέλει ἀκολουθεῖν μοι, μετανοείτω καὶ ἐλθάτω πρός με καὶ ἀπαρνησάσθω (deny) ἑαυτὸν καὶ ἀράτω τὸν σταυρὸν καὶ φερέτω αὐτὸν ὀπίσω μου.

   If anyone wishes to follow me he must repent and come to me, he must deny himself and take up his cross and carry it after me.

2. εἶπέν μοι, Ἔλθε πρός με. λίαν ἐχάρην ὅτε τούτους τοὺς λόγους ἤκουσα καὶ ἦλθον πρὸς αὐτὸν καὶ ἐλθὼν εὗρον χαρὰν μεγάλην ἐν αὐτῷ.

   He said to me, 'Come to me.' I was very glad when I heard these words and I came to him. When I had come I found great joy through him.

3. εἶπεν τῷ λεπρῷ, Ὕπαγε εἰς τὸν οἶκόν σου καὶ ὅρα μηδενὶ μηδὲν εἴπῃς.

   He said to the leper, 'Go home and see that you say nothing to anybody.'

4. προσήνεγκεν ἑαυτὸν τῷ θεῷ ἵνα ἡμᾶς σώσῃ ἐκ τῆς ἁμαρτίας καὶ ἵνα ἡμεῖς ἅγιοι ὦμεν καὶ ἀγαπῶμεν ἀλλήλους.

   He offered himself to God so that he might save us from sin and so that we might be holy and might love each other.

5. Ὅπου ἐγὼ ὑπάγω οἴδατε τὴν ὁδόν. λέγει αὐτῷ Θωμᾶς, Κύριε, οὐκ οἴδαμεν ποῦ ὑπάγεις· πῶς οἴδαμεν τὴν ὁδόν; λέγει αὐτῷ ὁ Ἰησοῦς, Ἐγώ εἰμι ἡ ὁδὸς καὶ ἡ ἀλήθεια καὶ ἡ ζωή. οὐδεὶς ἔρχεται πρὸς τὸν Πατέρα εἰ μὴ δι' ἐμοῦ.

   'You know the way where I am going.' Thomas said to him, 'Lord, we do not know where you are going: how can we know the way?' Jesus said to him, 'I am the way and the truth and the life: no one comes to the Father except through me.'

40.6

(a) Read Revelation 22:8–11, 17.

Notes

ἔπεσα – I fell, I fell down
δείκνυμι – I show, I reveal
σφραγίζω – I seal, I seal up
καιρός – time
ἐγγύς – near
ἀδικέω – I do wrong
ῥυπαρός – dirty, filthy

ἡ νύμφη – the bride
διψάω – I thirst, I am thirsty
δωρεάν – freely, as a gift, without payment

(b) Bible translations evaluation (6)

Consider these translations of the requests in John 4:7 and Luke 7:40

John 4:7 (Jesus said to her) Δός μοι πεῖν

NRSV and REB	'Give me a drink'
NJB	'Give me something to drink'
GNB	'Give me a drink of water.'
NIV	'Will you give me a drink?'
NLT	'Please give me a drink.'

Luke 7:40
ὁ δέ, Διδάσκαλε, εἰπέ, φησίν.

φησίν – he says (= he said). Διδάσκαλε : 'Rabbi!' or 'Teacher!' expresses respect, so the sense is: 'Rabbi', he said, 'please tell me.'

NRSV	'Teacher,' he replied, 'speak.'
NIV	'Tell me, teacher,' he said.
NJB	He replied, 'say on, Master.'
REB	'What is it, Teacher?' he asked.
NLT	'All right, Teacher,' Simon replied, 'go ahead.'

(Author's note: When I learned Latin and Greek at school, I learned that forms like δός and εἰπέ were imperative and used for commands. I got the idea that Greeks and Romans were rude and never said 'Please'! I needed to be told that such forms could express polite requests).

40.7

Revise lessons 33 and 34.

Lesson 41

μὴ κλέψῃς – do not steal
μὴ κλαῖε – do not weep, stop crying

41.1 Prohibitions

A prohibition is a negative command, 'Do not...'. In Greek, prohibitions can be expressed in two ways:

1. μή followed by a verb in the **aorist subjunctive**:
    Mk 10:19   μὴ φονεύσῃς, μὴ μοιχεύσῃς, μὴ κλέψῃς, μὴ ψευδομαρτυρήσῃς
    Do not murder, do not commit adultery, do not steal, do not give false evidence.

The verbs φονεύσῃς, μοιχεύσῃς, κλέψῃς, and ψευδομαρτυρήσῃς are all 2nd person singular **aorist** subjunctive active. The aorist is used because each forbids a single or definite act, or an activity that has not yet started.

2. μή followed by a verb in the **present imperative**:

    Mt 6:19   Μὴ θησαυρίζετε ὑμῖν θησαυρούς
    Do not keep storing up treasures for yourselves
    or Do not go on storing up treasures for yourselves
    Mt 6:25   μή μεριμνᾶτε τῇ ψυχῇ ὑμῶν
    Do not be worried in your mind
    or Don't keep worrying
    Mt 7:1   Μὴ κρίνετε, ἵνα μὴ κριθῆτε
    Do not judge, so that you may not be judged
    or Do not keep judging other people, so that you will not be judged
    Lk 8:52   Μὴ κλαίετε
    Do not weep or Stop crying
    Mk 9:39   Μὴ κωλύετε αὐτόν
    Do not stop him
    or Do not try to prevent him.

The verbs θησαυρίζετε, μεριμνᾶτε, κρίνετε, κλαίετε, and κωλύετε are all 2nd person plural **present** imperative active. The present is used because each concerns an action that is, or has been, going on.

So to a person who is already in the habit of stealing, one might say:

μὴ κλέπτε – do not steal, give up stealing

but to a person one hopes will not steal:

μὴ κλέψῃς – do not steal.

41.2 Indirect commands and prohibitions

'Do this!' is a **direct** command.
In 'He told me to do this', 'to do this' is an **indirect** command.
Here are three verbs often used to introduce commands.

1. ἐπιτάσσω – **I command** is followed by a dative case for the person commanded, and a verb in the **infinitive** for the action to be done:
   Mk 6:27 ἐπέταξεν ἐνέγκαι τὴν κεφαλὴν αὐτοῦ
             He commanded (him) to bring his head
   Lk 8:31 παρεκάλουν αὐτὸν ἵνα μὴ ἐπιτάξῃ αὐτοῖς... ἀπελθεῖν
             They begged him not to command them to go away.

2. διαστέλλομαι – **I give instruction to**, I command, is followed by a dative case for the person instructed and ἵνα with a verb in the subjunctive for the state or action required:
   Mk 5:43 διεστείλατο αὐτοῖς πολλὰ ἵνα μηδεὶς γνοῖ τοῦτο
             He gave them strict instructions that no one should know this.

3. ἐπιτιμάω – **I rebuke**, I tell not to, is followed by a dative case for the one rebuked and ἵνα with a verb in the subjunctive for the action that is forbidden:
   Mk 4:39 ἐπετίμησεν τῷ ἀνέμῳ
             He rebuked the wind
   Mk 8:30 ἐπετίμησεν αὐτοῖς ἵνα μηδενὶ λέγωσιν
             He told them that they should speak to nobody
       or   He told them not to speak to anyone.

41.3 Translate

1. ἐγὼ εἶπον αὐτῷ, Μὴ δῷς τοὺς ἄρτους αὐτοῖς. μὴ δίδου τὸν οἶνον αὐτοῖς ἀλλὰ δός μοι τὸν οἶνον. | I said to him, 'Do not give them the loaves. Stop giving them the wine but give me the wine.'

2. εἶπεν αὐτοῖς ὁ Ἰησοῦς, Μὴ κλαίετε, τὸ τέκνον οὐκ ἀπέθανεν. καὶ λέγει τῇ μητρὶ αὐτοῦ, Μὴ κλαίε.

Jesus said to them, 'Stop crying – the child has not died.' Then he said to his mother, 'Don't cry.'

3. ὁ βασιλεὺς εἶπεν τῇ θυγατρὶ τῆς Ἡρῳδιάδος, Ὅ τι ἐάν με αἰτήσῃς δώσω σοι. καὶ εὐθὺς ᾐτήσατο λέγουσα, Θέλω ἵνα δῷς μοι τὴν κεφαλὴν Ἰωάννου τοῦ Βαπτιστοῦ. καὶ ἀποστείλας στρατιώτην (soldier) ἐπέταξεν αὐτῷ ἐνέγκαι τὴν κεφαλὴν αὐτοῦ. καὶ ἐπετίησεν τῷ βασιλεῖ ὁ Κύριος ὅτι τὸ ἔργον τοῦ πονηροῦ ἐποίησεν.

The king said to the daughter of Herodias, 'I will give you whatever you ask me for.' Immediately she made this request: 'I want you to give me the head of John the Baptist.' So sending a soldier he ordered him to bring his head. The Lord rebuked the king because he had done the work of the Evil One.

41.4 Words

ὁ καρπός – the fruit, the crop
    καρποφορέω – I bear fruit
    καρπὸν δίδωμι – I yield a harvest, I produce a crop
σπείρω – I sow
    ὁ σπόρος or τὸ σπέρμα – the seed
ἡ δικαιοσύνη – the righteousness
δικαιόω – I acquit, I declare to be righteous, I accept as righteous, I justify
ὁ τόπος – the place
ἡ ὁδός – the road, the path, the way
ἕτοιμος – ready
    ἑτοιμάζω – I make ready, I prepare
τὸ αἷμα – the blood
    (When used metaphorically αἷμα is usually a symbol for death. See, for example, Mt 23:30, Acts 5:28.)
οὐ μή – not
    (This double negative is emphatic. It is found especially in emphatic denials:
    οὐ μή εἰσελεύσεται – he will **not** enter, he will certainly not enter.)
πίνω – I drink :   ἔπιον – I drank
πίνειν – to be drinking :   πιεῖν or πεῖν – to drink
ἡ εἰρήνη – the peace   εἰρηνικός – peaceful, peaceable
Like *shalom* in Hebrew and *salaam* in Arabic, εἰρήνη has a wider area of

meaning than the English word 'peace'. To wish a family εἰρήνη (Luke 10:5) is not only to wish that they may live peacefully, but also to wish that God's blessing may be on them. But in Matthew 10:34, οὐκ ἦλθον βαλεῖν εἰρήνην ἀλλὰ μάχαιραν – I did not come to bring peace but a sword, εἰρήνη corresponds closely to the English word 'peace'.

41.5 Translate

1. μὴ βάλῃς τὸν σπόρον σου εἰς τὴν θάλασσαν μηδὲ παρὰ τὴν ὁδὸν ἀλλὰ ἑτοίμασον τὴν γῆν αὐτῷ· καὶ ὅταν ἑτοίμη ᾖ τότε σπεῖρε τὸν σπόρον εἰς τὴν γῆν τὴν ἡτοιμασμένην καὶ καρπὸν δώσει. καὶ ὅταν καρποφορῇ χαρήσεις χαρᾷ μεγάλῃ. | Do not cast your seed into the sea nor along the road, but prepare the soil for it; and when it is ready then sow the seed into the soil that has been prepared, and it will yield a crop. And when it bears fruit you will rejoice with great joy.

2. χάρις ὑμῖν καὶ εἰρήνη ἀπὸ τοῦ θεοῦ τοῦ πατρὸς ἡμῶν ἐν ἀγάπῃ καὶ δικαιοσύνῃ. αὐτὸς γὰρ ὁ θεὸς ἀγαπᾷ ἡμᾶς καὶ ἔσωσεν ἡμᾶς διὰ τοῦ αἵματος τοῦ υἱοῦ αὐτοῦ. καὶ δικαιωθέντες διὰ πίστεως εἰρήνην ἔχομεν πρὸς τὸν θεόν. | Grace to you and peace from God our Father in love and righteousness. For God himself loves us and saved us through the blood of his Son. So having been accepted as righteous through faith, we have peace with God.

41.6

Read carefully:

Instructions, warning and promise

διεστείλατο αὐτοῖς ἵνα μηδενὶ μηδὲν λέγωσιν, καὶ ἑστηκὼς παρὰ τὴν ὁδὸν εἶπεν αὐτοῖς, 'Ἐὰν μὴ πίητε τὸ αἷμά μου οὐκ ἔχετε ζωὴν μένουσαν ἐν ὑμῖν καὶ οὐ μὴ εἰσελεύσεσθε εἰς τὴν βασιλείαν τῶν οὐρανῶν. ἀλλὰ τὸν πιστεύοντα ἐν ἐμοὶ καὶ πίνοντα τὸ αἷμά μου οὐ μὴ ἐκβάλω ἔξω· ὅτι καταβέβηκα ἐκ τοῦ οὐρανοῦ οὐχ ἵνα δικαίους καλέσω ἀλλὰ ἁμαρτωλούς, ὅπως εἰσέλθωσιν εἰς τὸν τόπον ὃν ἀπέρχομαι ἑτοιμάσαι αὐτοῖς.

41.7 Read John 2:1–12

v1 τῇ ἡμέρᾳ τῃ τρίτῃ – 'on the third day': this might mean 3 days after the meeting with Nathanael, or, on the third day of the week (Tuesday) which was considered propitious for weddings. ἐκεῖ – there.
γάμος – wedding.

v3 ὑστερέω – I fall short

v4 Τί ἐμοὶ καὶ σοί – 'What to me and to you?' a Hebraic expression appropriate when rejecting interference of any kind. ἥκει – it has come

v6 λίθιναι ὑδρίαι – stone jars. καθαρισμός – rite of purification. χωρέω – I have room for. μετρητής – measure (of quantity – about 9 gallons).

v7 γεμίζω – I fill   ἕως ἄνω – up to the top.

v8 ἀντλέω – I draw out (liquid). ὁ ἀρχιτρίκλινος – the president of the banquet, the master of ceremonies.

v9 ὁ νυμφίος – the bridegroom.

v10 μεθύω – I have plenty to drink, I am drunk. ἐλάσσων – less, inferior.

v12 οὐ πολλὰς ἡμέρας – lit. 'not many days': since 'many days' could mean 'a year', the negative perhaps means 'for a while' rather than 'for a few days.' (For accusative case indicating length of time see 37.3.6.)

41.8

Revise lessons 35 and 36.

Lesson 42

τῷ λόγῳ, τῇ καρδίᾳ: the dative case

42.1

λόγῳ – λόγοις, καρδίᾳ – καρδίαις, σοί – ὑμῖν,
τῷ παραπτώματι – τοῖς παραπτώμασιν   are all in the dative case.

Uses of the dative case

1. The dative case is used to show the person to whom something is given, or for whom something is done:

   Mk 5:19   ὅσα ὁ Κύριός σοι πεποίηκεν
   What great things the Lord has done for you

   Mk 1:30   λέγουσιν αὐτῷ περὶ αὐτῆς
   They speak to him about her

   Rom 16:27 ᾧ ἡ δόξα εἰς τοὺς αἰῶνας
   To whom be glory for ever

   Mk 9:5   καὶ ποιήσωμεν τρεῖς σκηνάς, σοὶ μίαν καὶ **Μωϋσεῖ** μίαν καὶ Ἠλίᾳ μίαν
   Let us make three shelters, one for you and one for Moses and one for Elijah

   Mt 23:31 ὥστε μαρτυρεῖτε ἑαυτοῖς
   Thus you witness against yourselves.

2. The dative case is used to show the thing with which something is done:

   Mk 1:8   ἐγὼ ἐβάπτισα ὑμᾶς ὕδατι
   I baptized you with water

   Mk 15:19 ἔτυπτον αὐτοῦ τὴν κεφαλὴν **καλάμῳ**
   They kept hitting his head with a stick

   Mk 15:46 καθελὼν αὐτὸν ἐνείλησεν τῇ **σινδόνι**
   Having taken him down he wrapped him in (with) the linen sheet

   Mk 12:13 ἵνα αὐτὸν ἀγρεύσωσιν **λόγῳ**
   So that they might trap him in a discussion

   Rom 5:15 τῷ τοῦ ἑνὸς **παραπτώματι** οἱ πολλοὶ ἀπέθανον
   By the wrongdoing of the one man the many died.

3. **The dative case is used to show the time at which something happened:**

Mk 2:24   τί ποιοῦσιν **τοῖς σάββασιν** ὃ οὐκ ἔξεστιν;
            Why are they doing on the Sabbath what is not allowed?

Mk 14:12   **τῇ πρώτῃ ἡμέρᾳ** τῶν ἀζύμων
            On the first day of the unleavened bread

Mk 16:2   **τῇ μιᾷ** τῶν σαββάτων
            On the first day of the week

Mk 12:2   ἀπέστειλεν πρὸς τοὺς γεωργοὺς **τῷ καιρῷ** δοῦλον
            At the (harvest) time he sent a slave to the farmers.

4. **The dative may be used to show the person to whom something belongs:**

Jn 3:1   Νικόδημος ὄνομα **αὐτῷ**
            His name was Nicodemus

Mk 2:18   οἱ δὲ **σοὶ** μαθηταὶ οὐ νηστεύουσιν
            But your disciples are not fasting

Jn 17:6   **σοὶ** ἦσαν κἀμοὶ αὐτοὺς ἔδωκας
            They were yours and you gave them to me
            (κἀμοί is a short form of καὶ ἐμοί).

5. **The dative is used after many verbs; for example, after:**

λέγω – I speak   ἐπιτιμάω – I rebuke, I tell not to
δίδωμι – I give   παραγγέλλω – I command
ἀκολουθέω – I follow   ἐντέλλομαι – I order, I command
ἀπαντάω – I meet   πιστεύω – I believe
ἀρέσκω – I please   προσκυνέω – I worship
ἀφίημι – I forgive   ὑπακούω – I obey
διακονέω – I serve, I minister to,   μέλει – it concerns, it is a matter of
      I care for   concern to.

Examples from Mark:

Mk 10:52   ἠκολούθει **αὐτῷ** ἐν τῇ ὁδῷ
             He followed him along the road

Mk 14:13   ἀπαντήσει **ὑμῖν** ἄνθρωπος κεράμιον ὕδατος βαστάζων
             A man carrying a jar of water will meet you

Mk 6:22   ἤρεσεν **τῷ Ἡρῴδῃ** καὶ **τοῖς συνανακειμένοις**
             She pleased Herod and the people sitting with him (his guests)

Mk 11:25 ἵνα...ἀφῇ ὑμῖν τὰ παραπτώματα ὑμῶν
So that he may forgive you your sins

Mk 1:13 οἱ ἄγγελοι διηκόνουν **αὐτῷ**
The angels ministered to him

Mk 8:32 προσλαβόμενος ὁ Πέτρος αὐτὸν ἤρξατο ἐπιτιμᾶν **αὐτῷ**
Taking him aside Peter began to rebuke him

Mk 8:6 καὶ παραγγέλλει **τῷ ὄχλῳ** ἀναπεσεῖν ἐπὶ τῆς γῆς
He tells the crowd to sit down on the ground

Mk 11:31 Διὰ τί οὐκ ἐπιστεύσατε **αὐτῷ**;
Then why did you not believe him?

Mk 1:27 καὶ **τοῖς πνεύμασι τοῖς ἀκαθάρτοις** ἐπιτάσσει,
καὶ ὑπακούουσιν αὐτῷ
He even gives orders to the unclean spirits and they obey him

Mk 4:38 οὐ μέλει σοι ὅτι ἀπολλύμεθα;
Doesn't it bother you that we are perishing?
or Don't you care that we are about to die?

Mk 12:14 οὐ μέλει σοι περὶ οὐδενός
You do not pay attention to anybody's status
or You are not worried about anyone
(Lit. It is not a matter of concern to you about no one).

42.2 Prepositions followed by a dative case

ἐν – in, among, by, with, towards
σύν – with, together with (with a person)
παρά – beside, with, at the house of, near, in the sight of
πρός – at, near to
ἐπί – on, upon (resting on), in, by, at, on account of, with a view to

Note that:
when a preposition is followed by the accusative case, the basic idea is often movement **towards** something;
when a preposition is followed by the genitive case, the basic idea is often movement **away from** something;
when a preposition is followed by the dative case, the basic idea is often of position or rest **at** a place.

42.3 ἐν

ἐν – in, among, by, with, under the influence of

1. ἐν – in, inside (of time or place):
   Mk 1:9   ἐν ἐκείναις ταῖς ἡμέραις
   In those days
   Mk 1:13   ἦν ἐν τῇ ἐρήμῳ
   He was in the wilderness
   Mk 2:23   ἐν τοῖς σάββασιν
   On the Sabbath day.

2. ἐν – into:
   Rom 1:25   οἵτινες μετήλλαξαν τὴν ἀλήθειαν τοῦ θεοῦ ἐν τῷ ψεύδει
   Who changed the truth of God into a lie.
   or Who exchanged the truth of God for a lie.

3. ἐν – among:
   Mk 15:40   Ἦσαν δὲ καὶ γυναῖκες... ἐν αἷς καὶ Μαρία
   There were also women...among whom was Mary.

4. ἐν – while:
   ἐν with the infinitive must usually be translated 'while...' or 'as...'.
   Mk 4:4   ἐγένετο ἐν τῷ σπείρειν...
   It happened while he was sowing...
   or As he was sowing...
   Lk 1:8   ἐν τῷ ἱερατεύειν αὐτόν
   In the course of his priestly duties
   or While he was doing his work as a priest.

Note also ἐν ᾧ – while, in the time during which

5. ἐν – by means of, with:
   Lk 22:49   εἰ πατάξομεν ἐν μαχαίρῃ;
   Shall we strike with the sword?
   Mk 4:2   ἐδίδασκεν αὐτοὺς ἐν παραβολαῖς
   He was teaching them by means of parables
   Acts 1:3   παρέστησεν ἑαυτὸν ζῶντα...ἐν πολλοῖς τεκμηρίοις
   He showed himself alive by means of many proofs
   or by means of many convincing actions
   Jn 1:26   Ἐγὼ βαπτίζω ἐν ὕδατι
   I baptize with water.

6. ἐν – under the influence of, under the control of:
   Mk 1:23   ἄνθρωπος ἐν πνεύματι ἀκαθάρτῳ
                  A man under the influence of an unclean spirit
           or A man possessed by an unclean spirit
   Mk 12:36 αὐτὸς Δαυὶδ εἶπεν ἐν τῷ πνεύματι τῷ ἁγίῳ...
                  Under the influence of the Holy Spirit David himself said...
           or David himself, inspired by the Holy Spirit, said...
   Mk 5:25   γυνὴ οὖσα ἐν ῥύσει αἵματος δώδεκα ἔτη
                  A woman being affected by a flow of blood for twelve years
           or A woman who had suffered from bleeding for twelve years.

7. ἐν – for, to :
   1 Jn 4:9   ἐν τούτῳ ἐφανερώθη ἡ ἀγάπη τοῦ θεοῦ ἐν ἡμῖν
                  In this way the love of God for us has been revealed
   Mk 14:6   καλὸν ἔργον ἠργάσατο ἐν ἐμοί
                  She has done a fine thing for me
           or She did a beautiful thing to me.

The preposition ἐν is used in a great variety of ways. We can only tell the best way to translate it by considering the context in which it is used and the meaning of similar or parallel passages.

42.4 σύν

σύν – with, together with (usually with a person)
   Mk 9:4   καὶ ὤφθη αὐτοῖς Ἠλίας σὺν Μωϋσεῖ
                There appeared to them Elijah with Moses
   Mk 2:26   καὶ ἔδωκεν καὶ τοῖς σὺν αὐτῷ οὖσιν
                And he even gave to those who were with him
   Mk 4:10   ἠρώτων αὐτὸν οἱ περὶ αὐτὸν σὺν τοῖς δώδεκα
                τὰς παραβολάς
                Those who were round him with the Twelve asked him about the parables.

Note also Luke 24:21, σὺν πᾶσιν τούτοις – in addition to all these things.

42.5 παρά

παρά – beside, with, at the house of, near, in the sight of

1. παρά – beside, near to:
   Jn 19:25   εἰστήκεισαν δὲ παρὰ τῷ σταυρῷ
                They stood near the cross.

2. παρά – with, among, at the house of:
   Jn 1:39 παρ' αὐτῷ ἔμειναν τὴν ἡμέραν ἐκείνην
   They stayed with him that day
   Lk 11:37 ἐρωτᾷ αὐτὸν Φαρισαῖος ὅπως ἀριστήσῃ παρ' αὐτῷ
   A Pharisee asks him to have a meal at his house
   or A Pharisee invited him to dine with him
   Rom 9:14 μὴ ἀδικία παρὰ τῷ θεῷ;
   Is there unrighteousness with God?
   or Can unrighteousness exist in God?

3. παρά – in the opinion of, in the sight of, before:
   Rom 12:16 μὴ γίνεσθε φρόνιμοι παρ' ἑαυτοῖς
   Do not be wise in your own eyes
   or Do not keep thinking how wise you are
   1 Cor 3:19 ἡ γὰρ σοφία τοῦ κόσμου τούτου
   μωρία παρὰ τῷ θεῷ ἐστιν
   For the wisdom of this world is foolishness in God's sight
   or For when God looks at this world's wisdom he considers it foolishness
   Gal 3:11 ἐν νόμῳ οὐδεὶς δικαιοῦται παρὰ τῷ θεῷ
   By means of the Law no one is justified before God.

4. παρά – from, from beside:
   Mt 6:1 μισθὸν οὐκ ἔχετε παρὰ τῷ πατρὶ ὑμῶν
   τῷ ἐν τοῖς οὐρανοῖς
   You do not have a reward from your heavenly Father.

42.6 πρός

πρός – at, near, on
   Mk 5:11 Ἦν δὲ ἐκεῖ πρὸς τῷ ὄρει ἀγέλη χοίρων
   There was there on the mountain a herd of pigs
   Jn 18:16 ὁ δὲ Πέτρος εἱστήκει πρὸς τῇ θύρᾳ ἔξω
   But Peter stood at the door outside.

42.7 ἐπί

ἐπί – on, upon (resting on), in, by, at, on account of, with a view to, in addition to

1. ἐπί – on:

   Mk 6:25   ἐπὶ πίνακι
               On a dish

   Mk 6:55   ἤρξαντο ἐπὶ τοῖς κραβάττοις τοὺς κακῶς ἔχοντας περιφέρειν
               They began to carry round the sick on mats.

2. ἐπί – at, because of:

   Mk 1:22   ἐξεπλήσσοντο ἐπὶ τῇ διδαχῇ αὐτοῦ
               They were amazed at his teaching

   Mk 10:22   ὁ δὲ στυγνάσας ἐπὶ τῷ λόγῳ ἀπῆλθεν
               Looking sad because of what was said, he went off
          or When he heard what Jesus said his face fell, and he went away.

3. ἐπί – in:

   Mk 9:39   οὐδεὶς γάρ ἐστιν ὃς ποιήσει δύναμιν ἐπὶ τῷ ὀνόματί μου
               For there is no one who will do a mighty work in my name.

4. ἐπί – close to, at:

   Mk 13:29   γινώσκετε ὅτι ἐγγύς ἐστιν ἐπὶ θύραις
               You know that he is near, at the gates
          or Know that he is near, at the doors.

5. ἐπί – about:

   Mk 6:52   οὐ γὰρ συνῆκαν ἐπὶ τοῖς ἄρτοις
               For they did not understand about the loaves
          or For they had not taken in the meaning of the loaves.

ἐπί has an extremely wide range of meanings. A translator must always take care to express its correct meaning in each context.

42.8

Summary of the common meanings of prepositions used with more than one case (see also lessons 37 and 39).

παρά – beside
    with accusative: beside, along, along beside, at the side of
    with genitive: from beside, from the side of, from
    with dative: beside, with, at the house of, in the sight of

ἐπί – on
    with accusative: on, on top of, against, at, onto
    with genitive: on, in, on account of, in the time of
    with dative: on, in, by, at

διά
    with accusative: because of, on account of, for the sake of
    with genitive: through, by means of, after

μετά
    with accusative: after
    with genitive: with

ὑπέρ
    with accusative: above, more important than, superior to
    with genitive: for, on behalf of, for the sake of, about

ὑπό
    with accusative: under, underneath, subject to
    with genitive: by (by a person)

κατά
    with accusative: down, according to, during, about, along
    with genitive: down from, against

περί
    with accusative: round, around, about
    with genitive: concerning, about, on account of

πρός
    with accusative: towards, up to, by, close to, with, against
    with dative: at, near to.

42.9 Read John 3:1-12

v1 Νικόδημος ὄνομα αὐτῷ – 'Nicodemus name to him' – a Hebraic way to express, 'His name was Nicodemus.' ἄρχων – ruler, member of the Sanhedrin. τῶν Ἰουδαίων – the Sanhedrin met on the Temple Mount in Jerusalem, the capital of Judea. The Galilee – Judea contrast is a feature of the next episode concerning Nicodemus (see 7:50-52). Note also that in John 5:1 the expression ἑορτέ τῶν Ἰουδαίων commonly translated 'a festival of the Jews' should perhaps be understood as 'a festival held in Judea', since it is noted that Jesus went up to Jerusalem.

v2 νυκτός – by night (for genitive expressing time: 39.1.2). οἴδαμεν – we know: the plural might refer to people generally, or to Nicodemus and the close disciples who would accompany a rabbi. ἐάν μή – unless.

v3 ἄνωθεν – from above (3:31, 19:11), but Nicodemus understands it in its other sense: over again.

v4 γέρων – old man.   κοιλία – abdomen, womb.

v6 σάρξ – flesh, physical nature.

v8 πνεῖ – it blows (πνέω). τὸ πνεῦμα – the wind, the spirit.

v10 ὁ διδάσκαλος – the teacher, the rabbi

v12 τὰ ἐπίγεια – things on earth.   τὰ ἐπουράνια – heavenly things.

42.10 Progress test 19

Read John 1:1-14 and answer the following questions:

1. In verses 1-5, which words are in the nominative case?
2. In verses 9-12, which words are in the accusative case?
3. In verses 3-8 and 12-14, which words are in the genitive case?
4. In verses 1-14, which words are in the dative case?
5. Translate these phrases in John 1:1-14:
   (a) ἐν ἀρχῇ
   (b) πρός τὸν θεὸν
   (c) δι' αὐτοῦ
   (d) χωρὶς αὐτοῦ
   (e) ἐν τῇ σκοτίᾳ
   (f) περὶ τοῦ φωτός
   (g) εἰς τὸν κόσμον
   (h) ἐν τῷ κόσμῳ
   (i) εἰς τὸ ὄνομα
   (j) ἐκ θελήματος
   (k) ἐν ἡμῖν

Check your answers in Key to Progress tests on page 334.

Lesson 43

εἰ ἐμερίσθη – if it has been divided
ἐὰν μερισθῇ – if it should be divided

43.1 εἰ, ἐάν – if

Study carefully:

1. (a) εἰ υἱός ἐστιν τοῦ θεοῦ
     If he is the Son of God
     or If he is in fact the Son of God

   (b) ἐάν τις πονηρὸς ᾖ
     If anyone is evil
     or If anyone should be evil

2. (a) εἰ τοῦτο ἐποιήσαμεν
     If we did this
     or If we had really done this

   (b) ἐὰν τοῦτο ποιήσωμεν
     If we do this
     or If we did this
     or If we were to do this

The clauses 1(a) and 2(a) are **definite**: they have verbs in the **indicative**.
The clauses 1(b) and 2(b) are **indefinite**: they have verbs in the **subjunctive**.

εἰ means 'if'. It is used chiefly in statements or clauses referring to the past, and in some that refer to the present. It is used when the thought in the speaker's mind is definite, or the statement clearly either true or untrue. Its force can often best be expressed in English by the use of 'in fact' or 'really'.

εἰ is followed by a verb in the indicative mood.

ἄν makes a statement indefinite:

Jn 14:7 εἰ ἐγνώκειτέ με, καὶ τὸν πατέρα μου ἂν ᾔδειτε
     If you had in fact known me **you would** also **have known** my Father.

ἐάν (εἰ + ἄν) is used when the idea in the mind is indefinite or uncertain:

1 Jn 1:10 ἐὰν εἴπωμεν ὅτι οὐχ ἡμαρτήκαμεν ψεύστην ποιοῦμεν αὐτόν
     If we say that we have not sinned we make him a liar.

ἐάν is followed by a verb in the subjunctive mood.
The difference between εἰ and ἐάν can be seen in Mark 3:25–26,

  ἐὰν οἰκία ἐφ' ἑαυτὴν μερισθῇ...
  If a family should be divided against itself...
  εἰ ὁ Σατανᾶς ἀνέστη ἐφ' ἑαυτὸν καὶ ἐμερίσθη...
  If Satan has in fact risen up against himself and has been divided...

43.2 Translate

1. εἰ υἱὸς εἶ τοῦ θεοῦ, ὕπαγε ὀπίσω μου. | If you are the Son of God, go away from me.
2. εἰ ὑμεῖς οἴδατε δόματα ἀγαθὰ διδόναι τοῖς τέκνοις ὑμῶν, πόσῳ μᾶλλον ὁ Πατὴρ ὁ ἐξ οὐρανῶν δώσει τὸ Πνεῦμα τὸ Ἅγιον ὑμῖν. | If you know how to give good gifts to your children, how much more will the heavenly Father give the Holy Spirit to you.
3. ἐὰν εἴπωμεν ὅτι ἁμαρτίαν οὐκ ἔχομεν ψευδόμεθα· ἐὰν δὲ ἐν τῷ φωτὶ περιπατῶμεν κοινωνίαν ἔχομεν μετ' ἀλλήλων. | If we say that we have no sin we are lying; but if we walk in the light we have fellowship with one another.

43.3 εἰ with the imperfect indicative

εἰ ἐπιστεύετε Μωϋσεῖ, ἐπιστεύετε ἂν ἐμοί
   (a) If you believed Moses (now), you would believe me
or (b) If you had believed Moses, you would have believed me.

Clauses with εἰ and the imperfect indicative refer 'to present time or to continued or repeated action in past time' (Liddell and Scott).

So in Galatians 1:10, with reference to the time that is present to the writer as he writes:

εἰ ἔτι ἀνθρώποις ἤρεσκον, Χριστοῦ δοῦλος οὐκ ἂν ἤμην
If I were still pleasing men, I would not be the servant of Christ.

But in 1 Corinthians 11:31, with reference primarily to past time:

εἰ δὲ ἑαυτοὺς διεκρίνομεν οὐκ ἂν ἐκρινόμεθα
If we had judged ourselves, we would not be being judged.

In John 18:36,

εἰ ἐκ τοῦ κόσμου τούτου ἦν ἡ βασιλεία ἡ ἐμή, οἱ ὑπηρέται οἱ ἐμοὶ ἠγωνίζοντο ἄν

the translator has to choose between:

   (a) If my kingdom were of this world my servants **would now be fighting** (compare RSV, REB, GNB)
and (b) If my kingdom were of this world my servants **would have fought** (compare NJB, Moffatt, Phillips).

Since the verb παραδίδωμι is used both of Judas betraying Jesus to the Jews

(Jn 18:2) and of Pilate handing him over to the Jews to be crucified (Jn 19:16), it is not easy to decide which way to translate John 18:36.

Note that some writers on New Testament Greek say that εἰ with the imperfect refers to present time. This is misleading. It would be better to add that in such cases it often refers to a present situation that arises out of a past situation. And it is necessary also to say that it can refer to continued action or attitude in past time.

43.4 Words

αἰτέω – I ask for
ὁ προσαίτης – the beggar
ἀνοίγω – I open
    ἤνοιξεν or ἀνέῳξεν – he opened
    ἀνοίξας – having opened
    ἠνοίγησαν or ἠνεῴχθησαν – they were opened, they opened
ἕκαστος – each
    εἷς ἕκαστος – each one
ἐμός – my   σός – your
ἡμέτερος – our   ὑμέτερος – your (p)
μᾶλλον – more (in importance or degree)
    πλείων...ἤ... – rather than
πλείων – more (in number or quantity)
    πλείων ἐκείνου – more than that
    πλείονα σημεῖα – more signs, more miracles
ὃ ἐάν – whatever
εἰ καί – even if

43.5 Translate

1. ἐὰν πλείονα τούτων αἰτήσῃς δώσει σοι ὁ Πατὴρ ὁ ἐμός.	If you ask for more than these, my Father will give (them) to you.
2. ὃ ἐὰν αἰτήσητε δώσω ἑνὶ ἑκάστῳ ὑμῶν.	Whatever you ask for I will give to each one of you.
3. εἰ ταῦτα ᾔτησαν, ἡ μήτηρ ἡ ἡμετέρα ἔδωκεν ἂν αὐτοῖς.	If they had asked for these things, our mother would have given (them) to them.

4. εἰ γὰρ πλείονα σημεῖα ἐποίησα ἐπίστευσαν ἂν ἐμοί.	For if I had done more miracles they would have believed in me.
5. εἰ καὶ μείζονα σημεῖα ἐποίησα οὐκ ἂν ἐπίστευσαν ἐμοί.	Even if I had done greater miracles they would not have believed in me.
6. ἠγάπησαν τὴν ἰδίαν δόξαν μᾶλλον ἢ τὴν δόξαν τοῦ θεοῦ.	They loved their own glory rather than the glory of God.
7. εἰ οὗτος ἦν ὁ Χριστός, ἤνοιξεν ἂν τοὺς ὀφθαλμοὺς τῶν τυφλῶν καὶ τὰ στόματα τῶν κωφῶν ἠνεῴχθησαν ἄν.	If this man was really the Messiah, he would have opened the eyes of the blind, and the mouths of the dumb would have been opened.
8. οἱ προσαίται οἱ ἐν Ἰερουσαλὴμ πλείονές εἰσιν τῶν ἐν Ναζαρέθ.	The beggars in Jerusalem are more numerous than those in Nazareth.

43.6

(a) Read John 15:18–27.

> v19 ἐκλέγομαι – I choose (out).   v20 μνημονεύω – I remember
> διώκω – I persecute, I pursue.
>
> v22 οὐκ εἴχοσαν – they would not have (εἴχοσαν is imperfect:- οσαν is sometimes found as an alternative for -ον: they). ἡ πρόφασις – the excuse
>
> v25 ἀλλ' ἵνα ... – but (this happened) so that ... ἐν τῷ νόμῳ – in the scripture: here the quotation is from Psalms, so νόμος has a wider meaning than Torah (Pentateuch).
> δωρεάν – freely, without cause, without reason.
> v26 ὁ παράκλητος – the helper, the encourager, the advocate.

(b) Bible translations evaluation (7)

In Luke 11:17b there are two parallel statements, and one element is missing from the second statement – a characteristic found in Hebrew style:

> πᾶσα βασιλεία ἐφ' ἑαυτὴν διαμερισθεῖσα ἐρημοῦται
> καὶ   οἶκος   ἐπὶ   οἶκον   πίπτει

We can see from the parallel of βασιλεία and οἶκος that οἶκος here means 'family' and implies 'ruling family'. The missing unit which must be supplied is διαμερισθείς 'divided' or 'in rebellion'. So the meaning is,

'Every kingdom in rebellion against itself is laid waste, and a ruling family split by rebellion collapses.'
> NIV   Any kingdom divided against itself will be ruined,
> and any house divided against itself will fall.
> NLT   Any kingdom at war with itself is doomed.
> A divided home is also doomed.
> NRSV Every kingdom divided against itself becomes a desert,
> and house falls on house
> NJB   Any kingdom which is divided against itself is heading for ruin,
> and house collapses against house.
> Note that ἐρημόω means 'I make desolate' (by 'ethnic cleansing'), I lay waste.

43.7 Progress test 20

Which of the following could be correct translations of the Greek?

1. καὶ εἶπαν αὐτῷ, Μὴ καὶ ἡμεῖς τυφλοί ἐσμεν;
   (a) They said to him, 'Are we also blind?'
   (b) And they said to him, 'We are also blind, aren't we?'
   (c) They said to him, 'We are not also blind, are we?'

2. Εἰ τυφλοί ἦτε, οὐκ ἂν εἴχετε ἁμαρτίαν.
   (a) If you were blind, you would not be guilty of sin.
   (b) If you had been blind, you would not have been guilty of sin.
   (c) If you are blind, you are not guilty of sin.

3. εἰ ἐκ τοῦ κόσμου ἦτε, ὁ κόσμος ἂν τὸ ἴδιον ἐφίλει.
   (a) If you had been of the world, the world would have loved its own.
   (b) If you really belong to the world, the world will love its own.
   (c) If you were of the world, the world would love its own.

4. εἰ μὴ ἦλθον καὶ ἐλάλησα αὐτοῖς, ἁμαρτίαν οὐκ εἴχοσαν.
   (a) If I did not come and speak to them, they would not be guilty of sin.
   (b) If I had not come and spoken to them, they would not be guilty of sin.
   (c) If I had not come and spoken to them, they would not have been guilty of sin.

Check your answers in Key to Progress Tests on page 334.

INTRODUCTION TO LESSON 44

Lesson 44 will help you to understand how Greek words are structured, and how groups of words are related to each other. Some of the words will be new to you. You are not expected to know or remember what they all mean, but what you see in this lesson will form a useful background to your continuing study of New Testament or Classical Greek. If you are interested in words and their meanings, and in New Testament exegesis, do not miss the 'comical warning'.

Lesson 44

δίκαιος – righteous
δικαιοσύνη – righteousness
ἀδικία – injustice, wrong

44.1 Word stems

Study the following groups of words. Notice how the endings (suffixes) and parts added at the beginning (prefixes) determine the meaning of each word within the general area of meaning indicated by the stem.

1. δικ – Words to do with justice, rightness, law, and courts

   δίκαιος – righteous, just, upright
   δικαιότερος – more righteous, rather righteous
   δικαιότατος – most righteous, very righteous
   (ἡ) δικαιοσύνη – righteousness, justice, uprightness, what is right
   δικαίως – justly, righteously
   (ἡ) δικαίωσις – justification, acceptance as righteous
   (τὸ) δικαίωμα – righteous act, righteousness, law, statute
   δικαιόω – I acquit, I declare to be righteous, I treat as righteous
   (ἡ) δίκη – justice, penalty, punishment
   (ὁ) δικαστής – judge
   (ἡ) δικαιοκρισία – righteous judgement
   (ἡ) ἀδικία – injustice, unrighteousness, wrong
   (τὸ) ἀδίκημα – unrighteous act, wrong
   ἀδικέω – I wrong, I do wrong to, I harm
   ἀδίκως – unjustly, unfairly
   ἄδικος – unjust

2. ἁγ – Words to do with holiness, reverence, purity

   ἅγιος – holy
   ἁγιάζω – I make holy, I sanctify
   (ὁ) ἁγιασμός – sanctification, making holy
   (ἡ) ἁγιότης – holiness
   ἁγνός – pure, chaste
   ἁγνῶς – purely, with a pure motive
   (ἡ) ἁγνεία – purity
   (ὁ) ἁγνισμός – purification
   ἁγνίζω – I purify

275

3. γνο – Words to do with knowing

γινώσκω – I know
ἀναγινώσκω – I read
ἐπιγινώσκω – I come to know, I recognize
προγινώσκω – I know beforehand
γνωρίζω – I make known
(ἡ) γνῶσις – knowledge, wisdom
(ἡ) ἐπίγνωσις – knowledge
γνωστός – known
ἄγνωστος – unknown
ἀγνοέω – I do not know, I am ignorant, I do not understand
(ἡ) ἀγνωσία – ignorance, misunderstanding
(ἡ) ἄγνοια – ignorance, lack of knowledge
(το) ἀγνόημα – act done in ignorance

Notice that α before a stem often, but not always, makes it negative. Grammarians call this α **alpha privative**.

In 44.2–6 we study common word forms, suffixes, and prefixes. These are given as guidelines, not as rules. They indicate what is generally the case, not what is always so. If you are in any doubt over the meaning of a word, study it in its context with the aid of a lexicon and concordance.

44.2 Nouns and their endings (suffixes)

1. To show actions:

-σις	f	ἀπολύτρωσις – redemption, βρῶσις – eating, καύχησις – boasting
-σια	f	ἐργασία – work, παρουσία – coming
-μος	m	ἀσπασμός – greeting, βασανισμός – torture, διωγμός – persecution.

2. To show the result of an action:

-μα	n	δικαίωμα – just act, law, ὅραμα – vision, πρᾶγμα – action, thing done.

3. To show the doer of an action:

-τηρ	m	σωτήρ – savior
-τωρ	m	παντοκράτωρ – ruler of all, almighty, ῥήτωρ – orator
-της	m	κλέπτης – thief, οἰκοδεσπότης – householder, master.

4. To show the means or instrument by which an action is done:
-τρον   n   ἄροτρον – plough,   λύτρον – ransom price.

5. To show the profession, position or class of person:
-ευς   m   βασιλεύς – king, γραμματεύς – scribe, ἱερεύς – priest
-ισσα   f   βασίλισσα – queen
-της   m   πολίτης – citizen, στρατιώτης – soldier.

6. To show quality:
-της   f   ἁγιότης – holiness, ἰσότης – equality,
             χρηστότης – goodness
-συνη   f   ἐλεημοσύνη – deed of mercy, alms,
             σωφροσύνη – moderation
-ια   f   ἀκαθαρσία – uncleanness, ἐλευθερία – liberty,
             πλεονεξία – greed.

7. To show the place where something is done:
-τηριον n   δικαστήριον – law court,
              θυσιαστήριον – altar, place of sacrifice
-ειον   n   μνημεῖον – tomb, ταμεῖον – treasury, store, inner room.

8. To show a smaller or younger type:
-ιον   n   παιδίον – a little boy, child,   τεκνίον – little child
-ισκος m   νεανίσκος – youth (νεανίας – young man)
-ισκη   f   παιδίσκη – young girl, maid, female servant.

44.3 Adjectives: prefixes and suffixes

A. Prefixes
1. Adjectives beginning with ἀ- or ἀν- – (not):
   ἄγαμος – unmarried   ἄγναφος – unwashed
   ἄγνωστος – unknown   ἀδιάλειπτος – unremitting, continual
   ἀδύνατος – impossible   ἄλαλος – dumb
   ἀνάξιος – unworthy   ἀνωφελής – useless.
   (ἄξιος – worthy)

2. Adjectives beginning with δυσ – hard, difficult:
   δύσκολος – hard, difficult   δυσερμήνευτος – difficult to explain
   δυσβάστακτος – hard to carry.

LESSON 44   277

3. Adjectives beginning with εὐ – good, well:
εὐγενής – well-born, noble
εὔθετος – suitable, fitting
εὐκοπώτερος – easier
εὐλογητός – blessed
εὐπρόσδεκτος – acceptable
εὔχρηστος – useful.

B. Suffixes

1. To show belonging or possession:
   -ιος   οὐράνιος – heavenly,   ἴδιος – one's own.

2. To show material:
   -ινος   λίθινος – made of stone,   ξύλινος – made of wood
   -εος/ους   ἀργύρεος – silver, made of silver   χρυσοῦς – gold.

3. To show inclination or tendency:
   -μων   δεισιδαίμων – scrupulous, reverent,
           ἐλεήμων – merciful   μνήμων – mindful.

4. To show aptitude or nature:
   -ικος   κριτικός – able to judge   φυσικός – natural,
            χοϊκός – earthy
   -ιμος   χρήσιμος – useful   ὠφέλιμος – helpful, useful.

5. To show passive force, capability, or ability:
   -τος   ἀόρατος – invisible   ὁρατός – able to be seen, visible.

44.4 Formation of adverbs

Most adverbs are formed with **-ως** or **-εως**:

ἀληθῶς – truly   ὁμοίως – similarly

ἡδέως – gladly, with pleasure.

But note also:

εὖ – well   εὐθύς – at once

ἥδιστα – very gladly   ταχύ – quickly.

(See also 35.1, 3.)

44.5 Verbs

Some verbs are formed from nouns and adjectives by endings like:
　　-αω　　-εω　　-οω　　-ευω　　-ζω　　-ιζω　　-υνω
The ending is not always a clue to the particular force or meaning, but the following are common.

1. **-αω, -εω, -ευω** – to show action or state:
   - ἀγαλλιάω – I exult
   - ἐάω – I allow
   - ἐρωτάω – I ask
   - τιμάω – I honor
   - κατοικέω – I inhabit, I dwell
   - ποιέω – I do, I make.
   - προσκυνέω – I worship
   - δουλεύω – I serve (as a slave)
   - ἡγεμονεύω – I govern
   - φονεύω – I kill
   - φυτεύω – I plant

2. **-οω, -αινω, -υνω** – to show causation or making:
   - δουλόω – I enslave
   - πικραίνω – I make bitter
     (πικρός – bitter)
   - ξηραίνω – I shrivel up
     (ξηρός – dry)
   - φανερόω – I reveal.
   - θανατόω – I put to death, I cause to be killed
   - πληθύνω – I multiply, I cause to increase
   - παροξύνομαι – I become angry

3. **-ιζω, -αζω** – to show intensive or causative action:
   - ἁγνίζω – I purify
   - βασανίζω – I torment
   - γνωρίζω – I cause to know
   - διαμερίζω – I divide
   - λιθάζω – I stone
   - ῥαντίζω – I sprinkle.

44.6 Verbs formed with prepositions

Many verbs are formed using the most common meaning of the preposition:
　　εἰς – into
　　εἰσέρχομαι – I go into, I enter.
But other verbs reflect less common meanings of the preposition:

ἀνά	ἀναβαίνω – I go up		
(up)	withdrawal:	ἀναστρέφω – I turn back	
		ἀναχωρέω – I go away	
	repetition:	ἀναζάω – I live again	
	thoroughness:	ἀναπαύω – I give rest to, I refresh	

ἀντί (opposite)	ἀντιλέγω – I speak against exchange: ἀνταποδίδωμι – I give back in return, I recompense

ἀπό (from)	ἀπέχω (1) – I am away from
	ἀπολύω – I release
	ἀφορίζω – I separate
	  return: ἀποδίδωμι – I give back
	          ἀπολαμβάνω – I take back
	  completion: ἀπέχω (2) – I have fully
	             ἀπόλλυμι – I destroy (utterly)

διά (through)	διέρχομαι – I go through, I travel through
	  distribution: διαγγέλλω – I proclaim (widely)
	              διαδίδωμι – I distribute
	  separation: διασπάω – I tear apart
	  succession: διαδέχομαι – I receive in turn
	  completion: διακαθαρίζω – I cleanse thoroughly
	             διαφυλάσσω – I guard carefully

ἐκ (out of)	ἐξέρχομαι – I go out, I come out
	  completion: ἐκπληρόω – I fill completely
	             ἐξαπορέομαι – I am utterly bewildered

ἐπί (on)	ἐπιτίθημι – I put on
	ἐπέρχομαι (1) – I come upon
	  opposition: ἐπέρχομαι (2) – I come against
	            ἐπιστρέφω – I turn back
	  superiority: ἐπισκοπέω – I oversee
	            (ἐπίσκοπος – overseer, bishop)
	  upwards: ἐπαίρω – I lift up, I raise
	  completion: ἐπιγινώσκω – I understand, I recognize, I realize
	            ἐπιζητέω – I seek for, I enquire, I demand

κατά (down)	καταβαίνω – I come down
	κατάγω – I bring down (to the shore)
	  opposition: καταράομαι – I curse
	            κατακρίνω – I condemn
	  completion: καταισχύνω – I make ashamed
	            κατεργάζομαι – I accomplish

	κατεσθίω – I eat up, I consume
order:	καταρτίζω – I set in order, I mend
	κατευθύνω – I make straight, I guide
after, behind:	κατακολουθέω – I follow after
	καταλείπω – I leave behind, I forsake

μετά	μεταδίδωμι – I share with, I impart
(with)	μετέχω – I share in, I partake of
	change: μεταβαίνω – I go from one place to another
	μεταμέλομαι – I change my mind, I repent
	μετανοέω – I change my attitude, I repent
	after, seeking: μεταπέμπομαι – I send for, I summon

παρά	παρακαλέω – I call to my side, I entreat, I comfort
(beside)	παραλαμβάνω – I take along (with me), I receive
	deviation: παρακούω – I fail to hear, I overhear
	παραβαίνω – I overstep, I transgress

περί	περιπατέω – I walk about, I live
(about,	περιβάλλω – I put around, I clothe
around)	excess, beyond: περιλείπομαι – I am left, I survive
	περισσεύω – I exceed, I abound

πρό	προάγω – I go in front of, I lead
(in front of)	beforehand: προορίζω – I determine beforehand, I foreordain
	προφητεύω – I speak beforehand, I prophesy

σύν	συνάγω – I gather together
(with)	συνεργέω – I work with
	totality: συγκαλύπτω – I cover completely, I veil
	συνθρύπτω – I break in pieces, I utterly crush
	συντηρέω – I keep safe

ὑπέρ	excess: ὑπερβάλλω – I exceed
(over)	ὑπερέχω – I excel, I am in authority
ὑπερνικάω – I conquer completely	

Lesson 44

ὑπό   ὑποδέομαι – I bind under (ὑπόδημα – sandal)
(under)   subjection: ὑπακούω – I obey
                           ὑπηρετέω – I serve, I minister to
                           ὑπομένω – I endure
            withdrawal: ὑπάγω – I depart
                           ὑποστέλλω – I draw back
                           ὑποστρέφω – I turn back, I return.

44.7 Useful stems in classical and New Testament Greek

As we saw in section 1, the stem of a Greek word will often help us to locate its area of meaning. It may also help us to understand technical words in English. Look, for example, at these stems:

γραφ	write	ὀνομ	name
δημ	people, live, inhabit	ποιε	do, make
ιατρ	cure, medicine, doctor	πορν	fornication, harlot
κρατ	power, sway, control	χρον	time
λεγ/λογ (1)	speak, word, reason	ψευδ	false, liar, pretence
λεγ/λογ (2)	gather, choose	ψυχ	soul, life, person

These stems can help us to unlock the meaning of many complex words like: chronology, democrat, psychiatry, onomatopoeia, pornography, pseudonym, graphology.

44.8 A comical warning

Words are used very flexibly. Precise meaning is fixed by context and by who the speaker is. For example, in the sentence: 'This is a useful table', we cannot understand 'table' unless we know know whether someone is talking about furniture or mathematics.

So when people talk about stems or roots of words and what the words might therefore mean, we must be careful. Be warned!

This warning is for all who wish to be astute (shrewd, carefully wise). The Greek word ἄστυ means city. But if you are astute, that does not mean you live in a city! (And the Latin word 'astutus' may have no link with ἄστυ).

This is a comical warning. I live in a village (κώμη), but it would be silly to say that a comical warning is one that comes from a village, or that it comes from a procession of revellers – κῶμος. So if someone says about a New Testament word 'Its root meaning is *this* , so we should understand it in *this*

way', be careful. You can only tell the meaning of 'comical' by seeing how it is used in the English language today, not by looking at its distant origins.
You have been warned. Be astute.

44.9

For further study of stems, roots, and word structures see Bruce M. Metzger, *Lexical Aids for Students of New Testament Greek,* new edition (T & T Clark, 1990) pp41–72, and for classical Greek grammar and word structures, *Reading Greek,* Joint Association of Classical Teachers' Greek Course, Part 1 *(Grammar, Vocabulary and Exercises)* (CUP, 1978) pp259–334.

44.10 Read 1 John 2

v2 ἱλασμός – propitiation : a sacrifice designed to restore a relationship after something wrong has been done.   v3 ἔγνωκα – I know.
v5 τετελείωται – it has reached its goal, it has been made complete.
v6 ὀφείλω – I owe, I ought (to).   v7 παλαιός – old.
v8 παράγομαι – I pass (away).   v9 ἕως ἄρτι – until now.
v10 σκάνδαλον – obstacle, cause of offence.
v13 νεανίσκος – young man (νέος – new young).
    νικάω – I overcome (νίκη – victory).
v14 ἰσχυρός – strong.   v16 ἐπιθυμία – desire lust.
    ἀλαζονεία – arrogance, pride.   βίος – wealth, possessions, life.
v18 ἔσχατος – last (decisive, critical?).   ἀντίχριστος – alternative Messiah, opponent of the Messiah.   γεγόνασιν – they have come into being (3p p perfect of γίνομαι).   ὅθεν – from which, whence.
v19 μεμενήκεισαν ἄν – they would have remained.   ἀλλ' ἵνα – but (they went out) so that.   v20 (τὸ) χρῖσμα – annointing.
v22 ἀρνέομαι – I deny.   v25 ἐπαγγέλλομαι – I promise.
v27 (ἡ) χρεία – need.
v28 σχῶμεν – we may have (ἔχω had an alternative form ἔσχω).
    αἰσχύνομαι – I am ashamed.   παρουσία – coming, arrival, presence.
v29 γεγέννηται – he/she has been begotten (has been born).

44.11

Revise lessons 37 and 38.

Lesson 45

νίπτω – I wash (someone or something else)
νίπτομαι – I wash (part of myself)

45.1

Study carefully:

1. (a) ἔνιψα τοὺς πόδας σου – I washed your feet
   (b) ἐνιψάμην τοὺς πόδας – I washed my feet
2. (a) ἐκάλεσεν αὐτούς – he called them
   (b) προσεκαλέσατο αὐτούς – he called them to himself
3. (a) ἐνδύσατε αὐτὸν τὰ ἱμάτια αὐτοῦ – put his clothes on him!
   (b) ἐνδύσασθε τὰ ἱμάτια – put the clothes on!
                   or put your clothes on!
4. (a) πέμπω αὐτόν – I am sending him
   (b) ἔρχομαι πρὸς αὐτόν – I am going towards him.

In each (a) sentence the action expressed by the verb is done by the subject to someone else:

    ἔνιψα, ἐκάλεσεν, ἐνδύσατε, and πέμπω are all **active** voice.

In each (b) sentence the action expressed by the verb specially involves or affects the person doing it:

    ἐνιψάμην, προσεκαλέσατο, ἐνδύσασθε, and ἔρχομαι are all **middle** voice (31.9C).

So in 1(a) ἔνιψα is 1st person singular aorist indicative active of νίπτω (I wash), and in 1(b) ἐνιψάμην is 1st person singular aorist indicative middle of νίπτω.

ἐνιψάμην refers to a washing of part of oneself. So ἐνιψάμην τοὺς πόδας means literally, 'I washed-for-myself the feet'. In English we say 'I washed my feet.'

Words that have to do with movement and feelings are often in the middle voice.

45.2 Words

νίπτομαι – I wash
προσκαλέομαι – I call to myself
ἀσπάζομαι – I greet
συνάγονται – they come together, they gather together
ἐνδύομαι – I put on (clothes)
δέχομαι – I receive
κάθημαι – I sit down
ἐκπλήσσομαι – I am astonished

αἰτέομαι – I request, I ask for
φοβέομαι – I fear, I reverence, I feel awe
ἐφοβήθη – he was afraid
ἅπτομαι – I touch
σπλαγχνίζομαι – I feel sorry for, I feel compassion
σπλαγχνισθείς – moved by compassion, feeling sorry for

45.3 Translate

1. ἀσπάζονται ἡμᾶς
καὶ ἡμεῖς δεχόμεθα αὐτούς.

   They greet us and we receive them.

2. ἐὰν μὴ νίψωνται τὰς χεῖρας καὶ τοὺς πόδας, οὐκ ἐσθίουσι τοὺς ἄρτους οὐδὲ ἐνδύονται τὰ ἱμάτια.

   Unless they wash their hands and their feet they do not eat the loaves nor do they put on their clothes.

3. σπλαγχνίζεται τοῖς λεπροῖς
καὶ λέγει αὐτοῖς, Μὴ φοβεῖσθε.
ὃς ἂν ὑμᾶς δέχηται καὶ
ἐμὲ δέχεται.

   He feels compassion for the lepers and says to them, 'Do not be afraid. Whoever receives you also receives me.'

4. συνήχθησαν πρὸς αὐτὸν πάντες
οἱ Φαρισαῖοι καὶ ἐξεπλήσσοντο
ἐπὶ τῇ διδαχῇ αὐτοῦ· ἔλεγεν γὰρ
Αἰτεῖτε καὶ δοθήσεται ὑμῖν.
καὶ ἔλεγον αὐτῷ, Διὰ τί ἡμεῖς
οὐ δεχόμεθα; ἀποκριθεὶς εἶπεν
αὐτοῖς, Διότι κακῶς αἰτεῖσθε ἵνα
τὸ θέλημα τὸ ὑμέτερον ποιῆτε.

   All the Pharisees gathered round him and they were astonished at his teaching for he said, 'Ask and it will be given you.' They said to him, 'Why do we not receive?' In reply he said to them, 'Because you ask with a bad motive so that you may do your own will.'

45.4

λήμψομαι – I will receive, I will take (λάμβανω)

Note that many verbs have a middle form in the future tense. They are often verbs where the action concerns oneself rather than, or as well as, someone else (verbs of perception and movement). Here are some common examples:

ἀκούω – I hear	ἀκούσομαι – I will hear
ἀναβαίνω – I go up	ἀναβήσομαι – I will go up
γινώσκω – I know	γνώσομαι – I will know
εἰμί – I am	ἔσομαι – I will be
ἐσθίω – I eat	φάγομαι – I will eat
ὁράω – I see	ὄψομαι – I will see
πίπτω – I fall	πέσουμαι – I will fall

Note also:

ἐλθών – having gone   ἐλεύσομαι – I will go, I will come.

45.5
Read carefully:

1. A great prophet

Ἀκούσονται τὴν φωνὴν τοῦ προφήτου καὶ ἐλεύσονται πρὸς αὐτὸν καὶ ἄρτον φάγονται μετ' αὐτοῦ. καὶ ἔσται μέγας καὶ πολλοὶ ὄψονται τὴν δόξαν αὐτοῦ καὶ ἀναβήσονται εἰς Ἱεροσόλυμα, καὶ πέσουνται πρὸς τοὺς πόδας αὐτοῦ καὶ γνώσονται ὅτι ὁ θεὸς ἀπέστειλεν αὐτόν.

2. Jesus heals the sick and teaches the crowd

Προσκαλεσάμενος τὸν τυφλὸν καὶ ἀσπασάμενος αὐτὸν εἶπεν αὐτῷ, Ὕπαγε, νίψαι τοὺς ὀφθαλμούς. ἀπῆλθεν οὖν καὶ ἐνίψατο καὶ οἱ ὀφθαλμοὶ αὐτοῦ ἠνοίγησαν. ὁ δὲ Ἰησοῦς πάλιν προσεκαλέσατο αὐτὸν καὶ ἐκάθητο πρὸς τοὺς πόδας αὐτοῦ. συνάγονται οὖν πρὸς αὐτὸν οἱ Φαρισαῖοι καὶ ἰδόντες τὸν ἄνθρωπον ἐκεῖ καθήμενον καὶ γνόντες ὅτι νῦν βλέπει, ἐξεπλήσσοντο καὶ ἐφοβοῦντο.
Καὶ πάλιν πολλοῦ ὄχλου συνηγμένου προσκαλεσάμενος τοὺς ἰδίους μαθητὰς λέγει αὐτοῖς, Σπλαγχνίζομαι ἐπὶ τὸν ὄχλον ὅτι εἰσὶν ὡς πρόβατα μὴ ἔχοντα ποιμένα. καὶ ἤρξατο διδάσκειν αὐτοὺς λέγων, Ὃς ἂν ἐμὲ δέχηται οὐκ ἐμὲ δέχεται ἀλλὰ τὸν Πατέρα τὸν ἐμόν.
Καὶ ἐκάθητο περὶ αὐτὸν ὄχλος καὶ ἦλθεν πρὸς αὐτὸν λεπρὸς λέγων ὅτι Ἐὰν θέλῃς δύνασαί με καθαρίσαι. καὶ σπλαγχνισθεὶς ἐκτείνας τὴν χεῖρα ἥψατο αὐτοῦ καὶ λέγει αὐτῷ, Θέλω, καθαρίσθητι. καὶ εὐθὺς ἐκαθαρίσθη ὥστε ἐκπλήσσεσθαι πάντας τοὺς περὶ αὐτὸν κύκλῳ καθημένους.

45.6

Read Mark 1:1–13

Notes

τὸ πρόσωπον – the face
κατασκευάζω – I prepare, I fix
βοάω – I shout
ἡ τρίβος – the track, the road
εὐθύς – straight, smooth, level
ἡ χώρα – the district
ἐξομολογέω – I confess
αἱ τρίχες – the hairs

ἡ ζώνη – the belt
δερμάτινος – made of skin, leather
ἀκρίς – locust
τὸ μέλι – the honey
ἰσχυρός – strong
κύπτω – I bend down
ὁ ἱμάς – the strap
ἡ περιστερά – the dove

Lesson 46

Translating – Romans 1:1–7

46.1

Read Romans 1:1–7.

Notes
κλητός – called
ἀφορίζω – I set apart
κατὰ σάρκα – according to the flesh
ὁρίζω – I mark out
ἡ ὑπακοή – the obedience
τὰ ἔθνη – the Gentiles, the nations

46.2 Translating long sentences: Romans 1:1–7

Romans 1:1–7 is one long sentence. In present-day English we seldom write long sentences. So when we translate a passage like Romans 1:1–7 we must divide it into shorter sentences. We shall decide how long the sentences must be, by considering:

1. the thoughts in the Greek that have to be expressed in English
2. the style of writing that is appropriate for the passage
3. the readers for whom we are translating.

Romans 1:1–7 is the beginning of a letter. Paul puts his words of greeting at the end of the first sentence (v7). If we divide this long sentence into several shorter sentences we may decide to put the words of greeting at the beginning, where they come in an ordinary English letter.
 Study the two following translations and the notes on them.

46.3 Romans 1:1–7 – Translation A (numbers refer to notes)

Dear Christian friends in Rome,
 You are all loved by God and called by him to be holy[1]. May you know the grace and peace which come from God our Father and the Lord Jesus Christ[2].
 I, Paul, am a servant of Jesus Christ. He called me and made me an apostle[3]: I have been set apart for the preaching of the Good News of God[4]. This Good News God promised beforehand through his prophets, by means of the sacred Scriptures. It is about his Son our Lord Jesus Christ: his human descent was from David, but in divine holiness he was shown to be the Son

of God by the mighty act of his resurrection from the dead.

Through him I received grace and was made an apostle so that people of every race might learn to trust and obey God[5], for the sake of Jesus. You are among them, for you also[6] have been called to belong to Jesus Christ.

Notes:
1. This first paragraph is from verse 7. In an English letter we usually begin with the greeting.
2. This is a passage of some importance for New Testament theology. Grace and peace come ἀπὸ θεοῦ πατρὸς ἡμῶν καὶ κυρίου Ἰησοῦ Χριστοῦ. God our Father and the Lord Jesus Christ are so closely linked as the source of grace and peace that Paul uses ἀπό only once. He does not say ἀπὸ θεοῦ... and ἀπὸ κυρίου... as if there were two separate sources. I have avoided the GNB translation: 'May God our Father and the Lord Jesus Christ give you grace and peace', for (i) it does not so clearly show the Father and the Lord Jesus as a single source of blessing, and (ii) it is a little bit more likely to be misunderstood as if the Father gives grace and Jesus gives peace.
3. κλητὸς ἀπόστολος – It is not clear whether these words express (i) one complete idea, or (ii) two separate ideas. We might translate (i) 'called to be an apostle', or (ii) 'called by him and made an apostle'.
4. In making a sentence end here, I have repeated the reference to the Good News in the next sentence so that the linking together of the ideas is made clear.
5. εἰς ὑπακοὴν πίστεως – The aim of Paul's apostleship is to produce the obedience which is the proper outcome of faith. I have attempted to express these ideas simply by 'to trust and obey God'.
6. καὶ ὑμεῖς – 'you also' – I have not translated και ὑμεῖς as 'you too', because when read aloud it would sound the same as 'you two'. Our translation must be clear when it is heard as well as when it is seen. Look at John 1:33 REB: 'he who is to baptize in Holy Spirit'. The translators have used capitals to indicate to the reader that John means 'the Holy Spirit'; they seem to have forgotten that the hearer cannot distinguish between 'Holy Spirit' and 'holy spirit'.

46.4 Romans 1:1-7 – Translation B

Dear Christian friends in Rome,

You are loved by God. He called you to be holy[1]. Grace and peace be yours. They come from God our Father and the Lord Jesus Christ.

I, Paul, am a slave of Jesus Christ. He called me. He made me an apostle. I have been set apart to preach the Good News of God.

God promised beforehand to send this Good News. He made his promise through the prophets. It is written in the holy writings.

The Good News is about his Son our Lord Jesus Christ. As a man his descent was from King[2] David. As a holy and spiritual being[3] he has been shown to be the Son of God. This was shown by the mighty act of his resurrection from the dead.

Through him I have received grace and was made an apostle. For his sake I preach. I lead people of every race[4] to trust in God and obey him. You also are among those who have been called by Jesus Christ[5].

Notes:
1. The sentences and paragraphs are shorter than in translation A. Paul's one long sentence is made into five short paragraphs. Translation B is for those who are not used to long sentences. When translating the New Testament one needs to try various kinds of translation, read them out aloud to various groups, and see which they can understand best.
2. ἐκ σπέρματος Δαυίδ – 'from the seed of David'; that is, descended from David. Paul and his readers knew David was a king. If our readers may not know this we may think it best to translate Δαυίδ as 'King David'.
3. κατὰ πνεῦμα ἁγιωσύνης – 'according to the spirit of holiness'. This is parallel to κατὰ σάρκα – 'with reference to his human descent'. So κατὰ πνεῦμα ἁγιωσύνης may mean 'with reference to his holy and spiritual nature'. But this is a difficult passage for a translator to be certain about. πνεῦμα ἁγιωσύνης could perhaps be a Hebrew idiom for the Holy Spirit. Paul might mean: 'He was designated and shown by the Holy Spirit to be the Son of God.'
4. ἐν πᾶσιν τοῖς ἔθνεσιν – 'among all the Gentiles, among people of every race'. Paul uses τὰ ἔθνη most often of the Gentiles, that is of all people who are not Jewish by birth. NIV translates, 'among all the Gentiles', but most recent translations use the more general sense of ἔθνη as 'nations': so GNB, 'people of all nations'. NEB, rather strangely, has 'men of all nations'. Paul says nothing here about men, so it is a pity to translate τὰ

ἔθνη in a way that might make women feel they were left out. In REB note the change to 'people of all nations'.
5. κλητοὶ Ἰησοῦ Χριστοῦ – 'called of Jesus Christ'. Does this mean 'called by God to belong to Jesus Christ' (translation A) or 'called by Jesus Christ' (translation B)? We cannot be certain. Paul most often speaks of God the Father as the one who calls people. But in Romans 1:7, Paul uses ἀγαπητοῖς θεοῦ to mean 'loved by God', so here in Romans 1:6 he may be using κλητοὶ Ἰησοῦ Χριστοῦ to mean, 'called by Jesus Christ'.

46.5

You will have seen that it is often very difficult to know the best way to translate a passage of New Testament Greek. We have to consider the meaning of the Greek carefully. We may need to weigh up what learned commentators say. Even so, we may have to confess that we cannot be absolutely certain.

We have also to consider carefully the people we expect to read or listen to our translation. How they use the language into which we are translating will be a guide to us in choosing the style of translation we need to make.

46.6 Read John 1:14–18

v14 (ἡ) σάρξ : flesh, person, human being. Compare the range of meaning of *basar* in Hebrew: flesh, body, man, person.
ἐσκήνωσεν – he lived, he dwelt: we have no equivalent English word, since σκηνή usually means 'tent'. 'He tented among us' is not natural English. When we see that ἐσκήνωσεν... is followed by καὶ ἐθεασάμεθα τὴν δόξαν (and we saw his glory) it becomes clear that, as 1:1 recalled the opening of Genesis, 1:14 recalls the conclusion of Exodus when the tent (or tabernacle) was filled with God's glory: καὶ δόξης κυρίου ἐπλήσθη ἡ σκηνή – 'and the tent was filled with the glory of the Lord.' μονογενής only (child), unique. παρά – from, from beside (balanced by εἰς τὸν κόλπον 'close to the bosom' in v18). πλήρης – full. χάρις – grace, mercy, gift. ἀλήθεια – what is real, genuine and reliable (or, when contrasted with a lie, truth).

v15 κέκραγεν – he called out (perfect 3p s from κράζω).
ἔμπροσθεν – before.
πρῶτος – first: πρῶτός μου – before me, superior to me.

v16 πλήρωμα – fullness.
καὶ χάριν ἀντὶ χάριτος – yes, grace upon grace (a similar use of ἀντί for something added on is found in Greek literature in a phrase meaning 'one sorrow on top of another').

v17 ὁ νόμος – the Torah (Ps 119 illustrates how it was experienced as being a blessing).

v18 πώποτε – ever. ὁ κόλπος – the chest, the bosom.
ἐξηγήσατο – he revealed, or, he has revealed.
 (In religious literature ἐξηγέομαι occurs with the meaning 'I reveal.') In v18 most manuscripts have ὁ μονογενὴς υἱός – 'the only son' (compare 3:16–18). A few early manuscripts have μονογενὴς θεός which is hard to understand since 'only child' is not a term that naturally goes with 'God', nor is 'unique, one of a kind.' See also 47.5 and 50.5.

46.7

Revise lessons 39 and 40.

Lesson 47

εἶπες ὅτι ἐσθίει – you said that he was eating

47.1 Indirect statements: 1. ὅτι followed by a verb in the indicative

Compare carefully:
(a) Ἐσθίει μετὰ τῶν ἁμαρτωλῶν
   He is eating with the sinners.
(b) εἶπες ὅτι Ἐσθίει μετὰ τῶν ἁμαρτωλῶν
   You said, 'He is eating with the sinners.'
(c) εἶπες ὅτι ἐσθίει μετὰ τῶν ἁμαρτωλῶν
   You said that he was eating with the sinners.

Compare (a) and (c). (a) is a direct statement. In (c) there is an indirect or reported statement, 'that he was eating...'. Notice that in Greek the tense of ἐσθίει (present) remains the same when the sentence is reported. But in English we do not say, 'you said that he is eating', but 'you said that he was eating.'

Now compare (b) and (c). They differ only in the capital E which indicates spoken words. The New Testament was originally written in capital letters (uncials). When written in uncials there would be no difference between sentence (b) and sentence (c). In translating, we should have to make our own choice between (b) and (c).

So in 1 John 1:6, EAN EIΠΩMEN OTI KOINΩNIAN EXOMEN MET AYTOY, we have to choose between using (a) direct speech, or (b) indirect speech, in our translation.

(a) Direct speech:
   If we say, 'We have fellowship with him...'
(b) Indirect speech:
   1. If we say that we have fellowship with him...
   or 2. If we claim to have fellowship with him...
The style of 1 John suggests we should use direct speech (a) when we can.

Translate:

1. θεωροῦσιν ὅτι προφήτης εἶ σύ.	They see that you are a prophet.
2. ἐθεώρουν ὅτι προφήτης εἶ σύ.	They saw that you were a prophet.

3. τυφλὸς ἦν καὶ νῦν βλέπει. | He was blind and now he sees.
4. οὐκ ἐπίστευσαν ὅτι ἦν τυφλός. | They did not believe that he had been blind.

47.2 Indirect statements: 2. Using accusative and infinitive

Compare:

(a) Σὺ εἶ ὁ Χριστός
'You are the Messiah'
(b) ἐγὼ σὲ λέγω εἶναι τὸν Χριστόν
(Lit. I say you to be the Messiah)
I say that you are the Messiah
(σέ is accusative form of σύ; εἶναι is present infinitive of εἰμί).

In Mark 8:29:
Ὑμεῖς δὲ τίνα με λέγετε εἶναι;
'Whom do you say that I am?'
(τίνα is accusative of τίς; με is the accusative form of ἐγώ).

Note also 3 John 14:
ἐλπίζω δὲ εὐθέως σε ἰδεῖν
I hope that I will see you soon
or I hope to see you soon
(ἰδεῖν – to see – is aorist infinitive).

Hebrews 3:18:
τίσιν δὲ ὤμοσεν μὴ εἰσελεύσεσθαι...;
To whom did he swear that they would not enter...?
(ὤμοσεν is 3p s aor indic active of ὀμνύω – I swear; εἰσελεύσεσθαι is future infinitive middle of εἰσέρχομαι – I enter).

47.3 Indirect requests – ἵνα followed by a verb in the subjunctive

Compare:

(a) Δός μοι τὸν ἄρτον (direct request)
'Please give me the loaf'
(b) θέλω ἵνα δῷς μοι τὸν ἄρτον (indirect request)
(Lit. I wish that you would give me the loaf)
I want you to give me the loaf.
(In (a) δός is 2p s aor imper active, and in (b) δῷς is 2p s aor subj active, of δίδωμι).

In Mark 13:18,
 προσεύχεσθε δὲ ἵνα μὴ γένηται χειμῶνος
 But pray that it may not happen in winter.

Translate:

1. παρεκάλουν αὐτὸν ἵνα αὐτοῦ ἅψωνται. — They begged him that they might touch him.
2. παρακαλοῦσιν αὐτὸν ἵνα αὐτῆς ἅψηται. — They beseech him to touch her.
3. θέλομεν ἵνα τοῦτο ποιήσῃς ἡμῖν. — We want you to do this for us.
4. δὸς ἡμῖν ἵνα καθίσωμεν μετὰ σοῦ ἐν τῇ βασιλείᾳ σοῦ. — Please grant us that we may sit with you in your kingdom.
5. προσεύχεσθε ἵνα μὴ ἔλθητε εἰς πειρασμόν. — Pray that you may not go into temptation (testing).
6. Τί σοι θέλεις ποιήσω; Θέλω ἵνα εὐθὺς δῷς μοι ἐπὶ πίνακι τοὺς ἄρτους ἐκείνους. — 'What do you want me to do for you?' 'I want you to give me at once those loaves on a dish.'
7. Τὸ θυγάτριόν μου ἐσχάτως ἔχει, ἵνα ἐλθὼν ἐπίθῃς τὰς χεῖρας αὐτῇ. — My daughter is dying. Please come and lay your hands on her.

47.4 Indirect questions

Compare:
(a) πότε ἔρχεται;
    When is he coming?
(b) οὐκ οἶδα πότε ἔρχεται
    I do not know when he is coming.

Mk 3:2   παρετήρουν αὐτὸν εἰ…θεραπεύσει αὐτόν
         They watched him to see if he would heal him
         (Direct form: θεραπεύσει αὐτόν; – 'Will he heal him?')

Mk 12:41 ἐθεώρει πῶς ὁ ὄχλος βάλλει…
         He watched how the crowd was putting…
         (Direct question: πῶς βάλλει; – 'How is it putting…?')

Mk 13:35 οὐκ οἴδατε…πότε ὁ κύριος τῆς οἰκίας ἔρχεται
         You do not know when the master of the house will come
         (When he does come, you will say: ἔρχεται – 'He is coming').

For indirect commands and prohibitions, see lesson 41.2.

47.5 Read John 1:14–18 again and note its chiastic structure.

A	Καὶ ὁ λόγος σὰρξ ἐγένετο	PRESENCE
	Καὶ ἐσκήνωσεν ἐν ἡμῖν,	REVEALING
B	Καὶ ἐθεασάμεθα τὴν δόξαν αὐτοῦ,	SEEN GLORY of the
	δόξαν ὡς μονογενοῦς παρὰ πατρός,	FATHER'S ONLY SON
C	πλήρης χάριτος καὶ ἀληθείας.	FULL of GRACE
	D Ἰωάννης μαρτυρεῖ περὶ αὐτοῦ	
	καὶ κέκραγεν λέγων,	
	Οὗτος ἦν ὃν εἶπον,	JOHN'S
	ὁ ὀπίσω μου ἐρχόμενος	WITNESS
	ἔμπροσθέν μου γέγονεν	
	ὅτι πρῶτός μου ἦν.	
C'	ὅτι ἐκ τοῦ πληρώματος αὐτοῦ	FULLNESS
	ἡμεῖς πάντες ἐλάβομεν	of
	καὶ χάριν ἀντὶ χάριτος·	GRACE
	ὅτι ὁ νόμος διὰ Μωϋσέως ἐδόθη,	
	ἡ χάρις καὶ ἡ ἀλήθεια	
	διὰ Ἰησοῦ Χριστοῦ ἐγένετο.	
B'	θεὸν οὐδεὶς ἑώρακεν πώποτε·	GOD not SEEN
	ὁ μονογενὴς υἱὸς ὁ ὢν εἰς τὸν κόλπον	but by
	τοῦ πατρὸς	the FATHER'S ONLY SON
A'	ἐκεῖνος ἐξηγήσατο.	REVEALED

In an extended chiastic structure it is the balance of key ideas and words that is important rather than equality in the number of lines. Notice how C is brief and introduces the key ideas of fullness and χάρις καὶ ἀλήθεια. C' expands these ideas beginning with fullness and moving on to χάρις. In the closure of C' the key words χάρις καὶ ἀλήθεια are repeated, which helps us to be sure of the literary structure.

In B, immediately before 'full of χάρις and ἀλήθεια' we have μονογενοῦς παρὰ πατρός, so in B' immediately after ἡ χάρις καὶ ἡ ἀλήθεια we have a sentence containing ὁ μονογενὴς – ... εἰς τὸν κόλπον τοῦ πατρός. Since in B μονογενής clearly means 'only son', when we have to choose between μονογενὴς θεός in some manuscripts and μονογενὴς υἱός in others the careful chiastic structures we see in 1:1–2, and 1:3–10, as well as here in 14–18, must be taken into account as evidence in favour of ὁ μονογενὴς υἱός.

47.6
Revise lessons 41 and 42.

Lesson 48

The Influence of Hebrew and Aramaic

48.1

In the time when Jesus taught and the Gospels were written, three languages were in use in Galilee and Judea: Hebrew, Greek and Aramaic. We know from the Dead Sea Scrolls and from the Mishnah that Hebrew was the main language for religious instruction. It was the language of the rabbis except for one or two who had a Babylonian background and used Aramaic. Hebrew enjoyed a period of revival after the Maccabees gained a measure of independence. It was almost certainly the language of the home. Greek was a lingua franca from Spain in the west to Persia in the east. Some of the written material from Masada, where the most patriotic Jews resisted the Romans, was written in Greek. The second lingua franca, from the Mediterranean to Mesopotamia, was Aramaic.

When my granddaughter, who lives in Spain, was eight years old she could talk to people in Spanish, English or French. So I know it is easy for people to grow up using three languages. I have also noticed that sometimes, when my daughter is thinking in Spanish, it shapes the way she uses English. When I was in Uganda I used the expression 'slowly by slowly' rather than 'gradually'. 'Slowly by slowly' is English influenced by East African idiom.

When I taught Mark's Gospel (1966–1972) I knew enough Hebrew to say to my students 'Mark's Greek is Greek written by someone who was thinking in Hebrew.' I was interested to discover recently that when Robert L. Lindsay translated Mark into Hebrew he found that Mark's Greek constantly gave him the right word order for Hebrew. He concluded that Mark was probably first drafted in Hebrew and then translated into Greek. Now that I know more Hebrew, I find that problems in interpreting words or passages in the Gospels can often find a reasonable solution if they are translated into Hebrew.

The Gospels contain many Hebrew words written in Greek. For example, Ἀμήν (about 100 times), Ὡσαννά (5), Σατανᾶς (15), Ῥαββεί (16, of which 8 are in John), κορβάν, ῥακά, βάτος (Lk 16:6), σίκερα (strong drink), Ηλι (my God: but also a short form for Elijah, hence the confusion recorded in Mt 27:46–47).

Besides the evidence of Hebrew words and idioms, there is also the evidence of literary forms and constant quotations from or allusions to the Hebrew scriptures. We have seen that whoever wrote John 1:1–18 was someone deeply immersed in Hebrew styles of composition. Jesus himself frequently taught using parables. We know of almost 5,000 rabbinic parables recorded in Hebrew – and only two in Aramaic.

What about Aramaic? Ἀββα is an Aramaic word (Mk 14:36) but it occurs frequently in Hebrew writings of the period. In English we can use 'sputnik' or 'en-suite' without anyone thinking we are speaking Russian or French. Εφφαθα (Mk 7:34) is Aramaic, but there are words like ταλιθα and κουμ (Mk 5:41) which could reflect either Aramaic or Hebrew.

In the past, the idea that Aramaic was used by ordinary people rather than Hebrew was sometimes strengthened by mistranslations. In John 19:20 it is recorded that the notice on the cross was written Ἐβραϊστί and in Latin and Greek. For example, NIV (1979) 'in Aramaic, Latin and Greek'. NRSV translates in the obvious way: 'in Hebrew', but has a footnote 'That is, Aramaic'; ('In Aramaic' would be Συριστί). In 1997 Matthew Black, who had earlier written *An Aramaic Approach to the Gospels and Acts* wrote that the evidence of the Dead Sea Scrolls confirms the view that Hebrew was 'a spoken vernacular in Judea in the time of Christ' and that we must allow for the possibility that Jesus used Hebrew as well as (or instead of) Aramaic. Professor David Flusser of the Hebrew University of Jerusalem, after indicating that there are hundreds of Semitic idioms in the Synoptic Gospels that can only be from Hebrew, concluded that there are no Semitisms which could only be Aramaic without also being good Hebrew.

48.2 Hebrew poetry

Hebrew poetic style is full of *repetition* and *parallelism*. Almost any chapter of Proverbs or Job will illustrate this. Note the *parallelism* in Luke 12:48. We indicate the pattern of this parallelism by the letters ABAB:

A παντὶ δὲ ᾧ ἐδόθη πολύ,
B πολὺ ζητηθήσεται παρ' αὐτοῦ·
A καὶ ᾧ παρέθεντο πολύ,
B περισσότερον αἰτήσουσιν αὐτόν.

Note the *repetition* in Matthew 6:19–20. We indicate the pattern of this repetitive parallelism by the letters ABCABC:

A Μὴ θησαυρίζετε ὑμῖν θησαυροὺς ἐπὶ τῆς γῆς,
B ὅπου σὴς καὶ βρῶσις ἀφανίζει

C   καὶ ὅπου κλέπται διορύσσουσιν καὶ κλέπτουσιν·
A   θησαυρίζετε δὲ ὑμῖν θησαυροὺς ἐν οὐρανῷ,
B   ὅπου οὔτε σὴς οὔτε βρῶσις ἀφανίζει
C   καὶ ὅπου κλέπται οὐ διορύσσουσιν οὐδὲ κλέπτουσιν·

Notice that in this section we have used the words repetition and parallelism in this order: repetition, parallelism, parallelism, repetition. The order of the words is on the pattern ABBA. Normally in a text-book if we say, 'Let us consider points (a) and (b)', we then discuss point (a) first. The order ABBA is typical of Hebrew poetry. It is called **chiasmus**. Read Matthew 7:6 and note the **chiastic** order. We might be tempted to translate this as:

Do not give what is holy to the dogs. (A)
Do not cast your pearls before pigs   (B)
lest they trample on them with their feet   (B)
and lest they turn and savage you.   (A)

But once we notice the ABBA pattern we might try a more natural English order in our translation. For example:

Do not give what is holy to the dogs
– they may turn and savage you.
Do not throw your pearls before pigs
– they may trample them in the mud.

Notice also that while 'trample them with their feet' is a repetitive idiom, natural in New Testament Greek, it is not so natural in English poetry. 'Trample them in the mud' is not a literal translation, but it may be the best equivalent translation.

48.3 Repetition for emphasis

In Hebrew, words are often repeated to give emphasis. Note in Ecclesiastes 1:1, 'frustration of frustration'. In English we would not naturally use such repetition for emphasis. We might perhaps use the word 'utterly' to give emphasis, and translate the sentence: 'Everything is utterly frustrating'. Note in Revelation 1:6, εἰς τοὺς αἰῶνας τῶν αἰώνων. 'To the ages of the ages' would not be a good translation. We need something like: 'to all eternity', or 'for ever and ever'.

A common Hebrew idiom uses the repetition of a form of the infinitive to give emphasis. This kind of verb-doubling for emphasis is found in the New Testament rarely with the infinitive, more often with the participle. For example:

Mk 4:9 ῝Ος ἔχει ὦτα ἀκούειν ἀκουέτω.

The infinitive ἀκούειν gives emphasis to the imperative ἀκουέτω. In translating this we must find a way of emphasis that will suit the readers for whom we are translating. Consider the following possible translations:

(a) He who has ears, let him not fail to hear
(b) The person who has ears must really listen
(c) If you've got ears – *use them*.

In translations (a) and (b) we translate ἀκούω as 'hear' or 'listen'. But ἀκούω often also includes the idea of 'understand'. So we might also consider:

(d) Use your minds to understand what you hear

– although this lacks the force and directness of the Greek.

Some further examples of verb repetition in the New Testament:
Mk 4:12   βλέποντες βλέπωσιν καὶ μὴ ἴδωσιν
           (Lit. Looking they may look yet they may not see)
           They certainly look, but they do not see
Acts 7:34 ἰδὼν εἶδον τὴν κάκωσιν τοῦ λαοῦ μου
           I have surely seen the persecution of my people
        or I have indeed seen how my people are oppressed
Heb 6:13–14 ὤμοσεν καθ' ἑαυτοῦ λέγων, Εἰ μὴν εὐλογῶν εὐλογήσω
            σε καὶ πληθύνων πληθυνῶ σε
            He swore by himself, saying, 'I will certainly bless you and
            I will certainly multiply you'
         or He made himself the witness of his own oath: he said, 'I vow
            that I will bless you abundantly and multiply you greatly.'

A similar noun may also be used with a verb to give emphasis:
Lk 22:15 Ἐπιθυμίᾳ ἐπεθύμησα τοῦτο τὸ πάσχα φαγεῖν μεθ'
          ὑμῶν πρὸ τοῦ με παθεῖν
          I have really longed to eat this Passover with you before I suffer
          (Lit. ἐπιθυμίᾳ ἐπεθύμησα is 'with longing I longed' or
            'with desire I desired')
Jas 5:17 προσευχῇ προσηύξατο τοῦ μὴ βρέξαι
          He prayed earnestly for it not to rain
          (Lit. With prayer he prayed...).

But repetitiveness is very common in Semitic idiom and it is not always emphatic:
1 Pet 3:14 τὸν δὲ φόβον αὐτῶν μὴ φοβηθῆτε
            Do not be afraid of them

Mk 7:7 διδάσκοντες διδασκαλίας ἐντάλματα ἀνθρώπων
   Teaching as doctrines the commandments of men
   or While they teach people to obey the commandments men have given
   or While what they teach is merely men's rules.

48.4

In Semitic idiom, ideas are often placed side by side and linked together by 'and' where in English we would not use 'and'. Take, for example, Mark 11:1-2,

ἀποστέλλει δύο τῶν μαθητῶν αὐτοῦ καὶ λέγει αὐτοῖς, Ὑπάγετε...

At first sight we might be tempted to translate this, 'He sends two of the disciples **and** says to them, "Go...".' But the saying does not come after the sending. So in English we must not link the two ideas by 'and'. We might translate: 'He sent off two of the disciples with these instructions, "Go...".' Similarly, in John 1:48, ἀπεκρίθη Ἰησοῦς καὶ εἶπεν should be translated 'In reply Jesus said', or 'Jesus replied.'

Note also Matthew 22:4, οἱ ταῦροί μου καὶ τὰ σιτιστά (my bulls and my fattened animals)—the animals fattened up with corn (σῖτος) are probably the bulls. We should translate: 'My fat bulls'.

In John 1:14 and 17 we find χάρις and ἀλήθεια set side by side. Do they indicate two different things (a) grace (love) and (b) reliability (reality, truth), or does ἀλήθεια indicate the nature of χάρις so that ἡ χάρις καὶ ἡ ἀλήθεια in 1:17 has the sense of 'reliable love' or 'genuine grace'? The fact that in 16 and 17(a) the focus is strongly on χάρις, and the gifts God has given, suggests that χάρις καὶ ἀλήθεια expresses a composite idea rather than two separate ideas.

καὶ ἐγένετο – *and it happened*
Particularly in Luke's Gospel, the next stage of a story is often introduced by the words καὶ ἐγένετο. We do not usually need to express this in English, except perhaps by beginning a new paragraph:

Lk 2:15 Καὶ ἐγένετο ὡς ἀπῆλθον ἀπ' αὐτῶν εἰς τὸν οὐρανὸν οἱ ἄγγελοι, οἱ ποιμένες ἐλάλουν πρὸς ἀλλήλους, Διέλθωμεν...
   When the angels had gone away from them into heaven, the shepherds said to each other, 'Let us go...'

But see also lesson 48.11.

48.5 Commands: two examples of Semitic influence

1. Participles used for the imperative
New Testament writers sometimes follow Semitic idiom in using participles to express commands, where classical Greek authors would use the imperative. Note in Romans 12:9–10 ἀποστυγοῦντες (hating)... κολλώμενοι (cleaving to)... προηγούμενοι (showing respect, considering better than oneself). In our translation we might say: 'Hate... Hold on to... Show respect to...'

2. The future indicative used for the imperative
Lk 4:8   Κύριον τὸν θεόν σου προσκυνήσεις
  (Lit. You shall worship the Lord your God)
  Worship the Lord your God.

48.6

Note the use of οὐ ... πᾶς ... or πᾶς ... οὐ ... for 'none, not any':
1 Jn 2:21   πᾶν ψεῦδος ἐκ τῆς ἀληθείας οὐκ ἔστιν
  (Lit. Every lie is not of the truth)
  No lie comes from the truth
Mk 13:20   οὐκ ἂν ἐσώθη πᾶσα σάρξ
  No flesh would be saved
  or Nobody would survive
Acts 10:14   οὐδέποτε ἔφαγον πᾶν κοινόν
  I never ate anything that was ritually unclean.

48.7

εἰ (if) is used to introduce a strong denial:
Mk 8:12   εἰ δοθήσεται τῇ γενεᾷ ταύτῃ σημεῖον
  A sign will certainly not be given to this generation
Heb 3:11   ὡς ὤμοσα ἐν τῇ ὀργῇ μου,
  Εἰ εἰσελεύσονται εἰς τὴν κατάπαυσίν μου
  As I swore in my wrath,
  'They will certainly not enter into my rest.'

48.8 Prepositions and prepositional phrases

Note particularly:
1. ἐν used with the dative, for the instrument with which something is done (lessons 31.3, 42.3 (5)).

In Matthew 3:11, αὐτὸς ὑμᾶς βαπτίσει ἐν πνεύματι ἁγίῳ καὶ πυρί, baptism with the Holy Spirit is not something separate from the baptism with fire (cf. lesson 48.4). A translator would have to consider whether:
- (a) to translate, 'He will baptize you with the Holy Spirit and with fire', leaving it to a commentator to explain the Hebrew idiom; or whether,
- (b) to adopt a translation like: 'He will baptize you with the fire of the Holy Spirit', or 'He will baptize you with the fiery Holy Spirit.'

2. ἐν χειρί (by the hand of) – by means of, through.
   Gal 3:19   ἐν χειρὶ μεσίτου
   Through a mediator
   There is no reference to the mediator's hand!

3. εἰς (into) – as
   2 Cor 6:18   ἔσομαι ὑμῖν εἰς πατέρα
   I shall be to you as a father.

4. πρὸ προσώπου (before the face) – before, ahead of
   Lk 10:1   ἀπέστειλεν αὐτοὺς ἀνὰ δύο δύο πρὸ προσώπου αὐτοῦ
   He sent them on ahead of him in twos
   (ἀνὰ δύο δύο is probably also a Hebraism).

   Compare: ἀπὸ προσώπου – from
               κατὰ πρόσωπον – before, in the presence of.

48.9 Uses of the genitive case

Some of the uses of the genitive case we have studied in lesson 39 show Hebrew and Aramaic influence. Notice particularly:

μείζων δὲ τούτων (lit. greater of these)
The greatest of these
τὸ πνεῦμα τῆς ἐπαγγελίας (lit. the Spirit of promise)
The promised Spirit
ὁ κριτὴς τῆς ἀδικίας (lit. the judge of unrighteousness)
The unrighteous judge
τέκνα ὀργῆς (lit. children of wrath)
People subject to God's wrath.

See also the examples in lesson 39.1, section 7(b).

48.10

There are many New Testament words which can only be understood when their Old Testament and Jewish background is known. For example:

νομοδιδάσκαλος – teacher of the Law of Moses and of the Jewish religious tradition based on the Law of Moses

ψευδοπροφήτης – false prophet: that is, someone who claims to be a spokesman for God but isn't

γραμματεύς – scribe: custodian, copier, and teacher of the Old Testament Scriptures; teacher of the Mosaic Law, interpreter of Jewish Law and tradition

εἰδωλολατρία – worship of idols

περιτομή – circumcision

ἀκροβυστία – uncircumcision

θυσιαστήριον – the altar of sacrifice (in the Tabernacle, or in the Jerusalem Temple)

ὁλοκαύτωμα – whole burnt offering

τὰ ἔθνη – the Gentiles, all non-Jewish nations or people

Χριστός – Anointed, God's Anointed One, the Messiah

εἰρήνη – peace: used in the wider sense of the Hebrew word *shalom* for all the blessings of welfare and peace.

Notice also various Aramaic and Hebrew words, written in Greek letters:

'Αββά – Father, Daddy
'Ακελδαμά – Field of blood
'Αμήν – truly
'Ελωι– my God
'Εφφαθα – be opened
Ταλιθα κουμ – girl, get up
Βοανηργές – Sons of Thunder, Thunderers.

For a fuller discussion, see C. F. D. Moule, *An Idiom-Book of New Testament Greek* (CUP, 1959) pp171–191.

Some Hebrew words are plural in form, but singular in meaning. For example: *shamayim* (heaven). In the New Testament, especially Matthew, notice uses of οὐρανοί meaning heaven. So we translate ἡ βασιλεία τῶν οὐρανῶν as 'the Kingdom of heaven' (or, the heavenly Kingdom) and not as 'the Kingdom of the heavens'. 'Kingdom of heaven' is a Hebraic idiom for 'Kingdom of God'.

48.11 Translating New Testament passages influenced by Hebrew and Aramaic

Most of the New Testament writers were Jews. Their normal use of Greek was influenced naturally by their Hebraic background. When we find a Hebraism, the writer is most often using language that is normal for him. So we must usually translate into the normal idiom of our own language.

But when New Testament writers are quoting from the Old Testament we may wish to model the style of our translation on that of a well-known Old Testament translation, if one already exists in our own language.

Consider also Luke chapters 1–2. Luke 1:1–4 is a carefully constructed sentence in stylish Greek. From verse 5 onwards the language is much coloured by the Hebraic-Aramaic background. We may want to give some indication of this in our translation. For example, in verse 5 we might translate ἐγένετο as, 'it came to pass.' This is not modern English. It is English of the style of the Authorized Version, which itself follows Hebrew style more closely than a modern translator would normally do.

48.12

(a) Read Luke 1:5–7 (κατὰ Λουκᾶν 1:5–7):

Notes
ἐφημερία – division, priestly order
θυγάτηρ – daughter, female descendant
ἐναντίον – before, in the presence of
δικαίωμα – statute, law
προβαίνω – I go ahead : προβεβηκότες ἐν ταῖς ἡμέραις – old .
Compare (LXX) Genesis 24:1 προβεβηκὼς ἡμερῶν – advanced in years.
Luke reflects the Hebrew idiom (**in**) more closely than the LXX translator.

Apart from the Jewish names, notice that the following words and phrases show signs of Hebrew influence:
ἐγένετο – it came to pass, there was...
ἐν ταῖς ἡμέραις – note the use of 'day' to refer to time or age
γυνὴ αὐτῷ – a wife to him: meaning 'he had a wife'
ἐναντίον τοῦ θεοῦ – before God
ἐντολαὶ καὶ δικαιώματα – commandments and ordinances: these two words reflect a difference in Israel's religious law between basic commandments and a multiplicity of lesser laws and regulations.
τοῦ Κυρίου – of the Lord: that is, of Yahweh.

(b) A few Hebrew idioms:
   (i) A good eye (ὀφθαλμὸς ἀγαθός) indicates generosity (Prov 22:9)
   A bad eye (ὀφθαλμὸς πονηρός) indicates meanness (Prov 23:6)
   (ii) To 'put one's face' can mean simply to 'set off towards' (Gen 31:21)
   (iii) To be a 'son of' something is to have a certain character (see 39.1.7) so in Luke 10:6 υἱὸς εἰρήνης (ben shalom) is to be someone who is warmly welcoming.
   (iv) In Hebrew teaching the same point is often stated twice over to make it emphatic, but in slightly different words. In Matthew 5:42 τῷ αἰτοῦντί σε δός 'Give to the person who asks you' is immediately followed by 'and do not turn away from the person who wants to borrow from you.' It is clear from Leviticus 25:37 οὐ δώσεις 'you must not **give**' that the verb δίδωμι may be properly used in the context of lending.

   So Matthew 5:42 (a) may not refer to giving a gift but to giving a loan.

   (v) In Luke 6:22 we read, 'you are blessed when... ἐκβάλωσιν τὸ ὄνομα ὑμῶν ὡς πονηρὸν...' What is meant by 'cast out your name as evil'? Deuteronomy 22:14 'he causes to go out against her a bad name' suggests it means 'slander you'.

   Study whatever translations you have, looking at (i) Lk 11:34, (ii) Lk 9:51, (iii) Lk 10:6, (iv) Mt 5:24 and (v) Lk 6:22, and consider whether the translations have been done in the light of the Hebrew idioms that lie behind the Greek.

Lesson 49

γένοιτο – let it happen, may it happen
δεδώκει – he had given ⸱|→|

49.1

γένοιτο – let it happen
μὴ γένοιτο – may it not happen, perish the thought!

Lk 1:38 γένοιτό μοι κατὰ τὸ ῥῆμά σου
Let it happen to me according to your word

Acts 5:24 διηπόρουν...τί ἂν γένοιτο τοῦτο
They were perplexed wondering what this could be
or They wondered what this might mean
or They wondered where the matter might end.

Translate:

1. τοῦτο γένοιτο ἡμῖν.	Let this happen to us.
2. μὴ γένοιτό μοι.	May it not happen to me.
3. μὴ πονηρός ἐστιν ὁ θεός; μὴ γένοιτο.	Is God evil? Perish the thought!
4. τὸ ἀγαθὸν ἐμοὶ ἐγένετο θάνατος; μὴ γένοιτο.	Did what is good become a cause of death to me? Of course not.

49.2

ἁγιάσαι – may he sanctify (ἁγιάζω – I sanctify)
εἴη – may it be (εἰμί – I am)
πληθυνθείη – may it be multiplied (πληθύνω – I multiply, I increase)

Translate:

1. Αὐτὸς δὲ ὁ θεὸς ἁγιάσαι ὑμᾶς καὶ παρακαλέσαι ὑμῶν τὰς καρδίας. χάρις ὑμῖν καὶ εἰρήνη πληθυνθείη, καὶ ἡ ἀγάπη τοῦ θεοῦ εἴη ἐπὶ πᾶσι τοῖς πιστεύουσιν ἐν αὐτῷ.	May God himself sanctify you and comfort your hearts. Grace and peace be multiplied to you, and may the love of God be upon all who believe in him.

2. ἠθέλησεν ὁ Παῦλος, εἰ δυνατὸν εἴη | Paul wished, if it should
αὐτῷ, τὴν ἡμέραν τῆς Πεντηκοστῆς | be possible for him, to be
γενέσθαι εἰς Ἱεροσόλυμα. | in Jerusalem on the day of
| Pentecost.

49.3 Optative mood

Forms like the following are called **optative**:

δῷη – may he give
λογισθείη – may it be reckoned
ὀναίμην – may I be profited
στηρίξαι – may he strengthen

ἐπιτιμήσαι – may he rebuke
φάγοι – may he eat
γένοιτο – may it happen

They do not occur very often in the New Testament.
They are marked by   οι ,   ει , or   αι   before or in the ending.

The optative is used

1. To express a wish:
Mk 11:14   Μηκέτι εἰς τὸν αἰῶνα ἐκ σοῦ μηδεὶς καρπὸν φάγοι
May no one ever again eat fruit from you for ever.

2. To express a condition when the outcome is considered unlikely:
1 Pet 3:17   εἰ θέλοι τὸ θέλημα τοῦ θεοῦ
If the will of God should so will
or If God should want it to be so
1 Pet 3:14   ἀλλ' εἰ καὶ πάσχοιτε διὰ δικαιοσύνην...
But if you should suffer because of righteousness...

3. To express a hesitant question:
Acts 8:31   Πῶς γὰρ ἂν δυναίμην;
For how could I?
Lk 6:11   διελάλουν πρὸς ἀλλήλους τί ἂν ποιήσαιεν τῷ Ἰησοῦ
They discussed with each other what they should do to Jesus
Lk 22:23   καὶ αὐτοὶ ἤρξαντο συζητεῖν πρὸς ἑαυτοὺς
τὸ τίς ἄρα εἴη ἐξ αὐτῶν ὁ τοῦτο μέλλων πράσσειν
They began to ask themselves
which of them it could be who was about to do this.

49.4 Ways of linking words and parts of sentences together

1. καί...καί... – both...and... :

Mk 7:37 Καλῶς πάντα πεποίηκεν, καὶ τοὺς κωφοὺς ποιεῖ
ἀκούειν καὶ τοὺς ἀλάλους λαλεῖν
He has done all things well, he (both) makes the deaf to hear and the dumb to speak.

2. ... τε καί... – both...and... :

Mt 22:10 συνήγαγον πάντας οὓς εὗρον πονηρούς τε καὶ ἀγαθούς
They gathered together all whom they had found, both bad and good

Jn 2:15 πάντας ἐξέβαλεν ἐκ τοῦ ἱεροῦ
τά τε πρόβατα καὶ τοὺς βόας.
He drove them all out of the Temple,
both the sheep and the cattle.

3. οἱ μέν...οἱ δέ... – some...others...
οἱ μέν...ἄλλοι δέ... – some...others... :

Acts 14:4 οἱ μὲν ἦσαν σὺν τοῖς Ἰουδαίοις,
οἱ δὲ σὺν τοῖς ἀποστόλοις
Some were with the Jews, others with the apostles

1 Cor 7:7 ὁ μὲν οὕτως, ὁ δὲ οὕτως
One man in this way, another man in another way

Jn 7:12 οἱ μὲν ἔλεγον ὅτι Ἀγαθός ἐστιν, ἄλλοι δὲ ἔλεγον, Οὔ
Some said, 'He is a good man', but others said, 'No!'

4. μενοῦν or μενοῦνγε – no, rather; on the contrary:

Lk 11:28 μενοῦν μακάριοι οἱ ἀκούοντες τὸν λόγον τοῦ θεοῦ
No, happy are those who hear the word of God
or Rather, blessed are those who listen to God's word.

5. μὲν οὖν – so, so then, however: (often used to link on the next stage of a narrative)

Acts 15:3 οἱ μὲν οὖν προπεμφθέντες
So they, having been sent on their way

Heb 9:1 Εἶχε μὲν οὖν καὶ ἡ πρώτη...
So then the first also had...

Acts 25:4 ὁ μὲν οὖν Φῆστος ἀπεκρίθη...
However Festus answered...

6. οὐ μόνον...ἀλλὰ καί... – not only...but also... :
Jn 5:18 ὅτι οὐ μόνον ἔλυεν τὸ σάββατον,
         ἀλλὰ καὶ πατέρα ἴδιον ἔλεγεν τὸν θεόν
         Because he was not only breaking the Sabbath
         but was also calling God his own father
2 Tim 4:8 ὃν ἀποδώσει μοι...οὐ μόνον δὲ ἐμοὶ
           ἀλλὰ καὶ πᾶσι τοῖς ἠγαπηκόσι τὴν ἐπιφάνειαν αὐτοῦ
           Which he will give to me...and not to me only
           but also to all those who have loved his appearing.

7. μέν...δέ... (see also no.3)
When two ideas or words are compared or contrasted they are often linked by μέν... and δέ... . In English we often use 'but' for δέ. We do not have a word which quite corresponds to μέν. 'On the one hand' and 'on the other hand' are rather too weighty for μέν and δέ.
Heb 1:7–8 καὶ πρὸς μὲν τοὺς ἀγγέλους λέγει... πρὸς δὲ τὸν υἱόν...
           To the angels he says..., but to the Son...
Mt 9:37   Ὁ μὲν θερισμὸς πολύς, οἱ δὲ ἐργάται ὀλίγοι
           The harvest is great, but the workers are few
1 Cor 1:12 Ἐγὼ μέν εἰμι Παύλου, Ἐγὼ δὲ Ἀπολλῶ
           'I am Paul's man,' 'But I am of Apollos.'

49.5 Words

φρονέω – I think of, I have in my mind, my attitude is
ἐπιτιμάω – I rebuke (with dative); I warn (with ἵνα – that)
ὁ πρεσβύτερος – the elder, the older man
ὁ νεώτερος – the younger   μωρός – foolish
φρόνιμος – wise, sensible   ὑψόω – I exalt, I make high
ὑπερήφανος – proud   ὕψιστος – highest
σοφός – wise   ταπεινόω – I humble, I make low
   ἡ σοφία – wisdom

49.6

Read carefully:

          Different attitudes: old and humble, young and proud
ἐν δὲ ταύταις ταῖς ἡμέραις ἄλλοι ἄνθρωποι ἄλλον τι φρονοῦσιν. οἱ μὲν γάρ εἰσιν φρόνιμοι παρ' ἑαυτοῖς καὶ ὑψοῦσιν ἑαυτούς, οἱ δὲ ἄλλοι

ταπεινοῦσιν ἑαυτοὺς καὶ οὐχ ὑπερήφανοί εἰσιν ἐν ταῖς καρδίαις αὐτῶν εὑρίσκομεν γὰρ ἐν ἡμῖν ὅτι οἱ μὲν πρεσβύτεροι οὐχ ὑπερήφανοί εἰσιν οὐδὲ θέλουσιν ἑαυτοὺς ὑψοῦν, οἴδασιν γὰρ ὅτι κακά τε καὶ πονηρὰ ἔργα πεποιήκασιν· οἱ δὲ νεώτεροι οὐ τὸ αὐτὸ φρονοῦσιν, ὅτι σοφοί εἰσιν παρ' ἑαυτοῖς, ἀλλὰ οὐ παρὰ θεῷ. μενοῦνγε μωροί εἰσιν παρὰ θεῷ, καθὼς γέγραπται,

Ἡ γὰρ σοφία τοῦ κόσμου μωρία παρὰ θεῷ, καὶ πάλιν,

Ὅστις δὲ ὑψώσει ἑαυτὸν ταπεινωθήσεται καὶ ὅστις ταπεινώσει ἑαυτὸν ὑψωθήσεται.

οἱ μὲν οὖν νεώτεροι ὑπερήφανοί εἰσιν, ἐὰν δὲ οἱ πρεσβύτεροι ἐπιτιμῶσιν αὐτοῖς οὐ χαίρουσιν ἐπὶ τοῖς λόγοις αὐτῶν οὐδὲ θέλουσιν αὐτῶν ἀκούειν. μακάριοί εἰσιν οἱ νεώτεροι; μενοῦν μακάριοι οἱ πρεσβύτεροι.

49.7 δεδώκει – he had given

Compare:
(a) Mk 14:44   δεδώκει δὲ ὁ παραδιδοὺς αὐτὸν σύσσημον αὐτοῖς
The man who was betraying him had given them a signal
(b) 1 Jn 3:1   ἴδετε ποταπὴν ἀγάπην δέδωκεν ἡμῖν ὁ πατήρ
See what great love the Father has given us.

In (b), δέδωκεν (he has given), is perfect tense. It refers to a past action which has a continuing result ⊤ |→ : God showed his love, and goes on loving us.

In (a), δεδώκει (he had given), is *pluperfect* tense. It refers to a past action which had a result, but that result is now also in the past ⊤ |→ |
Judas had told them the sign; the result was that they could recognize the sign. When Mark told the story, that recognition was also in the past.

The marks of the pluperfect active are:
1. ε before the stem
2. the repetition of the initial consonant before the ε
3. κ between stem and ending
4. endings -ειν , -εις , -ει , -ειμεν , -ειτε , -εισαν
5. sometimes ε before repeated initial consonant
   (see below, Luke 11:22, ἐπεποίθει).

Note that the first three are also marks of the perfect active.

Where a perfect form has a present meaning the pluperfect form covers all past meanings:
οἶδα – I know   ᾔδειν – I knew, I had known
ἕστηκα – I stand   ἑστήκειν or εἱστήκειν – I was standing, I stood
πέποιθα – I trust   ἐπεποίθειν – I trusted, I relied, I had trusted

Lk 11:22   τὴν πανοπλίαν αὐτοῦ αἴρει ἐφ᾽ ᾗ ἐπεποίθει
             He takes from him all the weapons on which he relied.

Note also the pluperfect passive:
Mt 7:25 τεθεμελίωτο γὰρ ἐπὶ τὴν πέτραν
        For it had been founded on the rock.

49.8 Read Luke 18:9–14 The prayers of the Pharisee and Tax-collector

v9 πεποιθώς – trusting (πείθω – I trust). ἐξουθενέω – I despise, I count as nothing. οἱ λοιποί – the rest, other people.

v10 ὁ τελώνης – the tax-collector.

v11 σταθεὶς πρὸς ἑαυτόν – standing a little apart (the contrast in v13 is μακρόθεν ἑστώς – standing at a distance). Ὁ θεός – θεός is here vocative. The use of ὁ when speaking to someone is found in Greek, but is common in Hebrew. ἅρπαξ – a robber. μοιχός – adulterer. ἢ καί – or, or for example (giving an added example, cf. Mt 7:10, not an alternative).

v12 νηστεύω – I fast, I go without food. ἀποδεκατῶ – I tithe, I give a tenth. κτάομαι – I get, I gain.

v13 ἐπαίρω – I lift up. τύπτω – I strike, I beat. τὸ στῆθος – the breast, the chest. ἱλάσθητί μοι – this means more than 'Be merciful' or 'Be gracious'. It is an aorist imperative form of ἱλάσκομαι – I propitiate. Prayer was made at the time of sacrifice and offering of incense (Lk 1:8–10). His prayer has the sense 'Let the sacrifice bring me your forgiveness.'

v14 δεδικαιωμένος (perfect participle passive) – this means more than 'acquitted' or 'justified' since the perfect indicates a continuing result, it has the added sense of 'in a right relationship with God'. παρά – beside, rather than, in contrast to.

Notice (a) the careful parallelism of person, position and prayer;
(b) the elements of shock (i) that the Pharisee does not begin his prayer 'Blessed are you, our God', but by speaking of his own

goodness, and (ii) the despised tax-collector goes home right with God;

(c) the elements of chiasmus in the beginning and ending:

v10 (A) the Pharisee, (B) the tax-collector

v14 (B') this man (tax-collector), (A') that man (the Pharisee).

There is also a chiasmus in verses 11–13:

    σταθεὶς πρὸς ἑαυτὸν...

    μακρόθεν ἑστώς.

(d) Lk 18:11 (a) σταθεὶς πρὸς ἑαυτὸν ταῦτα προσηύχετο
        standing by himself these things he prayed

or, should it be: (b) σταθεὶς ταῦτα πρὸς ἑαυτὸν προσηύχετο
        standing these things to himself he prayed

The evidence of manuscripts and early translations is divided, and some omit πρὸς ἑαυτόν. There are two problems with (b) which may make us prefer (a) as UBS4 does:

  (i) the order in (b) destroys the balance of σταθεὶς προς ἑαυτὸν and μακρόθεν ἑστώς

  (ii) 'he prayed to himself' is strange, considering that the prayer is immediately addressed to God.

Compare these translations:

NRSV The Pharisee, standing by himself, was praying thus,

NJB   The Pharisee stood there and said this prayer to himself

NIV   The Pharisee stood up and prayed about[a] himself ([a]footnote: to).

REB   The Pharisee stood up and prayed this prayer

GNB   The Pharisee stood apart by himself and prayed

49.9

Revise lessons 43 and 44.

Lesson 50

ἵνα ἡ χαρὰ ὑμῶν ᾖ πεπληρωμένη ACKP...

50.1 Writing books by hand

Before the printing press was developed in the fifteenth century AD, books were written by hand. If another copy of a book was needed, someone had to copy it out by hand.

If twenty people each copied out two or three pages of this book, one can be sure that several of them would make some mistakes. If from one of those copies someone else made another copy, that second copy would be likely to contain: (a) the mistakes made by the first copier; and (b) some mistakes made by the second copier.

Each book of the New Testament was written by hand, either by the author or by a scribe who helped him as a secretary. When the person or congregation to whom it was first written wanted others to be able to read it, they had copies made. As the Church spread, more and more copies were made. We call these hand-written copies of books *manuscripts* (MSS for short).

None of the original manuscripts of the New Testament books has survived. The earliest complete MSS of the New Testament that we have date from the fourth century AD.

50.2 Early translations

As the Church spread from Palestine into Syria, Asia Minor, Europe and North Africa, Christians began to want copies of New Testament books in their own languages. So the New Testament was translated into various languages in Egypt, Syria, Italy, and other lands. These early translations we call *versions*.

50.3 Sermons, commentaries, and books

In the early centuries of the Church's growth, Church leaders and thinkers wrote many letters, sermons, commentaries on the New Testament, and other books. In them they often quoted from their text or version of the New Testament. So they can be helpful to us in our study of the text of the New Testament. We call these writers the *Fathers*.

50.4 Mistakes in MSS

All the MSS we have contain mistakes. Fortunately the mistakes seldom affect the main point of any story or doctrine. When there are differences between what one MS says and what another says, we refer to them as different *readings*. When there are different readings we want to find out, if we can, what the author originally wrote. We ask ourselves questions about the variant readings. Here are some of the questions we may want to ask:

> Which reading makes better sense?
> Which one is supported by the earliest MSS?
> Which one is found in MSS in the largest number of geographical areas?
> Which one seems to have been used by the early translators?
> Which ones are quoted by the early Fathers?
> Which reading shows the kind of language or thought which fits the rest of the author's writings?
> When we have studied widely and thought deeply, we will decide what we think the author wrote.

For a list of the main MSS, versions, and Fathers, see *The Greek New Testament,* 4th edition (United Bible Societies, 1993) p4* to p52*.

In 50.5–8, we will look at a few textual problems where what we have already learned may help us to decide which reading to adopt.

50.5 John 1:18

θεὸν οὐδεὶς ἑώρακεν πώποτε· μονογενὴς υἱὸς (or θεὸς) ὁ ὢν εἰς τὸν κόλπον τοῦ πατρός, ἐκεῖνος ἐξηγήσατο.

Some of the early MSS read μονογενὴς θεός or ὁ μονογενὴς θεός. They are supported by one or two early translations and several of the Fathers.

Most of the MSS, versions, and Fathers support the reading ὁ μονογενὴς υἱός. Which do we think John originally wrote?

The number of MSS, etc., that support a reading helps us very little. If I make a mistake in copying something and a hundred people copy from me, it is still a mistake. If one other person has made a correct copy, that will be right, even though the numbers are 101 to 1. Nor can the age of the MSS alone tell us which is right. If a mistake was made, let us suppose, in a copy made about AD 100, it will still be a mistake if it is found in an 'early' manuscript copied about AD 350. But if we find two readings which for other reasons seem equally possible, then we are likely to choose the one that has the earliest MS support.

In John 1:18 we have to ask ourselves whether John was likely to write:
(a) 'No one has ever seen God: the unique God who is close to the bosom of the father, he has revealed him' *or*
(b) 'No one has ever seen God: the only son who is close to the bosom of the father, he has revealed him.'

(a) μονογενὴς θεός. μονογενής means 'one of a kind, unique'. Elsewhere in the NT it means 'only (son or daughter)' and in Heb 11:17 it refers to Isaac who was not Abraham's only son, but was the one to whom the promises were uniquely given and the only son of Sarah. μονογενής is not an adjective that suits the noun θεός in this context. God can hardly be an only child, yet to say 'no one has seen God – the unique God has revealed him' is not logical.

(b) ὁ μονογενὴς υἱός makes better sense. When we study the other passages in which John uses μονογενής (John 3:16, 18) we see that he uses it with υἱός, and in John 1:14 μονογενὴς παρὰ πατρός naturally implies the idea of sonship. So the way John uses μονογενής confirms what seems the more logical reading. Why, then, did the editors of the Greek New Testament (UBS 3rd and 4th Editions) adopt the alternative reading θεός? Partly because it is found in two papyrus fragments (p66 and p75) which are among our earliest witnesses to the gospel text. The other reason sounds strange at first, but it illustrates a fundamental principle of textual criticism. They preferred θεός because it is the 'more difficult reading', the one which fits less well with John's usual way of writing. The argument is this: if John wrote θεός, a scribe would be strongly tempted to change to υἱός, but if John wrote υἱός, it is hard to explain how the alternative reading originated.

But this kind of reasoning needs to be questioned. Any error made in copying a sentence is likely to make it more difficult to understand. If I write, 'he saw the boy in the car' and someone misreads r as n his copy will say 'I saw the boy in the can.' In considering John 1:18 there are also special features that we need to notice.

For the phrase μονογενὴς θεός our earliest manuscript evidence has ΜΟΝΟΓΕΝΗΣ ΘΣ. In Hebrew biblical manuscripts God's name was often shortened. We see it for example in Hallelu-**yah**. In early Christian manuscripts words like θεός Χριστός, υἱός (when it refers to Jesus) and πνεῦμα (when it refers to the Holy Spirit) are often shortened. So the difference between ΘΣ (θεός – God) and ΥΣ (υἱός – son) is only one letter. Such a mistake can easily be made.

The other special feature is the chiastic structure of John 1:14–18. As we have already seen υἱός in verse 18 makes a close parallel with μονογενοῦς in verse 14.

50.6 Mark 15:8

ἀναβὰς ὁ ὄχλος – ℵ B D , Latin, and Coptic versions
ἀναβοήσας ὁ ὄχλος – most MSS and versions.

Did the crowd 'come up' or 'shout out'? In verse 13 Mark says οἱ δὲ πάλιν ἔκραξαν (they shouted **again**). Study Mark's use of πάλιν. He seems to use it carefully. If we read ἀναβοήσας, there is a mention of shouting for πάλιν to refer back to. If we read ἀναβάς, the πάλιν has nothing to refer back to.
Now study the use of ἀναβαίνω in the New Testament, and especially in Mark. Mark uses it of people moving, and he uses it with ἐκ, εἰς, or πρός, to show the place someone goes up from, or up to. He never has any use of ἀναβαίνω like the English idiom, 'I went up to him and said...'. In Mark 15:8 there is no mention of a place, and no ἐκ, εἰς, or πρός, For the English idiom of going up to someone, Mark uses προσέλθων. So when we look at the usage of ἀναβαίνω, it confirms what we have seen from our study of πάλιν. It does not seem likely that Mark wrote ἀναβάς. In my view, it is probable that he wrote ἀναβοήσας. Many recent translations, however, are based on the reading ἀναβάς. The editors of the UBS 3rd edition Greek text note that there is no other occurrence of ἀναβοάω in Mark, while ἀναβαίνειν occurs nine times. This is true, but does not prove anything – Mark could have used ἀναβοάω here and nowhere else in the Gospel. And the fact that several scholars agree on a reading does not necessarily mean that they are right. In matters of textual criticism it is rarely possible to be completely certain of the original reading. In each case we should carefully weigh the evidence before making our choice, and not simply accept what others have decided.

50.7 1 John 1:4

καὶ ταῦτα γράφομεν **ἡμεῖς**, ἵνα ἡ χαρὰ **ὑμῶν** (or ἡμῶν) ᾖ πεπληρωμένη.
Did John write:
    (a) 'We write these things so that **your** joy may be full' *or*
    (b) 'We write these things so that **our** joy may be full'?

The reading (a) ὑμῶν (of you), is found in A and C (fifth century MSS), K and P (ninth-tenth century MSS) and most other MSS and versions. The reading (b) ἡμῶν (of us), is found in ℵ and B (both fourth century MSS), in L (ninth century) and one Latin version.

One learned New Testament commentator said, 'A positive decision on the reading here is impossible'. Most recent commentators and translators have chosen reading (b) – 'our joy'. They believe that 'our joy' could have been changed to 'your joy'; the opposite change is less likely. In my view, however, 'your joy' is the best reading.

Notice first that John does not say γράφομεν (we write) but γράφομεν ἡμεῖς (**we** write). Look at 1 John 3:14, 16, and 1 John 4:6, 10, 14, 16, 17, and 19. John uses this emphatic ἡμεῖς to point a contrast with another person or group. So after the emphatic ἡμεῖς in 1 John 1:4, we expect mention of another person or group: ἡ χαρὰ ὑμῶν fits John's use of language; ἡ χαρὰ ἡμῶν does not.

Notice also that John here speaks of his purpose in writing. Study 1 John 2: 1,7–14 and 5:13. His purpose is expressed in terms of the people for whom he is writing. Study in the Johannine writings also John 20:30–31, 15:11, 16:24. When the purpose of writing or of Jesus in speaking is mentioned, it is always so that someone else may benefit – the readers or the hearers. This adds to the likelihood that John wrote ἡ χαρὰ ὑμῶν and not ἡ χαρὰ ἡμῶν (see J. H. Dobson, 'Emphatic personal pronouns in the New Testament', in *The Bible Translator*, April 1971, pp58–60).

50.8 Mark 1:41

καὶ σπλαγχνισθεὶς ἐκτείνας τὴν χεῖρα αὐτοῦ ἥψατο καὶ λέγει αὐτῷ, Θέλω, καθαρίσθητι·

All the MSS except one read σπλαγχνισθείς (moved by compassion). But D (a fifth-century MS) has ὀργισθείς (moved by anger). The REB translators preferred the reading ὀργισθείς, and comment: 'It appeared more probable that ὀργισθείς...would have been changed to σπλαγχνισθείς than that the alteration should have been in the other direction.'

What can we say about this from our study of New Testament Greek? σπλαγχνισθείς is an aorist participle (and so is ὀργισθείς). It stands in the sentence without a noun or pronoun. If we study this kind of use of an aorist participle in the New Testament, especially where the participle expresses a feeling, we shall make certain discoveries:

(a) in a phrase like ἀποκριθεὶς εἶπεν the action described by the aorist participle finds its natural completion or expression in the action of the verb (εἶπεν),

(b) this is particularly noticeable where the aorist participle expresses feeling.

Study the use of ὀργισθείς in Matthew 18:34 and Luke 14:21. In Matthew 18:34, the handing over of the man to the torturers is a natural outcome of the master's anger. In Luke 14:21–24, the gathering in of people so that there would be no room for those who had refused was a natural result of the man's anger. Study the use of σπλαγχνισθείς in Matthew 18:27, 20:34, and Mark 9:22. In each case the act of forgiving, healing, or helping, is a natural outcome and expression of compassion.

So when we consider Mark 1:41, we find that the evidence of all the MSS except one is supported by the way the gospel writers use the aorist participles σπλαγχνισθείς and ὀργισθείς, for the act of healing the leper can be seen as a natural result of compassion, but not a natural outcome of anger. We should almost certainly read σπλαγχνισθείς.

What should we say about the point made by the REB translators? As well as what we have said above, we might also ask them to consider:

1. that manuscript D contains a large number of errors,
2. that in Mark 1:43 there is an unusual word ἐμβριμησάμενος (warn sternly). It is possible that someone tried to explain this by writing ὀργισθείς in the margin of his manuscript, and that a later scribe wrongly inserted it in 1:41.

50.9 Textual criticism and the translator

When we are translating the New Testament, we shall sometimes need to study carefully what textual critics have said about the text. We will not always be able to be certain which is the correct reading. If the difference between two possible readings seems to make a real difference to the meaning of the passage, we may need to put the alternative in a footnote. Textual criticism is a task that demands years of study and familiarity with the language of the New Testament and the manuscripts and versions. We must, in general, respect the opinions of other scholars when we see that they are mostly in agreement, unless we can find clear and compelling evidence which they appear to have overlooked. Never forget that we are trying to find out what the original author is most likely to have written.

We never simply ask, 'Which reading is supported by most MSS, or most editors, or most translators?'

We are fortunate that the text of the New Testament rests on far more manuscripts than the text of any other ancient Greek book. But while this gives us a general confidence, it sometimes makes the study of variant readings very complicated.

Students who wish to learn more about New Testament textual studies are advised to study:

Bruce M. Metzger, *A Textual Commentary on the Greek New Testament,* 2nd edition (UBS, 1994).

F. G. Kenyon, *The Text of the Greek Bible,* 3rd edition (Duckworth, 1975).

K. Aland and B. Aland, *The Text of the New Testament,* 2nd edition (Eerdmans, 1989).

50.10 Read Luke 11:5–8 A reasonable request

v5 Τίς ἐξ ὑμῶν 'Which of you...' As in Matthew 12:11 this introduces a situation that is totally unlikely. μεσονυκτίου – at midnight, in the middle of the night. χρῆσόν μοι – let me have (χράω – I give what is needed, I supply, I lend).

v7 ἔσωθεν – inside, from within. κόπος – hard work, **trouble**. παρέχω – I bring about, I cause. κλείω – I lock. (ἡ) κοίτη – place to lie down.

v8 εἰ καί – even if, even though. διὰ τὸ εἶναι φίλον – because of being a friend. γε – yet, at any rate. ἀναίδεια – lack of shame (or, perhaps, avoidance of shame). χρῄζω – I need. ὅσοι – as many as, all.

The cultural backround is that, in a village, the community would care for visitors – helping each other. It would be inconceivably shameful not to help. Notice the surprise at the end – he does not give only 3 loaves, but all that the man needs (compare Eph 3:20).

50.11

Revise lessons 45 and 46.

Lesson 51

Culture and Translation

In this lesson we look at a few examples of passages where the translator needs to understand aspects of the culture of Palestine in New Testament times, and to think carefully about the cultures of those who will use the translation.

51.1 Matthew 20:13

οὐχὶ δηναρίου συνεφώνησάς μοι;
You agreed with me for a denarius, didn't you?

In Matthew 20:1–16, there is a parable about men working in a vineyard. Each one was paid a denarius. This was a Roman coin – and an adequate daily wage. The AV translated it as 'a penny'. Maybe in AD 1611 this was a reasonable translation. In England towards the end of the twentieth century a reasonable day's wage might be about £30. But if inflation continues, that too may become out of date as a day's wage. So in translating δηνάριον we might use 'a day's wage' as the nearest useful equivalent. Compare:

> REB 'the full day's wage' and 'the usual wage for a day'
> GNB 'the regular wage, a silver coin' and 'a silver coin'.

In translating passages which refer to money, quantities, and distances, we always need to think carefully about their cultural setting. A particular problem arises when the numbers are symbolic. In Revelation 21:16, for example, the symbolic meanings of 12 and 1,000 are lost if we convert the distances simply into 2,400 kilometres (see lesson 39.8).

51.2 Mark 7:27–28

τὰ κυνάρια ὑποκάτω τῆς τραπέζης.

In Greek κύων means 'dog' or 'cur'. In Palestine, dogs were scavengers, as they still are in many parts of the world. In Revelation 22:15, they are a symbol for perverts and criminals. No one would have wanted a dog in his home.

κυνάριον means 'puppy' (a young, little dog). In Palestine young puppies were sometimes kept in the home as pets. In Matthew's account, when Jesus spoke to the woman he did not use the word κύων. He used the word κυνάριον. GNB and NEB both translate κυνάριον as 'dogs'. Our knowledge of Palestinian culture confirms that 'little puppies' would be a much better translation.

All passages that have to do with animals demand particular care from the translator, since the cultural background against which people experience animals varies so much.

51.3 Luke 14:12

Ὅταν ποιῇς ἄριστον ἢ δεῖπνον.

The people of Palestine used to eat only two main meals: a breakfast in the early morning and an evening meal about sunset. We might therefore translate Luke 14:12: 'Whenever you make a breakfast or a dinner'. But Jesus is talking about meals to which visitors are invited. In England we seldom invite people to breakfast. The nearest cultural equivalent of ἄριστον here is 'lunch'. So the NEB translates, 'Whenever you give a lunch or dinner party'. But in any country where people eat only in the morning and evening we might translate, 'Whenever you invite people to breakfast or dinner', or 'When you make a special meal for people in the morning or the evening'.

Passages which concern meals, greetings, weddings, and household customs demand special care from the translator (see also lesson 39.1, section 7, on Mark 2:19, and the rest of this lesson).

51.4 Matthew 9:2

προσέφερον αὐτῷ παραλυτικὸν ἐπὶ **κλίνης** βεβλημένον
People were bringing to him a paralysed man lying on a κλίνη.

How should we translate κλίνη? GNB and NEB both have 'bed'. For English readers this may produce a picture of men struggling to carry a bedstead. Most of our beds are quite heavy. In Palestine people slept on a thin mattress, rather like a quilt. This is what Matthew means by κλίνη. It would be better to translate 'lying on a thin mattress' than 'lying on a bed'.

51.5 Mark 8:26

καὶ ἀπέστειλεν αὐτὸν εἰς οἶκον αὐτοῦ λέγων, Μηδὲ εἰς τὴν κώμην εἰσέλθῃς
He sent him home saying, 'And do not go into the village.'

Look at the Critical Apparatus at the foot of the page in your Greek New Testament. You will see the MSS contain several variations of reading.

As Mark told the story, are we to suppose that Jesus told the man not to go into the village? (See NRSV and GNB, based on the text above.) Or did he tell the man not to speak to anyone in the village? (See NEB, preferring the reading Μηδενὶ εἴπῃς εἰς τὴν κώμην.) Here is a problem where textual and linguistic study needs to be combined with cultural knowledge.

People in Palestine lived in walled towns (πόλεις) or in villages (κῶμαι) with the houses closely grouped together. So when we read a text which says, 'He sent him home saying, "Do not go into the village"', we are aware that there is a problem. How can a man go home without going into a village?

When we read the NEB text, 'He sent him home saying, "Do not speak to anyone in the village"', we see some arguments for it. Mark's Gospel is full of parallelism. Here he uses the two-stage opening of the man's eyes as a parallel to the opening of the minds of the disciples (vv27–30). That story ends with strict instructions, ἵνα μηδενὶ λέγωσιν περὶ αὐτοῦ. This makes Μηδενὶ εἴπῃς εἰς τὴν κώμην look like a suitable ending for verse 26.

But now study in the New Testament the uses of ἀπέστειλεν... λέγων, and ἀποστέλλει...καὶ λέγει. See, for example, Matthew 21:1–2, ἀπέστειλεν δύο μαθητὰς λέγων αὐτοῖς, Πορεύεσθε εἰς τὴν κώμην, and Mark 11:1–2, ἀποστέλλει...καὶ λέγει αὐτοῖς, Ὑπάγετε... . It looks as if when ἀποστέλλω is used with λέγει, it is followed by a verb telling someone to go. Commands like 'Don't speak to anyone' are more likely to be introduced by forms of ἐπιτιμάω or παραγγέλλω.

It looks as if Mark might have written something like: 'He sent him home saying, "Go home, but do not speak to anyone in the village."' One MS, D, reads, ...λέγων, Ὕπαγε εἰς τὸν οἶκον σου καὶ μηδενὶ εἴπῃς εἰς τὴν κώμην Although D is a manuscript with many errors, it might be that in this verse it preserves the original text.

51.6 Matthew 21:16

Ἐκ στόματος νηπίων καὶ θηλαζόντων
Out of the mouth of children and sucklings.

νήπιος means a child of any age less than adult. θηλάζω means, 'I suck at the breast.' In Palestine, besides receiving other food, boys were often suckled at the breast until the age of four or five. Children of such an age are well able to speak and sing. In many modern cultures children are weaned before they can express themselves much in speech or song. If we translate θηλάζοντες as 'sucklings' or 'babes at the breast', we shall cause a misunderstanding. We might translate the phrase: 'Out of the mouth of young children'.

51.7 Luke 24:30

λαβὼν τὸν ἄρτον εὐλόγησεν
Having taken the loaf εὐλόγησεν.

How should we translate εὐλόγησεν? As 'he blessed', or as 'he said the blessing', or as 'he gave thanks'? In English families if a prayer is said before a meal, people are more likely to thank God for the food than to bless God for the food. In a Jewish family one is more likely to bless God. So far as we can tell, Jesus would probably have said a prayer in which he blessed God as the giver of food: 'Blessed art thou, O Lord God...'.

We have a twofold problem when we translate εὐλογέω in the New Testament when it concerns food. If we translate it as 'give thanks' we leave out the aspect of blessing. But if we translate it as 'bless' or 'say the blessing' we may give the impression that the speaker blessed the food. In the New Testament εὐλογέω is used of God blessing people, and of people blessing God as the giver of things, not for the blessing of things.

In Luke 24:30 we might translate λαβὼν τὸν ἄρτον εὐλόγησεν as 'He took the loaf and blessed God', but in doing so we should be aware that this reflects a Jewish custom and may seem strange to many readers. It is partly the difficulty of translating from one language and culture to another that encourages people to read the New Testament in Greek.

51.8 Customs, culture, and translation

If we are to translate the New Testament effectively, we need to understand not only the culture of the people of Palestine at the time the New Testament was written, but also the culture of the people for whom we translate. In one Micronesian area people consider it very funny to see a person speaking with his mouth wide open. So a literal translation of Matthew 5:2, ἀνοίξας τὸ στόμα αὐτοῦ ἐδίδασκεν αὐτούς, would make them laugh. They need, as we do in English, a translation which says, 'He began to teach them.'
For further study of the problems of customs, culture, and translation, see E. A. Nida, *Customs, Culture and Christianity* (Harper and Brothers, 1954/Tyndale Press, 1963).

51.9 Read John 20:24–31

v24 Δίδυμος – Twin.

v25 ἐν ταῖς χερσὶν – in his hands, in his wrists (χείρ – hand, arm: in crucifixion nails were usually driven through the wrist. χείρ has a wider range of meaning than the English word 'hand').

v25 τύπος – pattern, mark, imprint. ἧλος – nail. δάκτυλος – finger. πλευρά – rib, side. οὐ μή : a strong negative.

v26 μεθ' ἡμέρας ὀκτώ – a week later (counting the Sunday at the beginning and the Sunday at the end, see 37.14). ἔσω – inside, indoors. εἰς τὸ μέσον – in the middle. Εἰρήνη : when used as a greeting εἰρήνη is equivalent to 'Shalom' in Hebrew.

v27 φέρε – Carry! Lift up! Here it has the meaning 'lift up and stretch out.' ἄπιστος – unbelieving.

v28. ἀπεκρίθη ... καὶ εἶπεν : a Hebraic expression.

v31 ἐν τῷ ὀνόματι αὐτοῦ – through his name: that is, through his person and his power.

51.10

Revise lessons 47 and 48.

Lesson 52

Ἄγωμεν ἐντεῦθεν – Let us go on from here

52.1

In *Learn New Testament Greek* you have laid a basic foundation for reading and studying the Greek New Testament, and for translating it. But in the study of language this saying becomes true: ὅστις γὰρ ἔχει, δοθήσεται αὐτῷ καὶ περισσευθήσεται· ὅστις δὲ οὐκ ἔχει, καὶ ὃ ἔχει ἀρθήσεται ἀπ' αὐτοῦ.

If we are not to lose the knowledge and skills we have gained, we must use them and add to them.

Nothing can take the place of a short time each day in which we read some of the New Testament in Greek. John's Epistles, John's Gospel, and Mark's Gospel are perhaps the books to read first. In this lesson we consider some books that you may find useful in your further studies, and some ways in which your knowledge of New Testament Greek may prove stimulating or useful.

52.2 The Hebrew background of the New Testament

A knowledge of Biblical Hebrew can greatly enrich one's study of the New Testament. You can learn Biblical Hebrew and gain an understanding of narrative and poetic literature from:

John H. Dobson, *Learn Biblical Hebrew*, 2nd Edition (Baker Academic / Piquant Editions 2005)

For an interesting introduction to the Hebrew influence on the teaching of Jesus, see:

D. Bivin and R. Blizzard, *Understanding the Difficult Words of Jesus* (Destiny Image Publishers).

For insights into the literary and cultural background of the parables, see:

Kenneth E. Bailey, *Poet and Peasant* and *Through Peasant Eyes* (Eerdmans / Paternoster Press).

52.3 A basic library for the reader and translator of the New Testament

The following books are essential:

1. A text of the New Testament: Η ΚΑΙΝΗ ΔΙΑΘΗΚΗ

Two editions are widely used and recommended at the time of going to press: Nestlé-Aland 27th edition and UBS 4th revised edition. UBS 4 has the same text as Nestlé-Aland 27, but a different apparatus. It cites fewer variant readings but gives more detailed evidence for those cited. Both Nestlé-Aland 27 and UBS 4 are available in a variety of bindings.

2. A lexicon or dictionary of New Testament Greek

Lexicons range from the pocket-sized to the very large. Useful for beginners is B. M. Newman (Ed.), *A Concise Greek-English Dictionary of the New Testament*. It is published by UBS (1971) and available either separately or bound together with the UBS 4th edition New Testament. For detailed study you will probably need to refer to a large lexicon, such as *A Greek-English Lexicon of the New Testament and Other Early Christian Literature*, edited by W. Bauer (translated W. F. Arndt and F. W. Gingrich) 2nd revised edition, published by Chicago, 2000; or *A Greek-English Lexicon*, edited by H. C. Liddell and R. Scott, 9th edition, published by OUP, 1968.

For those who are particularly concerned with translating the New Testament, the following books are specially recommended:
The Translator's New Testament (BFBS, 1973).
The Translator's Handbooks and *Translator's Guides* series (UBS).
E. A. Nida and C. R. Taber, *The Theory and Practice of Translation* (E. J. Brill for UBS, 1969).
E. A. Nida and Jan de Waard, *From One Language to Another* (Thomas Nelson, 1968).

For advanced study, the following books are recommended:
E. G. Jay, *New Testament Greek: An Introductory Grammar* (SPCK, 1974).
C. F. D. Moule, *An Idiom-Book of New Testament Greek* (CUP, 1959).
W. F. Moulton and A. S. Geden, *A Concordance to the Greek Testament*, 5th edition (T & T Clark, 1978).
J. H. Moulton and N Turner, *Grammar of New Testament Greek* (4 vols): (T & T Clark, 1976).
F. Blass and A. Debrunner, *A Greek Grammar of the New Testament and other early Christian literature* (translated R. W. Funk) (Chicago, 1961).

R. W. Funk, *A Beginning – Intermediate Grammar of Hellenistic Greek*
(3 vols: SBL, 1973).

B. M. Metzger, *Lexical Aids for Students of New Testament Greek,* new edition
(T & T Clark, 1989).

B. M. Metzger, *A Textual Commentary on the Greek New Testament*
(companion to UBS Greek New Testament, 4th revised edition (UBS 1994)).

52.4 Using a lexicon – a Greek dictionary

Make sure that you have learned by heart the order of the letters in the Greek alphabet (see 16.2). This will help you to find the words in the lexicon.

Most words are easy to find. Care and insight are needed when looking up verbal forms. If you want to find the meaning of αἴρομεν it is fairly easy to remember that the 1st person sing. pres. indic. is αἴρω. If we want to look up ἦραν or ἄρας we must remember that they are forms of αἴρω. If the verbal form has an augment, that is an ε before the stem, remember that the stem will follow the augment. So for πεπίστευκα we look up πιστεύω. For ἤκουσεν we look up ἀκούω, and for ἤγειρεν we look up ἐγείρω. Where a verb begins with a preposition, remember that the augment normally comes after the preposition, and if the preposition ends in a vowel, that vowel will probably be changed. So for προσεκύνησαν we look up προσκυνέω, and for ἐπεθύμησαν we look up ἐπιθυμέω.

B. M. Newman (Ed.), *A Concise Greek-English Dictionary of the New Testament*, gives help with irregular and unusual verb forms.

52.5 Reading the New Testament in Greek

When we can read the New Testament easily in Greek without needing to stop constantly to use a dictionary, it can bring us a feeling of being drawn closer to the actual people and events. There will also be an opportunity to understand some passages better than we can do in a translation. For example, in John 3, ἄνωθεν covers an area of meaning which includes 'from above' and 'again'. A translator usually has to choose one of these meanings and ignore the other. In John's Gospel, when we read σημεῖον we shall know that it is both a miraculous sign and a meaningful miracle.

52.6 Translation

The skill you have been learning will prove useful, whether or not you become directly involved in the work of Bible translation. You are now able to assess existing translations; to ask 'Does this express the meaning (not necessarily the words) of the original?' or 'Can this be understood clearly by those who will read it?' These critical skills will be useful whenever you are using language.

52.7 Preaching

Some of us who are readers and translators of the New Testament will also be preachers. Our efforts to learn New Testament Greek may help us in a variety of ways.

In translating we have learned to consider carefully the cultural situation of the first readers and also the cultural situation of the people who may hear or read our translation. This discipline should help us in sermon preparation to think carefully how to make the Good News we preach relevant to people in the circumstances in which they live today.

If we have found some of the strange grammatical terms in this course hard to understand (aorist, infinitive, consecutive and final clauses…), then we may understand better how hard it is for ordinary people to understand a sermon if it is full of words like justification, sanctification, Trinitarianism, or even references to the Greek text!

Our efforts to understand the Greek text clearly enough to translate it may also aid us to preach clearly from it. For example, in Ephesians 2:8–9 we will notice: (1) that Paul speaks of our salvation as being (a) οὐκ ἐξ ὑμῶν, , and (b) οὐκ ἐξ ἔργων.

This will suggest two themes that may be developed in part of our sermon: (a) that we are not saved as a result of anything that we are (character, position in society or church, inherited nature, developed talents, faith), and (b) that we are not saved by anything we have done (kindness to people, service to God, achievements).

We will notice: (2) that Paul says we are saved χάριτι. Our understanding of χάρις as free unmerited love will help us to see that Paul means that God saves us because he loves us freely. He does *not* mean that he has first given us something that could be called 'grace' and then saves us because we have grace.

So our study of New Testament Greek should help us to preach clearly from the New Testament, and hopefully will help us to avoid words that people cannot understand.

52.8 New Testament Greek and theology

There are many problems discussed by theologians and by the supporters of various sects where a knowledge of New Testament Greek may be of help to us.

Theologians have argued whether the first Christian message was:
(1) God's Kingdom is now present, or (2) God's Kingdom lies in the future but will soon come.
So far as Mark 1:15 is concerned, the argument is whether ἤγγικεν means: (1) 'has arrived' (J. B. Phillips), or (2) 'is at hand' (RSV).

In fact, it is a perfect tense and means, 'it has come near'. A perfect tense indicates a past action with a continuing result. Because it has come near, people can already respond to it. The emphasis is on present nearness rather than on future arrival. But because 'it has come near' is not precisely the same in meaning as 'it has already arrived', it is possible that the completion of its arrival might yet lie in the future. Perhaps the appropriate question to ask about the Kingdom in Mark 1:15 is not a question about the time of its arrival, but about how one can respond to what is already near.

Some theologians have argued that the gospels show that Jesus expected his return to be soon. If we read Mark 13:30–32 carefully in the Greek text, we will notice a contrast between ταῦτα (*these* things) and ἡ ἡμέρα ἐκείνη (*that* day). The destruction of the Temple was to be within one generation, but the time of Christ's return was unknown. If we can trust the evidence of Mark 13 and some of the parables, Jesus did not expect his return to be soon. Of course, an attentive reading of a good translation will also show this, but it is sometimes the careful attention to the Greek text necessary for the task of translation that makes us more sharply aware of what it actually says.

You may hear people argue that the first Christians baptized people *in* water. If you are involved as a New Testament Greek scholar you will at least know that the evidence in the gospels points to baptism *with* or *by means of* water (ὕδατι, or ἐν ὕδατι).

You might hear a Mormon argue that Revelation 14:6 is a prophecy about the book of Mormon – you will know that εὐαγγέλιον in the New Testament never refers to a book, only to a message that is proclaimed. You might hear a Jehovah's Witness argue that John 1:1 means that 'the Word was a god' – you will know that θεὸς ἦν ὁ λόγος means 'the Word was God.'

The more technical and detailed a discussion of points of New Testament theology becomes, the more likely it is that a theologian will refer to words or passages in the Greek text of the New Testament. Because you have worked through this study course you will be in a position to understand what is being said.

52.9 New Testament Greek, classical Greek, and modern Greek

If you wish to go on to study classical Greek or modern Greek, you will find that this course in New Testament Greek will enable you to understand most of the forms and constructions. It will also help you to use a lexicon to cope with the much greater range of vocabulary.

52.10 Read the New Testament – ἡ καινὴ διαθήκη

Ἀγαπητοί, πολλοὶ καὶ ἄλλοι λόγοι εἰσίν οἳ οὐκ εἰσὶν γεγραμμένοι ἐν τῷ βιβλίῳ τούτῳ. ταῦτα δὲ γέγραπται ἵνα ἀναγινώσκητε τὴν καινὴν διαθήκην καὶ ἵνα ἀναγινώσκοντες τὴν ἀλήθειαν εὑρίσκητε ἐν τῷ Κυρίῳ ἡμῶν Ἰησοῦ Χριστῷ.

Ἄγωμεν ἐντεῦθεν.

KEY TO PROGRESS TESTS

Test 1:   1(c)   2(a)   3(b)   4(a)   5(c).
Test 2:   1(c)   2(a)   3(c)   4(b)   5(a).
Test 3:   1(b)   2(b)   3(c)   4(c)   5(a).
Test 4:   1(b)   2(b)   3(a)   4(b). In 1(a), 2(a), 3(b), and 4(a) the translation follows the Greek order of words too closely.
Test 5:   1(a)   2(c)   3(b)   4(c)   5(c)   6(b)   7(c)   8(c).
Test 6:   1. In heaven. 2. God's angel. 3. God's words. 4. She knows that they are true. 5. Luke. 6. We are. 7. The angel's words and Mary's words. 8. Because they are true. 9. He who has the word of God and trusts in Jesus. 10. Those who have the apostle's book and read it.
Test 7:   1(c)   2(b)   3(a)   4(b)   5(b).
Test 8:   1(c)   2(b)   3(b)   4(a)   5(b)
Test 9:   1(c)   2(b)   3(c). 1(a), 2(a), and 3(a) follow the Greek order of words too closely.
Test 10:   1(c)   2(b)   3(b)   4(c)   5(c).
Test 11:   1(c)   2(b)   3(b)   4(b). 1(a) and (b), 2(a), 3(a) and (c), and 4(a) follow the Greek order of words too closely. 2(c) and 4(c) do not express the meaning of the Greek quite so clearly.
Test 12:   1(b) (c) (e)   2(a) (c) (d) (e)   3(a) (c) (e) (f) (g)   4(a) (b) (d).
Test 13:   1(a)   2(c)   3(c)   4(a)   5(b)   6(b)   7(a)   8(a) (c) (e) 9(a) (c) (d) (e).
Test 14:   1(c)   2(c)   3(a)   4(b)   5(b) (c) (e) (h) 6(a) (d) (f) (g).
Test 15:   1(b) (d) (e) (f) (h) (i)   2(a) (d) (e) (f) (g) (j)   3(a) (c) (e) (f) (h) (j) 4(b) (c) (f) (g)   (i) 5(c) 6(c).
Test 16:   1(b)   2(c)   3(a)   4(c)   5(b)   6(c)   7(c)   8(a).

Note on 6(c): Should we describe ὄντα as being 'active'? εἰμί is active in form but it has no passive. The ways people use language are so variable that strict grammatical classifications do not always cover the uses adequately. For example, ἐπορεύθη (he traveled) is 3rd person singular aorist of πορεύομαι. It is middle in meaning and passive in form. If we call it aorist passive we may cause ourselves confusion. Compare also the use of ἠγέρθη for 'he rose.' We often need to bear in mind this comment: 'We grammarians are always trying to bind the free growth of language in a strait waistcoat of necessity, but language laughs and eludes us' (A. Platt).

Test 17: 1(b), 2(c), 3(c), 4(b) or (c), 5(a), 6(d), 7(b), 8(c), 9(a), 10 All of them.
Test 18: 1(b), 2(a), 3(b), 4(c), 5(b) or (a), 6(c), 7 φαῦλα, τὸ φῶς, τὴν ἀλήθειαν, πολλά, αὐτόν, φανερόν, τὸ πλοίον, τὴν ψυχήν, αὐτήν.
Test 19: 1. ὁ λόγος, θεός, οὗτος, πάντα, ἕν, ὅ, ἡ ζωή, τὸ φῶς, ἡ σκοτία.
2. πάντα ἄνθρωπον, ἐρχόμενον, τὸν κόσμον, αὐτόν, τὰ ἴδια, ἐξουσίαν, τὸ ὄνομα.
3. αὐτοῦ, τῶν ἀνθρώπων, θεοῦ, τοῦ φωτός, αἱμάτων, θελήματος, σαρκός, ἀνδρός, μονογενοῦς, πατρός, χάριτος, ἀληθείας.
4. ἀρχῇ, αὐτῷ, τῇ σκοτίᾳ, τῷ κόσμῳ αὐτοῖς, τοῖς πιστεύουσιν, ἡμῖν.
5. (a) In the beginning. (b) With God. (c) through him. (d) Without him. (e) In the darkness. (f) About the light. (g) Into the world. (h) In the world. (i) In the name. (j) From the will (as a result of a decision or wish). (k) among us.
Test 20: 1(a) or (c)   2(a) or (b)   3(a) or (c)   4(b) or (c).

REFERENCE GRAMMAR & ACCENTS

Introduction

R. 1

As we learn languages, we notice that there are patterns that occur regularly, and ways in which words function together in groups. The regular patterns and functions of the words in a language may be called its grammar. Throughout *Learn New Testament Greek* you have been learning grammar, step by step, as you needed it. Now, much of what you have been learning is put together so that you can refer to it easily.

In using the reference grammar please bear in mind two important points:

1. **The reference grammar is primarily designed for use when you have already read through the course.**
Lessons 5, 12, 14, 20–26, 28, 31–33, 37, 39, 40, 42, 45, and 49 introduce you progressively to the ideas and grammatical terms which will enable you to understand this reference grammar. Also, the course material has been designed to lead you into a fruitful way of looking at and understanding Greek words. For example, by the time you have reached the middle of the course, you will look at a word like ἐποίησαν (ἐ-ποιη-σ-αν) and understand it: you will know at once the significance of ἐ- and of -σ-, who is indicated by -αν, and the basic meaning of the stem ποιε. If, instead of that, you have developed a habit of asking yourself, 'What tense is it?' you will have hindered your own progress. Greek tenses do not function in quite the same ways as tenses in Latin or in English. To give them tense names before we are quite at home with their meaning and functions may be seriously misleading.

2. **All languages are flexible and contain irregularities.**
No brief grammar of New Testament Greek could cover all the variations and irregularities. It is more important to develop a feel for the language than an extensive list of learned grammatical forms. No grammatical rules can classify all the variety of ways people actually use language. A strict application of English grammatical rules might suggest that the answer to the question, 'Who is there?' should be, 'It is I', but an English speaker is much more likely to answer, 'It's me.'

So, use the reference grammar after you have completed the course to sharpen your awareness of significant forms and endings.

Note that a list of the forms of a word is called a **paradigm**.

A list of the forms of a noun, pronoun, or adjective shows how it is declined – so different groups of nouns are called **declensions**.

Nouns like οἰκία, γλῶσσα, φωνή, προφήτης belong to the first declension (note dative plural -αις).

Nouns like λόγος, οἶκος, ἔργον belong to the second declension (note dative plural -οις).

Nouns like ἀνήρ, γυνή, ἐλπίς, οὖς belong to the third declension (note dative plural ends with -σι or -σιν).

A list of the forms of a verb shows how it is conjugated.

Summary of types of noun:

R.2

In this first table, after the accusative singular stem has been given, only the endings which must be added to it are given

		Singular				Plural			
		nom	acc	gen	dat	nom	acc	gen	dat
house	ἡ οἰκία	οἰκί-αν	-ας	-ᾳ	-αι	-ας	-ῶν	-αις
tongue	ἡ γλῶσσα	γλῶσσ-αν	-ης	-ῃ	-αι	-ας	-ῶν	-αις
voice	ἡ φωνή	φων-ήν	-ῆς	-ῇ	-αί	-άς	-ῶν	-αῖς
young man	ὁ νεανίας	νεανί-αν	-ου	-ᾳ	-αι	-ας	-ῶν	-αις
prophet	ὁ προφήτης	προφήτ-ην	-ου	-ῃ	-αι	-ας	-ῶν	-αις
word	ὁ λόγος	λόγ-ον	-ου	-ῳ	-οι	-ους	-ων	-οις
house	ὁ οἶκος	οἶκ-ον	-ου	-ῳ	-οι	-ους	-ων	-οις
work	τὸ ἔργον	ἔργ-ον	-ου	-ῳ	-α	-α	-ων	-οις
man	ὁ ἀνήρ	ἄνδρ-α	-ός	-ί	-ες	-ας	-ῶν	-άσιν
star	ὁ ἀστήρ	ἀστέρ-α	-ος	-ι	-ες	-ας	-ων	-σιν
woman	ἡ γυνή	γυναῖκ-α	-ός	-ί	-ες	-ας	-ῶν	(ξ)ίν
fish	ὁ ἰχθύς	ἰχθύ-ν	-ος	-ι	-ες	-ας	-ων	-σιν
guard	ὁ φύλαξ	φύλακ-α	-ος	-ι	-ες	-ας	-ων	(ξ)ιν
hope	ἡ ἐλπίς	ἐλπίδ-α	-ος	-ι				
leader	ὁ ἡγεμών	ἡγεμόν-α	-ος	-ι	-ες	-ας	-ων	μ-όσιν
ruler	ὁ ἄρχων	ἄρχ-οντα	-οντος	-οντι	-οντες	-οντας	-όντων	-ουσιν
knee	τὸ γόνυ	γόν-υ	-ατος	-ατι	-ατα	-ατα	-άτων	-ασιν
body	τὸ σῶμα	σῶμ-α	-ατος	-ατι	-ατα	-ατα	-άτων	-ασιν
nation	τὸ ἔθνος	ἔθν-ος	-ους	-ει	-η	-η	-ων	-εσιν
ear	τὸ οὖς	οὖς	ὠτός	ὠτί	ὦτα	ὦτα	ὤτων	ὠσί(ν)

336   LEARN NEW TESTAMENT GREEK

R.3

Note the following nouns, some of which are found only in the singular.

	ὁ πατήρ the father	ὁ βασιλεύς the king	ἡ πόλις the town	ἡ ἔρημος the desert
Singular				
nom	πατήρ	βασιλεύς	πόλις	ἡ ἔρημος
voc	πάτερ	βασιλεῦ		
acc	πατέρα	βασιλέα	πόλιν	τὴν ἔρημον
gen	πατρός	βασιλέως	πόλεως	τῆς ἐρήμου
dat	πατρί	βασιλεῖ	πόλει	τῇ ἐρήμῳ
Plural				
nom	πατέρες	βασιλεῖς	πόλεις	αἱ ἔρημοι
acc	πατέρας	βασιλεῖς	πόλεις	τὰς ἐρήμους
gen	πατέρων	βασιλέων	πόλεων	τῶν ἐρήμων
dat	πατράσιν	βασιλεῦσι	πόλεσιν	ταῖς ἐρήμοις

	ὁ Ἰησοῦς Jesus	ὁ Ζεύς Zeus	τὸ πῦρ the fire	τὸ φῶς the light	τὸ πλῆθος the crowd
nom	Ἰησοῦς	Ζεύς	πῦρ	φῶς	πλῆθος
voc	Ἰησοῦ	Ζεῦ			
acc	Ἰησοῦν	Δία	πῦρ	φῶς	πλῆθος
gen	Ἰησοῦ	Διός	πυρός	φωτός	πλήθους
dat	Ἰησοῦ	Διί	πυρί	φωτί	πλήθει

Hebrew names are usually found with only a single form.

So: Ἀβραάμ – Abraham   υἱοὶ Ἀβραάμ – sons of Abraham
Ἰωσήφ – Joseph   τῷ Ἰωσήφ – to Joseph

βορρᾶς – north, has a genitive ending in α:

Lk 13:29 ἀπὸ ἀνατολῶν καὶ δυσμῶν καὶ ἀπὸ βορρᾶ καὶ νότου
from east and west and from north and south

Summary of types of pronoun

R.4

For ὁ ἡ τό – the, οὗτος αὕτη τοῦτο –this, and ὅς – who, see 12.7

ἐκεῖνος ἐκείνη ἐκεῖνο – that, has the same endings as οὗτος.

Personal prounous

αὐτός – he, αὐτή – she, αὐτό – it, ἐγώ – I, σύ – you, ἡμεῖς – we, ὑμεῖς – you.

Singular					
nom	αὐτός	αὐτή	αὐτό	ἐγώ	σύ
acc	αὐτόν	αὐτήν	αὐτό	με, ἐμέ	σέ
gen	αὐτοῦ	αὐτῆς	αὐτοῦ	μου, ἐμοῦ	σοῦ
dat	αὐτῷ	αὐτῇ	αὐτῷ	μοι, ἐμοί	σοί
Plural					
nom	αὐτοί	αὐταί	αὐτά	ἡμεῖς	ὑμεῖς
acc	αὐτούς	αὐτάς	αὐτά	ἡμᾶς	ὑμᾶς
gen	αὐτῶν	αὐτῶν	αὐτῶν	ἡμῶν	ὑμῶν
dat	αὐτοῖς	αὐταῖς	αὐτοῖς	ἡμῖν	ὑμῖν

τίς – who?, τί – what?, τις – someone, a; τι – something, οὐδείς – no-one, μηδείς – no-one

Singular			Masc	Fem	Neut
nom	τίς	τί	οὐδείς	οὐδεμία	οὐδέν
acc	τίνα	τί	οὐδένα	οὐδεμίαν	οὐδέν
gen	τίνος	τίνος	οὐδενός	οὐδεμιᾶς	οὐδενός
dat	τίνι	τίνι	οὐδενί	οὐδεμιᾷ	οὐδενί
Plural					
nom	τίνες	τίνα			
acc	τίνας	τίνα			
gen	τίνων	τίνων			
dat	τίσι(ν)	τίσι(ν)			

μηδείς is declined like οὐδείς.

The endings of οὐδείς give you the declension of εἷς –one: εἷς μία ἕν.

τις –someone, a, and τι –something, are declined like τίς and τί but have no accents.

Summary of types of adjective
R.5

καλός – good, proper, beautiful
πολύς – much, many
πλείων – more, most, greater

ἅγιος – holy, pure, sacred
μέγας – big, great, important
ἀληθής – true, real, honest

	Masc	Fem	Neut	Masc	Fem	Neut
Singular						
nom	καλός	καλή	καλόν	ἅγιος	ἁγία	ἅγιον
acc	καλόν	καλήν	καλόν	ἅγιον	ἁγίαν	ἅγιον
gen	καλοῦ	καλῆς	καλοῦ	ἁγίου	ἁγίας	ἁγίου
dat	καλῷ	καλῇ	καλῷ	ἁγίῳ	ἁγίᾳ	ἁγίῳ
Plural						
nom	καλοί	καλαί	καλά	ἅγιοι	ἅγιαι	ἅγια
acc	καλούς	καλάς	καλά	ἁγίους	ἁγίας	ἅγια
gen	καλῶν	καλῶν	καλῶν	ἁγίων	ἁγίων	ἁγίων
dat	καλοῖς	καλαῖς	καλοῖς	ἁγίοις	ἁγίαις	ἁγίοις
Singular						
nom	πολύς	πολλή	πολύ	μέγας	μεγάλη	μέγα
acc	πολύν	πολλήν	πολύ	μέγαν	μεγάλην	μέγα
gen	πολλοῦ	πολλῆς	πολλοῦ	μεγάλου	μεγάλης	μεγάλου
dat	πολλῷ	πολλῇ	πολλῷ	μεγάλῳ	μεγάλῃ	μεγάλῳ
Plural						
nom	πολλοί	πολλαί	πολλά	μεγάλοι	μεγάλαι	μεγάλα
acc	πολλούς	πολλάς	πολλά	μεγάλους	μεγάλας	μεγάλα
gen	πολλῶν	πολλῶν	πολλῶν	μεγάλων	μεγάλων	μεγάλων
dat	πολλοῖς	πολλαῖς	πολλοῖς	μεγάλοις	μεγάλαις	μεγάλοις
Singular						
nom	πλείων	πλείων	πλεῖον/ πλέον	ἀληθής	ἀληθής	ἀληθές
acc	πλείονα	πλείονα	πλεῖον	ἀληθῆ	ἀληθῆ	ἀληθές
gen	πλείονος	πλείονος	πλείονος	ἀληθοῦς	ἀληθοῦς	ἀληθοῦς
dat	πλείονι	πλείονι	πλείονι	ἀληθεῖ	ἀληθεῖ	ἀληθεῖ
Plural						
nom	πλείονες/ πλείους	πλείονες/ πλείους	πλείω	ἀληθεῖς	ἀληθεῖς	ἀληθῆ
acc	πλείονας/ πλείους	πλείονας/ πλείους	πλείω	ἀληθεῖς	ἀληθεῖς	ἀληθῆ
gen	πλειόνων	πλειόνων	πλειόνων	ἀληθῶν	ἀληθῶν	ἀληθῶν
dat	πλείοσιν	πλείοσιν	πλείοσιν	ἀληθέσιν	ἀληθέσιν	ἀληθέσιν

REFERENCE GRAMMAR

Notes:

1. Many adjectives, e.g. ἀληθής, have only one form for masculine and feminine. Because they have only this common form and neuter form they are called adjectives with two terminations.

Other examples are:

m/f	n	m/f	n
χείρων	χεῖρον – worse	ὑγιής	ὑγιές – healthy
ἐνδεής	ἐνδεές – needy, poor	ἄτεκνος	ἄτεκνον – childless
ἀνάξιος	ἀνάξιον – unworthy	δύσκολος	δύσκολον – hard, difficult

2. πλείων sometimes has shorter forms (see the paradigm above).

3. For the uses, parsing, and variety of adjectives, see 28.1–3, 35.1–3, 37.1, 44.3.

Comparison of adjectives and adverbs

R.6

1. Adjectives

The comparative usually ends in -τερος, so:

ἰσχυρός – strong   ἰσχυρότερος – stronger, rather strong
σοφός – wise   σοφώτερος – wiser

The superlative usually ends in -τατος or -ιστος, so:

ὑψηλός – high   ὕψιστος – highest, very high
μέγας – great   μέγιστος – greatest
ἅγιος – holy   ἁγιώτατος – holiest, very holy, most holy

Note particularly:

ἀγαθός – good	κρεῖττον (κρεῖσσον) – better	
κακός – bad	χείρων – worse	
μέγας – great	μείζων – greater	μέγιστος – greatest
πολύς – much	πλείων – more	πλεῖστος – most
μικρός – little	μικρότερος – smaller	ἐλάχιστος – smallest, least

2. Adverbs

ταχύ, ταχέως – quickly   τάχιστα – very quickly

πολύ – much   μᾶλλον – more, rather   μάλιστα –most, especially
πλεῖον – more   πλεῖστοι – most
ἡδέως – gladly   ἥδιστα – very gladly
εὖ – well   βέλτιον, κρεῖσσον – in a better way

Note: εἰς τὸ χεῖρον (ἐλθοῦσα) – (having become) worse

Summary of important verbal forms

R.7

1. λύω – I untie, I loose, I break. Stem: λυ-

Active Indicative	Singular 1p	2p	3p	Plural 1p	2p	3p
Present —	λύ-ω	-εις	-ει	-ομεν	-ετε	-ουσιν
Future | •	λύσ-ω	-εις	-ει	-ομεν	-ετε	-ουσιν
Imperfect — |	ἔλυ-ον	-ες	-εν	-ομεν	-ετε	-ον
Aorist ⁀|	ἔλυσ-α	-ας	-εν	-αμεν	-ατε	-αν
Perfect ⁀| →	λέλυκ-α	-ας	-εν	-αμεν	-ατε	-ασιν
Pluperfect ⁀|→|	λελύκ-ειν	-εις	-ει	-ειμεν	-ειτε	-εισαν
Subjunctive						
Present —	λύ-ω	-ῃς	-ῃ	-ωμεν	-ητε	-ωσιν
Aorist •	λύσ-ω	-ῃς	-ῃ	-ωμεν	-ητε	-ωσιν
Imperative						
Present —	–	λύ-ε	-έτω	–	-ετε	-έτωσαν
Aorist •	–	λῦσ-ον	-άτω	–	-ατε	-άτωσαν

Note that the position of the accents shown in the tables of verbal forms in this and the subsequent sections (R.7.1–7) with shift in accordance with rule 4 on page 349, e.g. in table 1, the imperfect 1p is ἔλυον in the singular but ἐλύομεν in the plural (he accent shifting to the second syllable).

Infinitive
Present —   λύειν
Aorist •   λῦσαι

Participle
Present —   λύων — λύουσα — λῦον
Aorist ⁀   λύσας — λύσασα — λῦσαν

In a verb which has a shorter stem in the aorist, the aorist indicative often has the same endings as the imperfect.

Note, for example, from βάλλω – I throw (ἔβαλλον – I was throwing) ἔβαλον – I threw:

ἔβαλον   ἔβαλες   ἔβαλεν   ἐβάλομεν   ἐβάλετε   ἔβαλον.

But note also the forms of κατέβην – I went down, and ἔγνων – I knew:

κατέβην   κατέβης   κατέβη   κατέβημεν   κατέβητε   κατέβησαν
ἔγνων   ἔγνως   ἔγνω   ἔγνωμεν   ἔγνωτε   ἔγνωσαν

2. λύομαι – I am untied, I am loosed

Passive Indicative	Singular 1p	2p	3p	Plural 1p	2p	3p
Present —	λύ-ομαι	-ῃ	-εται	-όμεθα	-εσθε	-ονται
Future | ⁻:	λυθήσ-ομαι	-ῃ	-εται	-όμεθα	-εσθε	-ονται
Imperfect —|	ἐλυ-όμην	-ου	-ετο	-όμεθα	-εσθε	-οντο
Aorist ⁻:|	ἐλύθ-ην	-ης	-η	-ημεν	-ητε	-ησαν
Perfect ⁻|→	λέλυ-μαι	-σαι	-ται	-μεθα	-σθε	-νται
Pluperfect ⁻|→|	(ἐ)λελύ-μην	-σο	-το	-μεθα	-σθε	-ντο
Subjunctive						
Present —	λύ-ωμαι	-ῃ	-ηται	-ώμεθα	-ησθε	-ωνται
Aorist •	λυθ-ῶ	-ῇς	-ῇ	-ῶμεν	-ῆτε	-ῶσιν
Imperative						
Present —	–	λύ-ου	-έσθω	–	-εσθε	-έσθωσαν
Aorist •	–	λύθ-ητι	-ήτω	–	-ητε	-ήτωσαν
Infinitive						
Present —	λυέσθαι					
Aorist •	λυθῆναι					
Participle						
Present —	λυόμενος — λυομένη — λυόμενον					
Aorist ⁻:|	λυθείς — λυθεῖσα — λυθέν					

3. νίπτομαι – I wash (part of myself) – Middle

Present, imperfect, perfect, and pluperfect are the same in middle and passive. Future and aorist have different forms in the middle voice. Note the following:

Middle	Singular			Plural		
	1p	2p	3p	1p	2p	3p
Indicative						
Present —	νίπτ-ομαι	-η	-εται	-όμεθα	-εσθε	-ονται
Future ⫶	νίψ-ομαι	-η	-εται	-όμεθα	-εσθε	-ονται
Aorist ⫶	ἐνιψ-αμην	-ω	-ατο	-άμεθα	-ασθε	-αντο
Subjunctive						
Aorist •	νίψ-ωμαι	-η	-ηται	-ώμεθα	-ησθε	-ωνται
Imperative						
Aorist •	–	νιψ-αι	-άσθω	–	-ασθε	-άσθωσαν

Infinitive
Present — νίπτεσθαι
Aorist • νίψασθαι

Participle
Present — νιπτόμενος – νιπτομένη – νιπτόμενον
Aorist ⫶ νιψάμενος – νιψαμένη – νιψάμενον

Note that if you need to be able to parse verbal forms (see 33.12) these tables will assist you in learning. For example, if you wish to parse λυθησόμεθα (we will be loosed), by looking at (2) λυομαι you will see from the column it is in that λυθησόμεθα is in 1st person plural, and from the section and line that it is future indicative passive. Similarly νίψαι (wash!) is 2nd person singular aorist imperative middle.

4. καλέω → καλῶ; ἀγαπάεις → ἀγαπᾷς; φανερόει → φανεροῖ

When the stem of a verb ends in a vowel, the vowel combines with the initial vowel of the ending. These verbs have the same endings as λύω and νίπτομαι, except for the result of the contraction of the vowels. The following table shows the contractions that result from combining vowels, e.g. α + ει = ᾳ,   ε + ει = ει,   ο + ει = οι.

REFERENCE GRAMMAR

	End of Stem		
	α	ε	ο
Verb ending begins α	α	η	ω
ε	α	ει	ου
ει	ᾳ	ει	οι
ι	αι	ει	οι
η	α	η	ω
ῃ	ᾳ	ῃ	οι
ο	ω	ου	ου
ου	ω	ου	ου
οι	ῳ	οι	οι
ω	ω	ω	ω

5. ἵστημι – I cause to stand, I set, I establish

Note, for example:

Mk 9:36   ἔστησεν αὐτὸ ἐν μέσῳ αὐτῶν
          He set him in the middle of them

Mk 7:9   ἵνα τὴν παράδοσιν ὑμῶν στήσητε
          So that you may establish your tradition.

Active Indicative	Singular 1p	2p	3p	Plural 1p	2p	3p
Present —	ἵστ-ημι	-ης	-ησι	-αμεν	-ατε	-ασιν
Future |⁀	στήσ-ω	-εις	-ει	-ομεν	-ετε	-ουσιν
1 Aorist ⁀|	ἔστησ-α	-ας	-εν	-αμεν	-ατε	-αν
Subjunctive 1 Aorist •	στήσ-ω	-ῃς	-ῃ	-ωμεν	-ητε	-ωσιν

Imperative
Aorist •   στῆσαι (to establish – Rom 10.3)

Note also: στῆσαι – it shall be established

6. ἕστηκα – I am standing, I stand

Note, for example, Revelation 3:20: ἕστηκα ἐπὶ τὴν θύραν – I am standing at the door. In the perfect and pluperfect ἵστημι has a middle sense: I have caused myself to stand (that is, I am standing) and I had caused myself to stand (I was standing). ἵστημι also has second form of the aorist active ἔστην (I stood). The aorist passive ἐστάθην also means 'I stood'. Note the following forms:

Active Indicative	Singular 1p	2p	3p	Plural 1p	2p	3p s	Meaning (1p s)
Perfect (Present) —	ἕστηκ-α	-ας	-εν	-αμεν	-ατε	-ασιν	I am standing
Pluperfect (Imperfect) — |	εἱστήκ-ειν	-εις	-ει	-ειμεν	-ειτε	-εισαν	I was standing
2 Aorist ⁻|	ἔστ-ην	-ης	-η	-ημεν	-ητε	-ησαν	I stood
Subjunctive							
2 Aorist •	στ-ῶ	-ῇς	-ῇ	-ῶμεν	-ῆτε	-ῶσιν	

Imperative	(συ)	στῆθι	(ὑμεῖς) στῆτε –	stand!

Infinitive		
Aorist •	στῆναι – to stand	

Participles				
2 Aorist	στάς	στᾶσα	στάν	standing
1 Perfect	ἑστηκώς	ἑστηκυῖα	ἑστηκός	standing
2 Perfect	ἑστώς	ἑστῶσα	ἑστός	standing
Aorist Passive	σταθείς	σταθεῖσα	σταθέν	standing

Note also στησόνται – they will stand, ἐστάθην – I stood.

7. Principal parts

From a knowledge of the stem, the present, future, aorist and perfect indicative, and the aorist passive of a verb, it is usually possible to tell the meaning of any form of the verb that is encountered. Note the following:

Meaning	Present	Main stem	Future	Aorist	Perfect	Aorist Passive
untie	λύω	λυ	λύσω	ἔλυσα	λέλυκα	ἐλύθην
do	ποιῶ	ποιε	ποιήσω	ἐποίησα	πεποίηκα	ἐποιήθην
love	ἀγαπῶ	ἀγαπα	ἀγαπήσω	ἠγάπησα	ἠγάπηκα	ἠγαπήθην
exalt	ὑψῶ	ὑψο	ὑψώσω	ὕψωσα	ὕψωκα	ὑψώθην
pick up	αἴρω	ἀρ	ἀρῶ	ἦρα	ἦρκα	ἤρθην
throw	βάλλω	βαλ/βλη	βάλω	ἔβαλον	βέβληκα	ἐβλήθην
write	γράφω	γραφ	γράψω	ἔγραψα	γέγραφα	ἐγράφην
raise	ἐγείρω	ἐγειρ	ἐγερῶ	ἤγειρα	—	ἠγέρθην

REFERENCE GRAMMAR

judge	κρίνω	κριν	κρινῶ	ἔκρινα	κέκρικα	ἐκρίθην
go	βαίνω	βα/βη	βήσομαι	ἔβην	βέβηκα	—
drink	πίνω	πι	πίομαι	ἔπιον	πέπωκα	—
fall	πίπτω	πεσ	πεσοῦμαι	ἔπεσον	πέπτωκα	—
know	γινώσκω	γνο/γνω	γνώσομαι	ἔγνων	ἔγνωκα	ἐγνώσθην
become	γίνομαι	γιν/γεν	γενήσομαι	ἐγενόμην	γέγονα	ἐγενήθην
come, go	ἔρχομαι	ἐρχ/ἐλθ	ἐλεύσομαι	ἦλθον	ἐλήλυθα	—
put	τίθημι	θε	θήσω	ἔθηκα	τέθεικα	ἐτέθην
give	δίδωμι	δο	δώσω	ἔδωκα	δέδωκα	ἐδόθην
forgive	ἀφίημι	(ἀπο)ἑ	ἀφήσω	ἀφῆκα	—	ἀφέθην
cause to stand	ἵστημι	στη/στα	στήσω	ἔστησα	—	—
stand	—	στη/στα	στήσομαι	ἔστην	ἔστηκα	ἐστάθην
destroy	ἀπόλλυμι	(ἀπο)ολεσ	ἀπολέσω	ἀπώλεσα	—	—
perish	ἀπόλλυμαι	(ἀπο) ολο	ἀπολοῦμαι	ἀπωλόμην	ἀπόλωλα	—

Summary of types of participles
R.8

As an example of typical forms and endings of participles we use the participles of the verb λύω – I untie, set aside

λύων – untying (present participle active)

	Singular			Plural		
	Masc	Fem	Neut	Masc	Fem	Neut
nom	λύων	λύουσα	λῦον	λύοντες	λύουσαι	λύοντα
acc	λύοντα	λύουσαν	λῦον	λύοντας	λυούσας	λύοντα
gen	λύοντος	λυούσης	λύοντος	λύοντων	λυουσῶν	λυόντων
dat	λύοντι	λυούσῃ	λύοντι	λύουσι(ν)	λυούσαις	λύουσι(ν)

Declined with the same endings:

aorist participles which end in -ων

e.g. βαλών – having thrown ἰδών – seeing, having seen
ἐλθών – going, having gone.

Declined with similar endings:

present participles of words like:

ἀγαπάω – I love: ἀγαπῶν ἀγαπῶσα ἀγαπῶν

καλέω – I call: καλῶν   καλοῦσα   καλοῦν
δουλόω – I enslave: δουλῶν   δουλοῦσα   δουλοῦν

λύσας – having untied (aorist participle active)

	Singular			Plural		
	Masc	Fem	Neut	Masc	Fem	Neut
nom	λύσας	λύσασα	λῦσαν	λύσαντες	λύσασαι	λύσαντα
acc	λύσαντα	λύσασαν	λῦσαν	λύσαντας	λυσάσας	λύσαντα
gen	λύσαντος	λυσάσης	λύσαντος	λυσάντων	λυσασῶν	λυσάντων
dat	λύσαντι	λυσάσῃ	λύσαντι	λύσασι(ν)	λυσάσαις	λύσασι(ν)

declined with the same endings:

  aorist particples which end in -ας

e.g.   ἄρας – having picked up
       στάς – standing
       κηρύξας – having preached

λυθείς – having been untied (aorist participle passive)

	Singular			Plural		
	Masc	Fem	Neut	Masc	Fem	Neut
nom	λυθείς	λυθεῖσα	λυθέν	λυθέντες	λυθέντες	λυθέντα
acc	λυθέντα	λυθεῖσαν	λυθέν	λυθέντας	λυθείσας	λυθέντα
gen	λυθέντος	λυθείσης	λυθέντος	λυθέντων	λυθεισῶν	λυθέντων
dat	λυθέντι	λυθείσῃ	λυθέντι	λυθεῖσι(ν)	λυθείσαις	λυθεῖσι(ν)

Declined with the same endings:

  all participles ending with -εις

e.g.   ἀποκριθείς – answering   δοθείς – having been given
       σταθείς – standing.

λελυκώς – having untied (perfect participle active)

	Singular			Plural		
	Masc	Fem	Neut	Masc	Fem	Neut
nom	λελυκώς	λελυκυῖα	λελυκός	λελυκότες	λελυκυῖαι	λελυκότα
acc	λελυκότα	λελυκυῖαν	λελυκός	λελυκότας	λελυκυίας	λελυκότα
gen	λελυκότος	λελυκυίας	λελυκότος	λελυκότων	λελυκυιῶν	λελυκότων
dat	λελυκότι	λελυκυίᾳ	λελυκότι	λελυκόσι(ν)	λελυκυίαις	λελυκόσι(ν)

Declined with the same endings:

  most participles with -ως

e.g.   γεγονώς – having been made, having become

REFERENCE GRAMMAR

ἐληλυθώς – having come
ἑστηκώς – standing
but not ἑστώς – standing: ἑστώς ἑστῶσα ἑστός.

λυόμενος – untying (for oneself), being untied (present participle middle and passive)

	Singular			Plural		
	Masc	Fem	Neut	Masc	Fem	Neut
nom	λυόμενος	λυομένη	λυόμενον	λυόμενοι	λυόμεναι	λυόμενα
acc	λυόμενον	λυομένην	λυόμενον	λυομένους	λυομένας	λυόμενα
gen	λυομένου	λυομένης	λυομένου	λυομένων	λυομένων	λυομένων
dat	λυομένῳ	λυομένῃ	λυομένῳ	λυομένοις	λυομέναις	λυομένοις

Declined with the same endings:

all participles ending with -ος

e.g. ἐρχόμενος – coming (present participle of ἔρχομαι)
λυσάμενος – having untied for oneself (aorist participle middle)
γενόμενος – having become, having been made
(aorist participle of γίνομαι)
λελυμένος – having been untied (perfect participle passive).

δούς – having given, giving (once) (aorist participle active of δίδωμι)

	Singular			Plural		
	Masc	Fem	Neut	Masc	Fem	Neut
nom	δούς	δοῦσα	δόν	δόντες	δοῦσαι	δόντα
acc	δόντα	δοῦσαν	δόν	δόντας	δούσας	δόντα
gen	δόντος	δούσης	δόντος	δόντων	δουσῶν	δόντων
dat	δόντι	δούσῃ	δόντι	δοῦσι(ν)	δούσαις	δοῦσι(ν)

Declined with the same endings:

γνούς – knowing, realizing, perceiving, having known
(aorist participle of γινώσκω)

Accents

In printed editions of the New Testament you will find three accents, known as acute ´ (for example, τί), grave ` (τό) and circumflex ˆ (μενῶ). These accents were not part of the original New Testament text; they appear only in manuscripts from the ninth century onwards. The system was devised by classical Greek Writers as an aid to pronunciation, with ´ indicating a high tone, ` a low tone, and ˆ a rising and falling tone.

In a few cases accents distinguish words which would otherwise look the same, e.g. εἰ means 'if', but εἶ means 'you are'. It is possible to read the New Testament without knowing anything more about accents. The rules of accenting are complex, and most students do not need to learn them. For those with a special interest, the following summary provides a basic introduction.

Note that a long syllable is usually one which contains a long vowel (η, ω) or a diphthong. However, both -αι and -οι are regarded as short when they occur at the **end** of a word (so the final syllable is short in λόγοι, long in λόγους). On a diphthong it is customary to place the accent over the second vowel (τοῦτο).

Basic rules for accentuation

1. An accent may be placed above **one** of the last **three** syllables of a word (Jn 1:3 πάντα δι᾽ αὐτοῦ ἐγένετο)

2. If the last syllable of a word is **long**, an accent may only be placed above one of the last **two** syllables (πνεύματα, but πνευμάτων).

3. A **circumflex** accent may only be placed above one of the last two syllables of a word, and only over a **long** syllable (δῶμα, δοῦ, Ῥωμαῖοι).

4. In **verbs** an acute accent is placed as far back from the end as rules 1 and 2 allow (δίδωμι, ἐδίδουν). Where a verb is **contracted** (13.1) and the acute accent would have stood on the short contracting vowel, it is replaced by a circumflex on the contracted vowel (φιλέω becomes φιλῶ).

5. Apart from rules 1 and 2 there is no rule to show where accents are placed on **nouns**. It is necessary to learn the accent as you learn the word. But note that most frequently a noun keeps its accent on the same syllable in other cases as it is in the nominative case (ἀρχή, ἀρχῆς), unless other

Reference Grammar

rules demand a change (πνεῦμα, πνεύματος – but πνευμάτων [rule 2]).

6. When a word that naturally carries an acute accent on the **last** syllable is followed by another word **in the same clause**, the acute accent is replaced by a grave accent (τοὺς ἀδελφοὺς βλέπω, but βλέπω τοὺς ἀδελφούς).

7. In normal circumstances a word may carry only one accent. There are, however, a number of short words (for example ἐστι, με, τις, πως) which throw the accent they would have had back on to the word before, when this is possible. For example ἄνθρωπός τις – a certain man, δοῦλός τις – a slave, ἥψατό μού τις – someone touched me (note that the accent from μου has been thrown back onto ἥψατο and the accent from τις on to μου).

Two acute accents may not stand on adjoining syllables. So τόπος τις – a certain place (τόπός is impossible so τις simple loses its accent). But where a **two-syllable** word cannot throw its accent back, it retains it: ἐν τόπῳ τινὶ ἦν – he was in a certain place.

Words that throw back their accents are called **enclitics**.

8. ὁ, ἡ, οἱ, αἱ, εἰς, ἐν, ἐκ, οὐ and ὡς have no accents.

For a more detailed treatment of accentuation, see E. G. Jay, *New Testament Greek: An Introductory Grammar* (SPCK, 1974) pp11–12 and 273–77.

APPENDIX: SOME THOUGHTS ON THE TEACHING OF BIBLICAL LANGUAGES
(with special reference to New Testament Greek)

Some principles of teaching

1. Love your students.
2. Present material so that it can be clearly understood and rapidly and happily learned.
3. Take delight in the rapid progress that your students make and show them that you are delighted.
4. Assess what you do and give assessment sheets at various stages to your students. Take them seriously. Always aim to do better next time.

   "*If you don't try to improve, it is the beginning of the end.*"
   Sven-Göran Eriksson (after England beat Germany 5-1)

5. Never forget that smiles stimulate study and that laughter lubricates learning. Measure your forward progress in smiles per hour.
6. Always relate what you do to the aims and hopes that your students have. If they desire to read and understand Greek or Hebrew, do not spend time at the start teaching them to write. Once they are fluent in reading they will learn to write more easily.

Keep on learning about learning, memory and teaching

Be an avid reader of books about the brain and memory, about methods of learning, about teaching of skills as well as facts. Besides obvious books like *Accelerated Learning* (Colin Rose) and *Techniques of Language Teaching* (F. L. Billows), I have found useful points to ponder in *The Speed System of Basic Mathematics* (Trachtenberg – translated and adapted by Ann Cutler and R. McShane), in *The Inner Game of Music* (Barry Green with Timothy Gallwey), and an old copy (10p, second hand!) of *Philosophy and Psychology of Teaching Typewriting* (Russon and Wanous).

I nearly didn't buy Russon and Wanous because (a) it was so old and (b) typewriting seemed far removed from language teaching! Here are some of my gleanings:

'Motivation comes from early use of meaningful material.' 'Learning is faster… if the lesson is broken up into different elements.' 'It is desirable that some work each day be easy enough for the student to build up skill without a sense of strain.' ' A teacher must believe that the students can learn.' 'A teacher needs to display enthusiasm, to treat students considerately and to build up confidence.'

For an early plea to free students from being 'suffocated with the nonsense of grammarians' I have seen nothing to compare with Sydney Smith (*Edinburgh Review,* 1826) in his discussion of Hamilton's Method of teaching languages.

Read widely.

The setting in which learning takes place

Make the room not a classroom but a learning zone, or a Hebrew/Greek Fun Factory.

To learn well, students need to be relaxed, free from anxiety, attentive and actively involved. Words of welcome in Greek or Hebrew should be at or near the door. Greetings and wishes of peace, love and joy can be a useful part of every session between tutor and class.

Relaxation and a brain-wave pattern that is conducive to learning can be helped if sessions begin with classical music, preferably adagio movements from baroque music.

Flowering plants and foliage placed in pots around the room can contribute to a pleasant atmosphere. Seating that is in a crescent or half-circle shape can build a sense of fellowship while enabling displayed visual material to be seen.

Straight lines of desks or tables should be avoided. It is sensible to make the learning area as little like a traditional schoolroom as possible because so many people associate schoolrooms with pressure, anxieties, failures, rivalries – that is, with enemies of the learning process.

The learning zone should be attractive and offer a rich variety of peripheral learning opportunities. For example, a 'revision wall' could display the key points of past lessons with important parts of words picked out in clear contrasting colours. By the light switch, 'Let there be light' and 'and there was light' could be shown in the target language. Pictures showing inter-action, with headings in the new language, can be displayed. Empty space needs to be available for movement and games involving words and word cards. Have some new display material for each session.

'I am not a linguist.' 'I am no good at languages.'

Many people, when faced with an opportunity to learn a language, fear that they will not be able to cope. Time needs to be taken (a) to tell them that if they can speak and read their own language, they have all the linguistic ability they require to do a properly structured course in Greek or in Hebrew; (b) to explain the marvellous capacity of our brains with their billions of neurons; (c) to remind them that as children they did not learn words the first time they heard them – but they began to learn them! So it does not matter if we do not learn what is in a lesson, only that we become aware of the material in it, so that we give ourselves a chance to start learning. What we begin to learn in a lesson, we consolidate as we move forward.

People are also shy and afraid of making mistakes, so it is not enough simply to assure them that mistakes do not matter, but are part of the learning process. We must also give them confidence that, while they are beginning to learn, no one will be picked out to perform alone.

As a teacher you will often be asking yourself questions like, 'Is it time to introduce a movement activity?' and this may lead you into making mistakes. Hopefully the class will correct you. But, in any case, point out that you too are liable to make mistakes but you are still surviving – and so can they. Then say, 'Please do that bit again, so that I can get it right!'

When you hear a mistake, do not point it out – stress what is correct. For example, if you hear some people say 'word' when it should be 'words', say, 'Let's do that again and let me hear the 's' on words.' Give constant encouragement and praise.

Things that help learning
1. Build a belief that the learning group will succeed.
2. Set goals for lessons that focus on awareness rather than learning, e.g. 'to become aware of the personal endings on verbs, for example the ω of λέγω that indicates 'I'. Focus on acquiring *ability* to understand sentences rather than *knowledge* of words.
3. Give each person a name, and name card, in the target language and use it during the lessons. It should be a new name, not their own.
4. Use texts with side-by-side presentation so that as the Hebrew or Greek is read the English is in peripheral vision.
5. In class work have cards available to cover the English column. Write on them: καλύπτω τούτους τοὺς λόγους   so that when you ask τί ποιεῖς; they can see what to reply.

6. After you have all read and translated a passage with the English covered, then uncover the English so that you can read the Greek to them while they have access to the translation.
7. When you are doing a new drill or exercise (a) read a phrase, line or sentence to the class, (b) get them to read it with you (c) translate it in unison. In this way each part is looked at three times – but without any sense of having boring repetitions.
8. If you make additional tapes, if possible use a soft female voice. Most children learned early language from their mothers.
9. Play word and movement games.
10. Make songs to tunes that are well known.
11. Ensure that each lesson includes things to read, to listen to, and to see, and things that involve movement. When introducing new words, mime them whenever possible.
12. Sometimes look back four or five lessons and do a short section to see how much easier it has become.

Things to avoid
1. Criticism of the class or anyone in it. If you improve your skills as a teacher and increase your stock of visually displayed material, you will create opportunities to say quite genuinely, 'You are the best class I have ever had' or, at least, 'You are one of the best classes I have ever had.'
2. Do not produce test material which is likely to lead to mistakes. In language learning success leads to more success.
3. Do not introduce anything that will slow down progress through the lessons. In language learning the brain needs to take in a 'critical mass' of a language before it can get it sorted. It needs to be drowned in the new language!
4. Do not spend a long time answering questions. Treat every questioner courteously, but find strategies that allow you to be brief. Often language teaching material will have a 'trailer' for what is coming. A question about such a trailer may often be answered after the style of 'That is an excellent question – you will find the answer later in the lesson. Let's press on to find the answer.' Remember that uncompleted tasks are remembered better than completed ones, because the brain stays alert. Questions, from those who have done Latin or other courses, about grammatical descriptions and

tables may be answered by suggesting that in their own time they should consult the Reference Grammar and maybe a brief comment that grammatical terms are less misleading if you first see how the language functions.

5. So far as possible, avoid the need to turn your back on the class and use a blackboard. Material like key points of a lesson should be prepared beforehand on a flip chart. This saves time in the learning period; it also saves time because it can be used again next year. Smaller visual material like an aim or goal for a lesson may be put on an A4 or A3 sheet and displayed using blutack (Handy hints: for writing on flip charts make yourself a backing sheet with black lines ruled on to keep your lines level and your letters all the same height. For sheets put up with blutack (etc) put a strip of clear tape over each corner, then you can use the sheets time after time without damaging the corner.

6. So far as possible, avoid lecturing about the language. 'A competent teacher organises and directs learning activities.' ('Russon and Wanous.')

7. Do not stand between the students and visually displayed material. A walking stick provides a useful pointer that allows you to stand well to one side (suggestion: write 'early' biblical passages boldly on A1 or flip chart sheets – for example, John 1:3–10 will fit on a flip chart sheet. Then as the group does 'choral' translation with you, you are able to point at the word or part of the word as it is being translated. No one gets lost. No one says, 'Which line are we on?' It takes time to prepare but is well worth it. Add to your stock each year.

8. Avoid linguistic and grammatical jargon which ordinary people will not understand. Incomprehensibility is not a mark of profundity but of discourtesy.

9. Avoid teaching parsing at least until people have become expert at reading and translating. Accurate translating is the key to parsing. When a student can look at κληθήσονται and know that – ονται indicates 'they' and – θησ – here indicates 'will be', so that it can be translated 'they will be called', then it is not hard to describe 'they' as 3rd person plural and 'will be' as future passive. But remember that 3rd person plural has to be translated back as 'they' before it has a clear meaning for most people. So perhaps what we should aim at is accurate translation. Parsing can normally be left until a

language course is finished – as a means of understanding (a) the Reference Grammar and (b) scholarly comments found in books. Premature work on parsing slows down the learning process and the all-important acquisition of fluency in reading.

10. Avoid premature testing. A seed should not be pulled out of the ground to see if it has begun to sprout and form roots. With group learning the teacher sees and hears and monitors the learning as it takes place. 'The teacher needs to do very little testing to know how pupils are progressing. As time spent on testing is largely wasted, from the point of view of learning, this is a great advantage.' (F. L. Billows).

11. Avoid testing which is not related to the aims with which students embark on the course. If their major aim is to read biblical text with understanding, then testing should be of their ability to translate biblical text. Later testing can be on translation evaluation, textual criticism, etc.

12. Avoid testing which is unrelated to the ways in which words function and the ways in which language is most naturally learned. Language is most naturally learned through hearing meaningful conversations. In a learning course in biblical languages, learning and memory best take place through connected narratives and complete sentences. 'Words are very flexible symbols whose meaning shifts in different contests' (Graddol, Cheshire and Swann). So words should never be tested out of context. Consider, for example οἶκος. The range of meaning covers 'house, family, descendants' and more. If a student is asked to give a translation of οἶκος the likely answer will be 'house'. One wonders whether in Luke 11:17, the reference to a ruling family being in rebellion against itself is translated as 'and house falls on house' (NRSV) because for so many generations students have been taught to learn words from vocabulary lists and to translate them out of context.

Enjoy yourself

There are few joys greater than teaching effectively and seeing your students grow and burst into bloom. So enjoy yourself and invite them to share in your joy. Keep creating. Teaching is not about standing still and becoming safe. Have great expectations of what your students will achieve: 'There's a generation coming up behind me very swiftly, and my heart is to see them do things I was never able to do.' (Kevin Prosch: worship leader and music teacher)

John H Dobson
May 2004

SCRIPTURE INDEX

Index of Passages To Read

MATTHEW		1:29–34	207	15:18–27	272
6:9–13	170	1:35–39	137, 207	20:30–31	175
		1:35–42	214	20:24–31	325
MARK		1:43–51	130		
1:1–13	287	2:1–12	259	ROMANS	
11:9–11	180	3:1–12	268	1:1–7	288
11:27–30	103	3:8–13	156		
		3:13–21	220	1 CORINTHIANS	
LUKE		4:1–6	119	12:12–21	190
1:5–7	305	4:7–15	124		
11:5–8	320	4:17–24	108	1 JOHN	
18:9–14	312, 313	4:27–30	141	ch1	185
		4:39–42	141	1:1–3	84
JOHN		5:19–28	152	1:5–7	100
1:3–10	69	6:31–33	152	ch2	283
1:6–8	60	7:45–52	162		
1:11–13	175	9:1–12	233	REVELATION	
1:14–18	175, 291, 296	9:13–23	238	21:1–3	162
1:19–25	95, 201	9:24–34	248	22:8–11, 17	254
1:26–28	201	9:35–38	137, 248		
		9:39–41	248		

Index of Verses Quoted

GENESIS		PSALMS		MATTHEW	
1:14	291	17:30	220	2:8	221
27:35	131	(18:29LXX	220)	2:10	226
28:12	131	115:8	47	2:22	248
31:21	306	115:9–11	47	3:11	303
		119	292	4:6	242
LEVITICUS				5:2	324
25:37	306	PROVERBS		5:8	43
		22:9	306	5:12	245
DEUTERONOMY		23:6	306	5:14	21
18:15, 18	95			5:18	213
22:14	306	ECCLESIASTES		5:24	306
		1:1	299	5:42	306
JOSHUA				6:1	265
7:19	248	DANIEL		6:11	249
		7:13–14	152	6:19	255

6:19–20	298	**MARK**		3:21	245
6:25	255	1:2	245	3:24	231
7:1	255	1:4	240	3:25–26	269
7:6	299	1:5	248	3:32	231
7:10	312	1:8	77, 260	4:1	228
7:25	312	1:9	263	4:2	263
8:1	143	1:10	131	4:4	229, 263
9:2	322	1:13	247, 262, 263	4:5	231, 232, 236
9:26	234	1:14	330	4:9	299
9:33	243	1:15	197	4:10	225, 231, 264
9:37	310	1:16	229	4:12	300
10:34	258	1:19	211, 226	4:21	231
11:2	63	1:22	266	4:35	92
12:11	320	1:23	264	4:38	262
12:22	234, 235	1:27	262	4:39	256
12:23	155, 248	1:30	247, 260	4:41	226
12:35	137	1:31	241	5:5	240
14:28	228	1:34	227, 236	5:7	127, 225
15:28	225	1:36	247	5:11	265
15:33	236	1:38	220, 237	5:13	245
17:1	232	1:41	318–319	5:18	222
17:9	143	1:43	319	5:19	260
17:14	226	2:2	236	5:23	222
18:27	319	2:4	101	5:25	264
18:34	319	2:10	246	5:26	210, 245
20:1–16	321	2:12	235	5:36	210
20:13	321	2:14	231	5:38	210
20:19	21	2:16	247	5:41	298
20:34	319	2:17	220	5:43	256
21:1–2	323	2:18	261	6:2	101
21:16	323	2:19	242, 322	6:3	229
22:4	301	2:19–20	243	6:8	222, 229
22:10	309	2:22	206	6:22	261
22:42	242	2:23	263	6:25	247, 266
23:30	257	2:24	261	6:27	256
23:31	260	2:26	264	6:34	106
25:20	194	2:27	232	6:48	231
25:24	194	2:27–28	236	6:52	266
26:38	237	3:2	295	6:55	266
26:56	223	3:4	237	7:5	230
26:75	241	3:5	202	7:7	301
27:45	231	3:12	222	7:27–28	321
27:46–47	297	3:14	222	7:31	229
27:64	241	3:20	236	7:34	298

360 LEARN NEW TESTAMENT GREEK

7:37	309	12:41	295	6:40	231
8:4	246	13	330	7:12	220
8:6	262	13:15	252	7:24	101
8:7	226	13:16	229	7:40	254
8:11	245	13:18	295	7:42	210
8:12	302	13:20	302	7:47	210, 211
8:26	322	13:22	221	8:4	220
8:27–30	323	13:29	266	8:31	256
8:29	227, 294	13:30–32	330	8:52	255
8:30	256	13:35	295	9:51	306
8:31	210	14:3	144	10:1	303
8:32	262	14:6	264	10:5	258
8:33	244	14:12	261	10:6	306
8:34	237, 244	14:13	261	11:3	249
8:35–37	237	14:19	155, 156	11:11	248
9:4	264	14:21	246	11:13	211
9:5	260	14:24	247	11:17	272
9:7	241	14:36	298	11:22	311, 312
9:10	225	14:44	311	11:28	309
9:22	319	14:55	229	11:34	306
9:26	234	14:58	246	11:37	265
9:30	245	14:66	144	12:48	298
9:31	232	15:5	237	13:2	230
9:36	255, 349	15:6	230	14:12	322
9:39	255, 266	15:8	317	14:21–24	319
9:40	247	15:19	260	16:6	297
10:19	255	15:29	225	18:11	313
10:22	266	15:32	252	18:12	241
10:37	213	15:40	263	22:15	300
10:41	247	15:46	260	22:19	249
10:45	221, 248	16:2	261	22:23	308
10:46	229			22:35	241
10:48	211	**LUKE**		22:49	263
10:52	261	1, 2	305	23:39	155
11:1–2	301, 323	1:1–4	305	24:13	227
11:2	63	1:8	263	24:21	264
11:14	308	1:8–10	312	24:30	324
11:25	245, 262	1:20	248	24:44	197
11:31	262	1:38	307		
12:2	261	2:15	301	**JOHN**	
12:12	229	4:8	302	1:1	77, 330
12:13	260	4:22	155	1:2	61
12:14	246, 262	6:11	308	1:1–2	6, 32, 39, 70, 77, 91, 296
12:26	246	6:22	306		
12:36	264				

1:1–10	39	4:7	250, 254	18:16	265
1:1–18	298	4:12	155, 157	18:22	160
1:3	32, 349	4:15	250	18:36	270, 271
1:3–10	6, 47, 60, 70, 296	4:16	250	19:16	271
		4:16–17	109	19:19	163
1:3–18	175	4:29	155, 157	19:20	298
1:4	39	4:34	222	19:25	264
1:4–5	46, 47, 60	4:41	232	20:19	21
1:5	196	4:46	225	20:25	136
1:6–8	61, 70	5:1	232	20:26	232
1:7–8	110	5:18	310	20:30–31	318
1:9	47	5:39	110	20:31	60, 110, 175
1:10	32, 47	6:10	226	21:3	220
1:12	240	6:28	63, 76	21:11	214
1:14	301, 316	6:32	195		
1:14–18	175, 317	7:12	309	**ACTS**	
1:16, 17	301	7:31	241	1:3	263
1:18	315–317	7:41	163	2:4	101
1:19	240	7:50-52	268	4:19	210
1:19–25	95, 201	8:12	15, 152	4:24	114
1:19–37	60	8:31	160	5:24	307
1:21	92	8:46	232	5:28	257
1:22	146	8:53	241	7:27	246
1:26	263	9:2	223	7:34	300
1:27	240	9:5	152	8:31	308
1:29	147	9:16	245	9:2	221
1:30	247	9:35–38	248	9:31	206
1:32	131	10:16	213	10:14	302
1:33	289	11:6	226	11:28	246
1:39	265	12:5	241	13:5	225
1:41	92	12:19	245	13:32–33	197
1:44	92	12:27	237	14:4	309
1:47	212	13:13	160	15:3	309
1:48	147, 231, 301	13:34	90	18:13	229
2:5	249	14:7	269	18:16	265
2:15	309	15:9–10	90	25:4	309
3	328	15:11	318	25:10	226
3:1	261	15:12	222		
3:13	229	15:18	81	**ROMANS**	
3:16	234, 316	16:24	318	1:6, 7	291
3:16-18	316	17:3	222	1:25	263
3:18	316	17:6	261	1:26	229
3:21	223	17:15	222	3:23	241
3:31	268	18:2	271	5:15	260

6:14	231	3:20	320	1:4	220, 317, 318
9:14	265	5:6	242	1:5	10, 54
12:9–10	302			1:6	293
12:16	265	**PHILIPPIANS**		1:10	269
15:24	248	1:7	236	2:1	318
16:27	260	1:27	237	2:7–14	318
		2:9	231	2:10	54
1 CORINTHIANS		2:20	247	2:21	302
1:12	310			3:1	311
3:19	265	**1 THESSALONIANS**		3:14	308, 318
7:7	309	5:5	242	3:16	318
10:23	216			3:18	76
11:31	270	**2 THESSALONIANS**		3:23	90
12:29	155, 157	2:3	242	4:6	318
13:13	241			4:9	240, 264
14:5	101	**2 TIMOTHY**		4:10	318
14:9	148	4:8	310	4:14	195, 318
15:44–46	237			4:16	10, 25, 54, 318
15:45	237	**HEBREWS**		4:17	318
		1:7	114	4:18	206
2 CORINTHIANS		1:7–8	310	4:19	318
1:4	221	2:17	226	4:20	101
5:19	177	3:11	302	5:3	240
8:14	221	3:18	294	5:13	318
6:18	303	6:13–14	300		
8:14	221	9:1	309	**3 JOHN**	
		9:12	246	14	294
GALATIANS		11:17	316		
1:10	270			**REVELATION**	
2:7	226	**JAMES**		1:6	299
2:12	245	5:16	247	3:20	349
3:7	242	5:17	300	5:4	210
3:11	265			14:6	330
3:19	303	**1 PETER**		18:7	43
4:6–7	236	3:14	300, 308	21:16	246, 321
5:17	223	3:17	308	22:15	321
EPHESIANS		**1 JOHN**			
1:13	240	1:1–5	54		
2:8–9	329	1:3	195		
2:12	241				

SCRIPTURE INDEX

INDEX OF GRAMMAR & CONSTRUCTIONS

1. Grammar

Nouns
  Intro. 4–6
  9.6
  12.7
  28.1
  32.4
  37.1
  44.2
  R.2
  R.3
Cases
  12.7
  37.1–3
  39.1–3
  42.1
  Nominative
    12.7
    32.4
    37.1
  Vocative
    37.1–2
  Accusative
    12.7
    37.1, 3–15
    42.2, 8
    47.2
  Genitive
    12.7
    31.2
    32.4
    37.1
    39.1–13
    42.8
    48.9
  Dative
    12.7
    31.3
    37.1
    41.2

42.1–7
Number and gender
  12.7
  19.1
  28.1, 6
  37.1
Pronouns
  10.1–4
  13.4
  50.7
  R.4
Adjectives
  28.1–3
  35.1, 3
  37.1
  44.3
  R.5
  R.6
Adverbs
  28.5
  35.1–5
  44.4
  R.6
Numbers
  31.4
  35.6
  37.8
Prepositions
  17.1
  30.3
  36.5
  37.4–15
  39.2–13
  42.2–8
  44.6
The article
  12.7
  28.6
  30.3
  39.10

Stems
  44.7
Verbs
Parsing
  14.6
  26.4–5
  31.9
  33.12
  37.1
  R.7
Moods
  Indicative
    4.1–5
    5.1–6
    13.1–3
    14.1–6
    15.1–3, 5
    16.4
    17.2
    23.1–7
    26.4–5
    31.9A
    32.1
    33.12
    38.4, 5
    43.1–3
  Subjunctive
    11.1–8
    31.9A
    33.12
    36.1–7
    41.1–2
    43.1
  Imperative
    31.9A
    33.12
    40.1–4
    41.1

365

Optative
    49.3
Infinitive
    18.1–2
    24.6
    30.1
    31.7, 9A
    32.2
    33.7, 12
    36.5 (2)
    37.3 (7)
    38.4 (1)
    41.2 (1)
Participles
    8.1–3
    16.7
    19.1–2, 5
    Intro. 20–25
    20.1–5
    21.5, 8
    22.1, 3
    24.5
    25.1–3
    24.5
    25.1–3
    29.8
    31.7, 9A
    32.2
    33.5, 7, 11
    37.1
    48.5
    50.8
    R.8

Tenses
  Present
    4.1–5
    5.1–6
    8.1–3
    11.7–8
    13.1–3
    14.6
    17.2
    18.1
    19.1, 5
    20.1–3
    24.1, 2, 5, 6
    25.1, 2
    26.4, 5
    29.1, 2, 4, 8
    30.1
    31.1, 9B
    33.12
    34.3
    36.1
    40.1, 4
    41.1
    47.1, 4
  Future
    26.1, 2, 4, 5
    29.2
    31.9B
    32.3
    33.12
    45.4
    48.5 (2)
  Imperfect
    14.1–6
    15.1–3, 5
    23.7
    26.4, 5
    29.6, 7
    31.6, 9B
    33.12
    43.3
  Aorist
    17.2
    Intro. 20–25
    20.1–5
    21.1–5, 7, 8
    22.1, 3, 4
    23.1–7
    24.1, 2, 5, 6
    25.1
    26.4, 5
    29.1, 4, 6–8
    30.1
    31.9B
    32.1
    33.5, 12
    34.3
    36.1
    40.1, 4
    41.1
    50.8
  Perfect
    31.9B
    33.1, 2, 5, 7, 10, 12
  Pluperfect
    31.9B
    33.12
    49.7

Voice
  Active
    31.9C
    32.1–3
    33.11
    45.1
  Middle
    29.1, 2, 4, 6–8
    31.9C
    33.11
    45.1–4
  Passive
    31.1, 3, 6, 7, 9C
    32.1–3
    33.7, 11
Formation
    44.5–7

366   LEARN NEW TESTAMENT GREEK

2. Constructions and types of speech

Alphabet and capitals
2.1–3
16.1–3

Commands
36.7 (3)
40.1, 4
41.1, 2
48.5

Conditions
11.1, 4
43.1–3

Consecutive clauses
38.4, 6

Denial
48.7

Final clauses
11.1, 5
36.1, 5–7
38.6

Genitive absolute
25.1–3
39.1 (8)

Indirect speech
41.2
47.1–4

Permission
40.4

Prohibition
36.7
41.1, 2

Punctuation
13.6
15.4

Questions
13.6
15.4, 6
16.7
27.1–3
47.4

Requests
36.7 (2)
40.1
47.3

Wishes
49.1–3

Time
14.1
20.3, 4
21.5
23.1
25.1, 2
26.1
29.1
35.5
36.1, 2
37.3 (6)
39.7
42.1 (3)
42.3 (4)

Place
17.1–3
27.1
35.5
37.3 (6)
37.12
39.7, 8
42.2, 5–8

INDEX OF GREEK WORDS

The first entry will normally tell you the basic meaning of the word. Other entries will give further developments or discussion. The index covers words in the word lists and others that are discussed.

ἀγαθός
  28.1, 3
  R.6
ἀγαπάω
  11.2
  13.1, 10
  15.5, 8, 9
  18.1
  23.7
  30.1
  R.7.4
  R.7.7
ἀγάπη
  3.6
  6.6
  11.2
  39.1
ἀγαπητός
  46.4
ἀγγελία
  10.7
ἄγγελος
  10.7
ἁγιάζω
  29.10
  44.1
  49.2
ἅγιος
  28.2, 6
  44.1
  R.5
  R.6
ἁγιωσύνη
  46.4

ἀγοράζω
  21.9
ἄγω
  31.9
  35.7
  36.5
  38.8
ἀδελφή
  11.2
ἀδελφός
  7.9
  10.11
  11.2
ἀδικέω
  40.6
  44.1
αἷμα
  17.5
  41.4
αἴρω
  9.3
  22.1
  23.2, 5, 6, 7
  30.1
  40.1, 4
  R.8
αἰτέομαι
  45.2
αἰτέω
  21.9
  43.4
  48.12

αἰών, αἰώνιος
  21.9
  36.2
  48.3
ἀκάθαρτος
  23.2
ἀκοή
  32.7
ἀκολουθέω
  14.7
  40.4
  42.1
ἀκούω
  5.3, 4, 5
  8.1, 5
  15.5
  17.5
  19.3
  21.4, 5
  26.1, 4
  39.1
  45.4
  48.3
ἀκρίς
  45.6
ἀκροβυστία
  48.10
ἀλαζονεία
  44.10
ἄλαλος
  31.4
ἅλας
  28.2, 9

ἀλήθεια
  9.7
  13.8, 10
  35.4
  46.6
ἀληθής,
  ἀληθῶς
  3.1–4, 5
  9.7
  15.8
  28.1, 5
  35.1
  R.5
ἀληθινός
  9.10
ἁλιεύω
  36.5
ἀλλά
  7.1, 6
  49.4
ἀλλαχόθεν,
  ἀλλαχοῦ
  35.5
ἀλλήλοι
  13.7
  17.5
ἄλλομαι
  21.9
ἄλλος
  28.2
  49.4
ἁμαρτάνω
  23.2
ἁμαρτία
  9.7
  17.5

369

ἁμαρτωλός
37.7
ἀμήν
14.7
ἀμνός
22.6
25.7
ἄν
11.1-3
36.2
43.1
ἀνά
37.4, 8
44.6
48.8
ἀναβαίνω
22.1, 4, 8
23.7
26.5
37.8
50.6
ἀναβλέπω
37.8, 17
ἀναγγέλλω
17.5
ἀναγινώσκω
8.5
14.6
21.5
26.5
44.1
ἀνακράζω
38.2
ἀνάξιος
44.3
R.5
ἀναστάς
(ἀνίστημι)
34.1
ἀναφέρω
37.8

ἀνήρ
19.1, 3
R.1
R.2
ἄνθρωπος
1.2
7.5, 6
8.7
28.3
ἀνίστημι
6.6
34.1
37.8
ἀνοίγω
22.8
37.8, 17
43.4
ἀνομία
39.1
ἀντί
28.2
31.11
39.2, 12
44.6
ἀντίχριστος
44.10
ἀντλέω
21.9
41.7
ἄνωθεν
35.5
42.9
52.4
ἄξιος
33.13
39.1
44.3
ἀπαγγέλλω
10.7
23.7
ἀπαντάω
42.1

ἅπαξ
35.6
ἀπαρνέομαι
40.5
ἀπείθεια
39.1
ἀπεκρίθην
(ἀποκρίνομαι)
27.1
29.2
48.4
ἀπέρχομαι
17.3
21.9
ἄπιστος
37.2
ἀπό
10.7
17.1, 3, 5
39.2
44.6
ἀποδίδωμι
28.2
ἀποθνῄσκω
36.2
ἀποκαθίστημι
34.1
ἀποκρίνομαι
18.5
19.7
22.3
23.7
24.5
27.1
29.2, 4
R.8
ἀπόκρισις
16.8
25.7
ἀποκτείνω
38.2

ἀπόλλυμι
34.1, 3, 6
44.6
R.7.7
ἀποπλανάω
36.5
ἀποστέλλω
8.5
11.9
14.6
26.5
51.5
ἀπόστολος
6.1, 3, 4, 5
7.6
46.3
ἀποσυνάγωγος
38.23
ἅπτομαι
29.2, 6
36.1
ἀπώλεια
39.1
ἄρας, (αἴρω)
23.5, 6
ἀρέσκω
42.1
ἀριθμός
37.3
ἄριστον
51.3
ἀρνέομαι
33.13
44.10
ἄρτι
38.8
44.10
ἄρτος
24.1
38.4

ἀρχή
2.5, 6
3.2, 5
ἀρχιερεύς
17.3
33.8
ἀρχιτρίκλινος
41.7
ἄρχομαι
18.2, 3
20–25 Intro
29.2, 8
ἄρχων
42.9
R.2
ἀσκός
34.5, 6
ἀσπάζομαι
45.2
ἀστήρ
R.2
ἄστυ
44.8
ἄτεκνος
R.5
αὔριον
20.4
αὕτη
9.7
αὐτός
7.1–6, 9
9.7
R.4
ἀφίημι
34.1, 3
40.4
42.1
R.7.7
ἀφορίζω
44.6
46.1

βαθύς
21.9
βαίνω
R.7.7
see also
ἀαβαίνω,
καψαβαίνω
βάλλω
18.3
20–25 Intro
22.1, 3
23.1, 3–5, 7, 8
26.1, 4
31.9
33.12
R.7
R.8
βαπτίζω
13.1
15.6
31.1, 3, 6, 7, 9
32.1–3
33.12
48.8
βάπτισμα
39.1
βαπτιστής
15.6
βασιλεία
9.7
29.10
43.6
βασιλεύς
9.7
12.7
14.11
37.3
44.2
R.3
βιβλίον
7.3, 11
12.5

βλασφημέω
28.5
βλέπω
14.3, 7
19.1
48.3
βοάω
16.6
βορρᾶς
R.3
βρῶμα
36.7
γάμος
41.7
γάρ
12.5
γείτων
37.17
γενεά
37.2
γενετή
37.17
γεννάω
30.5
γένος
12.7
γῆ
9.7
12.7
γίνομαι
4.6
27.5
29.1, 4, 6, 8, 10
48.4, 12
49.1, 3
R.7.7
R.8

γινώσκω
8.5
22.1
44.1
45.4
see also
ἀναγινώσκω
γλῶσσα
13.4, 8, 10
R.1
R.2
γνῶσις
44.1
γονεύς
37.17
γόνυ
R.2
γονυπετέω
37.3
γραμματεύς
33.8
44.2
48.10
γραφή
19.9
γράφω
3.3, 5
21.5
26.5, 7
31.9
33.1, 2, 7
R.7.7
R.8
γυνή
19.1, 3
28.1
37.2, 3
R.1
R.2
δαιμόνιον
12.5

INDEX OF GREEK WORDS 371

δάκτυλον
23.8
δαπανήσασα
39.6
δέ
16.4
34.5
49.4
δεῖ
19.7
30.3
35–52 Intro
35.3
δείκνυμι
26.7
34.3
40.6
δεῖπνον
51.3
δέκα
31.4
35.6
δέκατος,
δεκάκις
35.6
δεξιῶν
35.6
δερμάτινος
45.6
δεῦτε
24.7
δεύτερος
35.6
δέχομαι
45.2
δέω
30.3
δηνάριον
37.8
51.1

διά
25.4
36.2
37.4, 15
38.5
39.2, 7
42.8
44.6
διαθήκη
13.6
28.2
διακονέω
36.2, 5
42.1
διακονία
36.2
διάκονος
36.2
διακόσιοι
35.6
διαλογισμός
9.3
διαστέλλομαι
41.2
διδάσκαλος
14.7
40.6
διδάσκω
14.7, 10
26.5
30.1
48.3
διδαχή
14.7, 10
δίδωμι
19.3
22.1, 9
26.7
30.1
31.9
34.1, 3
36.1

40.1
41.4
42.1
48.12
49.3, 7
R.7.7
R.8
see also
δός
διέρχομαι
21.9
δίκαιος
35.1
44.1
δικαιοσύνη
41.4
44.1
δικαίωμα
44.1, 2
48.12
δικαίως
35.1
44.1
δίκτυον
23.1
35.6
δισχίλιοι
35.6
διψάω
21.9
40.6
διώκω
43.6
δόλος
22.8
δόξα
26.2
39.14
46.6
δοξάζω
26.2

δός (δίδωμι)
31.9
34.1, 3
39.14
40.1, 6
41.7
47.3
δουλεία
36.2
δουλεύω
36.2
44.5
δοῦλος
32.7
36.2
δουλόω
36.2
44.5
R.8
δούς (δίδωμι)
22.9
δραμών
(τρέχω)
22.1
24.2, 5, 6
δύναμαι
22.8
27.1
29.1, 2
36.5
δύναμις
33.8
δύο
35.6
37.8
48.8
δύσκολος
44.3
R.5

372   Learn New Testament Greek

δώδεκα
31.4
35.6
δωρεάν
40.6
ἐάν
11.1, 2, 4
43.1, 4
ἑαυτόν
26.7
40.2
ἕβδομος
35.6
ἐγγίζω
33.1, 2, 8
52.7
ἐγγύς
33.8
40.6
ἐγείρω
26.2
28.8
R.7.7
ἐγώ
13.4
37.1
R.4
ἔθνος, ἔθνη
33.8
46.1, 4
48.10
R.2
εἰ
10.6
14.6
16.6
32.7
34.5
43.1–3, 4
47.4
48.7
49.3

εἰ
10.6
16.6
εἶδον (ὁράω)
22.4
24.2, 5, 6
27.1
εἴδωλα
32.5
εἰδωλολατρία
48.10
εἴκοσι
35.6
εἴληφα
(λαμβάνω)
33.3, 4
εἰμί
3.1
16.4, 10
19.5
26.1
28.8
30.1
36.5
45.4
47.2
49.2
see also ὤν
εἶπον (λέγω)
16.4
17.5
22.1
24.2, 5, 6
30.1
31.9
εἴρηκα (λέγω)
19.7
εἰρήνη
5.7
41.4
48.10

εἰρηνικός
41.4
εἰς
17.1, 3
36.5
37.3, 4, 6
48.8
εἷς, μία, ἕν
31.4
35.6
43.4
R.4
εἰσέρχομαι
17.4
47.2
εἶτα, εἶτεν
35.5
εἴτε
32.7
ἐκ, ἐξ
17.1, 3
39.2
44.6
ἕκαστος
32.7
37.8
43.4
ἑκατόν
35.6
ἑκατοντάρχης
35.6
ἐκβάλλω
18.3
23.4, 7, 8
30.1
ἐκεῖ
40.2
ἐκεῖθεν
35.5
40.2
ἐκεῖνος

15.8
20.7
52.7
R.4
ἐκκλησία
9.7
ἐκπλήσσομαι
45.2
ἐκτείνω
32.4
ἐλάσσων
41.7
ἐλέγχω
36.4
ἐλεύθερος
32.7
ἐλεύσομαι
(ἔρχομαι)
26.1, 2
31.9
33.12
ἐλθών
(εἴρχομαι)
17.2
22.1, 3
26.4
29.4, 8
30.1
45.4
R.8
ἐλπίζω
39.13
47.2
ἐλπίς
R.1
R.2
'Ελωι
48.10
ἐμαυτόν
40.2

INDEX OF GREEK WORDS

ἐμβαίνω
25.4
ἐμός
43.4
ἔμπροσθεν
35.5
39.2
ἐν
2.5, 6
17.1, 3
30.3
31.3
36.8
37.17
42.2, 3
48.8
ἕν
31.4
35.6
ἐναντίον
48.12
ἐνδεής
R.5
ἕνδεκα
35.6
ἐνδύομαι
45.1, 2
ἐνέγκαι (φέρω)
22.1
24.2, 5, 6
30.1
ἐνενήκοντα
35.6
ἐθάδε
19.7
21.9
ἐννέα
35.6
ἐντέλλομαι
42.1

ἐντολή
15.6
48.12
ἐξ
13.7, 8
ἕξ
35.6
ἐξέρχομαι
17.3
22.3
23.7
31.9
44.6
ἔξεστιν
30.3
ἐξηγέομαι
46.6
ἑήκοντα
35.6
37.3
ἐξίσταμαι
38.2
ἔξοδος
16.1
ἐξομολογέω
45.6
ἐξουσία
18.3
ἔξω
23.2
ἔξω (ἔχω)
26.1, 5
ἑορτη
42.9
ἐπαγγελία
44.10
ἐπαύριον
22.8
ἐπερωτάω
18.5
44.5

ἐπὶ
35.4
37.4, 12
39.2, 8
42.2, 7, 8
44.6
ἐπίγεια
27.5
ἐπιθυμία
44.10
48.3
ἐπιούσιος
29.10
ἐπιστολή
9.7
ἐπιτάσσω
41.2
ἐπιτίθημι
34.1
44.6
ἐπιτιμάω
41.2
42.1
49.3, 5
51.5
ἐπιτρέπω
40.4
ἐπιχρίω
37.17
ἑπτά
35.6
ἑπτάκις
35.6
ἑπτακισχίλιοι
35.6
ἐραύνησον
28.8
ἔργον
12.1–5, 8
13.8
28.1
52.6

R.1
R.2
ἔρημος
12.7
16.6
R.3
ἔρχομαι
17.1–3
22.1
24.2, 5, 6
26.1, 2, 5
29.2, 4, 6, 8
30.1
31.9
33.12
37.1
40.4
45.1, 4
R.7.7
R.8
ἐρῶ (λέγω)
18.5
26.1
ἐρωνάω
19.9
28.8
ἐρωτάω
16.4
23.2, 7
20–25 Intro
44.5
ἐσθίω
20–25 Intro
22.1
24.1, 2, 5, 6
30.1
45.4
49.3
ἔσομαι (εἰμί)
26.1
28.8
31.9

ἕστηκα
(ἵστημι)
R.8
R.9
ἐστίν (εἰμί)
3.1–5
ἔσχατος
28.2
ἔσχον (ἔχω)
19.7
26.5
33.5
ἔσωθεν
35.5
ἔτι
25.4
ἑτοιμάζω
ἕτοιμος
28.8
41.4
εὖ
44.4
R.6
εὐαγγέλιον
12.5
37.3 (5)
52.7
εὐθύνω
33.13
εὐθύς
35.1
44.4
45.6
εὐλογέω
37.3
48.3
51.7
εὑρίσκω
8.5
15.5
22.1

ἐφάπαξ
39.7
ἔφη (φημί)
16.8
23.9
34.1
ἐφημερία
48.12
ἔχω
8.5
15.5
19.2
26.1, 5
30.3
33.3, 5
44.10
ἑώρακα
(ὁράω)
23.9
31.11
ἕως
36.2
38.8
44.10
ζάω
20.9
26.2
30.1, 3
ζητέω
13.4
ζωή
20.7
26.2
ζώνη
45.6
ζῷον
26.2
ζῳοποιέω
26.2
ἤ
18.5
43.4

ἤ
10.5, 6, 7
ᾖ (εἰμί)
36.5
ἤγγικεν
(ἐγγίζω)
33.1, 2
52.7
ἡγεμών
R.2
ᾔδειν (οἶδα)
20.7
33.1
34.7
ἡδέως
R.6
ἤδη
31.8
ἥκω
41.7
ἦλθον
(ἔρχομαι)
17.2, 3
24.2, 5, 6
26.4, 5
29.6
33.12
ἡλικία
38.8
ἡμεῖς
9.11
10.1–4, 7
37.3
50.7
R.4
ἡμέρα
9.7
35.4
37.3, 14
39.1
48.12

ἡμέτερος
14.11
43.4
ἤμην (εἰμί)
16.10
ἦν (εἰμί)
2.5–6
3.1–4
ἦρα (αἴρω)
23.2, 6, 7
ἠρξάμην
(ἄρχομαι)
18.2, 3
29.2, 8
ἡψάμην
(ἅπτομαι)
29.2, 6
θάλασσα
23.2
θάνατος
36.2
θανατόω
36.2
37.6
44.5
θαυμάζω
24.7
26.7
θαυμαστός
39.14
θεάομαι
14.11
20.7
34.7
35.8
θέλημα
18.3
28.1
θέλω
6.6
18.3

θεμελιόω 49.7	ἴδιος 22.8 28.2, 6 30.3, 5	ἰσχυρός 45.6 R.6	κακός 28.1, 2, 6 35.1 R.6
θεός 2.5, 6 3.1, 2, 5 7.6 13.10 28.8 36.8 39.1 50.5 52.7	ἰδεῖν (ὁράω) 22.4 30.1 R.8	ἰχθύς 31.6 R.2	κακῶς 35.1
		καθάπερ 32.7	καλέω 13.1, 4 14.6 15.9 19.5 36.5 R.7.4 R.8
	ἱερεύς 17.3 44.2	καθαρίζω 17.5	
		καθαρισμος 41.7	
	ἱερόν 17.3	καθαρός 9.4	
θεοσεβής 39.14	ἵημι 34.1, 3	κάθημαι 37.9 40.6 45.2	καλός 28.2 35.1 R.5
θεραπεύω 32.4	Ἰησοῦς 2.2 3.3, 5 R.3		
θεωρέω 19.7 40.6		καθίζω 37.9	καλῶς 28.5 33.3 35.1
θηλάζω 51.6	ἱλασμός 44.10		
		καθώς 15.8 20.7 22.4 30.3 37.9	
θησαυρός 41.1	ἱμάς 33.13 45.6		καρδία 9.1–7 12.7 19.1 37.1
θνήσκω 33.3, 5 36.2	ἵνα 10.8 11.1, 2, 5, 7 15.8 34.7 36.1, 5–7 38.6 41.2 47.3		
θρέμματα 21.9		καί 2.5, 6 10.7 43.4 48.4 49.4	καρπός 41.4
θρόνος 1.2 7.6			καρποφορέω 41.4
θυγάτηρ 48.12			κατά 30.3 35.4 37.4, 9 39.2, 5 42.8 44.6 46.1, 4 48.8
		καινός 13.6 15.8 28.1, 2	
θυσιαστήριον 48.10	ἵστημι 33.13 34.1, 3 49.7 R.7.5 R.7.6 R.7.7 R.8		
ἰατρός 35.2		καιρός 33.8, 10 40.6	
ἴδε 22.4 40.2		καίτοιγε 21.9	

376   Learn New Testament Greek

καταβαίνω
22.4, 8
23.7
25.1
30.1
40.4
κατάκειμαι
37.9
καταλαμβάνω
29.10
καταλλάσσω
31.3
κατασκευάζω
45.6
κατεσθίω
37.9
κατοικέω
37.9
44.5
κεφαλή
32.4
κηρύσσω
18.3
19.2
20.2, 3
21.3, 5
36.5
R.8
κλαίω
41.1
κλέπτω
41.1
κλητός
46.1, 3, 4
κλίνη
51.4
κοινωνία
10.7
κόλπος
46.6
47.5

κολυμβήθρα
37.17
κοπιάω
47.5
κοσμέομαι
28.8
κόσμος
5.7
7.10
14.6
26.7
κράζω
22.3
31.11
38.2
κρατέω
32.4
39.1
κρίμα
39.14
κρίνω
27.1
31.2
R.7.7
κρίσις
20.9
κριτής
27.1
κυνάριον
51.2
κύπτω
45.6
κύριος
10.7
19.7
23.9
37.1, 2
κύων
51.2
κωλύω
41.1

κώμη
44.8
51.5
κωφός
32.4
λαλέω
13.4
31.4
λαμβάνω
8.5
22.1
26.5
30.1
33.3, 5
45.4
λαός
33.8
λέγω
4–6 Intro
4.1–7
5.1–6
8.1–3
9.9
11.8
14.1–6
18.1
19.1, 5
22.1
24.2, 5, 6
26.1, 4
28.6
30.1, 3
42.1
47.1, 2
λεπρός
30.4
λίθινος
41.7
λίθος
23.2
λογίζομαι
49.3

λόγος
2.5
4–6 Intro
6.1–5
9.9
13.8
28.1
52.7
R.1
R.2
λοιδορέω
39.14
λύχνος
37.10
λύω
33.13
R.7.1
R.7.2
R.7.3
R.7.7
R.8
μαθητής
14.2, 7
μακάριος
8.3, 5
9.4
20.5
23.1
μᾶλλον
35.3
43.4
R.6
μαρτυρέω,
μαρτυρία
μάρτυς
11.9
15.6
μάχαιρα
31.3
42.3

INDEX OF GREEK WORDS 377

μέγας, μεγάλη,
  μέγα
  28.1
  37.3
  38.2
  R.5
  R.6
μεθερμηνεύω
  16.3
μεθύω
  41.7
μείζων
  20.7
  25.4
  48.9
  R.6
μέλει
  42.1
μέλι
  45.6
μέλος
  32.4
μέν
  32.7
  49.4
μενοῦν,
  μενοῦνγε
  49.4
μεντοι
  24.7
μένω
  6.6
  27.1
μερίζω
  43.1
μέρος
  32.4
μέσος
  33.13
  37.8

μετά
  10.7
  25.4
  35.4
  37.4, 14
  39.2, 9
  42.8
  44.6
μεταβαίνω
  20.9
  44.6
μετανοέω
  40.2
  44.6
μετάνοια
  39.1
  40.2
μετρέω
  48.4
μή
  11.2, 6
  13.7, 8
  27.3
  34.5
  41.1, 4
  49.1
μηδέ
  13.7
  27.1
μηδείς,
  μηδεμία,
  μηδέν
  31.4
μηδέποτε
  35.5
μηκέτι
  25.4
μήτηρ
  19.3
μήτι
  27.3, 5

μία
  31.4
  35.6
  R.4
μικρός
  R.6
μιμνῄσκομαι
  39.1
μισέω
  14.6
  43.6
μνημεῖον
  33.3
  44.2
μνημονεύω
  43.6
μονογενής
  36.4
  46.6
  47.5
  50.5
μόνον
  35.3
  49.4
μύριοι
  35.6
μωρός
  49.5
ναός
  37.3
νεανίας
  44.2
  R.2
νεκρός
  26.7
  36.2
νεκρόω
  36.2
νεώτερος
  49.5

νήπιος
  51.6
νίπτω,
  νίπτομαι
  31.9
  37.17
  45.1, 2
  R.7.3
νομοδιδάσ-
  καλος
  48.10
νόμος
  22.8
  31.11
  33.8
  43.6
νύμφη
  28.8
νυμφίος
  28.8
νυμφών
  39.1
νῦν
  19.7
  26.7
  36.2
νύξ
  39.1
  42.9
ὁ, ἡ, τό
  2.5, 6
  7.9
  8.2, 3
  12.7
  19.1, 2, 5
  20.5
  28.3, 6
  30.3
  39.10
  49.4

378　　　　Learn New Testament Greek

ὅ
  10.5, 6, 7
ὁδοιπορία
  47.5
ὁδός
  41.4
οἶδα
  27.1
  33.1, 2
  34.7
  49.7
οἰκία
  17.3
  R.1
  R.2
οἰκοδομέω
  23.7
οἶκος
  17.3
  43.6
  R.1
  R.2
οἶνος
  34.5, 6
  37.3
ὀκτώ
  35.6
ὀλίγος
  35.3
  37.3
ὁλοκαύτωμα
  48.10
ὅλος
  13.7
  28.2
  39.14
ὅμοιος,
  ὁμοίως
  35.1
  37.17
  44.4

ὁμολογέω
  16.8
  33.13
ὀνίναμαι
  (ὀναίμην)
  49.3
ὄνομα
  11.9
  12.7
  31.4
  42.9
  48.12
ὄπισθεν
  35.5
ὀπίσω
  31.11
  33.13
  39.2, 3
ὅπως
  36.5, 6
ὁράω, ὄψομαι
  22.8
  24.2, 5, 6
  30.1
  40.2
  45.4
  48.3
ὀργίζω
  50.8
ὀρθός, ὀρθῶς
  35.1
ὁρίζω
  46.1
ὄρος
  19.7
  31.4
ὅς, ἥ, ὅ
  10.5, 6, 7
  11.1–3
  12.8
  39.12
  43.4

ὅσος
  30.5
  38.2
ὄσφρησις
  32.7
ὅταν
  36.2
ὅτε
  16.6
  36.2
ὅτι
  8.4
  30.3
  38.5
  47.1
οὐ, οὐκ, οὐχ
  7.1, 6
  11.2
  27.3
  41.4
  48.6
οὐδε
  16.4
  27.1
οὐδείς,
  οὐδεμία,
  οὐδέν
  17.5
  27.5
  31.4
  R.4
οὐδέποτε
  35.5
οὐκ
  see οὐ
οὐκέτι
  25.4
οὖν
  16.4, 6
  49.4

οὐρανός
  7.6
  48.10
οὖς, ὦτα
  10.5
  32.4
  48.3
  R.1
  R.2
οὗτος, αὕτη,
  τοῦτο
  2.5
  3.3
  7.6, 8, 9
  12.8
  52.7
οὕτως
  20.10
  27.5
  28.5
  30.3
  35.1
  38.1, 4
  49.4
οὐχ, οὐχί
  see οὐ
ὀφθαλμός
  14.11
  32.4
ὄφις
  36.4
ὄχλος
  22.4
  33.8
ὀψέ, ὀψία
  31.8
ὄψῃ (ὁράω)
  22.8
  42.9

INDEX OF GREEK WORDS 379

παθεῖν (πάσχω) 30.1, 3	παραλαμβάνω 30.5 44.6	πέραν 33.14	πιστεύω 7.1 8.1, 5
παιδίσκη 25.2	παράπτωμα 42.1	περί 14.11 16.6	30.1 33.1, 2, 5
παλαιός 28.1	παρίστημι 34.1	22.4 37.4, 13	37.3 42.1
πάλιν 18.5 29.2 50.6	παρρησία 35.4 πᾶς 17.5	39.2, 10 42.8 44.6 περιβλέπομαι	49.7 πίστις 31.4 46.3
πανταχοῦ 35.5	21.8 22.4	31.8 περιπατέω	πλανόω 31.11
πάντοθεν 35.5	39.7 48.6	13.4 14.6	πλείων 28.1
πάντοτε 35.5	πάσχω 30.1, 3	18.5 22.4	43.4 R.5
παρά 30.3	πατήρ 12.7	23.7 44.6	R.6 πλῆθος
32.7 37.3, 4, 7 39.2, 6 42.2, 5, 8 44.6	19.3 26.7 29.10 37.2 R.3	περισσός, περισσότερος 35.1 περιστερά	R.3 πληθήνω 44.5 49.2 πλήρης
παραβολή 22.4	πειρασμός 47.3	20.7 34.7 45.6	30.5 33.8 46.6
παραγγέλλω 42.1 51.5	πέμπω 20.2, 7 25.7 30.1	πηγή 21.9 πηλός	πληρόω 13.1, 9 33.7, 8, 10
παράγω 37.11	45.1	37.17 πίνω	50.7 πλήρωμα
παραδίδωμι 31.1, 4 34.1 43.3	πεντακόσιοι 35.6 πέντε 33.3	40.6 41.4 R.7.7 πίπτω	31.11 πλησίον 21.9
παράδοσις 31.4 34.1 37.9	35.6 πεντήκοντα 35.6 37.8	32.4 40.6 45.4 R.7.7	πλοῖον 25.4
παρακλητος 43.6	πέποιθα 49.7		

πνεῦμα
13.11
19.7
23.2
27.5
46.4
48.9
πνευματικός
38.7
πνέω
27.5
πόθεν
22.8
27.1
ποιέω
12.5
13.1–3
15.1–3
19.1
20–25 Intro
20.1–5
21.1–5, 7, 8
22.3
26.4
30.1
31.9
32.1
33.12
36.1
40.1
44.5
49.3
R.7.7
ποῖος
18.5
πόλις
12.7
23.2
R.3

πολύς, πολλή, πολύ
28.1
30.3
35.3
38.4
41.2
R.5
R.6
πονηρός
12.5
28.1
48.12
πορεύομαι
29.2, 6, 7, 8
31.9
πότε
27.1
35.5
36.2
ποτίζω
32.7
ποῦ
27.1
πούς
32.4
πράσσω
36.4
πρεσβύτερος
49.5
πρό
22.8
39.2, 4
44.6
48.8
προάγω
31.8
44.6
προβαίνω
37.3
48.12

πρόβατον
19.2
πρός
2.5, 6
3.1, 4
17.1, 3
36.5
37.4, 5
42.2, 6, 8
45.1
προσαίτης
37.17
43.4
προσέρχομαι
50.6
προσευχή
48.3
προσεύχομαι
29.2, 4, 6–8
30.1
31.9
48.3
προσκαλέομαι
45.1, 2
προσκυνέω
19.3, 7
20–25 Intro
36.5
42.1
44.5
προσκυνητής
19.7
προσπίπτω
32.4
προστίθημι
48.4
προσφέρω
40.2
πρόσωπον
45.6
48.8

πρότερον
40.6
πρόφασις
43.6
προφήτης
1.2
4.5
7.11
R.1
R.2
πρῶτος
20.7
28.2
31.11
34.7
35.6
πτύω
37.17
πτῶμα
36.4
πῦρ
48.8
R.3
πώποτε
31.11
πῶς
27.1
ῥήγνυμι
34.5
ῥῆμα
49.1
ῥυπαρός
40.6
σάββατον, σάββατα
38.2
σάρξ
30.5
32.4
46.1

INDEX OF GREEK WORDS

σέ (σύ)
13.4
σεαυτόν
16.6
40.2
σημεῖον
36.5
52.4
σιτιστός
48.4
σκηνή
28.8
46.6
σκηνόω
30.5
46.6
σκοτία,
σκότος
9.10
10.7
13.4
σός
43.4
σοφία, σοφός
49.5
R.6
σπείρω
41.4
σπέρμα
41.4
46.4
σπλαγχνίζομαι
45.2
50.8
σπόρος
41.4
σπουδή
35.4

στάδιον
37.3
39.8
σταυρός,
σταυρόω
23.2
στηρίζω
49.3
στόμα
32.4
51.8
στρέφω
20.7
35.7
42.9
σύ
13.4
37.3
R.4
συγχράομαι
47.5
συκῆ
22.8
σύν
42.2, 4
44.6
συνάγω
44.6
45.2
συναγωγή
17.3
συνίημι
34.1
συντίθημι
38.8
σφραγίζω
40.6
σχίσμα
38.8

σῴζω
20.2
26.2
30.1
32.3
33.1
38.7
σῶμα
28.2
32.4
R.2
σωτήρ
26.2
44.2
σωτηρία
19.7
26.2
τάλαντον
33.3, 5
ταπεινόω
49.5
ταῦρος
48.4
ταχέως
35.1
τάχιστος,
τάχιστα
35.1
R.6
ταχύς, ταχύ
35.1
44.4
τέ
49.4
τεκνίον
12.5
13.7
44.2
τέκνον
12.5
19.1

28.1
48.9
τελέω
33.7
τεσσαράκοντα
35.6
τέσσαρες
35.6
τέταρτος
35.6
τετέλεσται
(τελέω)
33.7
τετρακόσιοι
35.6
τηρέω
15.6
τίθημι
32.7
34.1, 3
R.7.7
τιμάω
20.9
44.5
τις, τι
10.6
31.4
39.1
τίς, τί
10.6
15.6
16.6
27.1
37.15
47.2
50.10
R.4
τοιοῦτος
38.2

382   Learn New Testament Greek

τόπος 19.7 41.4	ὕδωρ 13.11 31.3, 4 52.7	ὑπό, ὑπ', ὑφ' 31.2 37.4, 10 39.2, 13 42.8 44.6	φέρω 22.1 24.2, 5, 6 30.1 40.2
τοσοῦτος 38.4	υἱός 17.5 19.3 26.7 30.3 39.1 48.12 50.5	ὑπόδημα 33.13 44.6	φημί 23.9 34.1 40.6
τότε 35.5 36.2		ὑστερέω 39.1 41.7	φιλέω 26.7
τρεῖς 31.4 35.6		ὕψιστος 49.5	φοβέομαι 37.3 41.7 45.2 48.3
τρέχω 22.1 24.2, 5, 6	ὑμεῖς 9.11 10.1–4, 7 39.10 42.1 R.4	ὑψόω 36.4 49.5 R.7.7	
τριάκοντα 31.4 35.6			φόβος 34.6 37.3
τριακόσιοι 31.4	ὑμέτερος 43.4	φαγεῖν (ἐσθίω) 20–25 Intro 22.1 24.1, 2, 5, 6 30.1 31.9 49.3	φρέαρ 21.9
τρίβος 45.6	ὑπάγω 27.5 44.6		φρονέω, φρόνιμος 49.5
τρίς 35.6	ὑπακοή 46.1, 3		φωνέω 19.9 22.8 40.1 42.9
τρισχίλιοι 35.6	ὑπακούω 42.1 44.6	φαίνω 9.10 29.10	
τρίτος 35.6	ὑπέρ 20.7 34.7 37.4, 11 39.2, 11 42.8 44.6	φανερόω 14.11 20.7 34.7 36.4 44.5 R.7.4	φωνή 16.7 19.3 22.3 R.1 R.2
τρίχες 45.6			
τροφή 47.5			
τύπος 35.6			
τυφλός 32.4	ὑπερήφανος 49.5	Φαρισαῖος 42.5	φῶς 3.6 10.10 12.7 13.4 R.3
ὑγιής R.5	ὑπηρέτης 28.8 37.3	φαῦλος 36.4	
ὑδρία 24.7 41.7			

φωτίζω 9.10	χείρων R.5 R.6	ψεύδομαι 17.5	ὤν, οὖσα, ὄν (εἰμί) 19.5
χαίρω 5.7 37.3 40.2	χίλιοι 35.6	ψευδοπροφήτης 48.10	20.3 25.2 28.6
χαμαί 37.17	χρεία 32.7	ψεύστης 8.4 15.3	ὥρα 19.7 20.7
χαρά 5.7 35.4 37.3 40.2 50.7	Χριστός 10.7 40.6 48.10	ψηλαφάω 14.11 44.10	ὡς 22.4 35.1
	χωλός 32.4	ψυχή 38.2, 7 41.1	ὥσπερ 26.7
χάρις 31.4 46.6 52.6	χώρα 45.6	ψυχικός 38.7	ὥστε 35.1 38.1, 2, 4
	χωρέω 41.7	ὦ 37.2	
χείρ 14.11 32.4 48.8	χωρίον 47.5	ὦ (εἰμί) 37.17	ὦτα see οὖς
	χωρίς 7.10 29.10 39.2	ὧδε 40.2	

Also by John Dobson:

Learn Biblical Hebrew

A satsified learner comments:

"Happy is the class whose teacher is bold enough to take this humane and scientifically sound approach to learning biblical Hebrew."

2nd revised (updated) edition
ISBN 978-1-903689-25-7 or
978-0-8010-3102-1, h/c
ISBN 978-1-909281-20-2 or
978-1-909281-19-6, p/b
229x152mm p/b, 400pp
With free MP3 audio downloads

PIQUANT editions
www.piquanteditions.com

Baker Academic
www.bakeracademic.com